BOARDINGHOUSE

Women

BOARDING

HOW *Southern Keepers,*
Cooks, Nurses, Widows,
AND *Runaways Shaped*
Modern America

HOUSE WOMEN

ELIZABETH S. D. ENGELHARDT

The University of North Carolina Press
CHAPEL HILL

This book was published with
the assistance of the Greensboro Women's Fund
of the University of North Carolina Press.

FOUNDING CONTRIBUTORS
Linda Arnold Carlisle, Sally Schindel Cone, Anne Faircloth,
Bonnie McElveen Hunter, Linda Bullard Jennings,
Janice J. Kerley (in honor of Margaret Supplee Smith),
Nancy Rouzer May, and Betty Hughes Nichols.

Design by Lindsay Starr
Set in MillerText
by codeMantra

Manufactured in the United States of America

Cover image © Wojciech Skóra—stock.adobe.com.

Library of Congress Cataloging-in-Publication Data
Names: Engelhardt, Elizabeth S. D. (Elizabeth Sanders Delwiche), 1969– author.
Title: Boardinghouse women : how southern keepers, cooks, nurses, widows, and
    runaways shaped modern America / Elizabeth S. D. Engelhardt.
Description: Chapel Hill : University of North Carolina Press, [2023] | Includes
    bibliographical references and index.
Identifiers: LCCN 2023023195 | ISBN 9781469676395 (cloth ; alk. paper) |
    ISBN 9781469676401 (paperback ; alk. paper) | ISBN 9781469676418 (ebook)
Subjects: LCSH: Boardinghouses—Southern States—History—19th century. |
Boardinghouses—Southern States—History—20th century. | Boardinghouses—Social
aspects—Southern States. | Women in the hospitality industry—Southern States. |
Women—Southern States—Social life and customs. | Women—Southern States—
Economic conditions. | Women—Political activity—Southern States. | BISAC: SOCIAL
    SCIENCE / Women's Studies | COOKING / History
Classification: LCC TX909.2.S68 E54 2023 | DDC 910.46/409—dc23/eng/20230601
    LC record available at https://lccn.loc.gov/2023023195

Reflection must show that where there are men and women, birth and death, the cooking and the eating of three meals in each twenty-four hours, the resigning of the body to that glimpse of Nirvana which we call sleep, the rising from it to greet a new day and a new round of petty happenings, there must be much of the simple domestic life common to all mankind.

—Grace MacGowan Cooke and Alice MacGowan,
*Aunt Huldah: Proprietor of the Wagon-Tire House and
Genial Philosopher of the Cattle Country* (1904)

There is no business in the world where so little sound business policy enters as in the keeping of boarders. It is a business that demands capital, push, energy, tact, executive ability, and liberal management, but it is the one business in the world where there is an attempt made to take everything out and put nothing in. The same methods applied to any business would ruin it, and we see the result. A successful boarding-house keeper is a modern wonder.

—Anonymous, "A Mismanaged Business,"
Christian Union (1889)

Contents

Acknowledgments

IN 2014, LABOR HISTORIAN Melissa Walker and her colleague Anita Rose, both professors at Converse College in Spartanburg, South Carolina, invited scholars and food writers interested in southern food studies to gather at their Okra to Opera conference. Academic conferences rarely live up to their promise—for every transcendent panel there are two awkward encounters around the book exhibit or lobby and another desperately off-track roundtable, or so it can seem. But now and then, a Brigadoon of conferences convenes. Panels are lively, meals encourage conversation, coauthorships are hatched, and sessions break down into energizing discussion as presenters and audience merge and everyone takes part. Perhaps a late-night picnic materializes in the lobby of the bed-and-breakfast at which many are staying, and just maybe the conversation goes late into the night. That is what that gathering in Spartanburg was for me.

Becca Sharpless, Marcie Cohen Ferris, Elizabeth Sims, Leni Sorensen, Ronni Lundy, Carrie Helms Tippen, Erica Abrams Locklear, and others were there. Becca and I started listing boardinghouse keepers in southern food: Mary Randolph, Craig Claiborne's mother, Sema Wilkes. Others called out their grandmother or great-aunt or third cousin. That bed-and-breakfast in which we were staying? One other guest was a traveling salesperson who stayed every three weeks or so. Another came once a year for an extended stay to see family. We were short-term guests, welcomed into a home that had been repurposed from its origins as a single-family luxurious house meant to display the wealth of its cotton-broker owner. I left Spartanburg with my eyes open to the overlooked story of southern boardinghouse keepers. Once I started to ponder boardinghouses and the women behind them, I realized they are everywhere, woven through the past and present and even future of food and culture in the US South.

Becca has been a friend and fellow scholar with me all the way. My thanks go to her and to Andrew Warnes for excellent reads of the manuscript. Psyche Williams-Forson and Diane Flynt have given me shelter and writing retreats along the way—as well as friendship and good fellowship. Ted Ownby, Lisa Jordan Powell, Jolie Lewis, Mickey Jo Sorrell, Malinda Maynor Lowery, and Corban Davis have each offered cups of coffee and conversation at key moments. Elaine Maisner grabbed the manuscript from my hands so that she could set up review as one of her last acts before retirement. That she handed editing off to the exemplary Mark Simpson-Vos on her way out the door means I benefited from two of the best that UNC Press has to offer. I am grateful for everyone on the team there.

The camaraderie and support of colleagues and friends at the University of North Carolina at Chapel Hill, including the Institute of the Arts and Humanities, my home department of American studies, and everyone in the dean's office who has had to hear me talk about this between our meetings, helped this project along. Intellectual partnerships and research assistance offered by archivists and librarians of our Wilson Library are one of the best reasons to be at UNC. It's an honor to be back in my home state for this project; extended family in Henderson and Transylvania Counties occasionally found their way onto these pages, none better than my father, whose chemical engineering background helped me understand why a fire engine exploded in Brevard in 1909, and my grandmother who quietly insisted to a federal census taker that she was indeed a boardinghouse keeper—something no one in the family thought she had done. My mother's childhood memories of their busy home made much more sense.

BOARDINGHOUSE
Women

LIKE NO OTHER BUSINESS IN THE WORLD

KATHLEEN CLAIBORNE refused to see her family face ruin in Depression-era Mississippi. To make ends meet, she took in boarders in the small towns in which she and her husband lived. A revolving cast of white southerners sat around Claiborne's table. The round table was walnut; Claiborne set it with her wedding china and linens. When not being used for meals, it hosted bridge parties and other social rituals. Claiborne and her family may have been hanging on to their status by their fingertips, but strangers around the table would not have known it by the surroundings.

Years later, her son Craig Claiborne, the American food writer, recalled the scene. In his telling, his mother's decision to take in boarders was logical, "because a rooming and boardinghouse was one of the few paths a properly brought up and aristocratic young southern woman could follow while holding her chin and prestige up." Craig's father, Luke, was always looking for the next big thing. When his gambles did not work, they would pack up the family and find a new situation—a new house where the scene would repeat.[1]

Good food and hospitality in Claiborne's Mississippi did not require expensive ingredients and materials, but they did need the steady hands of sophisticated cooks and an intentional host. Craig remembered his mother filling both roles. For him, a spoon captured Kathleen's character: "In my youth [my mother] performed what seemed to be Sisyphean tasks to keep her family intact. One of my most cherished possessions is, curiously and unsentimentally, perhaps, a silver spoon monogrammed with her initials that was given to her as a wedding gift." He continued, "Mother stirred all her sauces with this spoon, so much so that the lip, once a perfect oval, is worn down by an inch or so. It is, more than any other object, a symbol of the labor that she spent in providing bread and clothing in those awful days when my father had lost every cent that he owned along with a good deal of pride."[2] The constant, across all the moves and upheavals, was that his mother would hang out a shingle, take in boarders, and fire up her kitchen.

Though her work included stirring the sauces, Kathleen Claiborne played just a small part in the boardinghouse's labor. Despite the family's financial misfortunes, she never lost her social and racial privilege and always hired help for the kitchen. African American women and men (remembered, but nameless in Craig's memoir) cooked, served, and cleaned up after guests. Their essential presence allowed Kathleen to keep the house's reputation as "the most 'genteel' boardinghouse in the Mississippi Delta."[3] Material trappings—china, linens, and the walnut table—served one purpose. The presence of Black laborers and the household's policing of segregation served another. Together, they formed a structure of labor, profit, and racial division embedded in boardinghouses, the larger southern economy, and southern foodways.

Craig, who in many ways invented the role of *New York Times* food critic, eventually credited his mother and her Mississippi boardinghouse table for his refined palate and food acuity. He did not do the same for the Black women and men who labored in her boardinghouses. Claiborne used his column to elevate southern cuisine to national and global prominence. His 1985 profile of North Carolina chef Bill Neal and his Fearrington House restaurant sparked a national celebration of innovations in southern food; today, many regard it as a founding text of the vibrant southern foodways movement.[4] The peculiar twenty-first-century identity of "foodie" also rests on the search for regional, innovative, and artisanal treatments of food. Craig Claiborne and his generation of food journalists and chefs paved the way for today's food media.

A home in Indianola, Mississippi, now boasts a historical marker attesting to Kathleen Claiborne's hosting skills and flavors of her table.[5] It rightly notes that Craig's accomplishments began at his mother's boardinghouse table. Yet Kathleen could not have done what she did without the Black women who were in her employment making the boardinghouse run. They too were boardinghouse women, and they too deserve credit for changing American culture and food. Part of the original sin that haunts southern foodways today is the chronic erasure of names and talents of people of color who labored and created in white-owned or white-operated boardinghouse kitchens and in businesses of their own. When I tell people I'm writing about boardinghouses, the Claiborne model is what people often picture: a white woman who cooked well (or could hire people who cooked well), was property-rich but cash-poor, and who faced a loss of class status if she worked outside the home took in a small number of respectable boarders found not by advertising but by word-of mouth recommendation. It turns out that such a representation is a relatively small proportion of the overall boardinghouse story.

I KNEW A FAMILY STORY concerning the early years of the Ecusta paper mill in Brevard, North Carolina, at which so many in my white Appalachian family worked. While my grandfather helped build and then worked at the factory, the family took in some single male workers to their rental home on the road to the factory site. My grandmother Iva Sanders Whitmire cooked for the men alongside her own young children; my mother remembers piles of extra laundry and an unsettled family routine. I always heard this was only for a short period of time (it may well have been), and it was a temporary strategy until my grandparents saved enough money to move and, later, build a family house of their own. It certainly was never suggested that my grandmother embraced the role or made it part of her identity.

I was surprised, then, to open the 1940 census and find a single word in her "Occupation" column: boardinghouse. She listed it as a private boardinghouse, with two lodgers on the day she was interviewed. One lodger was her brother, and the other was a nineteen-year-old white woman from the neighboring community of Sylva, Ellen Mosby. Along with lodging in the home, Mosby identified her occupation as boardinghouse cook. And while my grandfather brought $600 into the family as income from his job in the mill, my grandmother told the census taker that she too worked fifty-two weeks of the past year. She reported an additional $360 of income for the family. In other words, at least for a moment in her life, my grandmother claimed a profession and made visible her workplace.[6]

Today the family remembers Iva's panfried chicken and her extraordinary ability with vegetables fresh from the garden—squash, okra, half runners, and cabbage. But we also talk about how shy she was, how reluctant to speak in public, and how her employed life mostly took place after my grandfather's early death. We do not remember her as a businesswoman and certainly not as a boardinghouse keeper. We should.

My grandmother lived in Brevard. Twenty miles away lies Hendersonville, the market town in which I grew up. There, I learned, Anne Gover was the proprietor of much larger boardinghouses than Claiborne's or Whitmire's. In 1908, Gover moved from running a smaller boardinghouse on South Main Street to "a large, rambling structure, one of the largest of its kind in Hendersonville," on the corner of Fourth and Washington Streets.[7] Eventually the dining room of Gover's Kentucky Home (not to be confused with the Old Kentucky Home that Julia Wolfe ran in nearby Asheville), while continuing to have lodgers, also seated an impressive 220 diners at a time, larger than many restaurants then and now.

Longtime employee of the business Henry Stephens was its pastry chef. Stephens was one of the many African Americans in western North Carolina who participated in the burgeoning resort economy that Gover's lodgings targeted; he and fellow chefs commanded a large-scale kitchen in the back of the house. He recalled, "When I was chef at the Kentucky Home there were nine cooks in the kitchen. Meals were served family style on long tables. The platters were piled high with delicacies and the tables were loaded. There were ten waiters to pass the food. . . . And all a body could eat for one dollar." Gover's formidable business relied on the skills Stephens and his fellow food professionals brought to the endeavor.[8]

By 1926, Hendersonville also boasted five Jewish boardinghouses. The county was advertised as the Catskills of the South in the robust US Jewish press. Summer camps established then survive to the present day. Collectively, Hendersonville boardinghouse keepers, including the Horowitz and Rubin families, hired a shohet in the summers to oversee the killing of poultry and cattle and to ensure boardinghouses provided kosher meals. The keepers played key roles in ensuring safe travel and religious freedom for Jews in the South.[9] They remind us that the South is and has always been a diverse place.

That diversity extended to boardinghouses' clientele. Leaving her childhood home in Brevard, Jackie Mabley found work as a comedian. While touring with fellow Black performers across the Jim Crow South, boardinghouses provided them safe accommodations on the road. In off seasons, Mabley opened her own home to other theater performers in need of the same. When not onstage, Mabley chose menswear and surrounded herself with other queer performers.[10]

From Claiborne's genteel house to Whitmire's ad hoc business while a factory was being built, to Hendersonville's tourist and summer camp support operations, to networks of places for performers to stay, boardinghouses took lots of forms. This quick tour helps us appreciate how integral they were to the southern economy for decades, especially for women and non-white people. Boardinghouses are—perhaps surprisingly—at the heart of what we now define as southern culture. They were engines of innovation for generations of creative people; they played a key role in the invention of southern food; and they deserve to take center stage in our stories of the diverse South.

Both the scholarship and the myths center northeastern and urban boardinghouses and conclude that the era of boardinghouses ended when the twentieth century began. But socially sanctioned Jim Crow practices and violently enforced legal segregation continued in southern states through the first six decades of the twentieth century. Workplace rules and customs kept Black southerners in domestic labor longer than in other parts of the United States. To travel safely, to survive, diverse non-white, queer, and non-Christian southerners sometimes benefited from and sometimes became boardinghouse women to carve out much-needed spaces. North Carolina was no exception—and these women's efforts shaped today's twenty-first-century American culture.

Flexibility across Time and Place

Whitmire, Stephens, Horowitz, Rubin, and Mabley were all from North Carolina (Claiborne was from Mississippi), and their boardinghouse experiences took place in the 1900s. I could have opened just as easily with six boardinghouse women influencing and shaping American culture from the coastal cities of Charleston, South Carolina, or Savannah, Georgia, rather than Hendersonville and Brevard, North Carolina. The story of southern boardinghouses is not just a twentieth-century one; it stretches across centuries too.

So, we could have begun with women like the "kind and charming" widowed Mrs. Galluchat in whose establishment on Charleston's King Street journalist Anne Royall stayed in the 1830s and was taken by her coffee, food, and respectability, enough to make a plea in print that the widow receive more customers and even marriage offers. A contemporary of Galluchat, the free-born Black pastry chef, caterer, and boardinghouse keeper Eliza Seymore Lee, managed her many businesses from a nearby Tradd Street headquarters and along the way trained the next generation of chefs in the cosmopolitan city. Down in Savannah, working-class white woman Sema Wilkes took over a railroad boardinghouse that she and her husband lodged in. Along with Black women like "Lessie Bates, Mildred Capers, Denise Coleman, Mrs. Dempsey, Virginia Foster, Laverne Gould, Cassandra Johnson, Susie Mae Kennell, Florrie Simpson Leach, Cecelia Maxwell, Rose Marie Mobley, Millie Parrish, Exedene Walker, Linda Wright, and a host of others," Wilkes turned a modest boardinghouse kitchen into a storied restaurant named an American Regional Classic by the James Beard Foundation.[11]

The story could also be told from urban New Orleans, one of the many places where boardinghouses and brothels blurred, as everyone from Tennessee Williams to the real estate owners and madams of Storyville discovered, along with businesses advertised as hotels or bars but functioning as boardinghouses and hospitals during the yellow fever years. Ida May Beard, who lived out the dissolution of her marriage to a con man in rough gamblers' boardinghouses in the railroad towns Ronceverte and Bluefield, and Margaret Montague, who wrote novels from her elegant room in White Sulphur Springs, would make a case for West Virginia for this story.[12] In your small town. In your big city. Using an extra room for the weekend. That's the point. Boardinghouse women were everywhere, despite their stories being long undervalued. The idea of boarding was so flexible and useful that it persisted while evolving and stretching along the way. In fact, boardinghouses never left. They are still around us. This book helps us to see again the women who created boardinghouse culture. Seeing them, in turn, lets us learn from them—their business models, their ability to nurture or shelter radical social transformations, and their contributions to the foods we eat and share. And that continuity from past into present gives us paths into chosen futures.

When Ecusta finally closed in Brevard, North Carolina, in the 1990s, one of my favorite cousins found a job working shifts in Travelers' Rest, South Carolina. He did not want to sell his house in Brevard (it was our grandmother's home), but the commute was long and tricky during bad weather and after twelve-hour shifts. His aunt lived a little farther down the road in Spartanburg. She owned a dry-cleaning business, generally cooked a lot of food, and had an extra room in her house for her nephew. For years, Cecil stayed there on weeknights, coming home to Brevard for weekends. Was his aunt a boardinghouse keeper? Today's food economy is peppered with experimental businesses—pop-up markets, shared spaces, events- and subscription-based companies. Homeowners in resort coastal and mountain towns, not to mention the hip neighborhoods in metropolitan areas, make extra cash through companies like Airbnb, Vrbo, and others.[13] Building off existing resources and skills, without requiring new or formal capital, these side gigs push us to ask: How might stories of boardinghouses help twenty-first-century communities?

The boardinghouse women whose voices and stories are the backbone of this book worked in, managed, or owned boardinghouses. Some stayed as guests. Some cooked and others ate; some presided over parlor and table while still others scrubbed stairways and wrung out laundry. Some made fortunes, others leaped from business into marriage, some launched careers as writers or activists, and some plotted political change. A few women here used boardinghouses to reinvent themselves—recover from divorce, heal from illness, change their gender identity or racial identification, or explore their sexuality beyond society's limitations. Some women explicitly used their boardinghouse experiences to shape southern and American culture writ large; others used boardinghouses as refuges of safety against the parts of society that threatened their very existence. Boardinghouses shine a light into hidden corners of culture and society, what Grace MacGowan Cooke and Alice MacGowan called "simple daily life," and show it was instead the "modern wonder" an anonymous *Christian Union* writer described—like no other business in the world.[14]

From the eighteenth to the twentieth centuries, entrepreneurial women ran boardinghouses across the southern United States—from Virginia to Mississippi to North Carolina to Texas. Some women took the idea of the South to boardinghouses they opened in California or New York City. Run by Black, Native, and white women, rich and poor, immigrant and long-term resident, some boardinghouses were not only thriving businesses but also sites where women could reinvent themselves and develop trades and skills, sometimes in ways that led to important changes in American culture and society. Although boardinghouses in cities like New York, Paris, and San Francisco have long lived in America's imagination as places of adventure, vice, and the enforcement of social class, people are far less familiar with the boardinghouses in and of the American South—much less so the extraordinary women who used them to reinvent southern cuisine, to invent new business models, and to engage in politics, sometimes scandalously, or even treasonously.

Boardinghouses prove to be places of immense innovation, entrepreneurship, and artistry, often led by powerful, ingenious women who broke out of expectations and convention to leave lasting impact on their communities and American culture. We just haven't looked closely at their stories before.

How to Recognize a Boardinghouse and Its Keeper

People running or staying in boardinghouses did not spend much of their daily lives worrying whether the establishments were real boardinghouses. Indeed, it would have been hard for them to do so. Southern boardinghouses did not follow a unified architectural blueprint. While Lowell, Massachusetts, created purpose-built boardinghouses as part of its early mill expansion and those buildings later became models for sex-segregated dormitory living around the United States, boardinghouses never required specific architecture to function. Some textile mills in the South—as well as other industrial sites, from furniture or food processing factories to company-built coal towns—did occasionally build dedicated boardinghouses. Because most companies were white-owned, lodging in the boardinghouses was almost exclusively confined to white employees. But even there, establishments varied: some were for men only, some for single women; some were for middle management; some were mixed-gender or a combination of short- and long-term residents. Most small factories and towns and cities supporting them did not invest in new buildings for workers. People of color who helped build, clean, and support the industry lived in boardinghouses too, but not ones captured in official town records.[15] So, if we looked only at purpose-built structures, we would miss the majority of the South's boardinghouses.

Single-family homes could hide boardinghouses behind their shutters, especially in southern communities, as people without liquid resources but with real estate, owned or rented, could build a business by opening their doors to boarders. Social strictures could push keepers to avoid advertising and downplay any physical signs that might give away their circumstances.

As we look from a historical distance, physical traces of boardinghouses are scarce on the landscape of southern communities. Home renovation can reveal houses divided or repurposed for boarders. Some former single-family homes passed through their boardinghouse stage into afterlives as apartments. Many no longer exist at all.[16]

Beyond purpose-built dorms and repurposed single-family homes, keepers took in boarders in all types of buildings. In resort towns or tourist locations, any family space could become a boardinghouse during the travel season—push the family into a single room, buy extra supplies and settings for the table, and advertise for boarders. At railroad stops and ports, ramshackle buildings often had bars or restaurants downstairs and boarders up rickety staircases on floors above. Some hotels became boardinghouses with a change of management (and vice versa); there are even cases of the same building holding both a functional hotel and a boardinghouse when a keeper rented out a floor to run as her boardinghouse. Mary Hamilton ran a boardinghouse without walls: tents to sleep in and a lean-to with open sides as a kitchen. Enterprising keepers looked at old boats, tents, cabins, and shacks in cities, towns, depots, ports, and wide places on the road and saw boardinghouses.[17] Sometimes what the business owner or guests called the place was enough—a practice that leaves the historical record blurry and messy but also rich and fascinating. Boardinghouses, in other words, were everywhere.

Further frustrating those who would like an easy census, boarding-houses proved equally flexible in terms of services offered. Many keepers offered lodging to unrelated people in a house in which they too lived, included communal meals at set times, took care of the cleaning and laundry for their boarders, and offered longer-term stays than competing hotels or inns. Limiting the discussion only to businesses that did all those things, however, would erase many of the boardinghouses and their keepers across the South—because other keepers lived off-site, managed multiple homes, outsourced laundry, or rented to their own family. They too should count.

The colloquial "boardinghouse reach" assumes a communal table with a shared mealtime for which individual boarders had to fend for themselves to get enough food from the "family-style" service of bowls and platters in the center of the table. But boardinghouses often had customized food for lodgers—à la carte service or off-time cooking, which brings them closer to contemporary restaurants. They could have café tables seating two or three rather than a single large table. Meals might be included, but some boarders chose to eat elsewhere instead. Nor did one have to be a lodger to take meals at many boardinghouses. Some boardinghouses made as much money on box lunches to go as they did on meals in the dining area. At some boardinghouses, laundry was included and done on-site; at others that was an outsourced service. Rooms could be furnished or not; the amount of privacy one's room afforded varied widely.

Family members sometimes rented from each other even as other lodgers began as strangers. Some boardinghouses had lodgers who stayed years, while some establishments catered to short-term travelers, with one- or two-night stays, similar to nearby hotels or inns. Feminist scholar Susan Strasser, in her classic book on women's housework, *Never Done*, wrote, "Current debates about the American family often rest on the assumption that new kinds of family structures—single-parent families, single-person households, unrelated adults living together—are replacing the nuclear family, which in turn supposedly replaced the extended family. In fact, unrelated adults have often lived together."[18] Boardinghouses are some of the places where they did.

In the late eighteenth and early nineteenth centuries, stagecoach inns, taverns, and boardinghouses vied for lodgers. Anne Royall, traveling from New York State down the East Coast, through Georgia, west to Mississippi, and then north to Ohio before coming back across West Virginia to Washington in the 1830s, stayed in all three types as well as in friends' guest rooms. She lodged with private families and at mail stops in taverns. At one point, she stayed in a home that was part boardinghouse, part cattery (for cats in needs of homes), run by a bachelor.[19] The story is more interesting if we focus on her as a boardinghouse traveler rather than on cataloging what counts as boardinghouses in her stays.

The forms boardinghouses took were still flexible when the twentieth-century boardinghouse women profiled here lived and worked in them. The Great Depression pushed Della McCullers to close the restaurant she ran in a hotel and to open a boardinghouse with a jukebox and inside and outside seating. In the northeastern United States, where most boardinghouse scholarship has focused, consensus holds that the era of the boardinghouse gave way to apartments and tenements around the turn of the twentieth century.[20] Certainly, the post–World War II housing boom made private residences, owned or rented, more available to more Americans of all races, including in the Sunbelt. However, some of that new housing allowed southern boardinghouse women to carry on. In other words, a straight-line chronology oversimplifies the boardinghouse story in the US South. Rather than proceed chronologically, I have chosen to organize the chapters that follow along themes to allow the messiness to reveal unexpected continuities—between Anne Royall and Della McCullers, for instance, but also between today's generation of side hustles and that bachelor who made a living caring for cats and people.

Boardinghouse keeper is a relatively but not perfectly gendered phrase. Women running food and lodging businesses were likely to identify as boardinghouse keepers and be called the same by others. Some men took on the term, but they were more likely to call their establishments inns, taverns, or hotels and themselves innkeepers, tavern keepers, or hoteliers (and, it should be noted, they were very likely to rely on the labor of women and people of color rather than do the work themselves). In one case, tracking the same building over a decade of its existence through the city directory finds it called a boardinghouse and run by a woman, changing to a hotel run by a man, and then morphing back to a female-helmed boardinghouse a few years later. Married heterosexual couples ran boardinghouses; so did sisters, single people, and unrelated business partners. People used boardinghouses to pass—to make their own sense of intersecting identities. They explored sexualities with resulting consequences—some positive, some negative. They named their race or changed their class, at times easily and at other times deeply unsuccessfully. They introduced themselves as the men or women they were, regardless of the sex assigned them at birth; only ones who were partially successful or questioned pop up in the historical record.[21] I keep the focus on self-identified women in boardinghouses, though, because background gender politics of American society made the space of boardinghouses particularly filled with possibility for women at a time when other spaces were not.

The written archival record of the US South has gaps and erasures. Institutional racism in society means that who could own, open, or profit from boardinghouses—and who would later be celebrated for the innovations the spaces made possible—tended to be white women rather than women of color. When formal archives hold traces of nonwhite people in boardinghouses, the record is often refracted through dialect or finding aids written by white curators.

This fall, I sat in the Carolina Inn with family descendants of Alice Lee Larkins, discussed in chapter 2. Known to the family as Allie, Larkins is remembered for her feistiness, spirit, and accomplishments that had come down over the years. A family member who bears one of her other nicknames, "Leila," as a middle name shared clippings of poetry Alice published, using it as a pseudonym. We talked about her carrying a pistol and defending and protecting her niece and daughter from unworthy men. While they had a photograph of Alice taken around the time that she was closing her boardinghouse, it is stiff and posed, and you can barely glimpse her curls and attention to fashion. We have many polished studio portraits of Jackie Mabley dressed as her best-known character, the old lady "Moms," but rarer ones of her offstage in suit jacket and tailored silk shirt. Photographs of Julia Wolfe on the steps of her Asheville boardinghouse are in the archives of the Thomas Wolfe Memorial, but her curiosity shows more in letters she wrote to her friend the writer Wilma Dykeman. A grainy newspaper image even shows us Lola Walker between her days as a chorus girl and before the suit her boardinghouse aunts brought on her behalf went to trial, but flirty photos that were introduced as exhibits in the trial are lost to us. It may seem odd to you, reader, that this book does not reproduce these and other images.

I made that decision in part because of what we do not have—and because of what we cannot see in what we do have. First, no images exist in public archives of Malinda Russell, of Frank Gibert and Cora Douglas, or of Della McCullers, and we do not even have the names of all the enslaved women who cooked in Mary Randolph's kitchens and developed her famous plan there—Black or queer keepers and lodgers whose stories are key to this book and to understanding boardinghouses and the innovations in them. Equally, the locations of the racially and religiously diverse keepers' houses where Anne Royall stayed, the tents surrounding Mary Hamilton's backwoods kitchen, and the cots, unfurnished rooms, and fly-by-night arrangements Ida May Beard had to stay in when her husband was running from the law have not been preserved in our photographic archives. With this book, I aim to disrupt narrow visions of who the South's boardinghouse keepers were and what kind of places they kept. Second, photos or portraits we do have can only hint at the lives and limitless possibilities behind the closed doors of boardinghouses. Allie Larkins was much more alive in the conversation with the Blackwell family than in her portrait; Texie Gordon's boardinghouse is now a parking lot. Mary Ellen Pleasant kept her innermost thoughts private; Lola Walker did not achieve fame and fortune; and some keepers will forever be anonymous. Their power and influence, however, remain.

I focus in this book on southern cultures, but not, perhaps, as some enthusiasts might assume. "Southern" here allows for people who use a geographical definition to say they live in southern communities. It makes space for people who use ideas of southern culture (always inflected with race) to call themselves or their establishments "southern" wherever they are located. And it allows for people who would lead with all kinds of other aspects of their identities first—mountain or coast; race, religion, or culture; state or city—but who clearly thrived, contributed, and existed in and among others in or of southern cultures. Women's crucial roles in business, politics, and culture were nurtured and enacted inside the walls of boardinghouses—and examples in southern boardinghouses are especially nuanced and fraught because the South was and is especially nuanced and fraught. Boardinghouses reveal the agency and the vulnerability of communities of color in the South who faced legal segregation and threats to travel and mobility across the centuries. As such, boardinghouses and their keepers could be radical engines of social change and spaces for shelter and reinvention. In others' hands, these spaces could facilitate the violence and structural racism of the US South. Boardinghouses ran the gamut from keen to nervous enforcement of social structures. Southern boardinghouse keepers, then, are particularly important as case studies—in part because they have been heretofore mostly absent in American cultural memories. Even as widespread boardinghouse culture waned in the rest of the United States after the turn of the twentieth century, boardinghouse culture in the South persisted until Jim Crow fell. Southern boardinghouse keepers, then, are also important because they had more time to influence the rest of us.

THE CHAPTERS that follow each focus on a pair of charismatic women. Most are boardinghouse keepers, but some are boarders, employees, and family members. Some are widowed; some divorced. Some used boardinghouses to leave their past behind, whether in terms of racial identity, gender, or class; some found the freedom to love who they wanted or resist expectations they hated. Some found that boardinghouse tables were places of influence, politics, or culture not otherwise available to them.

The first three chapters illustrate the power of the boardinghouse model for women deploying it. When Mary Randolph and Malinda Russell, two of America's culinary pioneers, were running kitchens in southern boardinghouses in the early 1800s, their boardinghouses provided simultaneously public and private spaces that proved perfect crucibles for culinary and authorial work, which led to them helping to invent southern food. Young Alice Lee Larkins, who carried a gun in her bodice to fend off marriage proposals from her boarders in nineteenth-century Wilmington, North Carolina, and Julia Wolfe, the woman on whom the most famous southern boardinghouse keeper in fiction, Eliza Gant, was modeled, created business models that were cooperative and required little formal capital. Fictional Texan Huldah Sarvice used her many boardinghouses in cattle country to provide nursing and childcare to the sick, elderly, and orphaned of her community. And college-town keeper Texie Gordon used her training as a nurse to create a boardinghouse for which caretaking was a central premise. Sarvice and Gordon used expectations of women's caretaking to expand social safety nets for their boarders. Through their boardinghouses, these six women and ones like them helped invent southern food, expanded how businesses could be created beyond formal capital, and worked through gendered expectations to change education and health care in American culture.

The middle three chapters turn to the hidden or taboo functions of boardinghouses; women were very aware of the in-between spaces and how they could be used. One of San Francisco's first millionaires, Mary Ellen Pleasant, funded abolitionist causes with her boardinghouse profits. Her politics were very different from those of Mary Surratt, hanged for her role in the assassination of Abraham Lincoln after running the boardinghouse in which the plot was hatched. Both, however, used their boardinghouses to advance their political causes and transported ideas of the South beyond geographical limitations as they did so. Sarah Hinton's grandmother tried to commit her to a mental institution when she resisted working in the boardinghouse and embracing her grandmother's conservative religious teachings that favored white southerners. Lola Walker was supposed to help in her aunt's Asheville boardinghouse, was seduced there, and then ran away to be a chorus girl before her aunt sued the man who lured her away. Hinton and Walker made space for new definitions of sex, romance, and careers in southern and American communities. Lives like theirs ultimately helped dislodge restrictive definitions of gender and sex. Jackie Mabley was raised in mountain boardinghouses in western North Carolina and became a patron of Black boardinghouses as she launched her comedy career across the South and then in Harlem. Along the way she made space for queer women like herself to have homes. Frank Gibert closed his successful saloon and came to Washington, DC, to be a writer; he intended to leave behind the time in his life when he was known by the female name Frances Harris. Mabley and Gibert show that if people wanted to reinvent themselves, embrace their truest selves, love or marry or remain single, or travel safely regardless of their identity, successfully navigating a boardinghouse could be the key to doing so. Women used boardinghouses to engage in the nation's most fraught political debates, especially around race; they challenged ideas of sex and female autonomy; and they allowed people to move around the world safely, sometimes by reintroducing their truer selves to the world.

The final two chapters focus on the footprints of boardinghouse women in rapidly changing American culture. They launched writing careers, carved out businesses in or despite the South's industrialization, and shaped new restaurant cultures out of their backdoors. Women like Anne Royall and Ida Beard stared down impoverished widowhood and abandonment to create "rooms of their own" in boardinghouses and change their circumstances with their pens. Mary Hamilton cooked in extraordinarily rough boardinghouse kitchens for large numbers of loggers and sawmill workers. Della McCullers was unapologetic about her skills, capabilities, and successes in the world of restaurant culture in the urban twentieth-century South, running her restaurant, community center, and juke joint as a boardinghouse near Shaw University in Raleigh, North Carolina. Hamilton, McCullers, and keepers like them helped create the southern lunch, a heretofore unexamined legacy of boardinghouse women. Women developed careers for themselves that others said were not possible, wove their businesses into emergent markets, and changed restaurant culture and its food along the way. In so doing, boardinghouse women found new energy and resources for engaging the wider world, models we live with today.

Who are today's inheritors of boardinghouse women's innovations? Rather than look to the physical spaces that resemble old ideas of boardinghouses, nostalgia-filled bed-and-breakfasts that dot tourist destinations, I turn to the spirit of boardinghouse women instead. The conclusion traces the boardinghouse story in folks who engage in today's sharing economy of Airbnb and pop-up restaurant experiences—creating new businesses without needing formal capital to launch. In assisted living facilities and private dorms, caring and nurturing continues while still largely relying on the labor of people of color. Finally, new twists on boardinghouse ideas dot the landscape, from modern teacherages to intentional pairings of elder-care and youth chaperoning to all manner of side hustles investing in community formation across southern and American communities and into the future. Boardinghouse women have much to offer today's twenty-first-century world.

PEOPLE TELL ME STORIES of the boardinghouses and boardinghouse keepers in their lives all the time. I have been graced with the story of a great-aunt who fell on hard times but who always left the cookie tin in reach

of nephews and nieces who visited. I have learned about the Parisian boardinghouse keeper who found ways to make southern college women less
homesick on study-abroad experiences by trying to cook foods from Alabama or Texas. I have listened to tales from traveling salesmen who started
their careers in boardinghouses around the last days of textile and furniture
factories in the piedmont South. I have heard about boardinghouses on
edges of college towns that proved perfect for self-professed countercultural
misfits. Stories of epic vacations where people found themselves in eccentric
boardinghouses; of historical markers that celebrate books written while
authors boarded on the site; and of all kinds of food, good and bad, served
at memory's boardinghouse dining rooms have been offered to me.[22] But
they are always told as half-remembered, partial stories. By the time you
finish this book, I hope you can truly see and learn from the boardinghouse
keepers or their descendants who surround you. My own family boardinghouse keeper, my grandmother Iva Whitmire, would remind me to sit down
and humbly listen, make a plan with others, have another serving but also
give one, and then get busy creating whatever future we most need now.

THE INVENTION OF SOUTHERN FOOD

Mary Randolph and Malinda Russell

RICHMOND, VIRGINIA, in the first decades of the 1800s was the bustling seat of Virginia government. Its proximity to the federal capital, as well as its position as a crossroads for the many prominent Virginians such as Thomas Jefferson and appointees of George Washington who served in the federal government and needed to travel between home and work, meant its social life was dynamic. Wealth flowed through the city, especially that generated by the sale of humans in slave traders' auction houses but also from the exchange and transportation of agricultural goods and natural resources out of the interior of the state and region to markets around the Atlantic World and beyond. An invitation to dine at Moldavia, one of the finest private homes in the city, or, later, choosing to pay for a meal or lodging at the Queen boardinghouse meant good food and good conversation led by one of the most skilled hosts in Richmond, Mary Randolph (1762–1828). The food was prepared by some of the most accomplished cooks in the city, even if they were not acknowledged or paid at the time. In both places, Moldavia and the Queen, trappings of Randolph's white wealth and class were translated into daily life. Political debates, business deals, and cultural exchanges took place around the establishments' tables. After twenty years of providing Richmond hospitality, Randolph channeled her cooks' and her own experience onto the pages of a cookbook that set the contours of regional southern cooking and the possibilities afforded to enterprising women by southern boardinghouses.[1]

Cold Springs, Tennessee, in the 1850s left a lighter impression on the national historical record than Richmond. For people seeking a quiet retreat for their health or looking to participate in the relatively new American idea of vacationing, the developing community on Chuckey Mountain may have been just what they sought. A congenial boardinghouse, run by a hardworking and resilient keeper, could provide the escape from daily life its occupants were seeking. One boardinghouse offered a keeper, Malinda Russell (ca. 1812–?), who had previously worked as a professional laundress. Russell cooked using techniques learned from a mentor who taught the plan outlined in Mary Randolph's book—and, Russell added, her knowledge was dynamic as she had "since learned many new things in the art of Cooking" as well. Her cooking was popular enough that she later ran her own pastry shop. For twenty years, she developed recipes and built up her business endeavors. As war broke out, eastern Tennessee proved a bad place to be an outspoken (by her own characterization) female business owner, especially if that owner, like Russell, was a free Black woman. In the overwhelming violence of the 1860s, Russell fled the state, threatened by a mob targeting her for her race and politics. As she ran, she could not carry much. But she did have recipes, honed by years of experience. She compiled them into *A Domestic Cook Book* and published it in Michigan, where she landed; today it is the earliest published cookbook we have found by an African American woman.[2] The cookbook allows us not only to recognize her considerable achievements but also to restore to the historical record the hands and minds of a key set of women in southern cuisine and boardinghouses, including Mary Randolph's: expert African American food professionals, free and enslaved.

Mary Randolph and Malinda Russell, both boardinghouse keepers, wrote cookbooks that retained historical value across more than a century. They were far from the only ones. Eliza Leslie, whose *Directions for Cookery* sold 150,000 copies, wrote eight other nineteenth-century cookbooks from a home base in Philadelphia. Leslie and her mother opened a boardinghouse upon the death of Leslie's father. Leslie's teacher Elizabeth Goodfellow and famed Charleston baker and boardinghouse keeper Eliza Lee both communicated cooking knowledge through apprenticeships, cooking schools, and lessons to other women. Sarah Elliott, their nineteenth-century contemporary in North Carolina, inserted a note at the end of the "Soup" section of her cookbook, *Mrs. Elliott's Housewife*, that addressed women who for "pecuniary aid or pleasure" needed to open a boardinghouse—one wonders if she had close experience with doing so herself. In the twentieth century, Kathleen Claiborne and Elizabeth Beard ran boardinghouses while raising sons Craig Claiborne and James Beard, who subsequently wrote cookbooks (and influenced American food profoundly). Sema Wilkes and Mary Bobo turned their Savannah, Georgia, and Lynchburg, Tennessee, boardinghouse experiences into successful restaurants and then cookbooks, catching the beginning of a late twentieth-century southern food renaissance.[3]

Boardinghouses offered women opportunities to develop trades in ways that would influence American culture for generations. When Mary Randolph and Malinda Russell ran their kitchens in southern boardinghouses during the first half of the nineteenth century, there was no such thing as "southern food" that a person could walk into a home or restaurant and order. It would not be until they each published cookbooks—and people like them organized menus, wrote stories and advice columns, and generally started speaking up for it as a thing to be desired—that "southern food" became a recognizable American tradition. Boardinghouses provided a simultaneously public and private space that proved the perfect crucible for these women's culinary and authorial work.

When I say boardinghouse keepers and their cookbooks helped invent southern food, let me recognize up front that I mean something broader and more diverse than the pop culture versions of southern food: grandma's biscuits, fried chicken, and sweet tea. I also do not mean that before the boardinghouse women discussed here prepared them, no one was eating those and other southern foods. Boardinghouse keepers were by no means the only people involved as southern food started to cohere. Increasingly across the eighteenth and nineteenth centuries and into the twentieth, people came to associate an aggregation of foods and the methods by which they were cooked, served, and shared as representative of southern cultures.[4] People began requesting such meals, thinking nostalgically of them and the places they ate them, and making an expanding series of cultural and social judgments around them. But amid the larger process, the boardinghouse table was a hub of activity—and, because of its ubiquity and particularity, a key one.

In the early years of the twenty-first century, one story of the invention of southern food played out in debates among scholars and other experts over whether it should be elevated to the status of a cuisine. If that elevation were to happen, the argument continued, then something needed to explain why other regions in the United States failed to establish their own cuisines. Proponents first suggested that in the South people ate at home longer, and thus the region's restaurant culture was slow to develop. As a result, people retained more local recipes and preferences than they did in other parts of the United States. That, then, explained the coherence and sophistication of southern food as a cuisine—unlike those in other parts of the United States that moved quickly to homogeneous national restaurant cultures or to copying French or other cuisines, southerners ate in relative isolation and thus formed distinct foodways.[5] Homogenizing pressures that flattened food in the rest of the country never got purchase in the rural South.

More recent scholarship has uncovered the long histories of sophisticated restaurants in southern port cities and luxury vacation spots, challenging that earlier story. In addition, even in sleepier small towns or up-country cities, fewer and fewer people were truly food self-sufficient. In railroad depots, stagecoach stops, taverns, general stores, and courthouse squares, prepared food could be found. Home gardens and farms were supplemented by salt, spices, coffee, tea, crackers, or prepared dishes, depending on a family's means. Traveling nurserymen brought newly developed seeds and rootstocks from one location to another, adding to the ingredients available in any given location. Existing in the space between mythical, completely isolated home kitchens and overwrought, bustling public restaurants, between kitchen gardens and general stores or markets, boardinghouses and their keepers stood. They served and charged boarders and diners to eat outside of the home but did so from within their own houses. Just as celebrity chefs writing cookbooks today generally craft recipes with home, not restaurant-scaled, serving sizes, boardinghouse cookbooks spoke to home cooks but participated in industrial and market-based worlds.[6] Boardinghouses expertly combined the domestic and public in foodways.

Paying close attention to boardinghouse women gets us closer to something hard to find in myths of southern food: records of daily practice. This too is what makes keepers influential in southern foodways: they had to produce meal after meal. Boardinghouse food is food that works—in many senses of the word. It was local, but it was often paired with shortcuts from processed foods as they became available. Recipes had to be dependable; customers had to be satisfied; cooks had to produce finished meals on time with enough variety to keep people coming back. So boardinghouse food in the South included biscuits, but it also featured corn bread, hot rolls, and other baked goods. Chicken might be fried, but it and other meats were stretched to hashes or stews or cold salads the next day. Some recipes found renown, while some were never written down. Boardinghouses were bridges between the aspirational and the actual. Although some went to great lengths to hide the work involved, boardinghouses and their cookbooks let us see laboring bodies (often African American but also otherwise less privileged) behind the food. They allow for the deep history of ethnically, racially, and economically diverse people living and eating in the South, even if for great expanses of time a whites-only definition of southerners was being violently enforced. As such, they expose structures of power encoded in ideas of southern hospitality, popular culture, and foodways.

Such ideas of southern culture proved to be unmoored from geography and powerfully transportable. As scholars, we talk extensively of the ways that "southern" moves around the globe—in music, entertainment, literature, business campaigns, and stereotype. But what were early mechanics of that movement? How did southernness become a recognizable export? I propose that the daily boardinghouse table, with its compromises, combinations, and blends of foods, was one of the keys. If southern food was being created out of even some of the dishes on a daily table, then a southern boardinghouse or a southern meal might be spotted on the basis of only a few elements. It did not have to be pure, essential(ist), or authentic. It could be partial, messy, and diverse. But if enough was present, an idea of the South had traveled.

And it was not just the food. Some elements of southern cuisine cohering involved intimate interactions around a table—manners, expectations, and practices inherent in the act of eating together, recipes shared by a community of cooks whose knowledge was carried to new locations. Boardinghouse food was food-in-relation, by which I mean an accumulation of conversation, shared experience, and exchange. Perhaps the growing season that supplied a San Francisco boardinghouse was different, but its cook still could serve a gumbo by being creative with ingredients. Or perhaps a boardinghouse in Havana, Cuba, cooked from locally grown ingredients, but its advertisement could promise southern manners and hospitality with a side of slow-cooked greens. In other words, in boardinghouses people experienced food outside of their home environments.[7] With the requirement of home cooking loosened, then, when they traveled or when establishments moved outside geographically bound definitions of the South, people were equipped to identify, recognize, and value southern food.

Race haunts all these movements and definitions. Structures of wealth, law, and privilege shaped who could travel freely and where they could go for most of the centuries of American boardinghouses. Systems of work and class shaped who cooked and who was served in public and in private. In the twentieth century, accumulated ideas of cuisine and culture influenced what got called southern and what got labeled "soul." Whatever the era, the very statement "I want southern food today" was likely in and of itself a coded request.

To see these dynamics in their earliest development, we can look to the lives of Mary Randolph and Malinda Russell, the similarities and differences in their Richmond and Cold Spring environments, the popular culture surrounding them, the habits of workers and guests in their houses, and the cookbook legacies they left behind.

Mary Randolph's Life and Work: Defining Southern Food

When Mary Randolph was born in 1762, her father was a plantation owner and legislator. Her mother brought wealth and Virginia political connections to their union. Together they had thirteen children, of whom Mary was the eldest. Thomas Jefferson's parents raised Mary's father, and the families' links continued when Mary's brother married one of Jefferson's daughters. That brother became governor of Virginia, while Mary married a first cousin once removed and embarked on her own influential life.[8]

Mary—called Molly by friends and acquaintances—and her new husband, David Meade Randolph, took up residence at their property called Presquile on the James River. Geographically it was not far from Virginia's cities, but Randolph's daily routine in the early years of her marriage was that of a rural plantation owner—including overseeing enslaved workers. She gave birth to eight children, four of whom lived to adulthood. While she must have had a busy life inside with young children and hosting duties, Randolph's subsequent recipes suggested that she or people whose labor she took also paid close attention to seasons, tides, and flavors of Virginia's land. Her cookbook imagined some readers in similar environs, telling cooks who would make "Mazagan Beans" to "gather them in the morning, when they are full-grown" and suggesting the best way to have beef in summer was to choose the animal "about the middle of February" and fatten it on corn through spring, directions that would not have worked for housewives who purchased from markets or city sellers.[9]

In 1795, George Washington appointed David Randolph as a US marshal for Virginia. The job requirements pushed the Randolphs to move to Richmond. Around 1800 they built their downtown home and christened it Moldavia, a portmanteau of their names—Molly and David. Mary's role, which she seems to have embraced, was to host dinner parties and facilitate long evenings of conversation. Enslaved men and women brought from Presquile to work in her new urban kitchen, along with Randolph herself, must have had quite a learning curve. Now, rather than using ingredients produced or harvested in season in nearby fields and wilderness, they had to adjust to interacting with food suppliers in markets. Living in Richmond also meant more constrained spaces for kitchen and food-processing work, even with generous lot sizes. It likely meant frequent large parties for whom to cook. Randolph's cookbook reflected these realities alongside the seasonal window. For instance, a summer beef recipe also gave directions for "housewives" purchasing meat for the preparation, including the benefits of finding Jewish butchers who, to Randolph's mind, understood freshness better.[10] Randolph's growing reputation as a host testified to her and her cooks' successful transition to the realities of planning and executing meals in a city.

Soon, though, another major upheaval arrived, this one more negative. David was a Federalist, so when anti-Federalist Thomas Jefferson was elected president, David was fired. Mary's close family connections to the Jeffersons (and David's slightly more distant ones) did not mitigate political differences. It was an economic setback as well as one of social prestige. The Randolphs sold Moldavia and regrouped. David spent the next few years traveling, some of it in Europe.[11] What was Mary Randolph to do? The solution she hit upon not only helped turn their fortunes around in the short term but resulted in a publication that outlined southern food for decades to come.

On February 29, 1808, Randolph placed an announcement in the *Richmond Gazette* that she had "established a BOARDING HOUSE in Cary street, for the accommodation of Ladies and Gentlemen.—She has comfortable chambers, and a stable well supplied for a few Horses." Her family was initially skeptical, a sister-in-law noting to the rest of the family when Mary did not immediately get boarders. But Randolph's vision paid off. Catering primarily to fellow elites, especially men in town to conduct state business as legislators, judges, and other government appointees, Randolph turned her reputation as a top host into a business filling the gaps in the family's finances. Both Randolph and the house came to be known as the Queen. One visitor to her table, Samuel Mordecai, praised Randolph as full of energy and industry. Mordecai raved, "There were few more festive boards than the Queen's. Wit, humor and good-fellowship prevailed, but excess rarely." Perhaps influenced by nostalgia, he remembered that "social evenings were also enjoyed, and discord never intruded" in all the times he attended Randolph's board. Her parlor and dining room table were the place to see and be seen, hash out the latest political controversies, and, not least, indulge in food and drink that rivaled any to be found in the still relatively young United States.[12]

Fifteen successful years later, Randolph closed the Queen and moved to Washington, DC. There she began work on her manuscript. Hard-won lessons of food tastes and fashions, combined with expertise from women and men who worked in her kitchen, made it to the page. *The Virginia Housewife* employed local ingredients, recipes we embrace today as central to southern cuisine, spices from across the Atlantic World, techniques from European kitchens, and advice for fellow women running kitchens large and small. It first appeared in 1824. Randolph passed away in 1828, but her book lived on. Nineteen editions were published between the 1820s and 1860s; *The Virginia Housewife* long remained in print and only grew in reputation across the nineteenth century.[13]

Food historian Karen Hess described *The Virginia Housewife* as "the earliest known southern cookbook in print, regarded by many as the finest work ever to have come out of the American kitchen." To Hess, Randolph's work documented Virginia cookery of her time and then was instrumental in mythmaking about nineteenth-century southern food. Two subsequent influential cookbooks, Lettice Bryan's *Kentucky Housewife* (1838) and Sarah Rutledge's *Carolina Housewife* (1847), paid homage to Randolph not only in title but also in structure. Southern food scholar David Shields calls the three together "Southern cooking's founding books." More specifically, Randolph's recipes for "barbecue shote," catfish and other specific fish, field peas, rice, and local vegetables are often used to trace the development of such quintessential dishes within southern foodways. Specific seasonality of ingredients, from beans to ducks to seafood, signaled Randolph's Virginia location; her insistence that one ought to pay attention to the exact moments when ingredients were at their best aligned with belief systems of skilled chefs across the centuries.[14] It also spoke specifically to developing southern foodways across the region, in which ingredients could vary but attention to microclimates and hyperlocal seasons was widely shared.

Randolph and people in her kitchen did not create in a vacuum. They were in a system of suppliers, growers, and other food processors, in Richmond and beyond. Food historian Leni Sorensen paints a picture of Randolph sending out "kitchen staff with scullions to carry items or load the wagon" to do the daily marketing. Like many small cities of the era, Richmond bustled with food entrepreneurs, some of whom competed with home cooks and boardinghouse keepers like Randolph for raw ingredients, others of whom provided foods already processed or expertise to augment what could be made at home. Randolph's friend Mordecai detailed in his Richmond memoirs a crowded city of taverns, oyster houses, coffee shops, pastry shops and bakeries, and hotels offering a range of foods for dining in or taking out and a diversity of food professionals who cooked in their own establishments or catered in others'. For raw ingredients, Randolph's shoppers may have gone to either of the "two city markets—the old market in Shockoe Valley, ten blocks or so east from her home, or the new one at 6th and I Street (now Marshall St.)—and along the way the many grocers who offered imported foods, spices, and wines." Sorensen further points out, "Randolph herself likely would not have gone with them but would have sent her male major-domo to represent her interests with the vendors. We don't know who that man was—white or black—free or slave."[15]

Nor was Randolph the only woman involved in creating food for sale, although her elite social class most likely separated her from this sisterhood of food professionals. Richmond's community included women like professional baker Nancy Byrd, about whom Mordecai wrote, "A name that carries its own passport to distinction. No dinner nor supper party could be complete unless she had a finger in the pie. She held undisputed sway over the dessert, with the rolling-pin for her sceptre." Mordecai also remembered Mrs. Gibson's Coffee House fondly for its tea, coffee, chocolate, and conversation. In later years, the coffee shop became a tavern and then an "'oyster and beef-steak house, with other refreshments,' under a skilful mulatto woman, whose canvas backs, soras, and other delicacies attracted many customers."[16] Food in Richmond was not confined to private spaces; rather, the give-and-take between public establishments and kitchens within homes was frequent and dynamic. Somewhere in these circulations, long-term boardinghouse tables helped create southern food that worked. As Randolph's cookbook showed, market purchases responded both to daily needs and to long-term economical preparations.

In cooking her way through *The Virginia Housewife*, Sorensen mapped technical innovations in Mary Randolph's kitchens, supply chains in Richmond and across Virginia for acquiring ingredients, seasonal thinking the cookbook required, and networks of free and enslaved African American experts upon which Randolph's boardinghouse drew. Dishes Randolph prioritized utilized specific Virginia flora and fauna. As a reading of Randolph's recipes suggests and Sorensen's research proves, cooks in her boardinghouse never lurched from meal to meal. Subsequent devotees (including Malinda Russell) of the system dubbed it a "plan" and adopted it into their own philosophies and practices. The substance of Randolph's kitchen staff's plan involved thinking days, weeks, and even seasons ahead. To make mincemeat pies at Christmas, for instance, one needed to think about the type of piglets procured in the spring. What one fed them in summer and how they were processed in fall all could determine if a cook had quality ingredients at hand in early December.[17] Readers valued the book for its honest (albeit economically and racially privileged) outline of a year in cooking. The *Virginia Housewife* plan reflected realities of food preparation in the nineteenth century. Its principles helped Randolph run an efficient boardinghouse. Cooking by the plan allowed cooks to minimize waste (in this example, using all the hog by processing the head meat even if it would not be used until months later) and stockpile necessary ingredients cheaply so that expensive replacements did not have to be sought at the last minute when boarders clamored for a dish.

Of all the people in this book, Mary Randolph has perhaps been written about the most.[18] Even as *The Virginia Housewife* introduced readers to Virginia flavors and ingredients, it also outlined systems of food preparation and rhetorics of good food and good hosting for the nation. Like her fellow boardinghouse keepers who wrote cookbooks, Randolph bridged worlds—reaching variously between public and private, southern and American, large and small, urban and rural, and consumer and producer. Her boardinghouse cookbook and others like it deserve reframing as a result. Rather than finding the phenomenon of keepers writing cookbooks curious, we might find it a reasonable outcome. From this perspective, boardinghouse keepers were, in fact, best positioned to write cookbooks for wide audiences in the nineteenth and early twentieth centuries.

Prevailing Ideas about Boardinghouse Food

Part of why, even in the many celebrations of cookbooks like Randolph's, the boardinghouse background of authors has been hard to acknowledge was the force of belief about how terrible food at boardinghouses was. The industry of boardinghouse vignettes, jokes, plays, songs, movies, novels, poetry, and short stories, which stretched across the whole century, emphasized over and over that the resting state for the food was nearly inedible. English-woman Frances Trollope's tour across the United States in 1827 confirmed European readers' image of bustling, class-mixing, rustic Americans with equally low-brow palates in a blur of city boardinghouses, private homes, and hotels. Trollope's route took her through New Orleans to Cincinnati and from there through Wheeling, West Virginia; New York; Philadelphia; Baltimore; and Washington, DC. To hear her tell it, female boarders every-where in the United States suffered in identical urban spaces where they "must rise exactly in time to reach the boarding table at the hour appointed for breakfast, or she will get a stiff bow from the lady president, cold coffee, and no egg." Trollope continued, "The fasting, but tardy lady, looks round the table, and having ascertained that there was no egg left, says distinctly, 'I will take an egg if you please.' But as this is addressed to no one in particular, no one in particular answers it, unless it happen that her husband is at the table before her, and then he says, 'There are no eggs, my dear.'" Bringing the point home, Trollope concluded, "Whereupon the lady president evidently cannot hear, and the greedy culprit who has swallowed two eggs (for there are always as many eggs as noses) looks pretty considerably afraid of being found out. The breakfast proceeds in sombre silence."[19] To Trollope, the stinginess of serving and lack of honest conversation was damning.

Trollope was equally dismissive of foods Americans ate when they indulged at more plentiful tables, saying, "The ordinary mode of living is abundant, but not delicate." She commented particularly on heavy meats and lack of coherent thought behind groaning tables: "They consume an extraordinary quantity of bacon. Ham and beef-steaks appear morning, noon, and night. In eating, they mix things together with the strangest incongruity imaginable. I have seen eggs and oysters eaten together; the sempiternal ham with apple-sauce; beef-steak with stewed peaches; and salt fish with onions."[20] Trollope's descriptions of hotel and public foods were generic; she rarely named places or even towns in which meals took place. Her vignettes made it very difficult to distinguish between tables and across regions of eating in the United States, but they drove home her conclusion that American boardinghouse food was bad.

Boardinghouses in southern communities or using ideas of southern hospitality came in for criticism also. In 1846, Maria Georgina Milward published a short story in the *Southern and Western Literary Messenger*. Titled "Mrs. Sad's Private Boarding-House," it highlighted contemporary stereotypes about food to establish the boardinghouse keeper's character and the mood in the house. Mrs. Sad served "tough beefsteak" with "forced etiquette" and pretended to offer second servings while making people fear the consequences if they accepted.[21] Naive boarders who did not know to insist on more food fell ill and starved.

Most often, though, boardinghouse food was used as punchlines for jokes. The nineteenth-century northeastern urban world caricatured by illustrator Thomas Butler Gunn took generalized dismissals of all "Americans" by European travelers going from city to city such as Frances Trollope and the regionally specific parsimony of Milward's story further. Gunn's *Physiology of New York Boarding-Houses* recounted his adventures in a wide range of establishments in 1850s New York neighborhoods. Having left a successful caricaturist career in England, Gunn arrived in New York City and joined its dynamic press culture. His book was widely reviewed and sold out its first print run in less than a month. Part humor, part guide, Gunn's work resonated with lodgers across metropolises with its portraits of boardinghouse challenges, including the perils of vegetarian, cheap, and bad food.[22]

In other publications, southern boardinghouse food "jokes" took on regionally specific political resonance—for example, the background violence and racial politics of slavery. An 1864 "Unpleasant Reminiscence" published in an abolitionist paper recalled a large boardinghouse "on the bank of the lower Mississippi" with a keeper known for being "deep in the mysteries of French cookery" for her excellent table. Seven weeks after taking up residence, the author watched as a dead body was fished from the cistern storing the kitchen's cooking water. African American Jack Tarpley had tried to escape his enslavers two weeks earlier and apparently fell into the well after blindly jumping over a fence while being chased. "French coffee, our rich sauces, and our excellent gumbos" had for those two weeks been made with the "rich and ropy" cistern water. Published in a prominent New York magazine in the Civil War era, the "Reminiscence" defied typical bad food jokes. The story's gentleness about the keeper and most of the food credited her cooking expertise while pointing out the corroding influence of southern slave systems. In this piece, slave economies were dangerous and full of unintended consequence, but the food would have been fine otherwise.[23] Food, like the very definition of hospitality or luxury, got swept up in overarching systemic violence.

Nothing was more quintessential to jokes about bad boardinghouse food, though, than hash. The original mystery meat dish, hash took a starring role in cartoons, songs, and jokes about boardinghouses. "Confessions of a Hash Eater" played on fears of drug addiction and compared actually liking the dread dish to "insanity." A song written by students at the University of Virginia, parodying a popular Gilbert and Sullivan song, proclaimed,

If you want a receipt for that popular mystery
Known to the world as boarding-house hash,
Take all the ingredients in natural history,
Mix them together without any splash.

Combining mystery meats and stinginess of ingredients, hash became everything wrong with the boardinghouse table. Assumed to be terrible in flavor, poor in quality, insufficient in amount, and undifferentiated across all locations, boardinghouse hash in turn stood in for all that was bad in American food history.[24]

An article in the *National Police Gazette* from 1889 renamed products sold as "prime country sausages" closer to their actual origins: "trotting sausages," a reference to the gait of hardworking urban delivery horses they once were. Tracing meat in boardinghouse sausages to horses rather than to pigs or cows, the article challenged readers to "just imagine a prime country sausage . . . kicking its driver through his hat!" It helpfully and gruesomely provided illustrations of a life cycle from racing horse to delivery animal to meat grinder to boardinghouse table. A year earlier, a joke in the American boardinghouse volume of Puck's Library, drawn from the first successful humor magazine in the United States, suggested a piece of steak rejected for being too tough for otherwise inured boarders was used as a doormat before being buried in the backyard. "Two months later a beautiful rubber-tree sprang from the ground," the authors cracked. Tough poultry and worrisome salted fish balls ("hand grenades" and "slung shots," quipped Puck) joined the list of nearly inedible meats on offer at the boardinghouse table of popular culture.[25]

In the pages of magazines and in stage routines, tough meats were joined by dishes so closely associated with boardinghouses you could spot one by the appearance of the other. Stewed prunes headlined the list. Perhaps digestively useful to mitigate other inedible dishes, prunes were also known to be cheap, available year-round, and easy to fix. None of that made them more acceptable to jokesters. An otherwise kind article about an ideal boardinghouse signaled its difference from others by advertising itself as "pruneless." Even when boardinghouse dinners featured unobjectionable ingredients, problems persisted. A central one involved stingy serving sizes. Immediately following Puck's joke about tough steaks was a cartoon of six adult boarders watching a keeper at the head of a table slice a measly dessert with a tiny spot in its center. The caption read, "A new game at our boarding-house—who will get the strawberry?" Other jokes turned on how keepers could cut razor-thin slices of cake or pie such that a single, small dish served a whole table.[26]

One humor piece appealed to many, judging from how many times it was reprinted. College women at Vassar called it "A Domestic Euclid" and placed it in *Good Housekeeping*. A Chicago publication called *Brick*, serving "stone and clay industries," titled the same piece "Brick Boarding-House Geometry" and suggested bricklayers were the real boardinghouse experts. Stephen Leacock, a Canadian economist and humorist and a contemporary of Mark Twain, was its original author. Leacock first published "Boarding House Geometry" in a journal titled *Truth*; he republished it in a collection of essays, *Literary Lapses*, in 1910. Set up as a series of propositions, theorems, and axioms, the piece argued, "A pie may be produced any number of times," "Any two meals at a boarding-house are together less than one square meal," and "All boarding-houses are the same boarding-house." Once all boardinghouses were declared interchangeable in popular culture, "QED," it concluded, the weight of stereotypes and generalizations threatened to make it nearly impossible to distinguish differences, be those in quality, region, or memory.[27]

Especially in the southern boardinghouse story, too easily accepting stereotypes of terrible, cheap, and indigestible foods risks perpetuating a whole set of oversimplifications about public food culture. We also may then fail to understand why keeper cookbooks were popular. Jokes, bad travel stories, and generalizations made it hard to see the strength of boardinghouse knowledge in cookbooks over time. No wonder cookbooks by accomplished boardinghouse keepers have been remembered for everything except their boardinghouse roots. To tease out details of boardinghouse keepers shaping southern food, Randolph and popular culture are not enough. Malinda Russell helps tell the rest of the story.

Malinda Russell's Food Knowledge

While Randolph's *Virginia Housewife* made an immediate impact from the moment of its publication, forty years later, another cookbook made a quieter landing upon its release. Its significance, however, has grown in the intervening century and a half. By the time Malinda Russell picked up her pen in Michigan, she had twice had savings stolen, lost at least one business and possibly property, and found herself violently separated from the security of hard-won community networks. But she held years of experiences and expertise and could write a cookbook. Today scholars struggle to find Russell in the historical record.[28] But her publication stands all the more precious for its contribution to the southern food story.

Russell likely had few resources with which to begin her boardinghouse. Born in eastern Tennessee to a free Black family, Russell used her early years to save enough money to begin the process of emigrating from the United States to Liberia. She was nineteen years old. We do not know the political convictions or connections that led Russell to contemplate this path, though she was in company with both white and free Black Americans who concluded that for African Americans, leaving was a more viable path than staying. Russell, however, made it only as far as Lynchburg, Virginia, before being robbed by one of the people with whom she traveled. In retelling the story, Russell did not linger over details, instead focusing on how she regrouped and responded. She said, "I commenced cooking, and at times traveling with ladies as nurse." She gave evidence that her "fine disposition and business-doing habits" served her well to get back on her feet—and, not coincidentally, added accomplishments to her record that would augment her future boardinghouse. It was probably during this part of Russell's career that she learned to cook from a fellow African American woman named Fanny Steward, who, Russell said, taught by the "plan of the 'VIRGINIA HOUSEWIFE.'"[29] The plan, referencing Mary Randolph's book, prepared Russell well for future challenges.

Russell soon married and settled into life in Virginia. She and her husband, Anderson Vaughan, had a child, whom she described in her cookbook as being "crippled" with "the use of but one hand." (We do not know if that was a congenital condition or the result of an accident at some point during her son's early years.) Russell described married life in Virginia as a happy time. To help support the young family, Russell "kept a wash-house." She quoted an advertisement she used to garner customers: "Malinda Vaughan, Fashionable Laundress, would respectfully inform the ladies and Gentlemen of Abingdon, that she is prepared to wash and iron every description of clothing in the neatest and most satisfactory manner." After detailing the care with which she treated clothes and customers as well as her experience with the business, the ad concluded, "She hopes to receive, as she shall exert herself to deserve, a sufficiency of patronage to insure her a permanent location." In other words, the advertisement managed to speak to previous experience as well as to future business plans. Russell did not say in her cookbook whether she successfully moved into a brick-and-mortar location. After only four years, her marriage ended abruptly when her husband died. Again, Russell declined to reveal emotions or details. She focused instead on her actions: Russell took back her maiden name and faced life as a young widow raising a child.[30] Rather than sink under the weight of her burdens, Russell regrouped.

She wrote, "I returned to Tennessee and, after the death of my husband, kept a boarding-house on Chuckey Mountain, Cold Springs, for three years. My boarders and visitors were from almost every State in the Union, who came to the Springs for their health." The 1840s and 1850s in the United States saw Americans begin to experiment with vacationing and leisure to counter the effects of work. Mountains and springs saw new visitors, some seeking health, some escaping disease before catching it, and others enjoying a moment of rest between work projects. Tennessee was at the center of this new form of travel and leisure. Given the era, it is likely that her boarders were white, but the archive is silent on this matter.[31] Regardless, Russell's opening a boardinghouse to host vacation travelers put her at the forefront of a growing industry in the United States.

After three years, Russell changed tack one more time: "After leaving the boarding-house, I kept a pastry shop for about six years." This seemed a wise business decision because it enabled her to put aside "a considerable sum of money" for future support of herself and her son. A full-scale exploration of nineteenth-century southern bakeries has yet to be published. But thanks to related work we know that jobs in baking and pastries were viable paths for some African American businesswomen in the early century. It would be interesting to know whether Russell had employees and, if so, how many. Did she rent or even own a purpose-built store, or did she make do out of her home or an empty business space? Did she have daily walk-in customers, or did she mostly focus on special events or commercial accounts? In whatever way she organized her business, Russell continued to perfect her recipes and refine her accomplishments in the kitchen, likely based in Greeneville, Tennessee.[32]

Then, in 1864, Russell lost her savings and investments yet again. This time it was "a guerrilla party, who threatened my life if I revealed who they were." Russell explicitly blamed the attack on her own "Union principles"; it must have been a truly terrifying time. Tennessee, and especially the eastern part of the state, was a crossroads for soldiers of indeterminate allegiance and informal organization. She and her son left Tennessee, seeking a way out of the South, "being attacked several times by the enemy" on the way north. Eventually, they settled in Michigan "until peace is restored." In May 1866, as she penned the introduction to her cookbook, Russell still wanted to return to Greeneville. Tennessee was home, and in Greeneville some of her property might be reclaimed. But for the present, she focused on her cookbook.[33]

Russell's *Domestic Cook Book* was a quirky, disorganized collection that relied on readers' background cooking knowledge. Russell began with cakes and moved into cookies, puddings, cordials, jellies, and preserves. The cookbook had no subsections, and latter pages included other cakes and jellies forgotten earlier. Sweet dishes dominated over savory ones for the first thirty-five pages. After that, some beef, chicken, pork, and turkey dishes were given, followed by a small number of vegetable recipes. Three pages of directions for medicines, cleaning solutions, and salves interrupted before giving way to a couple of ice cream recipes. The cookbook ended with a recipe "To Preserve Milk" and one "To Preserve Eggs." A few recipes were single sentences; most were three to four lines long. "Calf Head Soup" took Russell ten lines to outline, as did mince pies, and ice cream took her eight. Butter pastry and green tomato preserves got longer descriptions at eleven lines each. Recipes like "Delmonico Pudding" expected readers to have facility with flavorings, judgment as to the temperature at which pudding set, and comfort with boiled icings. Some recipes were downright terse, such as "Green Corn Bread," which in its entirety read, "Three dozen ears of corn grated, one egg, milk, a little salt." A couple of recipes included hints for the less-prepared in terms of skills or finances, such as "Charlotte Russe," which proposed that snow could help gelatin set if one did not have access to ice. She wrote when cooking everywhere in the United States was labor- and attention-intensive and where equipment (and staffing) varied widely from kitchen to kitchen—deferring to individual readers' expertise made sense.[34] With her list of recipes and with her comments on them, Russell showed that she valued and refined recipes that worked.

For a busy business owner, knowing that a dish would consistently turn out—would be good, nourishing, not require too much undivided attention while cooking, and make good use of its ingredients—was an invaluable feature of a recipe. Russell banked on such features being attractive to purchasers, whether they were actively running their own boardinghouses or simply cooking for themselves. Readers who ran boardinghouses would learn practical recipes from her, but so too would the much larger pool of readers who did not. Behind Russell's emphasis on the consistency and reliability of her recipes lay the real challenges of running a household in the nineteenth century, however large or modest.

Russell's cookbook demonstrated a second crucial detail of rapidly cohering southern foodways: networks and exchanges of food knowledge by women over time. As with many women's recipe boxes, Russell's cookbook credited some recipes to other women ("Mary's Jumbles," "Mrs. H's Pudding," and "Mrs. Roe's Cream Pie"). Were they friends? Mentors? Former boarders? Future customers? Russell maintained names with recipes, evidence that women with whom she had contact contributed to her knowledge base. In addition, some recipes were pinned to places (like the previously mentioned Delmonico Pudding, probably named after the most famous restaurant in the nineteenth-century United States, or a pudding simply called "Kentucky," her neighboring state). A few may have been cultural or political references, such as Washington Cake, Eve's Pudding, and "Miss Madison's Whim." Were recipes exchanged around her boardinghouse table? Garnered from newspapers or travelers passing through? We may have only her cookbook as evidence of her life, but glimpses of Russell's personality came along with it. A rare aside addressed the "great many ladies" who asked her how she made "cakes so light"—her answer involved managing one's oven well, although perhaps she held back some secrets. "I will say," Russell noted, implying there were things she chose *not* to say. She backed up her expertise in her introduction by asserting, "I know my Receipts to be good, as they always have given satisfaction."[35] Between the lines of Russell's *Domestic Cook Book* lay extensive Tennessee and Virginia networks; her food and southern boardinghouse food more generally existed in relationships between women.

Relationships in domestic spaces in the US South, though, were and are fraught. Russell does not say more about how easy or hard it was to create and sustain her networks. But in her study of Black domestic workers in white southern homes, *Cooking in Other Women's Kitchens*, historian Rebecca Sharpless documented the isolation felt by African American women who cooked in private white households across the US South between 1865 and 1960. Frequently enveloped in rhetoric about family and care that foreclosed honest assessment of the expectations of employees, such working conditions often prevented workers' attempts to form alliances to advocate for better wages, treatment, and ownership of one's own recipes or practices. The domestic nature of home spaces made it hard to define them as workplaces at all, leaving employees without advocates in the public realm. Russell faced challenges as a businesswoman, but at least she was not laboring in others' homes.[36]

At the same time, because cooking and cleaning were seen as such inherently domestic or private tasks, even when women doing those tasks were in formally organized workplaces they could be overlooked. Labor historian Dorothy Sue Cobble studied the difficulties faced by early twentieth-century waitresses trying to organize as a labor force in public diners, cafés, and restaurants. Laundry workers faced similar dilemmas.[37] Women's supposed inherent proclivities to nurture and the assumptions that they naturally belonged in homes rather than in the worlds of business added a layer of gendered inequalities to those of race and class against which it proved difficult to mount resistance.

The binary of public versus private could not be sustained in the spaces of boardinghouses. Their very nature was simultaneously both/and/also, not either/or. Boardinghouses were simultaneously akin to public restaurants and industrial hotel kitchens on the one side and private, small family home cooking on the other, with their own particularities exploding any lingering binaries. Boardinghouse tables held both national tastes and local ingredients, shared dishes and individual requests. They allowed capitalist market exchange and family or interpersonal barter, things bought, and favors traded. Boarders and employees were exposed as they walked down hallways or napped in parlors, but they were at their most intimate in places they slept and bathed. Because of these uncertainties, boardinghouses could function as spaces of change and spaces of effective resistance, as later chapters will show. In practice, though, the boardinghouse as a work site could enforce an unequal status quo—because it allowed an owner to use an even wider range of justifications against change. Owners could, for instance, pay less because work took place at home; they could skimp on hiring specialized employees, arguing (incorrectly, of course) it was work anyone could do. They could let long-term employees go (or in pre–Civil War times, be sold) abruptly, effectively evicting them from housing at the same time.

Mary Randolph suggested an embrace of social hierarchies in the introduction to her cookbook. She wrote, "The government of a family bears a Liliputian resemblance to the government of a nation." Her metaphor was detailed: imagining the role of a treasury department, enshrining good practice into "inviolable law," and calling for regulation for smooth governance. Other nineteenth-century women writers used American ideas of women's expert running of homes to argue for larger societal and political roles. Randolph instead suggested that no matter how small a reader's home circle was, that individual should manage it seriously, as if it were a governmental matter. The effect was to affirm that no matter the size or complexity of a household, her book's methods, recipes, and recommendations were for it. Bringing the experience of cooking for a full boardinghouse everyday into the pages of a cookbook required readers to accept that such experience would help with their own challenges. Randolph ended her introduction with a wish that her book would most help the "young inexperienced housekeeper."[38] She may have had professional and larger-scale experience, but she spoke to people starting out making meals in their own family homes.

Randolph seems to have had an unusually intimate knowledge of daily sounds, rhythms, smells, and temperatures in kitchens for a woman of her race and social class. Sorensen thought as much: "Probably more than most house mistresses she would have spent a good deal of time in the kitchen throughout the day; after all she was running a business." Randolph did not assume that she was writing for fellow boardinghouse keepers, women who would put in similar hours in the kitchen. Instead, her cookbook's introduction suggested three tasks for "the mistress" to perform in an ordinary day. She needed to corral family and guests to their seats for early breakfast, so that only one service was needed (this was because for enslaved workers, "no work can be done till breakfast is finished"). Then, while workers ate, she should "[wash] the cups, glasses, &c.; arranging the cruets, the mustard, salt-sellers, pickle vases, and all the apparatus for the dinner table" (because careful "ladies" did this better than clumsy "servants"—this had an air of suspicion of theft about it too). Finally, she needed to "go in to give her orders."[39]

Giving orders encompassed examining fresh ingredients, measuring out stored dried ingredients (probably from locked pantries or containers to which the "mistress" held keys), and gathering sauces, wines, and other necessary items. Randolph firmly stated, "The mistress must tax her own memory with all this: we have no right to expect slaves or hired servants to be more attentive to our interest than we ourselves are." It was a rare reference to enslaved people in the book. Some give-and-take between workers and boss had to happen—what was in season, what guests wanted, how long it had been since a given dish was served, what leftover ingredients could be repurposed for the day ahead. Not only did Randolph's advice economize in the kitchen, but it also increased efficiency and "comfort" for the person in charge. Not following her plan risked cooks interrupting the "mistress" throughout the day as they discovered the next ingredients needed. Randolph made a strong conclusion: "The prosperity and happiness of a family depend greatly on the order and regularity established in it."[40]

In practice, Randolph promoted social hierarchies that were inseparable from racial hierarchies. Young housekeepers to whom she wrote were unlikely to be poor or women of color. *The Virginia Housewife* assumed enslavement was unremarkable and would continue. Such callousness erased knowledge, skill, and contributions of men and women forced to labor in her kitchen and on the recipes. Randolph did not have to mention slavery explicitly; she only had to invoke concepts of "taste" and "management." Taste, possessed by ladies of intellect, trumped the expertise and physical labor of cooks, in Randolph's equation. Enslaved men and women servants in Randolph's household rarely appeared in the cookbook, though she and her husband were listed as enslaving nine men and women during the time the boardinghouse was operating. Along with their names, the expertise, voice, and agency of these people were systematically erased—folded under the primacy of the "housewife's" taste and management.[41] In the swirl of celebratory stories of southern food, Randolph's cookbook has been remembered as southern more for its food than for the labor systems of racial and social inequalities that produced it, but that must change.

Perhaps few kitchens ever ran with the precision Randolph and the staff agreed was ideal. Nonetheless, *The Virginia Housewife*—memorized by white women Randolph imagined as her audience and developed by experts she never named—informed and guided many kitchens as they produced reliable daily dishes.

Many kitchens would have looked more like one featured in an 1856 article in the African American newspaper the *Provincial Freeman*. Titled "Domestic Life in South Carolina," it spoke against the system of southern slavery. With a dateline of Columbia, South Carolina, the article's opening paragraph turned to "life in a boarding house." The article profiled "Big Sylvie," an "intelligent cook" who presided over kitchens for Eliza, a Quaker woman who owned the boardinghouse. Despite Eliza, her family, and most boarders being "privately speaking, of northern principles," Eliza forced enslaved Sylvie to work in terrible conditions. The dirty kitchen was located below the dining room, and "Big Sylvie never leaves the kitchen; she lives there, she sleeps there, adjusts her toilet there, smokes there, boards there, drinks there, and—whenever she can get enough of the favourite beverage—gets drunk there." The article outlined rape, beatings, and wage theft of an African American "laundress" who had arranged to rent herself out from her "owner," offenses that haunted the boardinghouse—and the corrupting, corrosive effect on previously well-meaning white people trying to run a business in a slave state.[42] The women and men who developed and then disseminated Randolph's system likely had experience with or stories of friends or family who lived through similar horrific conditions for living and working as the ones Sylvie faced in her kitchen. Malinda Russell's autobiographical writing in the introduction of her cookbook, while presented with as hopeful an outlook as possible, similarly testified to the difficulties of life in slave states for any person of color.

The matter-of-fact way that Russell presented her credentials through knowing Randolph's plan suggested she was confident that people knew what she meant. I have not found Fanny Steward, Russell's teacher, in the historical record. However, ephemeral traces of the networks in which both women lived do remain. One appeared in a memoir written by Susan Dabney Smedes from 1887. The white Smedes, writing in the post-Reconstruction era, largely set out to persuade her readers how "kind" and "compassionate" her father was, especially to the people he enslaved in prewar Virginia. She particularly described her father's butler, George Orris. According to Smedes, Orris "was quite equal to the trust committed to him. It was only necessary to say to him that a certain number of guests were looked for to dinner, and everything would be done in a style to suit the occasion." Orris's professionalism and competence at running a large private kitchen and delivering appropriate and luxurious foods to the family's guests was attributed to Randolph's plan. Smedes claimed George had memorized every recipe from *The Virginia Housewife*, having been "trained by that lady herself." She further said Orris was one of Randolph's enslaved kitchen staff when he was younger and then presumably was sold later, ending up in her family's kitchens. Would Orris have said he was trained by Mary Randolph? Or would he have thanked the fellow workers in the kitchens with whom he trained? More likely, those professional women and men were Orris's mentors and guides, not Mary Randolph. Regardless, the association with Randolph (Smedes added, "Virginia tradition says that Mrs. Randolph had spent three fortunes in cooking") emphasized a transmission of luxury, culinary prowess, and management skill.[43] The boardinghouse diminished in memory, but the system persisted.

Russell took what she learned in Virginia from Steward with her when she relocated to Tennessee. Did she train employees at her boardinghouse or pastry shop? David Shields has documented how Eliza Lee, a free Black caterer, baker, and boardinghouse keeper in Charleston, South Carolina, created an apprenticeship program that included training enslaved women for white household work. Advertisements in Charleston papers showed the value of Lee's training. Skilled African American cooks, especially in simultaneously public and private, industrial and domestic boardinghouse kitchens, built networks of knowledge by learning from each other and naming their processes in public statements.[44] Such networks held the possibility of mobility or agency, even moments of strategic resistance, for women and men who could deploy them in workplaces during their enslavement and most especially beyond. As much as boardinghouse cookbooks should be remembered for their role in the cohering of southern food, they should also be valued for the role they played to connect and maintain networks of people who produced, shaped, and invented that food.

I WOULD LOVE to see records of how many boarders stayed with Mary Randolph at the peak of her boardinghouse years. Political elites who lodged elsewhere in Richmond regularly dined with her and her boarders too. If Randolph kept a registry or log, it has been lost. Thus, it is hard to know how many regularly sat down to eat at the Queen—but we might reasonably guess, when adding in some food for staff, that her staff often had to cook for twelve or more. Even if we do not know the size of Malinda Russell's house, we do know she had experience not only cooking for tourists there in season but also cooking professionally, presumably larger batches in the pastry shop. Boardinghouses like Randolph's and Russell's required large purchases of foodstuffs, recipes that scaled easily, and dishes that could be carefully timed to come together at the right moments in busy, bustling kitchens for hungry, impatient diners.

Mary Randolph spent the final years of her life working on her cookbook at the Washington home of one of her children. Biographies of women and men enslaved by Randolph are harder to trace after the Queen's closing.

After Malinda Russell published her cookbook, she vanished from historical records. Did she make it back to family and property in Tennessee? Did
her son survive the upheaval of moving to Michigan? Did she survive the
war years into the brief hopefulness of Reconstruction? Did she witness her
home state's role in founding the Ku Klux Klan and establishing Jim Crow?
Might Michigan have proved a less complicated place for such an accomplished businesswoman? We simply do not know. Jan Longone, the scholar
who first wrote about Russell's cookbook, found it "astonishing" that copies have survived at all. Toni Tipton-Martin, for whom Russell's cookbook
formed the centerpiece of her *Jemima Code*, shared Longone's amazement
and obstacles. After frustrating attempts to corroborate details of Russell's
autobiography in historical records, Longone could only hope that future
scholars would have more success than she. So far that has not happened.

Nonetheless, both Randolph's and Russell's life stories strengthened
the argument that boardinghouses (and cooking for families, nursing, and
running a laundry business) provided viable paths for nineteenth-century
southern women, regardless of their race, ethnicity, social, and economic
positions. Randolph's and Russell's life stories together further showed that
boardinghouse keeping could lead to cookbook writing and participation in
putting the recipes and practices popular on southern tables onto the page
for distribution. Russell's cookbook may have been published in Michigan,
but it was practiced and developed in her southern boardinghouse. Recipes
Randolph claimed may have been the intellectual property of others, but
they and the system behind them were worked out in her boardinghouse.

All these women—Russell, the Queen's enslaved staff, and Randolph,
from their radically different positions within economic and racial hierarchies in southern cultures—were influenced by and helped shape ideas
of southern food from their view in boardinghouse kitchens. They created
meals that became recognizable, a shared palate of flavors, and a coherent
passport wherever southerners and southern cultures traveled. Southern
food did perhaps manage to cohere as a cuisine, not only because it lingered
in remote home kitchens among directly related family members but also
because it was shared in public kitchens that happened to be in businesses
that promised domestic privacy for let. It cohered because those boardinghouse kitchens were fast-paced crucibles of trade, industry, and invention.

For as much as Randolph's and Russell's stories tell us about the invention of southern food through their published cookbooks, they are relatively silent about business models of their boardinghouses. The fractured

historical record stubbornly remains mute about their individual hopes, dreams, motivations, frustrations, and daily life within the walls of the southern boardinghouses they led. Alice Lee Larkins and Julia Wolfe, two North Carolina boardinghouse keepers from opposite sides of the state, recorded glimpses of the business side of boardinghouses and the women in them.

CHAPTER 2

BOARDINGHOUSE KEEPERS AS BUSINESS INNOVATORS

Alice Lee Larkins and Julia Wolfe

ALICE LEE LARKINS (1840–91) had been a young bride. Her husband, Robert Houston, was a lawyer who worked with colleagues in Wilmington, North Carolina, and Washington, DC. When he died in 1870, his estate was tangled, and her rights to his assets were contested, despite their six-year marriage and two children. "Hopes of a happy home and noble life which smiled so beguilingly upon one where now are you all? Gone—Gone forever—!" the young widow cried in her opening diary entry. Alice had to persuade some of Robert's former connections to work on her behalf, a frustratingly slow process. As would characterize much of her widowed life, Larkins constantly weighed legitimate offers of help against those from men who could see only a young woman with prospects of money—men like a sheriff who, less than a month after Robert's death, "professed such strong friendship for my dead husband" that he wanted to advise her as to what he called the "best course." Unfortunately, that course was to be his mistress. As Larkins put it, he wanted her to "rent a suit [*sic*] of rooms in any part of the city and let him be responsible for the rent." It was the first of at least six proposals she rebuffed in her short diary. In reply to "Sheriff S." and with Fanny, a woman employed as her parlor maid, as witness, Larkins "evinced my appreciation of his kind words by ordering Fanny to 'show him out.'" Larkins added that she "gave him a further cordial invitation to stay out."[1] Such flashes of strength (and humor) run throughout the diary. In its pages, Larkins navigated the world of proper behavior for women of her social class and race.

Larkins's diary today is in the Southern Historical Collection at the University of North Carolina at Chapel Hill. Written between February 4, 1870, and November 6, 1871, it gives us a glimpse into the life of a boardinghouse keeper who went into the business because it was the best option for a young widow conscious of class status to earn money. It also reveals a woman who ended up enjoying the freedom and opportunities the business provided until she remarried and moved into the next phase of life, carrying the skills and lessons of the boardinghouse with her.

If one were challenged to name a famous southern boardinghouse and its keeper, Larkins would not come to mind. Instead, many might list fiction's Dixieland and its owner, Eliza Gant. Thomas Wolfe fictionalized his autobiography and published it in 1929. *Look Homeward, Angel* told of childhood in Asheville, North Carolina, and included a vivid portrait of a boardinghouse keeper based on his mother, Julia Wolfe (1860–1945). Faced with too many children to feed and a husband who drank, Eliza Gant looked at houses not as her husband did, as "picture of his soul, the garment of his will," but instead as "a piece of property, . . . a beginning for her hoard." Her husband thought that "the residence of anyone under his roof not of his blood and bone sowed the air about with menace, breached his castle walls." Specifically, "he had a particular revulsion against lodgers: to earn one's living by accepting the contempt, the scorn, and the money of what he called 'cheap boarders' was an almost unendurable ignominy." But to Eliza, "not merely to possess property, but to draw income from it was part of the religion of her family." She "was willing to relinquish the little moated castle of home; the particular secrecy and privacy of their walls," and, ultimately, she had her way.[2] Dixieland, known in real life as the Old Kentucky Home, came into being. Readers see Eliza Gant through the eyes of her son Eugene, fictional voice of Thomas. Eliza fed Eugene unpalatable soups, insisted he sleep at the drafty boardinghouse rather than in his father's home, and offered few gestures of love or understanding to the lonely boy. She was, to Eugene, not an easy woman. But she was a savvy businesswoman who turned to running a boardinghouse to accumulate capital.

Julia Wolfe ran the Old Kentucky Home boardinghouse on 48 Spruce, near downtown Asheville, from 1906 until 1920. After 1920, she stopped serving meals but still took in roomers. The Depression was hard on the business, and the death of Thomas, her youngest son, in 1938 was hard on her. Nonetheless, Julia lived in the home until her death at age eighty-five. Family members and friends worked to preserve the property and secure its heritage status; today one can tour its current reincarnation as the Thomas Wolfe Memorial, a National Historic Landmark and a North Carolina Historic Site and Museum. The site and its archive also make it possible to enter what Thomas's father dismissed as "Julia's barn" and focus not on Thomas but instead on Julia and the headquarters of this businesswoman's boardinghouse enterprise.[3]

Mary Randolph and Malinda Russell made visible the role of female boardinghouse keepers in the South in inventing southern food. However, because their archives are fragmented, they provided precious few glimpses into their boardinghouses as businesses. Larkins's and Wolfe's lives show how boardinghouses allowed certain women to create business models that were cooperative, required little formal capital but rather adaptation and invention, and responded flexibly to customer needs. Boardinghouse women's entrepreneurial innovations changed their own lives as well as those of people around them. In so doing, their boardinghouses provided key sites for southern business innovation more generally.

Alice Lee Larkins: A Widow Finds a Way in Wilmington

Some nineteenth-century diaries are taciturn to the point of offering little more than weather reports or records of death. Not so the daily diary of Alice Lee Larkins. Her voice leaps off the page. Born in 1840, she was not quite thirty when widowed; her two children were ages three and five. After a period of mourning, Larkins regrouped. She was funny, resourceful, deliberate, and feisty; she built a business that eventually supported not only herself but also her extended family. Pages of her diary record Larkins embracing a new life. Being a boardinghouse keeper rather than quickly remarrying proved to be an actual "best course"—and she wrote about it in no uncertain terms.[4]

When first widowed, though, Alice was at a loss—"If I but knew what way to turn!" Cousins in Wilmington suggested she move in with them, which she did temporarily. But, she noted, "they have persuaded me to quit home keeping," and "under pressure" from them and others, she gave up living on her own with her children, "but unwillingly for I cannot divest myself of this idea of committing an act that I'm to regret." Being dependent upon others did not sit well with Larkins. She mused privately, "I cannot get used to it and don't think I ever shall." Having had a taste of living away from family, the idea of returning to her childhood family circle chafed. She wrote, "There is so little congeniality between my family and myself—we are so utterly dissimilar in thoughts feeling & principles that I feel like an alien and I believe they regard me as such. . . . There is no one member of the whole family who understands me at all."[5] This was a low moment of pique in the diary—elsewhere Larkins demonstrated how close she became with at least the women in her immediate family.

That later closeness flourished only once she developed and executed a plan to maintain her independence. Larkins considered paths available to white women of her social class: teaching, nursing, and remarriage. "Mr. and Mrs. B," her cousins, suggested she "take charge of a school," and she interviewed for a teaching certificate. However, she could not find a situation that allowed her to keep her children close by. Her parents, concerned about her and the young children, pressured Alice to move back into their household, as they split time between Wilmington and the family's rural Lillington Hall. Reluctantly, she did.[6]

Life in the family fold involved cycles of visiting friends, going to church, and performing tasks Larkins described as "duty," such as nursing sick relatives. Privately in her diary, she began to lament what she called "this queer . . . feeling of dependence." Larkins clearly did not enjoy her new life; more than that, she did not like what it was doing to her personality and spirit. She wrote, "What a miserable good-for-nothing thing I am getting to be. I wish I had my old health spirits and hopes, but I believe I'm growing into a regular grumbler."[7] Something had to change.

Unfortunately, even more serious illness struck first her and then the family. Through early summer, as soon as she partially recovered, she dove into nursing family members. Larkins saw all but one pull through the first wave of illness. Briefly in late summer, she moved back into her own Wilmington home, but the respite did not last. Her time was occupied by correspondence with attorneys in Washington and visits to her legal team in Wilmington. The law practice owned by her husband had been neglected during the war and his illness after; the business was still entangled when he died, leaving a complicated mess for Alice to sort through. Soon, even those tasks could not be prioritized. Larkins wrote, "Oh! What a troubled household this is. Almost every member of this family ill and I just recovering from a severe attack. . . . It seems not improbable that more than one grave will be needed."[8] Larkins was sadly prescient.

As summer turned to fall, Larkins could hardly "steal a few hurried moments while watching and nursing the sick to write." She described the home (it is unclear, but probably this referred to Lillington Hall) as "a regular hospital," and she watched "every family in the village" face similar illness. By November 1870, Alice had suffered profound loss. Her son Percy and her father both were in those early graves she had predicted. She recorded their deaths after having "been full half an hour trying to compose myself to commence writing."[9] Alice grieved again, but this time, she also planned.

Larkins was keenly aware that virtually all support that patriarchal protection offered white women in the nineteenth-century South (a substantial amount, especially in the case of women of Larkins's class) was now gone—husband, father, son. Her remaining daughter was quite young; her niece was unmarried; her mother now joined her in widowhood.[10] For our purposes, the value of Alice Larkins's diary becomes clear in an extraordinary entry she made on November 19, 1870:

And now another duty rises up before me; one which now seems formidable to me, but I know that He who knows my heart and the motives which activate me will not withhold the means from me. Father's death leaves Mother and Little Rose homeless, and though neither of them realize the fact yet, the time will come very soon when they must. And by that time thank God, I shall have a home to offer them, if it is an humble one. This week unexpectedly I received my money from Washington and have deposited [it] in the bank until I can invest it in some manner to provide a home for them and myself. My physicians differ in opinions: one saying my lungs are diseased another that it is my liver, but they both agree upon one point that no sedentary life must be chosen by me, and as the only resort I am advised to open a private boarding house.[11]

And there it is in the moment. Right then, she decided to open a boardinghouse.

Between November and January, Larkins worried about her decision, writing, "I dislike that idea very much but see no other way." But she forged ahead, researching how to find boarders and how to open her business. In November she wrote, "These boarders of Mrs. C's are all quiet and steady and if I was sure of getting only that kind it would not be so bad." By January 1, 1871, plans were made: "I have taken possession of my new home; made new resolves and it is a new year in which I commence a new life." Despite hesitations and feeling "awkward" at the head of the table on the first day, Alice embraced the new role.[12]

Nine days and two additional boarders later, she was recording amusing stories. As she worked to convince Rose, her adolescent niece, to join her in the adventures, she said, "To commence, I gave her a high-colored picture of my first days experience in this as she calls it 'play-house'—my Biddy-like appearance encounters with draymen, boys, women &c, and was glad to hear a ringing laugh follow. I think I'll bring her round."[13]

Larkins was not alone on that learning curve in taking on full-time housekeeping for profit. Writing in the *Southern Cultivator* in 1872, "Mrs. Stayclose" gave advice on how to manage the "Trials of House-Keepers." She warned that even family "house-keeping does not only consist in ornamenting the front parlors and keeping up the flower-garden." She suggested women look to boardinghouse keepers for lessons in dividing duties into "Daily, Weekly, Quarterly, and Annual" tasks, promising this would at least help regularize the effort required. Mrs. Stayclose insisted that "ladies [should] procure one of our Southern cook-books prepared to suit our products and customs" (she recommended *Mrs. Hill's Southern Practical Cookery and Receipt Book*, but of course Mary Randolph's or Malinda Russell's would have worked too) for readers to have a chance at remaining "pretty even to fifty."[14]

Whether by dividing tasks on a yearly calendar or by managing employees efficiently, Larkins successfully expanded her capacity, taking on more boarders. Soon, she had the business enough under control that she could focus on other aspects of her new boardinghouse life.

In many ways, Larkins's boardinghouse story hews closest to nineteenth-century popular stories of how white southern women entered and navigated the business. Some of those traded in stereotype and myth; others held to core realities for some women's lives. Larkins emerged during the Reconstruction era a widow (her husband died at home, not in battle, but, like many of her generation, life before the 1870s looked quite different from life after it). She may have lost economic resources from her early life, but she retained the social capital to fight for the security she felt was her due. Larkins was well educated (not only did she qualify to teach, but her diary included poetry, occasional French and Latin terms, and biblical and literary references). She continued in the racial hierarchies of North Carolina's class structures in the postwar period, hiring African American men and women to work in her boardinghouse and writing about visits from "old servants" who knew her as a child "on the old plantations"—enslaved men and women saying complimentary things to the daughter of their former enslavers.[15] And she took on larger US racial and ethnic hierarchies, as evidenced by her joke comparing herself to female Irish domestics (her "Biddy-like" appearance). She and her family were deeply concerned with "respectability." Larkins herself seemed aware of the images surrounding her, as she knew her first boarders would set the tone for her and her business's reputation into the future.

Larkins never in the two years of her diary mentioned the new racial politics of her port city. She did not discuss terms by which she paid Black men and women working for her; nor did she mention their opinions about Wilmington life. Knowing Larkins was writing and working in Reconstruction-era Wilmington gives additional pointedness to absent Black voices in the diary. When Larkins was operating her boardinghouse, Wilmington was a diverse city pushing back against characterizations that confined African Americans to happy slaves longing for plantation days. Yet in the 1870s, the first-generation Ku Klux Klan was active on Wilmington's streets and in its media; social structures were shifting and unstable as newly freed African Americans joined long-term free Black residents, working-class whites, merchant-class whites, and formerly planter-class white elites to remake Wilmington's landscape. Successes of Black politicians, newspapers, and emergent wealth in the city eventually exploded in 1898, when a killing spree by white residents seized back gains made by Wilmingtonians of color. Massive societal changes were hidden in Larkins's diary but not in the city.[16] The Wilmington of Larkins's boarders could have led to a different America, but the language of her diary suggests complicity in, if not endorsement of, the racial order in which she was raised and that would prevail for a while longer.

After her father died and before her husband's estate troubles were resolved, Larkins keenly realized the economic fragility of her position. Albert Rhodes, writing in 1876 in the literary magazine the *Galaxy*, noted the near impossibility of accurately counting the number of widows who were boardinghouse keepers because "the desire to appear well is so strong, in many instances, that she who is engaged in this way will not admit it to the agent of the census bureau"—and thus she remained "a social widow surrounded with a few convivial friends" in records. However, to Rhodes, for many women who turned to keeping boarders, "it is a thin veil thrown over a catastrophe persistently ignored." He faulted the desperate need such women felt to "hold aloft that shabby flag on which she has inscribed 'genteel.'"[17] Not admitting to running a business by instead calling oneself a host for friends could be a useful strategy for securing some dignity, gentility, and social trappings of being a (white) lady despite economic fragility.

Especially in the post–Civil War South, with deeply unstable economic systems, large numbers of formerly enslaved people entering economic markets on their own behalf, and significant numbers of white women and men with less (and radically different) economic capital than they had in prewar years, southern widows of all races had strong incentive to define social class outside of economic categories. Formerly middle- or upper-class white women could be understandably nervous about admitting they needed to run businesses. Larkins's diary did not catalog details of the fraying of her family's social and economic net (other than through illness and death), but she clearly saw it happening. She took action.

A key innovation of boardinghouses as business models was the informal networks that successful ones deployed—of women, of existing and newly accrued capital, of suppliers and kitchen workers, of customer word-of-mouth, and of family and community contributions that were hard to quantify but crucial for success. The figure at the center of the web of networks was almost always the keeper. Her presentation, personality, and decisions set the tone for the entire establishment. As popular culture eagerly provided shorthand for "types" of widowed keepers, the old widow whose desperation made her greedy and miserly particularly hurt. This image suggested becoming a boardinghouse keeper was a move born of desperation by women already miserable and likely prematurely old and mean. Already established in 1846, when "Mrs. Sad," the title character in "Mrs. Sad's Private Boarding-House," offered up her stingy portions, the parsimonious boardinghouse keeper was recognizable. Beyond insufficient servings of food, Mrs. Sad, for instance, was tight in all her business decisions—saving money by limiting the comfort of her rooms, towels, blankets, and other hygienic necessities. Hiding the suffering under her roof, Mrs. Sad bordered on criminal in her approach. Evoking the Greek muse of tragedy, Milward described Mrs. Sad as "a tall, slim, Melpomene looking creature; habited in some faded remains of widowhood, drawling out each syllable to an immeasurable length and sighing at every close."[18] Young Edgar, the story's main character, had been warned by his mother to avoid public hotels. The country mother felt sure her son would be safer in a private house and insisted he find a boardinghouse instead.

By the end of the story both Edgar and his mother were in their graves. Mrs. Sad enacted "vigilant observance" of her boarders; with "a long drawn sigh," she maintained she was not to blame for Edgar's death in her boardinghouse. However, given that a former boarder still haunted the house's attic, insane and starving but "dreadfully alarmed whenever he catches a glimpse of Mrs. Sad," her protests did not mean much. Thomas Butler Gunn, in his satirical *Physiology of New York Boarding-Houses* from 1857, offered up his own version of Mrs. Sad and her boardinghouse with a description of an elderly widow who ran "the Mean Boarding-House" by stingily dispensing inadequate food, linens, and space to her boarders. Gunn made jokes out of seeing through the towels; Milward made tragedy out of the cold and hunger mean boardinghouses hid. The humor and pathos of stereotyped boardinghouse keepers lay precisely in their failures to provide nurture, care, and domestic safety undergirding many nineteenth-century ideas of ideal womanhood.[19] Women like Larkins wished to avoid such pitfalls.

For women opening boardinghouses, the expectations of female nurture and care were often at odds with the realities of grocery costs, late rents, home repairs, management, and staff pay. For southern women who in any way participated in the rhetoric of southern hospitality, with all its implied largesse, the tension could be even higher. To stave off the financial collapse that Rhodes called "catastrophe persistently ignored," women needed to develop business strategies and systems, even if they hesitated to call it business training and themselves businesspeople.[20]

Scholar Edith Sparks coined the helpful phrase "capital intentions" about women engaging with self-owned businesses in the late nineteenth century. While Sparks focused on San Francisco, her phrase is useful for southern boardinghouse keepers. Whether in San Francisco or Wilmington, most women could not qualify for loans, nor did they have liquid assets to deploy should they wish to open their own establishments. Women often could not open their own bank accounts, sign on their own behalf, or, in some places, even enter banks unaccompanied. In contrast, in addition to all that lay inside the bank doors, white men opening businesses could more often rely on handshake investments and significantly more unpaid labor in key early days—that of wives, daughters, and sons—than women could. As a result, women often needed solutions that would both provide income and still let them serve their families. Women were unlikely, in other words, to just back into business without a plan. As Sparks puts it, women had to be *intentional* when they entered business, taking care of others and themselves.[21]

American media was happy to help, publishing a stream of how-to articles to go with cautionary ones like "Mrs. Sad" and Gunn's how-not-to stories for women who were considering the step Larkins would take. Article after article appeared, with titles like "How to Be a Successful Boarding House Keeper" or "How I Made a Boarding-House Successful," all of which aimed at the goal enshrined in one title: "Making the Boarding-House a Business." Of a piece with the growth of the domestic science and home economics fields, how-to articles had a heyday from the 1880s until the 1910s. Many writers were descendants of earlier cookbook and advice manual authors, but in these pieces, they brought cooking school and college training to bear on the puzzle of running boardinghouses well. Just as Mary Randolph felt confident writing recipes that she did not necessarily cook on her own, some women giving advice about boardinghouse management never ran one—some had stayed as guests in them, and still others wrote from what they imagined them to be.[22]

Sarah Tyson Rorer, a prominent columnist, threaded this needle by assigning responsibility for successful boardinghouses simultaneously on keepers and guests. Rorer was one of the founding figures of domestic science and home economics. She was a key staff member for the *Ladies' Home Journal* and *Good Housekeeping*; her cookbooks and advice books were bestsellers; and her demonstrations at various World's Fairs and Chautauqua events were avidly covered by the press. In a column titled "The Boarding-House Table," she entreated guests to remember seasonality of ingredients and not make demands that could be fulfilled only by too expensive hothouse produce. Equally, she warned boarders not to expect to eat meat three times a day at a boardinghouse if they would expect it only once a day at home. "To those who board I would like to say: Study to be pleased," she warned.[23] It was plea to boarders to extend grace to hardworking keepers.

Rorer also dispensed advice to keepers. She emphasized judicious use of leftovers and training for employees such that even the simplest food was at its most palatable ("What is more appetizing for breakfast than a nicely poached egg on a dainty piece of well-toasted bread? The ragged sort, on bread burned and scraped, costs just the same"). Fellow columnist and high-profile Virginian author Marion Harland agreed, after admitting, "If I have not kept boarders, I have at least, for my sins, been kept as a boarder." Harland also advocated for cleanliness and economy, "carefulness in the household, by watching small leaks, by purchasing carefully, by planning judiciously." More than that, she asserted, "women with 'feelings' should not attempt to keep a boarding house, any more than should women without great strength of mind and body and large patience." Only that, Harland argued, could produce "success" in the boardinghouse business.[24]

Laurine Marion Krag was perhaps the most interesting magazine writer giving boardinghouse how-to advice. She called herself a "Woman on the Inside" with "Twenty Years' Experience" as a keeper when she wrote columns in 1905 and 1906. Her mother had kept boarders too, making Krag's experience multigenerational. Krag did not reveal where her boardinghouses were located and, in fact, chose to write generally for prospective keepers across the United States. She wanted women considering opening a house to "look the matter straight in the face without any rose-tinted glasses." She argued it would take three years' time and energy to build a strong business. Insisting women should do their own accounting and keep their own books, Krag recommended soliciting itemized bills from every grocer or supplier, against which one's own records could be checked. She admitted, "There is no respite from work," but despite the difficulties, she insisted it could be a dignified and viable one.[25]

Anna Green, writing in 1914 in "Making the Boarding-House a Business," struck a similar note as Krag. Green had responsibility for two younger sisters, both of whom were still in school. Green still had her family home, despite what she described as a "reversal in fortunes," so she opened its doors as a boardinghouse. Along with offering "good homey meals," Green focused on arranging space efficiently to minimize the number of employees needed and to save steps for the people left running things. In her words, she aimed to "use our heads to save our heels." She recommended choosing sturdy and easy-to-clean furniture and decorations and arranging them in logical ways. Green bought food in bulk and set up her pantry to preserve it as long as possible. But more than anything else, she agreed with Krag about learning basic accounting and record keeping. Green advised keepers to track not only bills and orders carefully but also menus, home repairs, recipes once worked out to the right scale, and fluctuating market prices for food. While Green maintained a rhetorical facade of "the boarders, or as I prefer to call them, my family," in every other way she embraced her role at the head of a business. She viewed success as the moment when "all expenses are met and there is still enough left to give me a salary and pay an interest on our capital invested."[26] Forty years after Larkins's era, Green spoke frankly about her business by embracing language of the marketplace.

Larkins did not list her reading in her diary, so I do not know if she ever turned the pages of magazines with advice and warnings about boardinghouses. However, over the course of Larkins's short diary, her ability to negotiate with the men, women, and youth who provided food, washing, fuel, and other supplies for her business improved with practice—and she came to look much more like the successful models celebrated in the pages of the women's press. Larkins regaled Rose with stories of her deliveries and her negotiations. She also honed her skills at reading people— prospective boarders, men bent on courtship, and business associates alike—minimizing the risk of being taken advantage of over the course of her business. Of one visitor, she acerbically observed, "I've been taking notes in my quiet way and the result I'm sorry to say is not complimentary to the notified parties. Item 1st. She has displayed lack of pride in transgressing all the rules of ettiquette [*sic*] by calling on me first; 2nd she talks too loud, too fast and employs the pronoun 'I' too often. 3rd she hasn't an honest open face and though her eye is open enough, there's the 'gleam' of the Rattle-snake without the i. 4th she is a tattler. 5th she is bold before new." She experienced her first theft in the boardinghouse (of her own wallet containing seventy-five dollars), but she decided not to prosecute the thief because she felt the woman must have really needed the money. Larkins did, however, rework her own security measures.[27] She spent time in her diary chronicling her changing levels of trust and sophistication as a businesswoman who needed to have a grasp of human nature in both personal and professional registers.

Boardinghouse keepers' business innovations involved translating their assumed skills at running a household and managing or performing nurture and domestic care. The change can be difficult to see because many keepers fought to maintain an illusion of naturalness. But women who ran successful boardinghouses developed viable budgets; navigated the public world of bills, supplies, and negotiations; and turned their assumed skills into actual ones. They built savings and social capital even if banks did not recognize them. Because of the particularities of locating businesses in boardinghouses, they also navigated issues specific to their roles as women who provided domestic space and service for pay.

Boardinghouse Marketplaces: Food, Lodging, and Marriage?

As often as articles discussed business skills of boardinghouse keepers, others busied themselves addressing marriage prospects of keepers, especially widowed ones. The marriage market had stakes as high as all the other markets that prospective keepers navigated. Indeed, 30 percent of the establishments that Thomas Butler Gunn satirized were headed by solo women, including, for instance, the "Tip-Top" boardinghouse, "The Boarding-House where You're Expected to Make Love to the Landlady," and the Southern Boarding-House, whose landlady Gunn called a "nominal" widow since her husband abandoned her almost a decade in the past.[28] A similar cultural imagination fueled questions from Larkins's circle of friends and acquaintances while she aimed to run a dignified, "tip-top" establishment. With the sheriff and other men offering marriage and making love to her as a matter of course, Larkins had to navigate expectations and reputation alongside the bills and budget of her table and lodging.

While opening a boardinghouse could make financial sense, especially for upper-class white women, they were keenly aware of the sexual stakes of inviting "strange men into the household." One caller told Larkins directly that "he fancies widows." She quickly dismissed him. As scholars have pointed out, because the association of boardinghouses with prostitution and brothels ran deep in southern culture generally, and because port cities like Wilmington had a concentration of brothels catering to sailors and other men traveling through the town, prospective keepers like Larkins needed to tread carefully. Historian David Silkenat used Larkins's story as a case study to note larger demographic patterns of female-operated boardinghouses expanding and moving closer to commercial districts over time (with Larkins's second location as good evidence thereof). He concluded that by century's end, the occupation of boardinghouse keeper was no longer considered so risky, thanks in part to successes like Larkins's; instead, it was viewed as "a vehicle for women's financial and personal empowerment." Larkin agreed. It was the type of empowerment that proved true in the opening lines of Larkins's diary: "Tonight I commence a new diary and with it almost a new life."[29]

Once boarders knew an establishment was not disreputable, then keepers could use interactions around parlors and tables in their houses to make their businesses more attractive. They often did so by flirting with an association of boardinghouses as places to meet future marriage partners. The assumption that keepers themselves must be seeking marriage ran deep. Anne Royall, in her travels through the southern United States in the 1820s, which are discussed more fully in chapter 7, did much to put this image foremost in peoples' minds. Royall, a widow herself, had been in a similar position to Larkins's at the beginning of her diary: widowed with her husband's estate unsettled. Royall's husband's relatives challenged his will (and her inheritance), and while the challenge was making its way in the courts, Royall took to the road. She earned money through writing and selling her *Black Books*, travelogues that were a mix of reviews and her pointed opinions. As she met keepers across the South (including in Wilmington), Royall assiduously took on the responsibility to classify for readers the ones she judged "marriageable."[30]

Royall cataloged where men seeking wives might profitably stay on their travels. If the keepers were young and beautiful and in addition had proved their domestic management and budgeting skills to Royall (to run a successful boardinghouse), who better to woo as potential helpmeets? In Milton, Virginia, she lodged at "a house kept by a fine, lively, smooth tempered widow." Royall continued, "She was tall, talkative, and fashionable, and I thought rather inclined to matrimony." Particularly impressive was the guinea fowl served for dinner, the first Royall encountered; it raised the landlady's reputation in Royall's eyes, leading her to conclude, "As the lady is a widow, gay, and lively, and keeps a good house, she deserves the patronage of the public, and a good husband to boot." In Charleston, she stayed with Mrs. Galluchat on King Street and raved, "She is a handsome young widow." Royall continued, "I hope she will receive the patronage of all the genteel widowers and bachelors who may visit the place." In this case, Royall did not explicitly suggest marriage, but it was easy to read between the lines of her advice (whether Mrs. Galluchat or the widow in Milton wished to remarry was unclear). She rated other women along the stage lines with whom they dined or stayed the night according to how "kind" or "obliging" or "hospitable" they were.[31]

Larkins's free time, both before and after the boardinghouse was up and running, was occupied fielding marriage proposals, regardless of whether she wanted them. It is unclear in the diary how much agency she had in this market, but if navigated successfully, having a desirable but unwinnable single woman in charge could draw customers to the door. The sheriff's offer to take her as his mistress came on the second day of her diary. Mere days after that, scarcely past her husband's death and within a month from the diary's opening, a former beau turned up and restated his case. For a few days, she was tempted, saying, "His words and voice have stirred feelings in my heart that are like resurrected objects—feelings which I thought long since dead and I cannot define them at all until I analyze them under the calm light of Reason and Reflection." But a week later, when the beau returned, she refused him. Her reason had everything to do with her sense of self-worth and intelligence: "I know my own heart and the calm sisterly affection I entertain for him is not the feeling to bestow with this hand. God help me and deliver me from ever prostituting myself thus for the sake of a home and luxuries. I am that man's superior in intellect and I must look up in love not down." On where Larkins got the idea that marriage frequently involved selling one's independence for the cover of a man's home and the bestowing of luxuries, the diary was silent. It has an intriguing whiff of the late nineteenth-century's women's movement and the free love theorists' arguments for marriage reform—but it could just as easily be a reflection of hard lessons from her own marriage or female family and friends' marriages and the difficulties of untangling her first husband's finances. Regardless, Larkins held firm to her independence—and her conviction held through her time as a businesswoman. Huffily, she noted another acquaintance "told me today that I'd be married in less than 6 months. I didn't express to her my opinion, but had one for all that."[32] Facing a full parlor and a rotating cast of boarders, family, and friends, Larkins repeatedly had to bite her tongue.

Four more marriage proposals followed, one from a notorious "woman hater" about whom Larkins sarcastically wrote, "What in the world can he see in me to love?" Another was from "such a 'puppy' in late years that I feel absolute contempt for the man. A perfect walking figure of Egotism—an animated statue of vanity—who could like him with all those 'airs' he sports so plainly?" A "formally and methodically gotten up 'offer'" inspired her to exclaim, "I've had quite enough of matrimonial experience to rest on it awhile. What has got into that man's head to address me—a woman at least five years older than himself [?]" Again, Larkins declared that marriage without love was little more than prostitution, saying, "Be my condition what it may I shall never marry any man I do not love, no matter how great might be the advantage to me in a pecuniary point of view. How any woman can thus legally prostitute herself I cannot understand for marriage without love is in my opinion nothing less." She wrote in her journal emphatically, "Sorry, I am not 'on market.'" By the fourth proposal, she admitted, "To save my life I could not keep my face straight during the 'trying ordeal'" of listening to the offer, behavior her niece Rose teased her about after. More to the point, Larkins's life *had* love and joy in it. She had found both through her boardinghouse: "Twelve months ago I was a homeless miserable waif: moneyless and sometimes I thought and felt friendless. Now, though plain and simple, I have a <u>home</u> and many friends; a home where I may take my dear old mother and work for her and care for her as she has always cared for me."[33] These were the joys and realities of her new life. She fended off more marriage proposals, for Rose as well as herself.

The most serious courtship came from a "Mr. S," largely because he was the first man Larkins struggled to figure out ("He worries me because he is the first man I ever met whose disposition I cannot understand"). She could not make a five-point list of his character as she had done for other boarders. He was a little dangerous, a little suave, a little kind: "I cannot analyze my feelings towards that man: I want to trust him—I like him—but that hateful 'gleam' prevents me. Strange—strange man! He pities a dumb animal—I have seen him bend and lift a bent or broken flower as if it were a human and yet—I believe that he would seduce a woman with no more compunction than I would pick a ripe apple." She wondered whether he was courting Rose but realized he had his eye on her all along.[34] Finally, Larkins agreed to go on a drive with him.

The following morning, her annoyance crackled on the page. Mr. S arrived to pick her up as darkness fell—late for propriety and social manners. A polite boardinghouse keeper had a reputation to maintain. What did Larkins do? She wrote in her journal the next morning, "It was quite twilight this evening when Mr. S came and though I did not quite like the idea of a night-ride with a stranger—I went and took along with me 'an ounce of protection' in the folds of my innocent looking chemisette. Wonder if he would feel complimented if he knew the proximity of that 'Colt's Revolver' to his immaculate white vest. He is one of the most fastidious, 'tasty,' neat men in appearance I ever met."[35] Riding around the Wilmington countryside with a gun in her bodice, Larkins was a woman in charge of her own body and her own decision-making. Mr. S vastly miscalculated this particular businesswoman, a fact Larkins made clear a month later. Mr. S sent flowers but addressed the accompanying card to "My dear child." Larkins fumed, "What an unconscious sarcasm! I believe he does regard me in the light of a simple weak child—but if he knew my past—if he could see the mountains of trouble which this 'child' has, utterly alone and unaided, <u>met and conquered</u> within the past ten days, how soon his opinion would change." It was the beginning of the end of Mr. S's prospects. He soon disappeared from the diary.[36] Humorous in her retelling and a window into her character, Larkins's navigation of Mr. S highlights the business calculations beyond money that women like her had to make. Social reputation, bodily safety, and personal respect were all fragile but necessary elements of her identity as a boardinghouse keeper.

By the final pages of the diary, Larkins had fully launched a new life along with the new career. Shrewd business decisions expanded her reach. She gave up her relatively quiet location, moving to "the noise and bustle of the heart of Town." She found "the change decidedly pleasant." As the diary closed, she had four additional boarders and meetings with both "business men and businesswomen." Yet another suitor was asking to be introduced.[37] Larkins's boardinghouses were indeed key to independence; the business model she embraced bridged her former life of dependency and shelter and helped her begin a new life of independent, intentional support not only for herself but for her family.

Alice Larkins's diary revealed personal interactions circling around the central figure of the keeper in establishing a successful boardinghouse business. As did fellow keepers, she built and used social networks inside and around traditional patriarchal hierarchies and expectations. However, Larkins never wrote in detail about practical aspects of her business—nor did she call herself a business owner. She did not list merchants with whom she traded or food she bought. She mentioned draymen and delivery people who came to the boardinghouse's doors, but she did not specify how often they came to her versus times she or her representative went to them. We do not know whether they extended her credit or whether she paid cash in hand. How much economizing did she do? Did she choose less-desirable cuts of meat or cheaper vegetables to meet her bottom line?[38] Did she hire women to do laundry on-site, or did she contract to send out for that work? The diary is silent about whether she had staff to serve or whether cooks put bowls and platters in the center of the table for boarders to serve themselves. The diary is also silent about how much longer Larkins stayed in business. It does not mark the day she closed the doors.[39]

Julia Wolfe as Eliza Gant: Most Famous Boardinghouse Keeper in Literature

Far across the state in the mountain town of Asheville, Julia Wolfe entered the boardinghouse business about thirty years after Larkins's boardinghouse diary ends. Wolfe had less formal education, and her husband often failed to bring in enough money to feed their family. Perhaps because of her family's economic struggles—or perhaps because American culture had accepted the figure of the boardinghouse keeper—Wolfe did not face the same risks to reputation and status when she opened her boardinghouse. Largely because of the short but famous life of one of her sons, Wolfe's archive is less fractured than Larkins's, filled with more accounting details, if fewer personal emotions. Her story thus complements Larkins's and addresses how boardinghouses could fulfill business aspirations of women even as other pathways to success were closed to them.

Lines between the fictional alter ego her son created for his mother and traces of the real woman in North Carolina's history—lines between Eliza and Julia—are admittedly blurry. It is complicated (and ultimately not the project here) to adjudicate which details in *Look Homeward, Angel* are "real" and which are fictionalized. Almost all scholars describe the novel as in some way autobiographical, but that is not the same as delineating what did and did not happen in Thomas Wolfe's own life. In the discussion that follows, records in Julia's own hand and in Asheville's contemporary accounts are balanced with passages from the novel that propose emotional reactions of a family to such records. Because Julia was not a diarist in the way Larkins was, her thoughts remain at a distance; because she was a thoroughgoing businesswoman, however, how she and her boardinghouse business innovations functioned are more visible.

Julia Elizabeth Westall was from a family with deep roots in Buncombe County, North Carolina, where Asheville is the county seat. She was born in 1860 and grew up in what one biographer described as grinding poverty. Julia did get some education, and that enabled her to work for a period as an elementary teacher. She was a book agent, selling books door-to-door, when she met her future husband, William O. Wolfe (known as W. O.). They married in January 1885. Julia was W. O.'s third wife; he had been divorced and widowed previously. Together, they had eight children, but the marriage was challenged by W. O.'s alcoholism and infidelities. While Julia had "boarded some local bachelors" and tourists early in their marriage, she turned to her larger boardinghouse plans after her children were born. Following youngest son Thomas's birth, Julia started looking for a place she could "not merely . . . possess" but also "draw income from." One former boarder described her as "short and stocky" with "eyes that would look right through you, and a thin slice of a mouth, under an imposing nose." More importantly, she was "commanding" and did not "tolerate any mischief"— at least from young men like the former boarder was at the time.[40] Unlike

Larkins, who had respectability and social capital to add to her attractive-
ness, and unlike women who could capitalize on existing property and fit
boardinghouses into their own residences, Wolfe hatched a more purpose-
ful two-part plan. Before she could find real estate in Asheville, she decided
to accumulate liquid capital and skills outside her hometown. She gambled
for both in St. Louis.

Reading about the 1904 St. Louis World's Fair, Wolfe had a hunch that
many residents of Asheville would also want to go. In the fictional budding
boardinghouse keeper's mind, "Eliza was fascinated at the prospect of combining travel with profit." Starting in April, coinciding with the opening of the
fair, Wolfe took a house on the outskirts of St. Louis, described in the novel as
"a white house on the corner." Explicitly taking advantage of her network of
acquaintances in and around Asheville, she promised a recognizable North
Carolina experience for travelers to St. Louis. Wolfe took along her children
but not her husband, and all summer they were in and out of the fairgrounds,
working, playing, and observing the wide range of humanity. They stayed the
whole summer, taking in boarders, until one of her twins, Grover, fell ill and
died. Soon after, Julia returned to Asheville with Thomas and her remaining children in tow. Grief is a deeply individual experience; Julia's approach
was to throw herself into her boardinghouse business. She had experienced
heartbreaking loss in St. Louis, but she returned with enough summer experience to move her plans forward and $500 in her purse.[41]

Wolfe wasn't alone. Working in food businesses, including boardinghouses, could give women much needed mobility. Oral histories and interviews from early generations of young women who left home and family
for careers as waitstaff show that part of the allure was that food service let
them see the country. Skilled waitresses and cooks could work all around
the United States, moving on to a new adventure as they saw fit, without
losing their reputations and without requiring independent wealth to do
so. Blanche Copenhaver, for instance, called herself a "born traveler" who
moved from place to place for more than twenty years because "I loved
seeing the country." Similarly, regardless of the curfews that Fred Harvey
wanted his waitstaff to keep, "Harvey Girls" traded the hard restaurant
work for the opportunities it afforded them to go where the railroad led. In
fact, if she followed the rules precisely and completed her entire contract,
a Harvey Girl earned a vacation and travel rights on the railroads before
beginning her next assignment.[42]

As a married woman with children and a husband who did not contrib-
ute much financially, Wolfe could not easily travel. But she was not the only

woman who let the fairs bring the world to them. An 1892 article published in *Railway Age and Northwestern Railroader* anticipated the 1893 Chicago World's Fair in similar terms. Worried about "World's Fair Schemes" of businesses capitalizing on fair attendees' fears of not finding adequate boarding or rail fare for their trips, editors sought to soothe readers by publishing information about two efforts to regularize the lodging and ticketing reservation process by relying on reputable businesses in the fair's hometown.[43] The article also pointed out a group of travelers in the late century who preferred staying in boardinghouses over hotels. If one reads between the lines of the piece, it is clear that Julia Wolfe was not the only entrepreneur in towns and cities across the United States dreaming up ways to get to the fairs while also making money.

Once returned to Asheville, Wolfe enacted her plan to use a boardinghouse to build a business network. She was not content with simply opening her home to others. By 1906, Wolfe purchased a building on Spruce Street already known as the Old Kentucky Home. It was a large space that promised quicker profits. From the beginning, her plan was to put any net gains from the business into acquiring other Asheville real estate she judged promising as investments. At first, she lived in the family home with her husband and tried to run her boardinghouse from afar. Soon, however, she moved into her business, leaving one of her daughters to run the household since her husband insisted he would not move. So entwined was her identity with the business, Wolfe did not allow herself to have even small luxuries in her own private quarters of the house. A "plain cot" without a headboard and a "single chair" were the only furnishings in her room.[44] Julia Wolfe became the face of her boardinghouse and the driver of its operations—roles she played for the rest of her life.

One thing that distinguished Wolfe from Larkins and the keepers to whom the advice columnists wrote was her deliberate approach to property. The Spruce Street boardinghouse was built in 1883 and was a single-family home for the first years of its existence. But by 1889 a widow owned it and had expanded it to eighteen rooms for boarders. An 1890 directory listed it as the "Reynolds," the last name of Alice Johnston Reynolds. At least three other female proprietors were at the helm through the final decade of the century. One owner, originally from Kentucky, gave the property its new name. Proprietors leading up to Wolfe included couples and single women; the consistent note during this part of its history was its function as a boardinghouse. Julia purchased the home in August 1906 for $6,500.[45]

Like so many other buildings across the South that served at least for a time as boardinghouses, Old Kentucky Home, then, did not begin as a boardinghouse. Negotiation for the sale included a request from the previous owner that Wolfe keep its name—a request she acquiesced to, recognizing value in its previously established reputation. Along with planting a garden, Wolfe put some of her early profits into expansion and alteration of the building—a better kitchen, more rooms, and the like. At its height, the property had 8,000 square feet of floor space and twenty-nine rooms. Scholar of Wilmington boardinghouses Glenn Perkins argued that in his southern city's case study, for the most part, "buildings were not designed to be boardinghouses; boarding's architectural function was based on adaptation rather than intention."[46] For both Wolfe and Larkins, in practice this meant they did not necessarily require (or even want) purpose-built boardinghouses. They did, however, want to find and enhance purpose-chosen spaces. In other words, both women looked to the spaces they rented or purchased with an eye to how they might successfully operate a boardinghouse within the walls. They gambled on location and then invested labor and resources into making interior spaces work. In practice, while limited by resources, such decisions were about sustainability in the career. Significantly, such choices make southern boardinghouse women harder to see from a historical distance and in fractured archival records, but for the women themselves, it was the easier (or only viable) option for the unbanked or for people with limited initial financial resources.

Julia had been looking for the right property, and Thomas described, through the thoughts of Eliza Gant, the types of calculations she might have been making. Her idea of a boardinghouse was not an inward-looking, private home space: it was always outward-focused, connected to the ebb and flow of business, commerce, and development that connected the house to Asheville, to the larger South, and to the world. First, Eliza looked at the town "in the pattern of a giant blueprint." She knew what each piece of property was worth, and she "watched the tides of traffic cannily; she knew by what corners the largest number of people passed in a day or an hour." She judged growth possibilities and future changes, most especially where routes might be straightened and made more efficient. Wolfe wrote, "Her instinct was to buy cheaply where people would come; to keep out of pockets and cul-de-sacs, to buy on a street that moved toward a centre, and that could be given extension." "Dixieland" fulfilled all these requirements: "It was situated five minutes from the public square, on a pleasant sloping middle class street of small homes and boarding houses," and Eliza was pretty sure that a straighter, more direct street would be constructed along its frontage soon. The house itself was "a big cheaply constructed frame house of eighteen or twenty drafty high-ceilinged rooms: it had a rambling, unplanned, gabular appearance, and was painted a dirty yellow."[47] None of that mattered to Eliza because it had already been converted by its current owners into a boardinghouse, so all she needed to do was put her own touches on the business. Real-life Julia jumped at the opportunity and made the purchase.

It was a crowded market, driven by Asheville's seasonal tourist cycles and thriving business and county government economies. Boardinghouse keepers needed to find ways to advertise their businesses; approaches ranged from subtle to explicit. If you could not afford to summer in one of Asheville's grand hotels or resorts or if you wanted more intimate lodgings, your plans still could take place in the city. All manner of boardinghouses stood ready to cater to visitors; proprietors needed to distinguish their properties from fellow boardinghouse keepers' offerings. Private houses, operating by word of mouth, found one audience; houses that advertised in the city directory, local newspapers, or railroad pamphlets found another.

The *Visitors Guide to Asheville, North Carolina*, an undated sixty-six-page pamphlet published sometime between 1893 and 1918, gave detailed descriptions of boardinghouses seeking residents. Mrs. S. Stephenson boasted that her "Carolina House" had a "table furnished with best that market affords"; she also pointed out that "electric cars pass the door" of her house from its North Main Street location. Mrs. William Turner's "Aston House" was a bit farther away, but she offered stoves in each room, as well as hot and cold water in the bathroom. Likewise, Mrs. F. E. Rice's location of her "Select Boarding" on Hiwassee Place had a lawn and a veranda. "Castle Rest," run by Mrs. Schirrmeister, featured "cooking in best of Northern Style" and steam heat to augment each room's fireplace.[48] If you stayed with Mrs. W. R. Bearden at "No. 15 Bearden Ave.," you could be "adjacent to grove of pines." Some keepers were terse, such as Mrs. L. V. Brown, who merely noted, "References exchanged"; others, like Mrs. C. B. Way of "Dell-Rosa," waxed poetic. She promised to "entertain a limited number of guests in quiet, comfortable, country style. They can have large, airy rooms on first and second floors, with open 'fire-places' or stoves. From the home farm she will furnish them fresh milk and butter, fowls, vegetables and fruits."[49]

Some families simply piled children into shared bedrooms for May through August and catered to one or two summer residents. Likewise,

Julia sent Thomas back to his father's house or crowded him into her room during the busy summer periods. If they were willing to endure temporary discomfort, families could earn enough extra cash to support them for the quiet parts of the year.[50] In the novel, Thomas Wolfe distinguished between home and business in a boardinghouse family through comparative portraits of the tables in each—with his father's home table overflowing with bounty and his mother's public table stingy and business-oriented. For young Eugene, contrasts between his meals with his father (cooked first by his mother and then, after Dixieland opened, by one of his sisters) and those he scrounged at the boardinghouse or on the various jobs he took to get out from under his mother's wing were stark. At his father's table, Eugene saw seasonal variety. Fall hogs and apples gave way to winter turkeys and citrus that, in turn, led to spring lettuces and radishes. Wolfe described a whole day of eating in spring:

> In the morning they rose in a house pungent with breakfast cookery, and they sat at a smoking table loaded with brains and eggs, ham, hot biscuit, fried apples seething in their gummed syrups, honey, golden butter, fried steak, scalding coffee. Or there were stacked battercakes, rum-colored molasses, fragrant ground sausages, a bowl of wet cherries, plums, fat juicy bacon, jam. At the mid-day meal, they ate heavily: a huge hot roast of beef, fat buttered lima-beans, tender corn smoking on the cob, thick red slabs of sliced tomatoes, rough savory spinach, hot yellow corn bread, flaky biscuits, a deep-dish peach-and-apple cobbler spiced with cinnamon, tender cabbage, deep glass dishes piled with preserved fruits—cherries, pears, peaches. At night they might eat fried steak, hot squares of grits fried in egg and butter, pork chops, fish, young fried chicken.[51]

At the boardinghouse, such sensuousness was not supported. For night after night of uninspired soup, Eugene blamed his mother's inability to keep African American workers. "Good soup," Eliza angrily insisted to her son who would rather eat anything else on the boardinghouse table. At Dixieland, the food was generic—unspecified soup—never described further, with none of the seasonal excess at his father's table; Eugene only noted that the more filled the house was with boarders, the longer he had to wait to even get a seat at the table and the smaller his own bowl of unsatisfying dinner was.[52]

Here the distance between novel and mother matters. One of Wolfe's former boarders recalled that the food she offered enticed customers on its strengths alone, with "many people" coming "just for a home-cooked meal." Good food fit into the marketing plan for a successful boardinghouse in a crowded vacation town. The boarder, Joe Wakefield, continued, "Mrs. Wolfe would serve fried chicken and heaping piles of mashed potatoes set at either end of her long dining room table. There were slabs of ham, fresh sliced tomatoes and a big piece of fruit pie or a cobbler for desert [*sic*]." The Appalachian excess on the home table in *Look Homeward, Angel*, in other words, seemed to come in part from the author's experiences at his mother's Old Kentucky Home boardinghouse table. Wakefield remembered people piling their plates so high they looked "like pigs, as they dove into their heaping platters."[53] This is a far distance from the fictional son with hurt feelings remembering lonely soup on the table.

Yet, even in the boarder's fond memories, Wolfe emerged as a consummate businesswoman, or, according to Wakefield, "Everything had a price, and everyone paid." Records show that Wolfe sourced some food on her table from her own backdoor garden, supplying most of the fresh food from there especially in the early years. Other supplies came from "fresh stock bought daily off the farmers' wagons." Best for purchasing produce, though, was Saturday night, when "prices came down." Given her and her family's long history in both the city of Asheville and its surrounding agricultural areas, Wolfe must have been an astute haggler and purchaser.[54] Her existing networks gave her significant advantages for launching her business.

Wolfe's ledgers, still in the house, now in the collection of the Thomas Wolfe Memorial, a North Carolina state historical site, show her following much of the advice given in Krag, Rorer, and Harland's how-to articles even as she surpassed the modest stated aims of the columnists. Wolfe kept meticulous records for each lodger, down to the number of cigars, books of matches, and extra servings of butter they had her provide. Mr. S. M. Smith had two cigars at five cents each on September 6, 1909. Wolfe procured postcards (ten cents) and stamps (two cents) for guests regularly. While the Lincoln and Fowler families were in residence, she ordered peaches as well as vegetables and milk from the Biltmore farm and dairy. Around World War I, Wolfe had to keep track of her bread tickets and sugar rations in the ledgers as well. For the house, she purchased bread, milk, ice, beans, apples, tomatoes (in September), buttermilk, potatoes, peaches, eggs (half a crate, so in bulk), and ten pounds of butter. She recorded paying waiters and porters (porter John Garvey received $0.50, while Ike, working as a waiter, received $1.50 in September, for instance).[55] Purchases were made almost daily. The ledgers give us a window into the operations and networks in which a busy boardinghouse keeper moved.

Building a successful boardinghouse business was not simply economizing or strategizing menus for the table. It also involved the parlor—creating the right tone and conversation to match patrons with their desires. Wolfe was strategic about fulfilling these other requirements for her boarders' satisfaction. If she had residents who were more literary or high-culture-oriented, she drew on her friends Wilma Dykeman and James Stokely. While Alice Larkins, with her education and innate social class, could orchestrate lively conversations in her parlor, Wolfe, with her scrappier background and more sheltered mountain childhood, drew from other resources. Dykeman and Stokely had been introduced to each other by Wolfe's daughter Mabel (and they remained lifelong friends with the extended Wolfe family). A powerful couple in North Carolina and Tennessee, they both were published authors. Wilma was also a working journalist and occasional professor. Wilma and Julia were especially close, traveling together later in life, despite Julia being at least a generation older than Wilma. Rather than trying to play the role of salon conversationalist herself, Julia asked friends to come sit in the parlor when such boarders were in the house. In other words, the networks and communal support around a boardinghouse were not only financial; they were also social and cultural. Wise keepers thought beyond traditional business arrangements for building their innovative models of "customer service."[56]

AFTER ALICE LEE LARKINS's diary ended in November 1871, the next concrete record of her life is a marriage certificate showing her joining with George Patterson Quinn on June 13, 1872, in Wilmington. Their nearly twenty-year marriage ended with Alice's death. She and George were both buried in Wilmington's Oakdale Cemetery, with Alice passing away in 1891 and George in 1893. One hopes that in George, Alice found her "ideal of manhood" and "noble qualities of heart . . . refinement and intelligence" that would add up to a "kind feeling manly heart to confide in and lean on."[57] Whatever the emotional keel of their marriage, Larkins closed her boardinghouse diary and its chronicles of joy and longing. Alice Larkins's diary nonetheless is a crucial document in the story of southern boardinghouses. Stereotypes of keepers can suggest that opening a house to lodgers was an option of last resort, a desperate decision one was forced to endure, and Larkins herself was not immune to those images. The same stereotypes argue that being a boardinghouse keeper aged a woman, made her mean, and brought out penury or unpleasantness. Alice Larkins proved that keeping a house could be financially viable, a path to independence, romance, and even fun.

Julia Wolfe lost much of her real estate wealth in the economic swings of the Great Depression, as, of course, did many American investors. Through a series of arrangements with banks and family members, however, she lived in the Spruce Street property through her life (even though she did not always own it). W. O. died in 1922, but her son Frank lived with her through her old age. She, Mabel, Wilma Dykeman, and James Stokely wrote letters back and forth as Julia traveled to New York City, and they planned future adventures together. Julia Wolfe passed away in New York, of a heart attack, in 1945. Both during and after her life, the property was almost lost several times: to developers, to an arsonist, and to the vicissitudes of the growing town.[58] North Carolinians are fortunate it is in public hands now. "Julia's barn," even if remembered under her son's banner, stands as testimony to the series of intentional business decisions that early twentieth-century southern boardinghouse keepers had to make to take care of themselves and their families. Wolfe's ambitious plan always viewed the intimate boardinghouse table part of a networks of markets, capital, and investments: a business, in the most ambitious sense.

Boardinghouses provided food and lodging to customers. They also had a third key element, sometimes delivered enthusiastically and sometimes with reluctance. That element was care. A deeply gendered concept, care might be explicit nursing and health care. It might be chaperonage and nurturing provided to the young, vulnerable, or naive. In what other ways were the definitions of boardinghouses stretched or expanded to fit into the lives and needs of their keepers, their communities, and their transient and long-term residents? With a deeper sense of the innovations around food and business in the southern boardinghouse story, the more intimate topics of person-to-person care inside and swirling around boardinghouses in southern popular culture can take center stage.

CARETAKING, NURTURING, AND NURSING

Huldah Sarvice and Texie Gordon

HULDAH SARVICE, the eponymous character in the 1904 book *Aunt Huldah: Proprietor of the Wagon-Tire House and Genial Philosopher of the Cattle Country*, took in orphans, abandoned wives, and weak or sick men trying to recover from drink or gunshots or both. No matter how difficult the case, Sarvice offered support and care during times of great need in the rough Texas town in which she lived and worked. The novel was cowritten by sisters Grace MacGowan Cooke and Alice MacGowan, who grew up in Tennessee and lived in boardinghouses, cooperatives, and artist communes in New Jersey, Texas, and California over the course of their long, productive lives. Cooke wrote *The Power and the Glory*, a novel that proposed that utopian boardinghouses could be respites for women in the textile industry, five years later.[1] Fictional portraits like Huldah's imagine the gendered emotions and expectations that real women navigated in opening or patronizing boardinghouses. In *Aunt Huldah*, Cooke and MacGowan portrayed crucial social safety nets provided in small towns around the border South and raised wider insights into nursing, nurture, and end-of-life caretaking in and around boardinghouses.

Georgia boardinghouse keeper Texie Gordon (1882–1962) trained as a nurse before opening her boardinghouse. She continued to work in a doctor's office while she welcomed her first lodgers. Even once she became a full-time boardinghouse keeper, she drew on customers' expectations that caregiving was part of her Athens, Georgia, boardinghouse offerings in the 1930s. In so doing, Gordon joined generations of women whose boarders simply assumed that they were naturally caring. Unlike the fictional Huldah, Gordon ran her boardinghouse in a college town.[2] That too raised questions about the role of keepers in nurturing the vulnerable in communities. A college town and county seat, Athens had rapidly expanded after the passage of the federal Smith-Lever Act in 1914. That act had spurred the expansion of land-grant universities such as the University of Georgia and enabled agricultural extensions and home demonstrations to strengthen. It also meant towns like Athens needed to rapidly develop support systems for college employees, students, and affiliated businesses.

Boardinghouses—and the nurturing they provided—became linchpins in the educational system. Across the country, including southern states, boardinghouses helped colleges grow. Before they committed to wholesale housing of students in campus dormitories, colleges entered formal and informal arrangements with boardinghouse keepers to feed, lodge, and look after students. Even at colleges that built dorms early in their existence, boardinghouses took on overflow housing for late-enrolling students or students who simply did not want to live in college housing options.[3] Colleges, especially in the late nineteenth and twentieth centuries, shaped policy, served as research engines, and trained leaders for the larger United States. Those schools eventually (mostly) took on the in loco parentis model; when they did, they learned from the boardinghouse keepers with whom parents had entrusted their children and young adults for years.

Boardinghouse keepers often were expected to be caretakers—of individuals and society—in the decades before those roles were folded into other social safety nets, from dorms to hospice, foster care to rehabilitation facilities. Ongoing challenges of poverty and weak commitment to federal governmental programs, as well as robust mythologies around purity and protection for southern white women, meant boardinghouse women played roles that persisted in southern ideologies well into the twentieth century (if not beyond). Individual keepers and boarders had a range of expectations placed on them and a variety of responses to the assumptions that they would be caretakers or chaperones. I do not assume that women are naturally nurturing or more caring than men, but I am interested in how individual keepers responded to suppositions about their skills and capabilities. In other words, the gender of keepers did not necessarily mean they were better or worse to potential patients and students, but their gender might have set societal expectations of their capabilities. How they responded is what is revealing. This small shift allows us to ask questions about why it matters that so many boardinghouses were run by women—and reveals that subsequent explicit public policy and implicit social codes were shaped by the lives of women in boardinghouses.

Huldah Sarvice's Open-Door Business

In *Aunt Huldah*, Huldah Sarvice lives in West Texas, in the Panhandle's cattle lands. She came to the area years earlier, with her husband, an alcoholic. By the time he died in a tragic drowning that also killed her two children, all that was left to Huldah was a single wagon tire. Twenty-five years old, "she turned her one talent to account and ever since kept a humble eating-house in one little town or another of the Texas cattle country." Rather than use a dinner bell, each day she calls her boarders and diners to eat using the wagon wheel. In her words, "I had gone to work cookin' fer a woman that was keepin' boarders, an' I set up that wagon-wheel by the front door, an' used to pound on the tire of it to call to meals. Seems like it would sound louder ef I had the wheel a-loose from the tire, an' 'twas no manner of account by itself thataway, so I took the tire a-loose." At the opening of the novel, Huldah is in her fifties and has run more than ten different establishments she called Wagon-Tire Houses.[4]

Her current Wagon-Tire House is in an old adobe that previously held a saloon and, before that, a hotel, arranged with individual door rooms facing onto the street. Because the only room with a lock is the kitchen, people come and go, sometimes staying a single night, sometimes living with Huldah for years. Events of the novel take place over the course of a year, except for a concluding chapter set a few years later. Sarvice's past, backstories of the boardinghouse's residents and diners, and a portrait of the small backcountry outpost on the verge of experiencing a boom all unfold. By the final page, the railroad has arrived, and the small settlement has become a full-fledged town with politicians, physical infrastructure (like streets, courthouses, and a police station), and fleshed-out social structures (such as an orphans' home, churches, schools, and doctors). Romance has blossomed between residents of the house and town; and Huldah has remained the moral backbone and caretaker of bodies and souls.[5] Her titular role as "philosopher" pushed readers to consider the female boardinghouse keeper as more than an inventor of southern food-that-works or an innovator of business models for people unable to follow more traditional paths. Sarvice, created by Cooke and MacGowan, suggested a need for nurturing and care, especially of the vulnerable, in nineteenth- and early twentieth-century southern communities, a need boardinghouse keepers could fill.

Basics of running the Wagon-Tire Houses, cooking and keeping house, are background activities in the novel. Instead, Cooke and MacGowen focused on Sarvice and the lives she influenced. Sarvice houses orphan children ranging in age from infancy to young adulthood; townspeople regularly dine with her; her open-door policy meant that men who had been drinking or people who were ill or injured could just turn up; and people across the county called her to their own homes for physical nursing and for her kind ear regarding life's cares and concerns. "Such were Huldah's daily duties!" the novelists said before listing them:

> To care for an infant less than four months old; to keep house, with such assistance as Narcissa [eleven years old] could give her; to prepare three meals daily and send one of the children to pound on the tire and summon such customers as cared to come; to doctor a sick animal when necessary, or a "sick human," as her word was, if one applied; to scatter as much sunshine as she could; to attend to the children's morals first, and, if time were, to their manners as well; to look after their souls, and not, if it could be helped, neglect their bodies.

Sarvice "invited responsibility," so later in the novel, when offered the chance to run a sedate "Orphans Home" full of socially acceptable children in a settled town, she chooses instead to be "Police Matron" and help the ones everyone else had given up on.[6]

Men like Lone Deatherage fell into the category of having been given up on by everyone. Deatherage was "a dangerous lunatic with drink, and whose every spree closed with an illness which, it seemed, would end his life." But "when one of his sprees occurred in Blowout, the Wagon-Tire House was his unfailing asylum, and Aunt Huldah his faithful nurse." Townspeople could not understand why she cared for him, but Huldah was unfailingly willing to give people second, third, and more chances. Deatherage ultimately proves to be the long-lost loving husband of a woman she had taken in, but even when there was not a neat, happy ending, Sarvice would say, "Honey . . . I've had them awful fellers to lay sick in my house; I've 'tended on 'em an' talked to 'em; I've had several that was brought to the Wagon-Tire House bad hurt, to die there." Shot by a lynch mob as he tried to protect his ungrateful brother-in-law, Deatherage finally swears off drinking, finds his way back to his estranged wife, and resumes his former identity as farmer, rancher, and family man, with his much more prosaic name, Bob Patterson.[7] While she did not count on making money off the injured or ill, Sarvice's reputation for kindness brought future customers to her boardinghouses, sustaining her business over decades.

Sarvice's medical skills were formidable, even if acquired through practice, not formal training. When called, "Huldah girded herself for the fray; and for more than an hour life was pretty much all hot water, mustard plasters, ammonia, herb teas and the various other weapons of her accustomed arsenal." Given that the credentialed doctor in town almost killed an orphaned baby by mistaking morphine for quinine because he was drinking, Sarvice's nursing was held in higher regard in the town than any other option.[8]

Published cookbooks, including those by boardinghouse keepers, supported the evidence of nursing skill that Cooke and MacGowan wrote into their fictional character. Keepers had reason to develop and collect recipes for sickroom foods and medicinal herbs. Stretching back to the earliest collections, recipe books were compendiums of household expertise that held science, medicine, and food knowledge together for families. Once they began to be published and distributed, cookbooks retained some of that earlier usage. Annabella Hill included a chapter called "Cooking for Invalids" and one titled "Medical Receipts" in her *Southern Practical Cookery and Receipt Book* from 1872. The first leaned heavily toward soft and easily digested puddings, custards, and gruels. The medical chapter covered burns, emetics, cures for coughs and colds, poisons, and more. She advised how to set up a sickroom and concluded, "A great deal of pain and suffering is inflicted upon the sick by a want of *consideration*, and not the wish or intention to be unkind. Never carry a sad, lugubrious face into a sickroom." For boardinghouse keepers, any of their rooms could suddenly be sickrooms; a good keeper was prepared. Malinda Russell listed some of her best medicines in her boardinghouse cookbook: Magnetic Oil, Black Ointment, "Sticking Salve," shampoo, hair oil, and recipes for corns, tooth cleaning, burns, toothache, and rheumatism. One recipe for Magic Oil included laudanum, chloroform, cayenne, and alcohol, among other things; one for Paregoric combined opium and licorice.[9]

People in boardinghouses in need of healing might not only be lodgers. Employees, family, and keepers themselves could fall ill. Many of Russell's recipes for medicines, it must be noted, could just as equally have been aimed at herself and fellow working women like Huldah Sarvice: two different cures for corns, one for burns, and another for rheumatism. Caring for the dying and the healing brought hazards to keepers themselves—long hours spent on one's feet, dealing with stoves, and going up and down stairs or bending over the laundry tub. Nurses joined patients in need of cures and remedies.[10]

Life ended sometimes around the Wagon-Tire House, and when it did, Sarvice was by the bedside. In the novel's rough border-town setting, many people had nowhere to go to die, no family, no home. Sarvice "sat by more than one such death-bed. 'Twould wring your heart to hear it."[11] In truth, though, boardinghouses could be homes of last resort for people without social networks across the South trying to avoid poorhouses, institutions, or the streets. In the era before hospice or nursing homes in towns and cities, on coasts, and in the backcountry, people breathed their last in boardinghouses. If they were lucky, someone like Huldah Sarvice waited on them, with kindness and understanding as they passed out of this life.

Sometimes they were not so lucky. Earlier fictional character Mrs. Sad, the boardinghouse keeper who starved her lodgers, allowed people to die in her care regularly. A Durham boardinghouse keeper, Martha Hinton, takes center stage in chapter 5. In her 1939 Federal Writers' Project interview, not only did she refuse to take responsibility for people in her care, but she also viewed those who needed it as people deserving only of scolding. When a lame man arrived at her doorstep in a snowstorm asking for charity, she told him he should just work harder. She proudly told her interviewer that she slammed the door on him. Despite being separated by a century, Mrs. Sad, notorious for her miserly portion sizes, and Hinton, unwilling to offer basic charity on a cold night, each allowed sick residents to waste away and die—perhaps even rushing inevitable death to turn over rooms more quickly to better-paying customers.[12] Not every keeper leveraged caretaking in their boardinghouse model, but most were judged against the expectation that they should.

Grace MacGowan Cooke, the cocreator of Aunt Huldah, is especially interesting in any conversation about gendered expectations because of her own life path. In 1906, Cooke filed for divorce from her husband and moved with her sister Alice to the East Coast. Her husband's response to the divorce petition noted that she particularly objected to domestic tasks that took her away from her life of "intellectual effort."[13] She joined a community of writers in the Northeast, including Sinclair Lewis, Edith Summers (later Kelley), and Upton Sinclair, committing the rest of her life to writing and art. Grace and Alice lived in Upton Sinclair's utopian Helicon Hall in New Jersey.

Located in a building that formerly was an equally idealistic boys' school, Helicon Hall featured atriums, library spaces, and comfortable lounges for conversation and artistic practices. Sinclair's vision was based in part on his reading of Charlotte Perkins Gilman's feminist writings calling for professionalizing housework. Sinclair proposed outsourcing labor of individual families to communal spots. This included communal kitchens that provided shared meals (with residents working shifts and nearby college students hired for bursts of manual labor), cooperative childcare, and more. On the night of March 16, 1907, Helicon Hall burned in a fire, injuring the MacGowan sisters, before its fullest vision could be realized. The building was a total loss, and the community dissolved.

Cooke and MacGowan, though, had caught the bug for artists' colonies and communal living. They resided in such communities for the rest of their lives, ducking traditional gendered expectations from then on. After the sisters left New Jersey to heal, they migrated across the country before landing in California. Grace never remarried but continued to raise her daughters and write collaboratively with other women. Once settled in California, the sisters were foundational figures in the artists' colony Carmel-by-the-Sea, sometimes called Helicon West.[14] Across her life, Cooke consistently looked to make space for her artistic practice; that she centered the interior life of a caring boardinghouse keeper for a novel makes sense. Having created Huldah Sarvice, Cooke and MacGowan crafted lives of nurture and care even if they refused mainstream pathways for southern white women. To get where they wanted to be, their path ran through boardinghouses.

Texie Gordon's Entrepreneurship

By the time Federal Writers' Project employee Grace McCune interviewed Texie Gordon in February 1939, available pathways for women had considerably expanded. McCune conducted more than forty interviews in Athens, Georgia. She talked to white and Black grocery store clerks, Jewish department store owners and shoppers of all backgrounds, a Syrian dry goods merchant, and various florists, bus drivers, city court clerks, tailors, undertakers, beauticians, and farmers. McCune left behind a portrait of interconnected caretaking economies in the college town.[15]

When McCune met her, Gordon was fifty-seven years old and had been running boardinghouses for sixteen years. McCune's supervisors, on reading the interview transcripts, noted in the records that Gordon was "rather successful" as a keeper—an understatement. Born on a Madison, Georgia, farm, Gordon lived there through the early years of her marriage, stayed after her husband died, and moved to Athens only after her son, who had been managing the farm, married and left. Gordon came to town with her mother and two daughters; a third daughter was already married. Upon first arriving, Gordon worked as a "practical nurse." A lower-status job than "graduate nurse," practical nursing was hard work for little pay. Gordon found the hours especially difficult because "I had to be away from home all the time, day and night, and I hated to leave mother and the children by themselves." Like Alice Lee Larkins, Gordon turned to boardinghouse keeping. She told McCune, "After thinking about everything that I knew how to do I realized that I was better at cooking than anything else, and that is when I thought of a boarding house."[16]

Like Julia Wolfe, Gordon did not just jump in. While Wolfe researched real estate and had her pilot house at the World's Fair, Gordon researched how to run a boardinghouse well. She created an apprenticeship for herself: "To get a little experience I worked seven months for a woman who ran a large boarding house." Only then did she rent "a large house and started to taking boarders." Of all the keepers we have met so far, Gordon was perhaps the least willing to gamble. So, to offset start-up costs for "furniture and linens," she "got a good cook, and then I went back to nursing." In this way, Gordon paid off her debts before devoting herself to the work full-time. She told McCune, "It was hard, but I have always been used to work, and I'd rather work hard any day than sit down and wait for someone else to do for me."[17] Her experience in nursing came with her to her boardinghouse and was one key to her success.

Talking to McCune, Gordon spoke fondly of an "old blind man" who needed eye surgery. Doctors in Athens had already told him they would donate their care of him, up to and including surgery, but they needed to know he had a place to recover. When others in town turned him down, the man arrived, desperate, on Gordon's doorstep.[18] Did he know Gordon had worked for years as a practical nurse? While she had mostly been employed by an obstetrician, she had general medical knowledge that could help a range of patients.

Gordon took the man in, embracing her nurse and caretaker role again.[19] Given the vast public health crises in the US South, especially in the late nineteenth and early twentieth centuries, this aspect of the southern boardinghouse story was crucial. Gordon hosted the ill man for more than ten weeks, giving him free room and board. She said, "I didn't miss the little he ate." Her boarders collected donated clothing for his hospital stay. Together, both she and her boarders looked in on him at night during his recovery, and soon he could "walk by himself" and live on his own. Gordon said to McCune, "I wish you could see how happy that old man is!" To drive home her point, she added, "We feel well paid for what little we were able to do." About her business model, she reflected, "I don't feel like I have lost anything in helping people."[20]

Gordon positioned her decision to take in an ill man as purely worth it. But any boardinghouse keeper who took in someone ill, especially a stranger whose family background the keeper did not know, had to calculate the cost of care versus the very real risk that it would never be paid. Some 200 years earlier, the problem was especially acute in port cities. Some passed laws to compel care for medically vulnerable sailors. According to Sharon Salinger in *Taverns and Drinking in Early America*, 1700s South Carolina had justices of the peace who allowed the "'Master or Mistress of any Publick House or Ordinary' to trust a seaman who was ill for the cost of his care until he was restored to good health," a better alternative than death on their streets.[21] Sailors were perhaps an extreme example of people unmoored from networks, but traveling salespeople and others in later centuries whose lives were upended by the Great Depression or general lack of a social safety net could still stand before a tired boardinghouse keeper and ask that keeper to make a snap decision about their care.

With her proximity to a modern hospital and her own medical training, Gordon was especially well positioned to make compassionate decisions about unhealthy boarders. For many boardinghouse keepers, however, the prospect of a sick or dying resident was precarious. A hundred years earlier, James Rees wrote about yellow-fever-plagued New Orleans. Because of the sudden onset of the disease and because of its seasonal sweeps through the city, Rees found that "boarding houses in New Orleans are conducted upon principles different materially from those of other cities in the Union."

He explained that a keeper needed to be "mother to her boarders," "nurse, and in many cases physician." Boardinghouse keepers were called on to save boarders' lives, "hence it is that in large boarding houses there exists a sympathy of feeling which is every way calculated to make one at home, though he be among strangers."[22] Another way of putting that, one that Rees as a boarder did not consider, was that keepers worried about too much death in their New Orleans houses. The balance was difficult: reputation for healthiness of an establishment had to pair with reputation for compassion and care in the face of illness. People had to want to stay not only with the keeper but in the company of fellow boarders. If too many were ill or if too many did not recover, then new boarders would not arrive at the door. Nursing helped businesses stay open year after year.[23]

Not all illnesses were physical. "The Old Landlady's Album," a fictional short story in *Catholic World* magazine in 1891, took on boardinghouse keepers who were asked to manage mental health care for unattached people in crisis. Elise, a Norwegian American who had spent some time in a theatrical touring company and then fell in love with a con man, turned up on the doorstep of a Nashville, Tennessee, boardinghouse. Caught in the throes of a worsening mental break, Elise disrupted the house with nightly terrors, wandered the grounds of the Capitol Building, needed rescuing from the roof and upper banisters, and eventually had to have sharp objects taken from her. One boarder cried, "There is *some* place for her besides your house, where she is not only dependent on your bounty but where she will seriously injure your business. Mrs. Trewhitt, I am sure, will prolong her holiday visit indefinitely if she hears there is a lunatic in the house." But the landlady refused to abandon Elise in crisis; fellow boarders pitched in to brainstorm, and together they found Elise a home with the mother of a boarder ("half a doctor and entirely a Christian philanthropist, with a large house and ample means and leisure"). Elise recovered enough to join a Catholic convent as a nun; the story ended with the landlady in her retirement "extol[ling] the delights of monotony" after twenty years of the emotional and physical labor entailed in nurturing, nursing, and caretaking.[24] Mental health care was a taboo enough subject that fictional portrayals like this can often be some of the best evidence of how patients managed to find care.

Race made a difference in that the network of hospitals, nursing homes, and medical care was built under the nation's systemic racism and inequalities. African American and other women from underrepresented groups had even fewer formal options for aging when families were not functioning as a safety net. Dressmaker Elizabeth Keckley fell on hard financial times late in life. Keckley had built a successful business, with clients from Washington, DC's elite, including most famously Mary Todd Lincoln. Needing to transition out of the physically demanding work of designing, managing a small factory of seamstresses, and fitting dresses to fussy customers, Keckley had hoped that the publication of her book, *Behind the Scenes; or, Thirty Years a Slave, and Four Years in the White House* (1868), would provide her an economic cushion. When it did not, she moved briefly to Ohio to run the Department of Sewing and Domestic Science at Wilberforce University. Eventually, she ended up moving back to DC, where she spent her final days in the National Home for Destitute Colored Women and Children. Earlier in her life Keckley had raised money to found the home and support it, not imagining that she would need it herself someday.[25]

Despite assumptions of the natural caring and nurturing instinct that filled nostalgic portrayals of southern (and American) women throughout the nineteenth and twentieth centuries, not every woman was eager to embrace the role. For many boardinghouses, food was not designed for invalids; business models were too fragile to allow for unanticipated sickroom needs; and care offered on busy days was deeply insufficient. Yet for many patients, the boardinghouse was a refuge of last resort. If your family was fractured or nonexistent, if your resources were too thin to pay for a sanatorium or home care, or if you fell ill in an unfamiliar community, you might have had to take your chances—to live or die in the boardinghouse in which you found yourself.

That boardinghouse might even be your own. End-of-life care could come for keepers themselves. Novelist E. D. E. N. Southworth surveyed the world of Washington City (now DC) in the middle of the nineteenth century. In her writing, she explored what women without means could do to age in place and in some amount of comfort. Her most famous novels, *Ishmael* and *Self-Raised*, told the story of a quintessential self-made young American man. Ishmael was kind, had a strong work ethic, and came from modest, almost nonexistent, means, but he was never too busy or ambitious to help others along the way. Ishmael was Southworth's stand-in for all that American masculinity could and should be. While he was center stage always in the novels, he provided two easily overlooked characters the means to a beneficial end of life. By wisely choosing Ishmael as their final boarder, Jenny and Nelly Downing found fully realized estate plans and care.[26]

Old ladies when Ishmael met them, the Downings were renting out portions of their family home. They chose not to have many boarders, which gave them the quiet they wanted but also the ability to form a meaningful friendship with the young lawyer: "He not only found a real home in his boarding-house, and a faithful friend in his servant, but a pair of aunties in his landladies." The Downings "had no relatives to bestow their affections upon, and so, seeing every day more of their young lodger's worth, they grew to love him with maternal ardor. It is not too much to say that they doted on him. And in private they nodded their heads at each other and talked of its being time to make their wills, and spoke of Mr. Worth as their heir and executor."[27] Jenny and Nelly approached Ishmael with this plan; he agreed. At the end of their lives, Ishmael was there. The boardinghouse became a place of care for boarders and for keepers. Given all that Ishmael represented for Southworth, her point was that to thrive and succeed, America needed definitions of manhood that recognized lessons learned from and with boardinghouse women.

Though separated by decades, Federal Writers' Project interviewers like Grace McCune shared with Southworth a desire to find stories of survival and compassion. McCune emphasized Texie Gordon's kindness. Gordon worked hard to hire and retain dependable help, because she knew how hard the work was. Like Huldah Sarvice, Gordon also knew that some guests and employees struggled to live honestly. Rather than change her philosophy, Gordon viewed occasional losses and theft as far less important than the good that accrued from trusting people. Gordon told McCune, "Oh, yes, I've lost money many, many times, and in large amounts too. When I've tried to help some of them out, especially if they were out of work, sometimes they have slipped out owing me a month's board, and some have beat me out of more than that. But for everyone that does that way, I usually find someone else that is a good honest player." Gordon contrasted one dishonest factory manager, who got months of free food before skipping out on his bills from both Gordon and the company's owners, with the "good many boarders" who left before paying but then "sent the money back" when their economic situations recovered. When hardworking girls on their lunchbreak accidentally overpaid, Gordon called them to return their money, earning the girls' lunchtime loyalty for years.[28] Gordon wanted McCune to see how the network of care stretched across Athens.

A cook might smuggle raw eggs out in her sleeves, but she also might get caught when Gordon tried to give her extra food to take home with her. Unlike Martha Hinton, who slammed the door on the one-legged man in need, Gordon freely gave hungry families boxes of groceries and a cold woman her daughter's best coat. Gordon's charity fit with her willingness for her boardinghouse to serve as a place for hospital patients to recover (a "step-down facility," it might be called today). Overall, Gordon's philosophy was simple: "I ask all my boarders to respect my house as they would their own home." For Gordon, her long career taught her that social and economic class was less important than having clients who understood that everyone was working hard in mutual networks of care.[29]

Gordon's interview revealed a deeply female network in Athens that she valued. Some of her boarders were men, and farmers and grocers with whom she worked included many men, but her fellow keepers, family, and people for whom she served as a role model were women. Gordon's daughter, recently widowed herself, was "here in town running a boardinghouse to try to get her boy and girl through the university." During the interview, a neighbor boardinghouse keeper stopped by, and the two women's conversation caused McCune to be self-reflective: "I wondered as I listened how the woman that I board with judges me; if I am rated as a good boarder or one of the kind that is so much trouble and expects too much for the money. It was my first time to listen to their side of the story and I enjoyed it." The neighbor was wearied by her unsatisfied boarders: "I can't cook a thing to please 'em, and they are threatening every time they come in to get 'em another place to stay. I just get so mad I don't know what to do."[30]

The two women turned to McCune. "Suppose you tell us just what kind of a boarder you are. Do you pay your board without grumbling? Are you hard to please? Does it take a lot of towels for you?" they grilled her. After the neighbor left, Gordon revealed that she had used the questions as a teaching moment, but not for McCune. "I'm a pretty good judge of people and you answered just as I wanted you to. She really is hard on her boarders," Gordon pointed out.[31] Lessons Gordon learned were freely offered. Gordon did not manufacture competition; she gave of herself when people asked and made space for them to return kindness to her. The model created by keepers like Gordon provided alternatives to capitalist competition: an ethic of nurturing that imagined success for a network of boardinghouse women across the South and the nation.

Gordon was not all treacle and sentiment, however. Her philosophy of kindness was also proven by its opposite: the fate left to women who tried to compete or trick her out of success. One woman "on the same street" kept asking for hints about how Gordon "managed so well," which Gordon generously gave. She offered details about balancing the books, labor she did herself, and personal touches that made a difference to individual boarders. Unsatisfied, the woman went to Gordon's landlord and "told the man I was renting from that she would give him $15 a month more than I was paying."

In response, Gordon simply gave up the house and moved to the location where McCune found her. Boarders followed her. Once the new house filled, former lodgers took rooms near enough to continue to eat with Gordon. Now bursting with lodgers and diners, Gordon concluded, "It never pays to try to undermine anyone, for in a very short time she was almost without any boarders at all." Rather than losing profits to her competitor, Gordon expanded her business. Her loyal customer base sustained her as much as she cared for them.[32]

Situated as she was near the University of Georgia, Gordon and her boardinghouse were influential not just for the nurture and care inside the building but also for the influence they had on staff, faculty, and students who dined at Gordon's boardinghouse. Across the South, students and university leaders benefited from and were shaped by boardinghouses in their communities. In turn, they went on to careers across the nation that carried those lessons with them.

Boardinghouses in College Towns

Texie Gordon interacted with university folks in the mid-twentieth century in her boardinghouse dining room. Such moments of contact were far from new, however. As far back as the 1820s, when Anne Royall toured the US South, she made a special point to see the state universities of Virginia and North Carolina. At the time, neither university had enough dorms for its students. In both, she wrote about the relationship between students and boardinghouses. Always a contrarian (it was how she sold her writing), Royall provoked hostile town-gown relations in Charlottesville, culminating with her town boardinghouse being stormed by students from the college who felt the town was using her to criticize them. In Chapel Hill, she worried about the power given by young white male students to women heading boardinghouse tables—who, she felt, were indoctrinating students to erode the separation of church and state, thereby ceding the power of universities to religion. What Royall found to be meddling interference, others may well have felt was moral, virtuous training. In both places, Royall's travel journals exploited the close relationship between boardinghouses and early college towns.[33]

Royall criticized women at the helm of college boardinghouses, but the colleges themselves often supported them, especially when they were widows of their professors. When male professors died, colleges sometimes chose to house students with willing widows, in effect to pay out insurance benefits to the wives left behind. In the 1890s, Julia Graves was one such widow. Her husband was a professor at the University of North Carolina at Chapel Hill (not a path open to women at that time), and she managed their household. Their house was located near one of the main entrances to campus. Before he passed away, the Graveses hosted other professors, college leadership, and students around their table to discuss the issues of the day.[34]

Then her husband died in 1899. Left with a house but no income of her own, she worried she would have to pull up roots and leave. One evening, a few months after the funeral, the dean dropped by. He brought an offer, endorsed by the college. If she would agree to board eight undergraduate students each year, the college would find students and arrange their stays. Parents, he said, would appreciate the home cooking and care her house could provide.[35]

Graves was not the only keeper to influence the history of the University of North Carolina. The Pickard family ran hotels and boardinghouses on East Franklin Street between the first years of the 1900s and the 1930s. Until the 1950s, the widow of the university doctor, Laura Abernethy, rented to students rooms next to the infirmary. Women like Fannie McDade, an accomplished laundress, and Louisa Cotten, musician Libba Cotten's mother, a "sought-after cook and domestic," supported Chapel Hill's boardinghouses with their labor. Such networks of women's work allowed universities to wait until their finances were stronger before embarking on major capital projects to build enough dormitories. As colleges and universities in the South were considering becoming fully coeducational, boardinghouse keepers again played a transitional role, providing chaperonage, rooms, laundry, and meals until the schools built women's dorms.[36]

For some students, boardinghouses were not just places for students to find housing. Boardinghouses offered jobs that allowed them to go to college in the first place. Joe Matheson was such a student. His education at Lenoir-Rhyne College in Hickory, North Carolina, resulted in a career with Duke Power. When he was interviewed in 1939 by Ethel Deal, Matheson described how he "washed dishes, mopped floors, and waited on the tables" at a boardinghouse to pay for his first year of college. His work had to be done twice a day, including Sunday. According to him, "I had to work hard there and had no leisure hours, but it was the only way." Matheson held the job through his junior year. By his senior year, he could afford to stay in a dorm, but he still worked a job the boardinghouse had trained him to do, busing tables in a café.[37]

Taking on responsibility for students, many of whom were away from home for the first time, added layers of work to already heavy loads of running boardinghouses. One can find similar arrangements across the South's university and college towns where the need to support youth and future leaders intersected with expectations about women's skill in nurturing and care. The college model is, indeed, often discussed as in loco parentis, but in housing, we might more properly describe it as *in loco maternis*.[38] Deeply gendered ideas of women's "natural" abilities to take care, to nurse, and to support allowed many women to become boardinghouse keepers in college towns with a robust customer base. Universities today are often some of the largest employers and real estate holders in their states; the boost that a college degree gave to graduates often propelled them to economic, political, and social achievements. Just as we have only now acknowledged the role of boardinghouses in the invention of food in the South, we ought to recognize the role of boardinghouses and their keepers in the prosperity of the nation and region.

IN THE EARLY days of her business, Texie Gordon moved locations a few times. But by the time Grace McCune interviewed her, she was mostly settled. Having gone through her own health scare, Gordon told McCune, "I am thankful that my health is so much better and that I can still run my boarding house, for it means my living to me and my daughter, and I only hope I'll be able to continue to work."[39] City directories show Gordon continued to run the boardinghouse at 363 East Hancock Avenue until sometime between 1942 and 1947. After 1947, she resided on Hill Street, three-quarters of a mile from her earlier address. She passed away in 1962, still in Athens, but was buried back in Madison, the county in which she was born, in the Jones Chapel Methodist Church cemetery.[40] Today the property on Hancock holds a government building and parking lot. The neighborhood is no longer residential, but the domestic support she provided surely helped shape today's Athens.

As Grace MacGowan Cooke and Alice MacGowan migrated from the East Coast to the West, Cooke spent time in southwest deserts with fellow writer Mary Austin. Did she meet real-life versions of her fictional Aunt Huldah while out in her own border-town rooms? When she needed to recover from injuries from the Helicon Hall fire, did she rely on friends and family, or on the staff and owners of lodging places for help? Cooke returned to the nurturing spaces of a boardinghouse in her later novel, *The Power and the Glory*. By then, she invested the ideal boardinghouse with her most utopian solutions to help tired and burned-out women across the US South.[41] In the hands of writers, interviewees, and diarists, boardinghouses held hope for the elderly, the sick, and the healers.

Malinda Russell and Mary Randolph used their boardinghouses as platforms to step forward as expert cooks. In so doing, they helped invent southern food. The spaces of boardinghouses and the recipes that men and women in their kitchens developed put words and practices around the foodways that lodgers and diners wanted. Southern boardinghouses, positioned as they were, in between the public and the private, helped southern food cohere as a concept as people learned to ask for it, consume it, and replicate it in their own home kitchens, cookbooks, or restaurants—their innovations are all around us today. Alice Larkins and Julia Wolfe used boardinghouses to become businesswomen. Unbanked and without significant liquid assets, neither woman was deterred by existing business structures that favored men with credit and cash. Their boardinghouse successes were two among many nudging American culture to see the talent and capacity of women to helm business enterprises. Women like the fictional Huldah Sarvice and the real Texie Gordon pushed health care and education where they lived to examine gendered expectations of providers—and simultaneously to recognize informal roles that befell women in communities when public options were insufficient. Boardinghouse women, through nursing and caring for students and workers outside of classrooms and parlors, provided a moral compass for future expansion of social welfare programs.

Cooking, lodging, and caring were the most visible aspects of boardinghouses through time. For boardinghouse keepers who were not natural caregivers or cooks, the assumption that women must be those things could be deployed to enable other aspects of boardinghouse lives. For keepers and lodgers who wanted political voices or sex lives that differed from community expectations or who yearned for truer ways of being, the in-between spaces of boardinghouses by their very nature could help. New ways of living inside the doors of southern boardinghouses augured new ways of living across American culture. While white women would not gain the right to vote in the United States until 1919 and Black, Indigenous, and other women of color would not until as late as the 1960s, women themselves wanted to have a voice in American politics long before that. Both Mary Ellen Pleasant and Mary Surratt used boardinghouses to intervene in their era's highest-stakes political debates.

USING BOARDINGHOUSES FOR POLITICAL ENDS

Mary Ellen Pleasant and Mary Surratt

PEOPLE AND IDEAS were on the move in nineteenth-century America, and southern boardinghouses and their keepers were no exception. Where economic booms and rapid population growth surged, women saw opportunities. Having a dozen shirts laundered in San Francisco at the height of the Gold Rush could cost as much as twenty dollars. A single turnip for dinner might require five dollars in cash. Imagine, then, the price for a clean bed in a private room of a congenial home where meals, linens, and laundry were included. Astute businesswomen looked at the situation and did the calculations in the other direction: imagine how much profit could come from providing customers a full-service boardinghouse. Mary Ellen Pleasant (1814–1904) was one such woman. She capitalized on her facility with laundry, reputation as a gourmet cook, sales background, and ability

to invest by starting a string of boardinghouses and related support businesses. To do so, she used public expectations of her innate "southernness"
to her own advantage, despite this quality being almost entirely fictional.
Pleasant built a fortune running exclusive boardinghouses that offered
her customers their fantasy of "southern hospitality," vertically integrated
her businesses, and invested wisely in business ventures and real estate in
downtown San Francisco. She leveraged those funds into activism for her
deeply held political beliefs—an understudied phenomenon that women
could deploy when they made and controlled their own capital. Pleasant
made a million dollars in the wild free-for-all that was the nineteenth-
century California economy and then used those funds to fight for abolition
and later integration around the United States and Canada.[1]

Mary Surratt (1823–65) also supported herself through running a boardinghouse. She too presented her establishment as full of southern hospitality. Surratt, like Pleasant, could and did make her own choices about how to
support political causes with her resources. However, Pleasant and Surratt
were on opposite sides of the nineteenth century's political spectrum. Surratt lived and died for her embrace of the Confederate States of America.
Her South was that of race-based politics, violence, and slave economies,
and she fought for it from her locations in Maryland and Washington,
DC. Surratt wore her southern identity defiantly, and it brought her early
death. During the Civil War, Surratt ran a boardinghouse located at 604 H
Street, NW. Today the building boasts a small historical marker but holds
a Chinese restaurant and karaoke rooms. Busy DC residents walk right by,
wrapped up in their everyday lives, rarely noticing one more piece of history
in their midst, surrounded as they are by so many representations of US
nation-state origin stories. But during the heart of the Civil War, her rural
Maryland connections and her political allegiances sent messages to potential Washington boarders ready to hear the conversation on offer within
her walls. Of course, even judged against other southerners fighting for the
Confederacy, Surratt was audacious in her participation in plotting against
the United States. Her role in the tragically successful conspiracy to assas-
sinate President Abraham Lincoln resulted in her being the first woman
executed by the federal government in the United States. That conspiracy
grew from her boardinghouse.[2]

In eras that made public participation in political life difficult for
women, boardinghouses could be locations of various political debates
and revolutionary actions across the political spectrum. In the hidden
spaces of a boardinghouse—the back hallway, private suites, storage

closets—everything from people to taboo ideas could be sheltered. These were ideal spaces, in other words, for new ideas to take hold. Further, boardinghouse women who advertised their businesses as southern show how the idea of the South spread around the nation and the globe, the consequences of which have shaped contemporary politics, another contribution of boardinghouse women to American culture today.

This piece of the southern boardinghouse story takes place in San Francisco and Washington, DC. Boardinghouse women like Pleasant and Surratt demonstrate how ideas of southernness move across place and time. As in the boardinghouse cookbooks and kitchens of Malinda Russell and Mary Randolph, where southern food came into focus, and the parlors and advertisements of Alice Lee Larkins and Julia Wolfe, where opportunities for southern women to make business innovations expanded, Mary Ellen Pleasant and Mary Surratt embraced and strategically deployed ideas of the South in political cultures through their boardinghouses and the customers they drew in. Boardinghouses were powerful tools by which women could enact and explore political agendas during times in the United States when institutional structures excluded them from voting and societal norms could discourage them from engaging in political speech in public. Mary Ellen Pleasant, having grown up in Nantucket, New Bedford, and Boston, Massachusetts, "passed" as a southerner in California. People thought she was southern and identified enough southernness in her establishments to confirm their beliefs, and that was sufficient. The South came with her when she immigrated to California, taking no space in her luggage, requiring little proof of possession, and ultimately proving expansive enough to fuel an enterprise and help fund a movement. Surratt's South hid in plain sight but also stretched to encompass her political participation despite her Catholicism, femaleness, and precarious status among her Union-supporting neighbors.

Women like Pleasant and Surratt used southern boardinghouses to finance and voice their political commitments. Despite fractures in the historical record, Pleasant's background illustrates how southern boardinghouses could be started with skills, networks, and ephemeral social assumptions even at great distance from the geographical South. Pleasant's pre-emancipation Underground Railroad abolitionist work and Reconstruction era civil rights work, financed by her business successes, open up a discussion of whose Souths are represented in southern boardinghouses and celebrations of southern hospitality embodied by boardinghouse keepers. For Surratt, boardinghouse basics—cooking, washing, and providing hospitality—made space for particularly vitriolic white southern race politics. Surratt's strategy was to insert herself in the war that was tearing the country apart.

Washington, DC, and boardinghouses have long histories together. More generally, politics and boardinghouses were interdependent across the country, including on federal, state, and local levels. Representatives, for example, lived in boardinghouses when engaged in governance at state and federal levels. While not a state capital, San Francisco and its boardinghouses hosted their fair share of political leaders and debates. Women hosted officials in boardinghouses for decades before they could run for and be elected to public roles themselves. Political boardinghouses ran the spectrum of each era's political beliefs—including the treasonous violence birthed at Surratt's establishment in her time. Surratt's boardinghouse voice made it possible for her to expand her freedom, but she wielded it to try to curtail the freedom of others. If successful, women like Pleasant would have lost rights under Surratt's vision. For both women, boardinghouses and the hidden spaces inside them relied on ideas of the South and made possible their articulation of politics inflected by some of those same ideas.

Fragments of a Life: Mary Ellen Pleasant's Ambiguous Biography

Existing documents about Mary Ellen Pleasant's early life place her in the US Northeast, among people with deep roots in Maine and Massachusetts. Nearing her death, she told an interviewer she was born free in Philadelphia; oral traditions passed on in California and among other biographers and her own earlier statements give some reason to question a Pennsylvania birth. Genealogical research has not yielded definitive answers. What is clear from the historical record and her narrative is that Pleasant's formative experiences took place in northeastern communities, not southern ones.

As a girl, Pleasant spent time on the island of Nantucket in the household of a Quaker woman, Mary Hussey. Perhaps she helped around the house (whether by choice or by financial arrangement, we do not know), thereby learning domestic skills. She assisted in Hussey's shop, a broadly stocked general store. Pleasant's most recent biographer, Lynn Hudson, explained that because the whaling economy regularly emptied the island of most of its men, "Nantucket proved an ideal locale for an ambitious, headstrong girl to learn business. Indeed, Nantucket Town was overrun with woman-owned shops." For the rest of her career, Pleasant trod in business realms seemingly without fear. This early training in accounting, sales, and marketing must have helped when she was ready to launch her California plans. Like Alice Lee Larkins's and Julia Wolfe's, Pleasant's eventual boardinghouse business benefited from more than her domestic abilities. Later in her young adulthood, Pleasant left Nantucket to live and work in Boston and New Bedford, Massachusetts. She married her first husband in Boston, perhaps while working in clothing shops.[3] During this time, she added to her business experience but also made lifelong connections in free Black and abolitionist communities.

Sometime between 1849 and 1852, Pleasant landed in San Francisco. She was not alone: California's population exploded with some new residents seeking wealth, others seeking freedom from slave states, and still others seeking simply to escape their past and start anew. Carrying some funds likely inherited upon the death of her first husband and married now to her second, Pleasant entered gold rush California with a few advantages. From the deck of the ship docking in San Francisco Bay, Pleasant looked out with capital to invest, the comfort of a safety net, and business skills from her years apprenticing in others' establishments. At the same time, it must have been a disconcerting environment after her years in northeastern Quaker and free Black communities. Black San Franciscans made up less than 1 percent of the city until the 1940s. In 1850, all of California was 92 percent male.[4] At the very least, we can say that Pleasant stood out. In hindsight, we can see how she worked that innate visibility to her advantage. But when she first landed, she looked out at an uncertain world.

For her first ten years in California, Pleasant worked in other people's households as cook and manager, earning wages that would have been exorbitant for the same jobs in other parts of the country. Reminiscent of her contemporary Malinda Russell, Pleasant was keenly aware of profits to be made cleaning others' clothes and linens. On the side, she purchased laundries, presumably outsourcing some of her own labor but also profiting off a need in the city. She may have made her first forays into the boardinghouse business in these years as well; she certainly forged connections to elite and wealthy San Franciscans when they dined in private houses in which she worked. She capitalized on these connections in coming decades. The laundry boom in the city was profitable but unstable. Pleasant sold her laundries ahead of the bust in that market; her business instincts were finely tuned to swings in California's economies.[5]

By the 1860s, Pleasant began to be listed in city directories as a board-inghouse keeper, presumably investing profits from the laundries, her own cooking, and other sources into boardinghouse properties and their out-fitting. Her public reputation shifted from employee to employer. From the 1870s through the 1890s, she owned and operated multiple boarding-houses, continued to cater dinners and events, and generally navigated the maturing economies of San Francisco and California. Her clientele was predominantly white, increasingly elite, and desirous of luxury—they paid well. In 1877, she moved into a new mansion valued at more than $100,000 when first built. The wealthy Bell family lived there with her. That they were white confused some, but Pleasant, no longer the boardinghouse keeper in residence, managed her various businesses and investments from the lux-ury of her own home on a hill above the city. The house's opulence and the occupants' lifestyle were tangible signs of their success.[6]

Even before she secured the financial stability reflected by the mansion, Pleasant spoke against the politics of pro-slavery white southerners in her public actions. Perhaps the most important detail about Pleasant's life, it is also frequently overlooked—even though it is easier to document than many details of her biography. It was so important she requested it carved on her gravestone: Mary Ellen Pleasant was a "Friend of John Brown." A committed abolitionist, she hid people escaping enslavement in her boardinghouses. Funds from her businesses (including the laundries, her own hiring out, and money from her first marriage) supported others on the East Coast working in the Underground Railroad.[7]

Easier to discuss in consequence than to thoroughly or exhaustively doc-ument, the Underground Railroad has achieved almost mythic status in our understanding of resistance in antebellum life. Women like Harriet Tub-man shepherded many to freedom. Activists like William and Ellen Craft, Harriet Jacobs, and Henry "Box" Brown cleverly devised ways to wrest free-dom for themselves and some of their families. Tubman, the Crafts, Jacobs, and Brown did not stop when they reached free states: they wrote mem-oirs describing their path out of the South. William Still collected and pub-lished some 800 stories from his time as a conductor and as a result of his research. We know countless others wrenched themselves out of enslave-ment and traveled to safer communities, even if we do not have detailed accounts from them about specific routes they took. Many remain name-less. A network of safe spaces, friendly homes, hidden rooms in the backs of businesses, and caches of supplies in outbuilding or barns facilitated peo-ple's journeys. Because this network relied on whispers and secrets, pinning down where those sheltered spaces were located is difficult.[8] However, what better place than in the halls of a busy hotel or boardinghouse? Boardinghouses, especially ones with shorter-term residents, had guests who either were too new or too oblivious (and may have additionally been too classist or racist) to know the names of all the employees of an establishment. One or two new faces could be mixed in without anyone becoming aware. With extra food, rotating linens, and flexible sleeping spaces (cots, mattresses, converted overflow hallways, and the like) at hand, who would notice if leftovers or extra bedding made their way to hidden temporary lodgers?

William Still, Philadelphia abolitionist and head of the Vigilance Committee of the Pennsylvania Anti-Slavery Society, documented as many stories from the Underground Railroad as he could. His book *The Underground Railroad*, first published in 1872, told of keepers of sailors' boardinghouses who were also conductors on the railroad. A man named Charles Gilbert hid out under Higee Hotel for a month—literally: the hotel did not have a cellar, Still said, merely pillars on which the structure was perched. Gilbert hid there on the dirt floor. Elsewhere, Cordelia Loney took advantage of her enslaver, Mrs. Joseph Cahell, when Cahell booked into a northern boardinghouse for a month. While there, Loney contacted railroad conductors and fled. Because the boardinghouse shared Cahell's "southern sympathies," fellow boarders tried to help Cahell find Loney—unsuccessfully. Another "fleeing girl of fifteen" came to a boardinghouse as "Joe," and guests were "wholly ignorant of the occupant of the upper room." They did not notice extra food sent up so that Joe could eat a Thanksgiving meal. In fact, they overlooked Joe entirely until he crossed at Niagara into Canada and arrived at a friendly boardinghouse. There, Joe reemerged as Miss Ann Maria Weems.[9] Boardinghouses supported and facilitated direct action that helped individuals but also collectively made a larger political statement against slavery.

For Pleasant, this was more than an East Coast activity supported from afar. California, despite being founded as a free state, allowed slaveholders to bring enslaved people to live and work in the state. Pleasant likely helped an ally, William West, make his San Francisco boardinghouse a shelter for enslaved people trying to escape. She sheltered men like George Mitchell and Archy Lee as their former owners tried to recapture them with help from California courts. Lee first hid in a hotel run by free Black professionals and then in one of Pleasant's homes. In private, she used her boardinghouse experiences, resources, and spaces to hide men like Lee. She also was active in public: funding conventions and buildings in which they could be held to promote abolition and later civil rights. A historical marker in San Francisco today notes that "she supported the western terminus of the Underground Railway for fugitive slaves" and hails her as "Mother of Civil Rights in California."[10]

In his years as a conductor on the Underground Railroad, William Still sent as many people as he could into Canada. The men whom Pleasant helped also had Canada as an ideal destination in mind. While many aimed for areas around Vancouver on the West Coast, the prime location for East Coast connections was Canada West in Ontario. Communities there such as New Buxton and Chatham, founded by free African Americans, were associated with *Provincial Freeman* editor Mary Ann Shadd Cary and the Ohio abolitionist John Brown. Mary Ellen Pleasant and her husband forged strong relationships with Chatham and Canada West. The Pleasants purchased property in Chatham; they were listed on the town's Vigilance Committee; and they were active around the planning and aftermath of John Brown's raid. What Lynn Hudson describes as various "legends" around Pleasant suggested she rode in advance of Brown's raid on Harpers Ferry or, more plausibly since she lived so far away, helped finance it. So far, Pleasant's participation has not been conclusively documented by scholars, but such is the nature of clandestine and illegal missions.[11] What is undeniably true is that boardinghouse keeper Mary Ellen Pleasant was a devoted activist for the rights of African Americans.

Closer to home in San Francisco and stretching into the Jim Crow era, Pleasant worked on behalf of her local community. In 1867, she brought suit to integrate city streetcars; coverage of this trial was the first time Pleasant was identified in print as a boardinghouse keeper. She endowed libraries and meeting halls in the heart of the town's Black community. She helped women in trouble, perhaps most famously by bringing a case against a state senator on behalf of an Irish American woman whom he called a prostitute. The woman claimed she was, in fact, the senator's wife; Pleasant took the woman's side. Less publicly, Pleasant seems to have supported women who needed housing or funds to escape violent or unsustainable situations. In general, she did not hesitate to enter lawsuits and legal proceedings to demand her and others' rights.[12] Her activism, on whatever the cause, was grounded in boardinghouse knowledge and spaces. In a change from the overwhelmingly white gold rush town that greeted her when she arrived, San Francisco benefited from Pleasant's political work to establish community and more just laws. To advocate for expansive freedoms, Pleasant worked in and through restrictive stereotypes about Black women that had roots in the South, even if Pleasant did not.

If you have heard of Pleasant today, it may have been as "Mammy Pleasant" rather than by her proper name. During her life and the century since her death, newspapers, magazines, oral tradition, movies, novels, and city and state histories called Pleasant "Mammy." Applied to her, sometimes the word implied caretaking and nurturing, especially of vulnerable or needy people in her orbit. Other times it was deployed to heighten mysteries around her life and business. Frequently, those calling her Mammy were spreading salacious rumors about Pleasant's role in illicit sex, brothel keeping, murder, blackmail, and tropes of stereotypical voodoo. It can be very difficult to find the woman behind the myths. At the end of her life, in an interview when she was eighty-seven years old, Pleasant firmly insisted people should try harder to find Mary Ellen Pleasant behind the mask of Mammy Pleasant. She told the interviewer in no uncertain terms, "Listen: I don't like to be called mammy by everybody. Put that down. I'm not mammy to everybody in California."[13] The pattern, however, was entrenched, and the late-in-life interview did little to dislodge the sobriquet in public memory.

Earlier in life, though, Pleasant allowed or even encouraged representations that implied she must be a southern mammy: a possible slave past, long-practiced cooking and domestic skills, and the role of trusted family advisor for wealthy elites. Frankly, given the social environment of nineteenth-century US cultures, it may have been virtually impossible for Pleasant not to be called Mammy by the mainstream press. As she appeared in newspaper accounts of lawsuits written by sensationalist courtroom reporters, she also pursued a public reputation for her businesses in advertisements and word-of-mouth marketing that required shorthand, catchy hooks. She recognized people's desire to hear a thrilling life story and responded by giving them what they wanted.

Before her death and in (dubiously sourced) biographies after, connections to prominent Virginia, South Carolina, or Louisiana families were floated. Those stories, both in print and in oral history traditions, claimed wealthy southern governors and/or enslavers in Pleasant's immediate family tree while also debating the darkness of her skin and simultaneously attributing overwrought stereotypical voodoo powers to her.[14] As they did so, her reputed origins moved farther south. How else, they asked, could she have learned to furnish so-called southern hospitality for her successful West Coast businesses? The logic was a classic tautology: circular and self-fulfilling.

Further confusing things, at other times Pleasant seemed content to obfuscate her private life herself. For years, she let San Francisco society believe that she was a mere employee in her main residence—housekeeper, maid, or cook to the Bell family. That she spent her childhood in Maine and Massachusetts; that her family connections were untraceable even in her era, much less in our own; that almost any vision of luxury and manners could fall under the rubric of southern hospitality; and that the mansion's deed was in her name and the Bell family were at most co-residents—none of this mattered for the mythmakers when it came to the islander shop clerk Mary Ellen Pleasant.[15] It is worth looking at how these ideas about southern Black women boardinghouse keepers in the nineteenth century made her politics possible.

Writing in 1933, some thirty years after she died, California memoirist Herbert Asbury claimed Pleasant arrived "preceded by her reputation, and was besieged by a crowd of men, all anxious to employ her, before she had so much as left the wharf at which her ship had docked." Asbury continued, "She finally sold her services" as a cook for "five hundred dollars a month, with the stipulation that she should do no washing, not even dishwashing." While Asbury provided no source for the anecdote, his story followed closely one printed in the newspaper the *San Francisco Call* in 1899. That version added, "When the rich merchants, richer miners, and good livers in town heard that there was a colored girl on the vessel and that she was 'one of the greatest cooks that ever came out of the south' there was an excited and tumultuous scramble." The *Call* story included the $500-and-no-dishwashing claim.[16]

The *Call* writer conflated Pleasant's next twenty years of work into a couple of days (claiming she changed her mind about the highest bidder and instead walked down the street and opened a boardinghouse that day). Asbury did not claim he witnessed the shipboard bidding scene. But his anecdote and similar ones dominated stories of her arrival. Did Pleasant know how to cook professionally when she arrived? Her first decade in California saw her taking jobs that built her domestic skills—cooking, cleaning, laundering, and running households, not exactly the ones most practiced in her Boston and Nantucket shopkeeping days. Regardless, she was willing to let stand the assumptions people held about her abilities simply because she was Black. Her expanding businesses and reputation as a boardinghouse keeper benefited.[17]

The term "mammy" was in flux in the nineteenth century, containing ideas of multiple roles Black women could be assumed to play. Confining

Black women to these roles was dismissive, if that was all they were allowed to do or be; nonetheless, almost all of these functions could be useful in a boardinghouse if actively used. Pleasant would have been six when the word "mammy" came into popular use in 1820; she was at the height of her influence when the Aunt Jemima character was introduced at the 1893 World's Fair in Chicago.[18] For Black women, for whom the images were almost inescapable and simultaneously mutable, the strategy to use rather than fight them made sense. It was another version of how boardinghouses allowed women to capitalize on what they already had. Pleasant was likely going to be called "Mammy" in San Francisco, even without southern formative experiences. People's racist nostalgia was more powerful than her actual biography in popular culture. Pleasant used the transportable idea of southernness and the natural skills it conferred to her advantage.

Pleasant's most enthusiastic biographer was Helen Holdredge. A former opera singer originally from Minnesota, Holdredge was an avid collector and biographer, but her work is problematic. Among her many publications was *Mammy Pleasant's Cookbook*, published in 1970. Prone to exaggerations but not to citations, Holdredge amplified sensational rumors about Pleasant. In the cookbook, for instance, unsubstantiated court case rumors of Pleasant's "black magic" and the story that Pleasant's mother was originally from Louisiana became chapters in which Holdredge claimed Pleasant lived and cooked with Marie LaVeau in New Orleans and then was hired as a free Black cook on a prewar plantation in upper Louisiana. Holdredge included "voodoo" and "plantation" recipes for both. Sausages, grits, and veal meatloaf were apparently "voodoo" recipes, while spoonbread, beaten biscuits, and black bean soup were on "plantation" menus. This was not respect for Caribbean religious practices; it was sensationalist capitalizing on tropes of dark, exotic magic (also a last gasp of its type, appearing in 1970 right as the soul food, Black Power era worked to change the narrative).[19] Holdredge instead presented bizarre romantic, fictional nostalgia about enslavers and their homes.

Holdredge claimed to base the cookbook on at least two undated recipe books she collected, but the publisher's preface of the cookbook said she "tested the recipes and equated them to smaller amounts, in some cases adding ingredients unknown to the cooks of that period."[20] Rather than reading it for a successful businesswoman's dependable recipes, like we could with Malinda Russell's or Mary Randolph's publications, here the cookbook says more about white readers' expectations of Pleasant. For instance, *Mammy Pleasant's Cookbook* implied that *only* by living in each region could she have known how to cook its dishes. If she served grits, black beans, or spoon-bread, she must have been living and cooking in places where those recipes were common. Other possibilities—studying cookbooks, experimenting in her kitchen to fill boarders' desires, or innovating her own specialties in her California life—were erased by the cookbook's premise.

Holdredge was not unique in treating Black women's cooking abilities with implicit derision. Toni Tipton-Martin defined the eponymous Jemima Code as "an arrangement of words and images synchronized to classify the character and life's work of our nation's black cooks as insignificant." She outlined consequences of labeling Black accomplishments as instinctual. Doing so "diminishes knowledge, skills and abilities involved in their work, and portrays them as passive and ignorant laborers incapable of creative culinary artistry."[21] Over and over, in media and culture, such characterizations erased the hard work and training of Black men and women working as culinary professionals.

Dismissals persisted even in the face of evidence to the contrary, such as Malinda Russell's description of her education by the *Virginia Housewife* plan; enslaved chefs like Hercules, who ran George Washington's kitchens, and James Hemings, chef for Thomas Jefferson, who had impressive Parisian training; and the numerous cookbook authors whom Tipton-Martin documented.[22] Pleasant may have had substantial culinary training and thus entered San Francisco with a solid reputation preceding her. It is also possible she developed expertise on the fly, once employed in the city. It is not impossible that Pleasant cooked by feel and intuition—and indeed, even today the most accomplished formally trained chefs benefit from their own intuition and natural ability at the job. Nonetheless, for Pleasant to manage multiple kitchens across private houses and her boardinghouses, as she did, required practical skills. She may not have contradicted people who assumed she had natural cooking skills by virtue of their ideas about "mammies," but eventually she had to put good dishes and meals on her tables to keep them coming back. Pleasant capitalized on people's willingness to find the newcomer a highly desired cook entering the San Francisco markets—and then set about proving those assumptions true.

Rather than speculate on how Pleasant honed her facility with various recipes, we could instead notice the polyglot table cultural memory ascribed to nineteenth-century San Francisco boardinghouse cuisine in general. Holdredge, by all accounts an avid collector of materials on her city, believed in the diversity of dishes on Pleasant's boardinghouse table. Other sections in Holdredge's cookbook offered "River Boat Fare," "Coastal

Steamer Cooking," "Los Alamos Rancho," and "Highland Fling" recipes. By the time Pleasant's most luxurious boardinghouse, the one at 920 Washington Street, was up and running, her reputation had evolved. No longer merely a great cook, Pleasant was heralded as a "gourmet chef" by her contemporaries. San Francisco's food sophistication had similarly evolved, with a bevy of French-trained chefs using a wider range of both imported and locally grown ingredients whose availability increased while prices fell as markets matured. Whether dining upstairs or down in her establishments, residents and customers were served "fine food and wines" by Pleasant and her staff. Her facility with flavors and local ingredients reached to the drinks on offer at her house as well: "including 'cordials made from wild clover that grew in profusion on Twin Peaks,' brandies made from elderberries and blackberries, and a concoction called Balm Tea, laced with 'paralyzing gin.'" Food scholar David Shields profiled several nineteenth-century San Francisco "culinarians" in his book by that title. They included Louisa Drouilhat, Pierre Trapet, and Jules Arthur Harder, all three known for parallel efforts to marry haute cuisine and California ingredients, and all three overlapping with Pleasant's time in the city.[23]

Clearly at some point in her business endeavors, Pleasant stopped doing the daily cooking. She soon owned more than one boardinghouse; she hired staff and insisted on their professionalism; and for much of her peak business years she lived off-site in her private home. But the idea persisted that because a Black woman was at the helm, the food would be great. Pleasant likely had a complicated relationship with this aspect of southernness and food in the boardinghouse environment. At most we can conclude she manipulated to her advantage an assumption she could not dislodge. That assumption allowed her to hide her important political activism behind the facade.

It was not just the food but also the laundry around which stereotypes clustered. A perverse power circled around laundry in American culture. Secrets and lies joined the physical soils to which cleaners were privy. Later in life, Pleasant was dogged by rumors that she blackmailed former clients with sexual secrets and other compromising information. The press called the situation the former boardinghouse keeper's "dirty laundry."[24] Pleasant struggled even after having significant financial success to shake free of the association. But laundry and Black women's assumed skills with it was another traveling idea from the US South that followed Pleasant to California and others around the world.

We do not know how Pleasant learned to clean clothes and household linens, although we might surmise she helped with the task in Mary

Hussey's Nantucket home, if Hussey did not hire it out. Given how great the needs were when she first moved to San Francisco, Pleasant likely oversaw, if not actively performed, washing in the households in which she worked. Fairly early in her time in San Francisco, though, Pleasant was already thinking beyond her individual body's capacity to labor. The son of one of Pleasant's laundry employees, interviewed in 1950, recalled at least three different locations his father told him about that Pleasant purchased and ran in the 1850s.[25]

Before she was a cookbook author, Malinda Russell likewise professionalized the "natural" skill that women who started boardinghouses were assumed to have. She advertised her laundry services for others in Abingdon, Virginia. Surveying advertisements for help and subsequent records of work, historian Rebecca Sharpless found that people who could cook were expected by employers to be skilled at laundry as well. Black cooks in the US South between 1865 and 1960, despite making efforts to resist, "did a variety of household chores. Most southern households had only one domestic worker at a time, and that one worker usually had her hands full." In 1880s Louisville, "90 percent of employers expected their domestic workers to do some combination of tasks, including cooking, washing, and cleaning," judging from employers' newspaper advertisements.[26]

Feminist Anna Julia Cooper in *A Voice from the South* described many southern Black women's work. In 1892, Cooper pleaded for people to remember "the pinched and down-trodden colored women bending over wash-tubs and ironing boards—with children to feed and house, rent to pay, wood to buy, soap and starch to furnish—lugging home weekly great baskets of clothes." Advertisements, popular culture images, and material objects paired stereotypical mammy images with washtubs. Even more than cooking, laundry could be done around other work—in the home if young children needed care, in stages if other jobs interrupted, and for most of the nineteenth century without a great outlay of equipment or advertising. That Russell advertised for business from ladies and gentlemen and that she aimed for a devoted storefront that would offer *only* laundry services put her at the cutting edge of the industry. Thousands of miles away, Pleasant joined Russell as a fellow innovator.[27]

Just as cooking changed rapidly in the nineteenth century, technologies for doing laundry changed also, especially in urban locations. In San Francisco, Chinese men entering the laundry business transformed cleaning in the city in the second half of the century. Rather than a single woman over a washtub, forward-looking entrepreneurs consolidated laundry into small service industries with multiple employees. Borrowing a term from industry more broadly, we could say Pleasant vertically integrated her business and, in Lynn Hudson's words, moved from being a laborer into running "an enterprise."[28]

Pleasant's husband, James, was consistently employed during this decade as a cook on merchant ships; he was unavailable to help Pleasant, even had he been so inclined. To expand, Pleasant had to assume significant risks and move quickly into employing a workforce beyond herself. It proved a worthwhile gamble. Pleasant's laundries supported the households (and increasingly boardinghouses) she ran, but they also allowed her to branch out to other customers, including people not employing her directly or staying in her houses. After the bubble in laundry prices passed (and Pleasant wisely got out of the business before prices collapsed), she had amassed more capital to pay forward into her next expansion. Accordingly, in the 1860s, she went more deeply into the boardinghouse business and for the second half of the century concentrated on luxury and the needs of professional and social elites as she designed her boardinghouse enterprise.[29] At that point, laundry moved to the realm of secrets and political leverage as Pleasant became ever more politically active. Her politics brought the South to account.

First, though, she created a network of information. The boardinghouse at 920 Washington Street was downtown, next to San Francisco's central plaza. That put it near banks, government buildings, and business headquarters driving the boomtown's impressive growth. Pleasant spent substantial funds to design and furnish its interior—purchasing "massive furniture," drapery, china, linens, glassware, and artwork, in addition to making sure the spaces worked well for their multiple purposes. The house gained a reputation as having "mysterious, lavishly furnished upstairs rooms which were set up as combined private dining and bedrooms"—suited for business deals, conversation, and intimate encounters that surely included physical pleasures. Others remembered the quantities of food and drink particularly, using the same adjective, "lavish." To run such an exclusive establishment, Pleasant invested in well-trained and discreet staff, another expense.[30] Hospitality on offer was material and concrete, but it simultaneously was ephemeral and constructed, relying on a woman called Mammy to deliver.

Other boardinghouses around the United States capitalized on related ideas about the South over the nineteenth and twentieth centuries. Mary and Susan Moore, with a third sister, ran a southern boardinghouse in New

York City, according to a nostalgic piece written upon its closing. Situated at 239 Central Park West for more than sixteen years and in existence for more than thirty, "Miss Mary's Boarding-house" provided "a southern home in New York, where the welcome was real and the willingness to help each other prevailed." Susan Moore, the final sister living, described the legion of boarders who were able to "come to New York from down home, get a start in the world, wed right here in my parlor, and go forth to big places." The white Moore sisters were important, but boarders and diners recognized the Georgia roots of the house in no small part through the efforts of an African American cook, Betty, whose last name the author James Young did not bother to give. Betty "worked on until the last day preparing fried chicken, the famous waffles, biscuits and gravy, and other southern dishes," her labor vital to the house.[31] In 1925, as furnishings were auctioned and final boarders left, Young reflected on it as an oasis of southern food, manners, politics, and conversation outside the geographical South.

Some six decades earlier, Thomas Butler Gunn profiled "The Boarding-house Whose Landlady Is a Southerner" in his *Physiology of New York Boarding-Houses*. Gunn claimed, "Only rich Southerners travel; and such as are induced by business or pleasure to seek northern cities naturally prefer the accommodation of Hotels rather than Boarding-Houses." Since he was about to profile southern boardinghouses and claim they were common enough to qualify as a type, he hinted customers still chose boardinghouses too. After establishing class (and implicitly race and politics) in his definitions of "southerner," Gunn continued, "Yet, as, among our list of Establishments, we have cognizance of one whose general characteristics savored of the sunny South; whose landlady prided herself on being 'no Yankee,' and whose boarders hailed mainly from the other side of Mason and Dixon's line, we accord it a Chapter." Gunn's southern keeper wore bright, garish colors and emphasized appearance over substance. Her house was "handsomely furnished," but, Gunn continued, "a general *untidiness*—thoroughly Southern in its way—and originating in want of system, pervaded everything."[32] Nonetheless, boarders from Arkansas, Kentucky, Louisiana, Texas, and Virginia passed through, as did New Yorkers like Gunn seeking a "southern" establishment.

For Gunn and the Moore sisters, at least some plausible familiarity with southern cultures can be tracked. Pleasant was not alone, however, in accruing southern identities and practices without close personal connections to the South. A short newspaper story from a *New York Times* correspondent, published in the *Atlanta Constitution*, identified a trend in the 1870s of fake "Southern ladies" opening boardinghouses in New York City. Banking on a reputation for being better than other keepers, southern keepers charged higher prices and were in greater demand. The author further suggested southern-run houses' popularity came from a belief that unlike local New York women, southern keepers were "free from stinginess." The correspondent concluded, however, that the *idea* of southernness was enough: "I suspect, however, that some of the persons who advertised as Southern widows, and the like, are nothing of the sort, but regular old stagers of Gotham, who hope in this way to attract boarders that would religiously shun them if they stepped out in their true colors." Cons and shams were not rare in American culture then (or now), but it is fascinating that people were so willing to believe that "southern" meant good food, housekeeping, and congeniality across decades.[33]

These beliefs were part and parcel of prewar myths of leisure and postwar nostalgia for plantations, and it did not matter that they were often untrue. Black women like Pleasant could *use* the common beliefs to draw increasingly elite and select customers for growing businesses.[34] Southern hospitality—a concept difficult to define but in common usage throughout the nineteenth century and into our present day—performed the work of bringing the most elite customers to Pleasant's San Francisco establishments. For Mary Ellen Pleasant, southern hospitality worked wonders to distinguish herself from other hotels and boardinghouses in the fast-growing city.

Indulgences of southern hospitality, operational in boardinghouses like Pleasant's, were not limited to food and drink. The promise hinted that hospitality had no taboos—anything and anyone you wanted. In other words, for those who wanted to hear it, there was an implication of intimacy, sex, and pleasure. Discussed more in the following chapter, what is most relevant here are rumors that Pleasant's boardinghouses might have been bordellos, brothels, places for intimate encounters. As Hudson documented, we are unlikely to know exactly what happened behind the closed doors of 920 Washington Street. And that was the point, both for her customers and for Mary Ellen Pleasant.

Ideologies of hospitality worked even or especially in locations far from actual southern plantation kitchens, including those of a San Francisco boardinghouse keeper with Maine and Massachusetts roots. Pleasant, Malinda Russell, Betty who cooked for the Moore sisters, and boardinghouse keepers and employees like them were well aware of structures of racism, white supremacy, and social power encoded in the phrase "southern hospitality." They used what they had to carve out livings for themselves and their families; some, in turn, used what was left to try to change hostile systems around them. In public and in private spaces inside her boardinghouses, Pleasant pushed back against darker, more troubling political messages lurking in southern culture as it spread through the United States and the globe.

Mary Surratt: Revolutions in the Hallways

Born nine years after Mary Ellen Pleasant, Mary Surratt had a much shorter life. However, the very set of decisions that led to her execution composed the political context that made Pleasant's political activism simultaneously dangerous and consequential. White supremacist politics that Surratt defended had less to do with food, laundry, and hospitality, but she placed them in her southern boardinghouse and used the space clandestinely for activism. Her boardinghouse at 604 H Street (the address then was 541 H Street) was just one of many such establishments throughout the city. In the 1860s, the H Street neighborhood was more residential than it is today. Surratt catered primarily to male residents, though she also made it home to her daughters and female employees. Those male boarders worked as government clerks and messengers. Some were travelers, representing others' interests in the city (today we might call them lobbyists). For some of her boarders, Surratt was just another boardinghouse keeper; her house was one of many lodgings from which to choose.[35]

Yet for others, including John Wilkes Booth, Lewis Powell, George Atzerodt, David Herold, and Dr. Samuel Mudd, the interior of Surratt's boardinghouse was a sheltered space from which to plan insurrection against the federal government. On July 7, 1865, Mary Surratt and three coconspirators were executed by hanging and others received life imprisonment for their roles in the assassination of President Abraham Lincoln—the assassination they planned at Surratt's H Street boardinghouse.[36]

Born Mary Jenkins, the girl who would conspire against the president was educated by the Sisters of Charity who ran an Alexandria, Virginia, Catholic school. She converted while in school, and her Catholic faith remained a constant in the rest of her life. Jenkins married John Harrison Surratt in 1840. When not away at school, Mary had grown up near Surratt's parents' land. John and Mary had three children while living on a farm in nearby Oxon Hill, Maryland. John was a difficult man who struggled with alcohol and anger, but Mary had few options once married.[37]

By 1852, John had purchased land in the community that would come to be known as Surrattsville. The first structure they built became an all-purpose building that served variously as a tavern, a post office, and a home for the family. They served food as well as drink; the building was at times called Surratt's Hotel. But it always drew customers from near and far, most generally being a community gathering spot to hear the latest news, gossip, and political debates. Archivists from the Surratt House Museum as well as scholars find that from its earliest days, the tavern's politics skewed southern, and "ample evidence" shows it was "a safehouse in the Confederate underground network which flourished in southern Maryland" once war broke out.[38]

Mary's life took a decisive turn in 1862, however, when John died suddenly. He left substantial debts, and Mary had few resources with which to settle them. She hung on for two years, but by October 1864, Mary had to make a change. She rented the tavern to an acquaintance to run, and she moved to a townhouse the family owned in Washington, DC. Facing a situation similar to Alice Lee Larkins's, Surratt needed to support herself and her children while settling the convoluted estate her husband had left. With no cash at hand, Surratt took in boarders. The large, comfortable house had three stories, plus attic rooms. Surratt advertised in November and December 1864 in the *Washington Star* but quickly found that word of mouth was sufficient to keep the house at full capacity.[39] Much like Mary Randolph, Surratt became a boardinghouse keeper who sat at the head of a table with lively political discussion. Unlike Randolph, Surratt's politics took a much darker turn.

Surratt operated the boardinghouse for less than a year, but in that time it served as a conduit of supplies, people, and political discourse that enabled the assassination of President Lincoln. The charitable interpretation that Surratt was merely a cash-poor widow following so many others of her kind into keeping boarders has been challenged by a theory that she was much deeper in the conspiracy all along—that title transfers that let the tavern and gave her the house meant she had knowledge of her son's espionage and that her financial decisions to furnish the house and take out mortgages to support it made no long-term sense but had high short-term political payoffs for a conspiracy in process. Its parlors and private bedrooms, like those of many boardinghouses, facilitated whispered conversations, closed-door meetings, and confidentiality—but rather than innocuous secrets of romance, job opportunities, or gossip, secrets at Surratt's were explosive. Fellow Confederate sympathizers, including female spies and male blockade runners, populated the hallways. John Wilkes Booth became a steady presence in the boardinghouse; he and Surratt's son and daughter became quite close during the spring of 1865.[40] Of particular note after the fact, Surratt herself traveled between Surrattsville, where the conspirators would soon seek shelter, and the boardinghouse on the day of the assassination. The boardinghouse subsequently became the center of investigators' focus as they tried to unravel details of the violent, political plot.

The relationship between political culture and boardinghouses was profound and long-standing, in DC and across the country. Surratt was not unique in gathering politically like-minded boarders under her roof. Journalist and travel writer Anne Royall had outlined desirable houses in both state and national capitals during her tours thirty-five years earlier. In Richmond, Virginia, for instance, Royall noted, "Mrs. Nelson keeps a good house, and has fine servants—so does Mrs. *Stanard*—and the Swan is a good house; these are all worthy of patronage." Royall used italics quirkily—whether as jokes, ease of typesetting, or special favor is lost to us today—but her description continued with details of how politicians chose their houses (for instance, Stanard's had representatives from the western part of the state where Royall lived previously). The city of Washington got similar treatment, and here Royall grouped "Boarding houses and Taverns" together. Good, orderly houses are run by "Messrs. *Williamson, Gadsby*, and *Brown*." Royall was "particularly pleased with landlady Brown and Williamson." Further, "Mrs. *Ball, Carlisle*, and *Myers* are still living, and receive boarders—also, Mrs. *Hungerford* and *Branan*, Mrs. *Elliott* and the two Mrs. *Peytons*. To these I must add as deserving patronage, Messrs. *Broadhead, Sawkins, Greer, Tims, N. Fletcher*—also Mrs. *Burk, Washington, Turner*, and *Gulven*—likewise the amiable Miss *Polk*." Then she noted, "It's impossible to put down a number of *mean* Boarding houses, all of which I could name; as there are always some mean men in Congress, whose taste and manners correspond so exactly with them, it would be a pity to part them."[41]

The North Carolina Collection at the University of North Carolina holds a printed broadside from the 1830s titled *A Directory of the Names of the Members of the Senate and House of Commons of the Present Legislature.* For that year's state representatives, it listed "Their Respective Boarding Houses, Politics, &c. &c." Indeed, each legislative body was sorted into columns according to members' names, politics, counties, and finally residences. Some hotels were listed: Litchfords', the Washington, Murray's, and the Eagle. But most of the representatives lived in boardinghouses. Keepers were primarily "Mrs." but included one or two called "Miss." At this remove, it is difficult to determine who among them were married, widowed, or never-married. Mrs. Shepherd, Haywood, Taylor, and Stuart joined the "Misses Pulliam." A couple of houses were listed by likely men's names: "Capt. Laurence's," "Mr. Hutching's," and "Dr. McPheeter's."[42] For voting citizens in the state, a broadside like this could guide them to lobby, conduct business, or exert political influence. For new lawmakers, it aided in securing lodgings. For aspiring keepers, it served as a model of how to market one's business. State capitals across the country had such practices, but it was in the nation's capital that the practice had the longest and most entrenched history.

Barbara Carson, in her classic work, *Ambitious Appetites*, described rows upon rows of DC boardinghouses. There were so many because for much of the early nineteenth century, Washington trailed other US cities in building grand hotels. For representatives, who needed to conduct business with some amount of privacy, taverns were difficult to manage, seeing as on any given night extra guests might cause people to share rooms—or even beds. Boardinghouses were a handy solution. While serving as vice president, even Thomas Jefferson boarded out. For him and others, DC's boardinghouses offered a wide range of quality of food, quiet or bustle, and political perspectives. Some keepers helped favored guests host parties at the boardinghouses and further their political ambitions; others insisted on no variance from the common meal with democratic first-come, first-served seating and dining principles.[43]

A contemporary of Mary Surratt, James Wormley, a free Black man, began with boardinghouses and liveries in Washington, using profits to build the luxurious Wormley Hotel aimed at high-profile political residents. Some hotel guests stayed entire legislative sessions. Others moved back and forth between the hotel and Wormley's other business, a rooming house that held regulars and hotel overflow. Much like Mary Ellen Pleasant and very much unlike Surratt, Wormley and his family donated to support political efforts to integrate the city, promote other fledgling businesses, and provide a safety net for the most vulnerable. However, Wormley's story holds deep political irony. In 1876, the political compromise that installed Rutherford B. Hayes as president and ushered in the end of Reconstruction was worked out in the Wormley Hotel.[44] Like all African Americans, Wormley's life was negatively impacted by the decisions made by longtime boarders at the hotel.

Choosing a boardinghouse was an important strategic decision that newly elected representatives had to make. Novelist John William DeForest, in his 1875 novel, *Honest John Vane*, made clear that his title character's decisions about boardinghouses had major consequences not only for John Vane's personal life but also for his political future. The novel's opening sentence read, "One of the most fateful days of John Vane's life was the day on which he took board with that genteel though decayed lady, the widow of a wholesale New York grocer who had come out the little end of the horn of plenty, and the mother of two of the prettiest girls in Slowburgh, Mrs. Renssaelaer Smiles." Soon, John fell for and married the eldest daughter. A simple but self-made man, John gave a speech against corruption that resulted in election to Congress. He and his new wife moved to Washington. She lived beyond their means, trying to compete in the city's boardinghouse society. John proved susceptible to corruption and political bribes as he too tried to keep up. No longer honest, his fall was swift and messy. The novel has been described as originating literary tropes of Washington's corrupting influence on innocents from the country; less noticed has been that the corruptions began in boardinghouses.[45]

A nonfiction version of DeForest's warnings about boardinghouses had played out earlier in the notorious Petticoat Affair of 1829–31, which saw President Andrew Jackson's cabinet torn apart over rumors about the wife of his secretary of war, John Eaton. Eaton had married the daughter of his boardinghouse keeper. Other wives of Jackson's cabinet refused to allow Peggy Eaton into society. The scandal consumed DC and reverberated into national politics.[46] Women may not have been able to vote or run for office, but from their boardinghouses they nonetheless influenced politics in deep and profound ways. How aware was Mary Surratt of DC society, and did she have plans to establish deep roots there, using expectations of southern hospitality and boardinghouse nurturing, with a dash of dirty laundry and secrets? Did she imagine herself in the company of DC's keepers who were powerful political brokers from their parlors or tables?

If it is hard at this historical remove to trace Mary Ellen Pleasant's specific connections to John Brown, it is equally hard to understand the details of how actively Mary Surratt participated in the assassination plan. In the time that has elapsed, some view her as a dupe or a scapegoat to a country in need of swift justice. Others have detected a whiff of sexism in interpretations by those who do not believe a woman could have been an active participant in the conspiracy. For the story of boardinghouses, these obfuscations and elisions are precisely the terrain in which politically active keepers could find space to operate.

Government investigators first knocked on the door of Surratt's boardinghouse at 2:00 a.m. on April 15, 1865, a little more than three hours after

Lincoln was shot. Her arrest took place in short order after the assassination. In the weeks that followed, investigators spent time combing through the house, its objects, and the stories of its inhabitants, including Surratt. She had made several mysterious trips to Surrattsville, carrying packages. A Black woman hired by Surratt named Susan Mahoney Jackson helped investigators make sense of the story the boardinghouse was telling—and exposed lies and contradictions that Surratt tried to pass as truths. Conspirators clearly met together at the boardinghouse, and more than that, Booth met in private conversation with Surratt at several points, including for longer than an hour on the day of the assassination. Much to the shock of many who thought the US government would never execute a woman, she was tried, convicted, and hanged soon after.[47]

MARY ELLEN PLEASANT lost most of her wealth before she passed away. A terrible fight with the Bell family who lived with her for years, as well as a series of bad investments and entangled assets, meant that Pleasant had to leave her mansion in San Francisco behind. Final decades of her life saw Pleasant recognizing the power of her life story in popular culture, as she attempted to take back her own narrative in the courts, in culture, and in her living spaces. Living in reduced circumstances, she agreed to interviews and profiles, hoping to rehabilitate her reputation and make some quick money. Unfortunately, the two aims were often at odds, and late profiles toggle between clear-eyed reflection on her life and sensationalist stereotype. She passed away in relative poverty and obscurity in 1904.[48] Biographer Lynn Hudson, though, following in footsteps of earlier Black feminist scholars, concluded, "The mystery concerning her past is a piece of evidence in itself," by which she meant gaps in her life story—details Pleasant herself chose to hide or which were too dangerous to speak—are all important to her story.[49] They are part of the boardinghouse story as well—in hidden spaces of corridors and in survival strategies of keepers. Inside her private chambers, inside her boardinghouse, Pleasant kept her own council. Perhaps she joyfully or tearfully reinvented herself. Perhaps she hated that people called her southern. Perhaps she laughed that her activism outlasted that of women like Mary Surratt. She certainly used multiple, contradictory stories in the public realm to carve a little space, mobility, and freedom for herself as a Black woman surviving despite virulent American slave systems and subsequent institutionally sanctioned racial inequalities.

Surratt's life ended swiftly and violently at the end of an executioner's rope in July 1865, a mere three months after the death of Lincoln.

Defenders, though, have worked to restore her reputation, efforts not unrelated to the long arc of Lost Cause narrative supporters trying to instill nobility to white southerners' fight for slavery. Karen Cox, one of our best scholars on women's participation in the successful proliferation of ideas of the so-called nobility of the Confederate cause and the subsequent construction of the Jim Crow South, has written about this extreme fetishization and has found, for instance, a corner of eBay that offers "Confederate hair" from notables including Surratt.[50]

For both Pleasant and Surratt, their afterlife has included popular culture remembrances of their boardinghouses. In 1874, a short article by "A Sufferer" appeared in the *Courier-Journal* of Louisville, Kentucky. Titled "A Plea for Poor Boarding-house Keepers," it ended with a very bad joke: "Poor creature, she should have much saintly patience! Mrs. Surratt was hung for keeping a boarding-house, and it would be a charity to hang some of the present day."[51] The Surratt house and museum in Maryland continues to support good research about her life and story. As recently as 2011, *The Conspirator*, a film with Hollywood star power, was produced about Surratt. The industry of Lincoln and Civil War books suggests her name will not fade from memory anytime soon. But the very nature of closed doors and quiet passageways of a woman-led boardinghouse means we will never know the precise conversations that led to the plot's unfolding.

Silences of Mary Ellen Pleasant's inner circle and promises of confidentiality and privacy behind the doors of her boardinghouse rooms mean that the extent of her political activism remains similarly obscured. Pleasant hid her money too well and kept her private thoughts too muted. But the idea of Mammy Pleasant entered public memory in as powerful a way as that of Mary Surratt. A play based on her life was performed across the United States and in London in the 1920s. *The Cat and the Canary*, a 1927 silent film based on the play, named one of its characters Mammy Pleasant to evoke a maid more in touch with the dead than the living. Howard Asbury included Pleasant in his adventuresome 1930s "informal history" of San Francisco, *Barbary Coast*. Novelists Frank Yerby and Michelle Cliff featured aspects of Pleasant's life in their works in the 1980s and 1990s. In recent years, San Francisco has reclaimed Pleasant as a businesswoman, investor, cook, and real estate owner. Her grave is marked, and the site of her mansion has a plaque.[52] The Underground Railroad worked because of the silences and hidden spaces, some of which were squarely inside boardinghouses across the United States and Canada. In southern boardinghouses around the nation, women's political voices emerged from people who had a hard time being heard in any other public forum of their time.

Boardinghouse spaces fostering political activism could also bring more personal explorations. Did Pleasant's boardinghouses really offer anything—and anyone—that wealthy customers desired? Did she give women who found themselves pregnant or abandoned a path back to self-worth and value? Was the nature of Surratt's relationship with John Wilkes Booth a more intimate one? Were her daughters free to explore their own romantic longings within the H Street boardinghouse? The possibilities of bodily autonomy, sexual expression, and resulting new definitions of southern and American womanhood are the subjects to which we turn next.

CHAPTER 5

SEX, DRINK, AND SEDUCTION

Sarah Hinton and Lola Walker

SARAH HINTON (b. ca. 1920s–?) was raised by her grandmother Martha Hinton in a boardinghouse in Durham, North Carolina. Sarah's mother, Susan, died when Sarah was an infant; her grandmother insisted that Susan was a bad child whose children were marked by the devil as evil. Sarah and her brother, Harry, lived alongside two cousins in their grandmother's house, children of Hinton's other deceased daughter, Jenny. Unlike Susan, Jenny was remembered by Martha as virtuous, kind, and the mother of equally angelic children.[1]

Not only did Martha express such beliefs to the grandchildren, but she backed them with actions. When Hinton was interviewed in the 1930s, she said about Susan and Harry, "I never let them play with Jenny's children, I kept them to themselves and made them work to keep them out of trouble and mischief." A devout Baptist, Hinton rejected anything that could possibly be construed as luxury, including hiring help for the work; as a deeply racist woman,[2] Hinton especially was never going to hire African Americans, the most likely domestic help available to her. Without employees to carry some of the load, she pushed work onto her "bad" grandchildren. Sarah and Harry must have performed hard labor essential to the running of the house—laundry, cleaning, errands, cooking—while their cousins played. One can only imagine the dynamic between the four children. As soon as he turned sixteen, Harry ran away to join the navy. Martha noted he lied about his age to do so, but really, who can blame him?

Unlike her brother, Sarah's fate was initially decided by her grandmother. According to Martha, "Sarah grew up rebellious like her mother before her, so at sixteen, to save her from disgracing me as her mother had done, I had her pronounced incorrigible and committed her to a mental institution." For this interview, family names were withheld "upon request" and pseudonyms inserted throughout the transcript.[3] It makes it difficult to trace the fortunes of the Hintons after the interview. But it is worth trying because countless girls like Sarah grew up in southern boardinghouses. Some embraced the role models their mothers, aunts, and grandmothers provided. Some mothers, aunts, and grandmothers were themselves what others might consider "fallen" or "bad," and girls chose either to follow them or to find a path away from boardinghouse hallways. For many others, interpretations of behavior and life choices were complex and shifting. How a grandmother's fears of "disgrace" were sufficient to confine a young girl against her will to an institution is perhaps hard to understand today. Sarah's story extended Alice Larkins's vague worries about how riding in a carriage with a man after dark could affect her respectability and reputation. In Sarah's story, a concrete example of life in a boardinghouse going wrong plays out.

Lola Walker (1886–?) did ride in carriages after dark with men.[4] Her subsequent life on the road, in the media, and on the witness stand illustrated very real consequences of fears expressed by Alice Larkins and Sarah Hinton's grandmother Martha. Names of girls growing up in boardinghouses can be harder to find in the archives than boardinghouse keepers' names. But some of their stories reveal intersections of sex, drink, reputation, and self that happened in boardinghouse hallways and back porches. Unlike Sarah's, we do know Lola Walker's real name—photographs of her and quotes by her were printed in newspapers during the trial she was involved in. Before she was known to readers around the country, though, Walker passed through one of Asheville's summer resort boardinghouses, one of many such girls at the turn of the century across the South. Lola came to her aunt Lynn Cullen's Montford Avenue boardinghouse in the summer of 1903 to stay, perhaps to work, and certainly to be safe with family. We know her name now because of a nighttime ride in a carriage she took with a wealthy Tennessee man named Colonel Richard "Dick" Edwards, later called by one newspaper "Millionaire Edwards." That ride and accompanying summer fling began with multiple rounds of drinks in a restaurant called the Red Room at the Battery Park Inn—champagne, cocktails, beer, and whiskey, consumed in great quantities. Summer evenings saw the party move to the dining hall of nearby Kenilworth Inn, where they continued to drink and were loud enough for the proprietor to intervene. One witness alleged Walker and a friend danced on tables and sang the latest hits while being cheered on by the larger group. "Beverages of no soft character" were "quaffed," said a newspaper delicately.[5]

Eventually, the party piled into a rented tallyho (a large buggy with at least three rows of seats in addition to the driver's) and headed out of Asheville up to Beaver Dam, a picturesque but remote drive north of town. On the dark road, drinking continued, now primarily beers and cocktails in bottles and flasks. Added to the revelry were "kissing and hugging," especially between Walker and Edwards. Thus began the summer affair between the seventeen-year-old and the man of the world that took place in and around her aunt's boardinghouse. According to Walker, Edwards proposed. She said they planned to run away and rendezvous in New York. When that went sour, Lola became a chorus girl and hit the road, causing her aunt Lynn and aunt Annie anguish. Three years later, the sensational story of a boardinghouse seduction of a chorus girl by a wealthy clubman entered the public record in a courthouse in western Tennessee when her two aunts sued on Lola's behalf. Jurors heard lurid allegations of sex, miscarriages, murder plots, bribery, and collusion. The trial garnered daily coverage in newspapers across the region and regular mentions in newspapers as far away as New York, Chicago, and Texas.[6]

For every story of a kindly keeper creating a true home for lodgers who quickly become dear friends, we should also remember the daughters caught up in more dangerous boardinghouse cultures. Sarah Hinton's and Lola Walker's stories reveal the perils and promise of girls growing up in boardinghouses. They found stolen moments of freedom, changing social mores, and generational struggles. Fractured families, broken along generational or religious lines, hid in boardinghouses. Alcohol, sex, and nighttime revelry led to lawsuits, ruined lives, and notoriety in the press and popular culture for girls who did not follow societal expectations. Some

girls and women, despite risks, sought to expand and embrace new definitions of sex, romance, and careers. Similar social changes were taking place
all over the United States. But in boardinghouses in the South, with elevated codes of religion and segregation and a particular veneration of racial
and sexual "purity" of white girls, gambles like the ones take by Sarah and
Lola were high-risk indeed. In boardinghouses, opportunities were concentrated for unrelated people of different genders, races, classes, and ages to
rub up against each other. Over time, their examples ultimately dislodged
the most restrictive definitions of gender and sex; we live in a world they
helped create.

Sarah Hinton's Boardinghouse Behaviors

Travis Tuck Jordan conducted the interview with Martha Hinton. Jordan
was head of the Federal Writers' Project Durham office, and her work in
the 1930s took her across North Carolina interviewing everyday people.
A published poet, Jordan had a keen eye for detail when she walked into
others' lives, even for a moment. Because of the program's emphasis on
sending interviewers around their regions, and because those interviewers were looking for conversational partners who had seen life in whatever
community they lived, a good number of people involved in boardinghouses
tell their stories in the files.[7] Federal Writers' Project interviews provide
glimpses into the struggles, joys, and diversity of growing up in boardinghouses. Martha Hinton's boardinghouse was a place with more struggles
than joys and a narrow definition of who was welcome. Deviation was
beaten and prayed out of residents, especially family members.

Reading Federal Writers' Project interviews is tricky business. Interviewers were as much products of their time as subjects were. Interviews
between white interviewers and African Americans are notorious for imposing dialect in the transcripts, for narrowing the conversation to memories
of slavery (whether appropriate to the individual's life story or not), and for
moments of evasion, performance, and dissemblance. Racial politics and
power differentials in the Jim Crow era came into the room along with the
people talking. Even when sharing racial or ethnic backgrounds, interview
participants faced gender, class, age, or religious expectations that needed
careful navigation.[8]

Jordan acknowledged the challenges she had connecting emotionally to
Martha Hinton as an interview participant. Sarah's story took up only about

one page out of the nineteen total pages in the interview (though its emotional effect is large). Sarah's mother, Susan, got a few more pages in the story; her grandmother Martha's life story dominated, but it was not easy for Jordan to hear.

Martha Hinton was a difficult woman for her interviewer to like. Jordan began Martha's description saying, "When she opened the door in answer to my knock I said nothing for several seconds, for the expression on the woman's face was so unexpected that it startled me." Jordan paused to outline her expectations, the pleasant view that crumbled in that moment of encounter. After all, Jordan had been told Martha Hinton was a long-established, well-known boardinghouse keeper in Durham. As a reader, I nod my head. Jordan had expected to find "a good woman," one who was kind, perhaps religious, but the type of religious faith that "warmed and tendered" a character.[9] Jordan hoped for boardinghouse stories filled with compassion and kindness, featuring keepers whom people admire, long to meet, or wish to honor in some way. We might expect it to be like sitting with Alice Larkins or Texie Gordon in their parlors late in life, having nice long visits and sharing funny, gently gossipy stories of successful granddaughters, eligible men, and strategizing mothers from boarding-house days. Jordan's experience interviewing Martha Hinton was very different.

Martha Hinton's face, Jordan continued, was "the coldest, most relent-less and stoic face I have ever seen. It is as unyielding as a block of granite." She had a "furtive, repellent look." Even "her grey eyes are cold, even bel-ligerent and as uncharitable as frosty ice on a winter morning." Standing blocking the door, Hinton's "thin lips were clamped together as close and unsmiling as . . . the bit of a steel trap, and there was no gleam of cordiality on her austere face nor in her frosty eyes"—extraordinary judgments rendered on the first page of an interview.[10]

Trying to break the ice, Jordan asked about geraniums on the stoop and a Christmas cactus in a window. In reply, Hinton gave her a lecture about wastefulness and only reluctantly let her inside. Soon, Hinton revealed that she had bought and paid for the house herself, through keeping boarders. She shut down the business because "I'm too old to cook." Using a racist epi-thet, she added no one was "going to be messing in my kitchen and carrying off my things." Indeed, furniture, old china, and other remnants from her boarding days were still in the house, piled up around Hinton. Jordan used the scene to position Hinton's views, including those on race, as equally outmoded.[11]

Jordan wrote, "The only modern thing in the house is a gas stove and electric lights and Mrs. Hinton resents both." Hinton's long-deceased second husband had gone behind her back to install them while she was briefly hospitalized; to her mind "it was sinful to be spending money on gas and electricity."[12] With the structure of the interview, Jordan built a case to show the particularities (clearly ones she found twisted or disturbing) of Hinton's religion and politics.

Born on July 20, 1859, in rural Person County, North Carolina, Hinton was raised Primitive Baptist. She described herself as good, in contrast to her own disobedient sister (who did things many now might find mild—like wading in a creek on Sundays or unraveling Hinton's knitting when she got mad at her). Her father allowed Hinton enough education to be able to "read the Bible and to write," and that "was all that was necessary," she noted. "I don't read trash," she said. "These novels and magazines with their filthy stories and indecent advertisements of women in underwear and showing their legs are sinful. You can't be a good woman and read such things."[13] Being a good woman was crucial to Hinton—it is a phrase Jordan recorded her saying over and over—and it became the ironic subtitle to the interview in the archives. Being a "good woman" also hinted at the generational struggle Sarah had with her grandmother, a struggle Susan clearly had as well.

Martha Hinton was young when she first married. She was seventeen, and her husband was a much older country doctor. It was not a happy marriage. But "the children began to come," she noted. She leaned toward Jordan and explained, "I hated having children . . . hated carrying them, it seemed so vile and indecent, it's a punishment the Lord puts upon women for some sin they've done." Hinton consistently spoke against any bodily pleasures—be they taste, touch, sound, or movement. She divided people into good and evil based on their embrace of pleasures. And she did so as judge and jury of others' inner thoughts, not even of actual behavior. One son, she said, was righteous; another may have fooled the rest of the world, but she knew he was evil.[14] She made the same judgments about her two daughters and two sets of grandchildren.

Soon Hinton was widowed and upon remarriage moved to Durham. Once there, Martha began taking in boarders. Members of her own family, much to her horror, drank "liquor and coco colas, dance, read trash instead of the Bible, play cards, go to baseball and football games, hunt and fish on Sunday, and sit in the movie houses looking at vile pictures." Martha fought an uphill battle as consumer culture across the South blossomed. North

Carolina's Piedmont, with booming textile mill economies, saw businesses flooding in, ready to separate workers from their cash by offering the food, music, movies, and leisure activities Hinton found so appalling.[15]

Susan, Sarah's mother and the daughter Martha did not like, wanted to look at herself in a mirror or play dress-up with a friend. When she turned fifteen, Susan asked for "twenty-five cents to go to some play they were having at the high school," another strongly punishable offense to her mother. Susan finally got a month's respite to stay with a wealthier aunt from "another town." The aunt bought Susan "fine clothes, silks and velvets; she let her curl her hair about her face and put silly high heeled shoes on her feet. She let her go to parties and picnics; even let her go buggy riding alone with men and taught her to dance." Unfortunately, Susan returned pregnant. That baby died, but Susan soon married and gave birth to Harry and Sarah. Sometime after the birth of Sarah, Susan passed away. Martha editorialized, "Her sinful beauty died with her."[16] Both Susan and her "good" sister, Jenny, died early, but not before each had two children—which is how the already reluctant mother, Martha Hinton, ended up a resentful grandmother, raising four grandchildren in a boardinghouse alongside lodgers.

Hinton, then, was guided by intolerance wrapped in righteousness as a boardinghouse keeper. Such rigidity and moral certainty directed her decisions about people under her roof. Repeating again and again that everything she did was because she was a "good woman," Martha dictated her lodgers' bedroom lives too. Upon finding a pack of cards in a room she rented to her youngest son, she blamed World War I for changing him, sending him back "with a cigarette swinging to his lips and slang words dripping from his tongue." Hinton grabbed a broom to sweep the cards onto a shovel and threw the "plaything of satan" into the fire. When he married, Martha bemoaned that his wife would not listen when she told her how bad she was too. The wife "cut her hair, danced, played cards, played the piano and sang indecent love songs"—and she "laughed" when her mother-in-law tried to fix her.[17]

Martha Hinton's impulse to control and tamp out rebellion played out in her absolute rejection of sensual pleasure. This extended to daily food. Hinton refused to fix food that paid attention to "new-fangled dieting," saying fried cabbage, onions, buttermilk, and collards were good enough for anyone. They are, of course, great foods, if cooked well. But Hinton seemed unwilling to approach food as anything other than expedient. Further, by the 1930s those foods were already old-fashioned. Processed milk was becoming popular; old-style buttermilk was no longer as easily available.

The era of reconstituted buttermilk was upon Hinton. Cabbage, onions, and collards were all cheap ingredients with long growing seasons. They could be cooked without much attention, especially helpful for a keeper who refused to hire from the most obvious pool of accomplished cooks, Black women. A sign of such foods is that recipes for them do not generally appear in the era's cookbooks.[18] Hinton blamed any stomach troubles in her children or grandchildren on eating at other people's houses, where they may have experienced sweet, savory, salty, and luscious tastes—along with human kindness and interactions. For Hinton, any pleasure was risky; any indulgence, especially by girls, could lead straight to sex, pregnancy, sin, and hell.

Imagine Sarah, living in a household run by a rigid grandmother who framed her codes of behavior in religious language. Imagine her being told regularly that she and her brother "were stubborn and wilful," inherently evil, sinful, and unredeemable, and thus had to work while their two cousins did not.[19] Further, Martha told Sarah and Harry almost daily about their mother's failures, sinfulness, and consignment to hell. Imagine them being cut off from extended family who seemed to thrive despite (or because of) making different life choices—like going to dances and enjoying the world around them. But also imagine being surrounded by that world and its pleasures—the blossoming of consumer and popular culture in the bustling new South. Movies, soda fountains, high school plays, radio, magazines and catalogs boasting the newest fashion, and even snack cakes and candies all around.

Then bring all of that into the doors of a boardinghouse. Perhaps packs of playing cards hid in rooms Sarah was asked to clean. Surely some tenant forgot to collect a flask of hidden liquor before packing up and leaving. Magazines or novels or newspapers with different perspectives fell out of someone else's trunk or suitcase. Sarah had to deal with laundry dirtied by any manner of behavior. Perhaps she picked up the latest slang by overhearing it; perhaps she shared a stolen kiss behind a parlor door. Certainly, loving grandparents did and still do raise children with strict religious codes. Some grandchildren so raised embrace tenets and structures to which their elders hew. But for some grandchildren, the concentration of conflicting worldviews within boardinghouse walls made for an explosive atmosphere.

What did Sarah do that worried her grandmother? Martha said only that she "grew up rebellious."[20] Whatever it was, Martha's radical step resulted in a permanent rupture between granddaughter, boardinghouse, and herself.

In the interview transcript, Jordan did not give the name of the institution in which Hinton confined her granddaughter. It could have been one of the large-scale mental hospitals in North Carolina, such as Raleigh's Dorothea Dix Hospital in the eastern part of the state or Morganton's Broughton Hospital in the west. Given the year and the shaky evidence of Sarah's behavior, it may well have been a facility explicitly for the reeducation and rehabilitation of girls declared delinquent.

Society, including policy makers in state legislatures such as North Carolina's, were worried about girls in the early twentieth century. As historian Mary Odem documented, the legal term "juvenile delinquent" came into widespread use as fears of unattached girls with disposable income rose. Immigrant girls, African American girls, and girls with marginalized religions or recently acquired class positions suddenly joined the white girls who might have cash to spend to make decisions on their own lives. Some were even becoming college educated and were speaking persuasively for themselves in public forums. At the same time, companies realized that it might be useful to have a new category of consumers and began marketing to girls. They enjoyed consumer items that gave pleasure to bodies or minds; they demanded to dress in what they liked, read what they wished, listen to the latest songs, go to movies, see the sights, and ride the rides. Teen girls replaced nineteenth-century views of young ladies. These new teen girls were simultaneously promising but unpredictable new consumers. Novels, sermons, government policy, advice manuals, magazine and newspaper articles, and songs all weighed the promises and perils of unleashing girls into the marketplace. Of course, children progressed to adulthood all along; what changed was the visibility and cultural worry over gender, race, class, and girlhood.[21]

If Sarah's incorrigibility was judged juvenile delinquency, Sarah may have ended up in the State Home and Industrial School for white girls in Eagle Springs, North Carolina, popularly called Samarcand Manor. Historian Karin Zipf's study *Bad Girls at Samarcand* gives evidence that Martha Hinton's suspicions of "bad" or "fallen" behavior would have been more than sufficient in the eyes of the state for Sarah to be confined. Hinton described the institution where she put Sarah as one in which "her rebellion would be curbed and she would have to work."[22] That described the mission statement of Samarcand almost exactly.

Ironically, if Sarah ended up at Samarcand, her daily work might not have differed much from life at her grandmother's boardinghouse. The "education" system at Samarcand nominally featured "three months of training in eight areas of domestic work, including 'plain sewing,' dress-making, 'domestic art' such as needlework, farming, milking, feeding pigs and chickens, laundry, and cooking and pantry work"—notably all skills that would not go astray in boardinghouse work. Zipf calls it a nominal plan because so many girls were given either special benefits that got them out of classes or punishments that kept them away from class that it is almost impossible to figure out who if any completed the whole program. Education fell far behind the efforts to curb rebellion, in other words. A much trickier concept, getting rid of rebellion at Samarcand took place by a publicly discussed honor system and a largely secret probationary system. Organizers tried to present the story that bad girls at Samarcand emerged as "good southern ladies."[23] In practice, though, individual experiences varied wildly—from being labeled a success and accruing special privileges and responsibilities as a result to being dismissed as criminally irredeemable and enduring isolation, beatings, and other punishments.

Poetic Dreams and Desires

Life in the grips of the Depression, especially in the US South, could be brutal and unforgiving, as individuals and families struggled to find enough food, afford housing, and hold onto emotional and physical health often while separated from extended family and home communities. People were caught in waves of social change, even if headed in the direction of finding more freedom and options, and the journey could be fraught. Travis Jordan wrote of such struggles in her poetry. Composed, revised, and often published across the same years as her work for the Federal Writers' Project, her poems stood as creative vignettes imagining internal lives of women and men in small-town North Carolina, often fictionalized as "Chilton."[24] In the swirl of newly available consumer goods, Jordan was one among many creative writers wrestling with the relationship between things and happiness, especially for women and teenage girls.

One poem, "Thalia Conway," centered on a main character whose life story was strikingly similar to Sarah's mother, Susan. Thalia's mother, Emma, opened the poem, saying Thalia "was born for trouble" because she was "conceived against my will / By a drunken father." That rape read as marital rape, and it echoed Martha Hinton, who had confided to Jordan her view that carrying children seemed "vile and indecent," especially since both her husbands drank. Regardless, Thalia "developed into a voluptuous girl" with beautiful eyes and lips. The poem continued,

> And at sixteen two men had possessed her body,
> But she was not ashamed.
> She grew to womanhood stained and soiled,
> Resentful of home restrictions
> And Chilton's piety.

Unlike Sarah's mother, who died after her unapologetic premarital sex and pregnancy (in Martha's words, "her sinful beauty died with her"), Thalia's story ended closer to the way Sarah's would: she got away from her family. Thalia

> packed her clothes and went away.
> Boldly announcing that she was goint to the city
> And run a bawdy house—her lifelong ambition.

Thalia "was never seen in Chilton" again. Sarah did not run a brothel—in fact, through some twists and turns, she became a librarian. But the emotional resonance for the mothers, Martha Hinton and the poem's Emma Conway, overlapped significantly. Martha Hinton condemned her granddaughter even at the time of the interview for being "vain and determined to have her own way, loving the pleasures of this world," and the way that Sarah made her own career sounded a lot like how Thalia Conway never looked back, even if librarian and madam are two quite different paths.[25] For young girls who did not choose to stay near their parents' moral compasses or play the roles assigned to them by community and town, "trouble" followed. But it is hard not to feel like another tragedy befell the constrained and pained mothers and grandmothers who could not follow or support their daughters' efforts for freedom.

At times, Jordan seemed to use poetry to understand psychic costs for women like Martha Hinton. Hinton wanted Jordan to know that she "had worked and slaved like a dog, put up with a drinking philandering husband." A poem variously titled "Tilly Woods" and "The Hill Woman" imagined a woman's insanity after a life spent cooking for and serving "working men." The poem opened, "For twenty years she lived a barren life / of isolation from the teeming world" as a proper "mountain wife." Tilly held her "desire," her "deep-hearted longings" inside, but "her heart seethed with rebellion." Eventually,

> One moonlight night they found her in the town,
> Stark nude, with staring eyes and streaming hair,
> "Come see," she cried, "my rosy-satin gown,
> My silver shoes,—I have another pair."

Sarah Hinton's mother, Susan, wanted a red dress and to wear her hair in loose curls. In Martha Hinton's words, Susan's "hair was curly and she wouldn't let it stay plaited and slicked tight back so she wouldn't be noticed so much, she would fluff it out when she got to school, and let it curl about her cheeks." Hinton continued, "Once she took a bran [*sic*] new dress I made for her and cut it into strings. She wanted a red dress, a bright red dress made the princess style they were wearing then with short sleeves. But, I told her she couldn't have it, that a good woman dressed quietly; they didn't wear clothes that showed the lines of their figure." That Jordan's poetic creation, Tilly, dreamed of freedom by way of pretty dresses, fun shoes, and unbound hair sounded a lot like Sarah's mother letting her hair free, wearing high-heeled shoes, and learning to dance unabashedly.[26]

The hard, unromantic work of a boardinghouse, almost by definition invisible to other community members because of its interior, domestic, or commonsense nature, could be turned into a narrative of success or reward. But it could also twist into a painful, low-payoff, repetitive life with few moments of relief. No wonder boardinghouse girls like Sarah and her mother in Durham, fictional Thalia in Chilton, and Lola Walker in Asheville dreamed of romance and escape.

Poetry was one window into the interior lives of girls; a moment of infamy, when a life story became an object of curiosity and investigation, was another. A major debate driving the Walker-Edwards trial in 1906 was deciding whether Lola was a naive girl caught up in dreams of romance or a worldly schemer plotting a path to fame, fortune, and freedom. Both were reasonable possibilities. Swirling around resort boardinghouses were stories, songs, and gossip about exciting romantic possibility. Lola's aunt's house Lynnoaks in Asheville was no exception. Caught up in the mess of the trial were lodgers, tourists, salespeople, business suppliers, and neighbors. They sat for depositions; some testified on the stand. Newspapers hinted the trial was a source of dinner party gossip and nervous speculation across Asheville.[27]

One person caught up in the trial was Julia Tennent, a neighbor and fellow boardinghouse keeper a few doors down at 111 Montford Avenue. Dr. G. S. Tennent, Julia's brother, was called as a witness for Dick Edwards's defense in the trial, and he testified to knowing Lola's aunt as a neighbor.[28] Hospitality ran in the family; G. S. Tennent and his wife, Emma, lived at and took in summer boarders at Antler Hall on the French Broad River in Biltmore in the 1880s. Another relative published a thirty-three-page novella in 1882 in the pages of the popular *Godey's Lady's Book* titled "Among the Mountains," about Asheville's boardinghouse culture. Mrs. S. S. Tennent's fictional magazine story foreshadowed Lola's summer dreams. A love story set in a boardinghouse, "Among the Mountains" centered on daughters of the keeper who met and married wealthy men who came to board. If Lola Walker read the magazines or talked to her aunt's neighbor, visions like Tennent's might have shaped her hopes and dreams when she started her own Asheville adventure.[29]

"Among the Mountains" opened with sisters Carrie and May Thornton discussing a decision they have made with their mother to open the family home to boarders. They have rejected opening a school: "You know the number of schools in Asheville, and the low price of tuition. . . . I don't think a school will do." Neither sister sewed well enough to support the family as a seamstress. May's "MS., alas! as soon as written and forwarded to publishers with all the buoyant hopes of a young and ardent authoress, are respectfully declined," so she could not support the family as a writer. And so, they concluded, "now there is nothing, absolutely nothing, for us to do, but to take boarders!"[30]

Carrie, nicknamed Cad, made peace with the decision first, feeling like the extra work and change of family arrangements in summer would make the rest of the year better. May, however, struggled with the idea. She worried,

"Yes, boarders, boarders, boarders! Don't speak Cad—don't interrupt me. I am trying to familiarize myself with the idea. The Asheville paper will doubtless appear with a puff—'We call the attention of our readers and of the public in general to the advertisement of Mrs. Thornton's Private Boarding House! We can testify most fully to the merits of this most estimable lady, who will furnish persons during the summer with cheap and delightful board. Rooms large and airy, table loaded with all the delicacies of the season, servants polite and efficient, daughters handsome, obliging and entertaining, etc., etc., etc.' Really though," with a look of horror, "mother will not advertise?"

Her sister assured her that, much like Mary Ellen Pleasant, Texie Gordon, or Alice Larkins, they would rely on word of mouth to find residents. May shifted gears to dream of how opening up their house to the public would change their daily meals: "Will we have ice cream for dinner every day, and cake always in the house? Oh, how charming it will be!" In addition, Carrie and her mother resolved "not to take children. Young married people, old married people, young men, young women, old bachelors, or old maids, will all alike be welcome." They pledged to call residents "guests," reasoning, "It *sounds* better than boarders, at any rate."[31]

Because of their home's convenient location, rooms filled quickly. Carrie, especially, assisted her mother in running the house. For the sisters and "guests," summer in the Thornton house included croquet on the lawn, picnics overlooking the French Broad River, and day trips to area sites.[32] They sang, told stories, flirted, and took advantage of all Asheville offered. The real city was well known to readers of fashionable magazines of Tennent's era, and the author drew on the positive associations for her story. Vanderbilts were visiting in the 1880s and by 1889 had started their grand home, the Biltmore estate. Battery Park Hotel opened its doors in 1886, and Kenilworth Inn joined it in 1890. More than 30,000 visitors per year vacationed in Asheville in the decade in which Tennent was writing; newspapers and magazines advertised all manner of boardinghouses, hotels, and inns for them.[33] Twenty years later, Lola Walker and Dick Edwards joined Asheville's still vibrant scene for their romantic summer.

Before opening the boardinghouse, fictional Carrie and May dreamed about having "a corner of the porch canvassed in, where pretty girls and their cavaliers can enjoy their innocent flirtations." Over the course of the novella, Carrie navigated multiple suitors, including a cousin who had broken off an earlier engagement with her to marry a belle from New Orleans. Wealthy Mr. Ross, the man to whom the New Orleans belle was formerly pledged, fled to the mountains to get over his heartbreak and meets Carrie. Walks on the house's "piazza" led to quiet conversations near rose trellises and arbors. The final scene of the novella saw Carrie step from the piazza into the boardinghouse library where she and Ross declared their love and intention to marry.[34] "Among the Mountains" began and ended in its Asheville boardinghouse, where love was reputably, safely nurtured between boarder and boardinghouse keeper. That is not what happened to Lola Walker.

Lola Walker: Boardinghouse Drinking

The piazza flirtations in which Lola Walker engaged proved much less innocent and held much greater consequence. Summer of 1903 was a typical one in Asheville, North Carolina. Tourists wandered town, some passing through for one-week vacations and others staying for the whole season. Hotels catered to wealthy visitors with amenities such as billiard rooms, elevators, wine rooms, and luxurious grounds. They hosted balls that drew attendees ranging from guests to individuals across Asheville society. Railroad companies invested grand sums in comfortable train cars on the lines and in advertising campaigns to lure travelers with convenient train schedules and luxury lodgings. The Grove Park Inn was still ten years away from opening, but its future owner, Edwin Grove, was already amassing property and spending his time in the Asheville area. His hotel would feature mild foods and tonic waters and ban alcohol—in large part to respond to the decadence he witnessed in Asheville and its society.[35]

With the entrance into Asheville of wealthy George Vanderbilt through his new mansion, Biltmore House, and the infusion of energy and industry into Biltmore Village supporting it and abutting Asheville itself, the city was even more on front pages of society journals. Amenities, luxuries, and cosmopolitan scenes expanded. Chefs drew from local foods but also imported fine ingredients from around the world; sommeliers and bartenders stocked cellars to quench guests' thirst on order.[36] Many came to Asheville for precisely the rambunctious times that a little alcohol, good food, and conversation in a beautiful place provided.

Not everyone who came to Asheville was vacationing. Hotels, inns, resorts, and boardinghouses of all sizes needed workers. Someone had to help with the extra work required in the peak seasons. Keepers drew on extended family networks and word of current employees to find additional staff. That is what brought Lola Walker to her aunt Mrs. Lynn Cullen's Lynnoaks boardinghouse on 103 Montford Avenue in 1903. Cullen seems to have been drawn to Asheville much in the same way that Julia Wolfe chose St. Louis for her first boardinghouse: it made good business sense. Cullen rented the property, taking over from a previous boardinghouse keeper. She seemed to have no family or personal connections to the mountain town; what she had was experience and skill as a businesswoman. Here was a community with plenty of customers, tourists, summer health-seekers, and traveling businessmen. Lynnoaks catered to all.

Walker's extended family, especially the women, had extensive experience in food and hospitality. Walker had previously lived with her aunt Annie Bauer in a boardinghouse in Chicago, worked as a bookkeeper for a café run by her mother and grandmother in El Paso, Texas, and generally moved from place to place after the death of her father. Staying with Cullen in Asheville may have seemed safe for the girl still struggling with grief. In an Asheville City Directory from 1904–5, both Cullen and Walker listed their residence as 103 Montford; Cullen's entry further identified her as a widow. The house, also spelled Lynn Oaks, was listed under "Boarding Houses," along with 119 others. Four other boardinghouses had Montford Avenue addresses, including those run by Mrs. Hannah Bryan and Miss Julia Tennent on the same block as Cullen's.[37]

The summer of 1903 proved volatile for Walker and her family. In competing testimony three years later, lawyers for Lola Walker and Dick Edwards disagreed about precisely how the clubman and boardinghouse girl first heard about each other. They agreed, however, that telephone calls between his hotel and her boardinghouse were flirtatious moments that led to them meeting in person. Cullen claimed, "The telephone rang and Lola answered it and told her that Dick Weaver wanted to bring Col. Edwards down." Weaver was the caller, so Cullen got on the line and quizzed him until she felt confident in her niece accepting a visit from Edwards. Weaver agreed to his role introducing the two, having told Edwards that Walker "was a gay jolly girl" who would "perhaps give him a good time." In Weaver's telling, he then passed the phone to Edwards, who then talked directly to Walker. Weaver thus witnessed the phone call that resulted in the couple's first date. Edwards said Walker told him, "You look good to me," and he replied, "You are a right peart little girl" over the phone, all before they ever met in person. They also agreed their affair lasted the whole summer, with clandestine meetings taking place in discreet corners of the Lynnoaks porches. Edwards testified that "the only time he called on Lola at her house . . . Lola asked him to accompany her to a more secluded place, and he went around the portico with her and took a seat in a hammock," where they stayed more than twenty minutes. Edwards claimed they made plans on the boardinghouse porches to travel together to New York. Her aunt insisted in testimony that the porch had "air lights" to keep it brightly illuminated— no dark corners in which to hide, in other words.[38] Whether in the open or in cozy seclusion, Walker and Edwards progressed to racier adventures around Asheville, both day and night.

After the nighttime buggy rides, the fun continued, with stops at a photographer's studio for portraits (some, the *Nashville American* reporter
said, did not "boast of a superabundance of clothing"). They not only took
carriages; Lola also hopped on a horse, cutting quite a figure riding "astride,
shortly after a tallyho ride, in a red skirt." Walker and Edwards spent evenings listening to music and dancing and rode by themselves as a couple in
closed carriages as well as among the infamous open-buggy group parties.
Eventually, the summer ended, and Edwards prepared to leave Asheville for
a trip to New York.[39]

Walker followed. "It was between 9 and 10 o'clock at night that Lola
slipped away from the house to take a train to join the defendant in New
York," testified her aunt Lynn Cullen. Cullen dashed to the railroad station
and tried to stop her. She even got on the train and tried to talk Lola out of
the berth in which she had barricaded herself. When she failed ("Plaintiff
told her that she was going to the Metropolis to marry Edwards and that
she would not be stopped"), Cullen turned to newspapers to cover the story;
she augmented the press by inserting notices in papers up the East Coast
line, with headlines like "Seeking a Trace of Her Eloping Niece," begging
for Lola's return. According to some accounts, Lola was a young innocent
misled by a nefarious man: at that time, "she was a 16-year-old girl, with an
abiding trust in humanity," said her lawyers. She thought she and Edwards
were engaged, and she innocently headed to New York to start her new life
as Mrs. Colonel Edwards.[40]

According to other accounts, theirs was strictly a business arrangement:
"Miss Lola was a young woman quite capable of taking care of herself,"
claimed lawyers for Edwards's defense. She dreamed of the stage, practiced
her high kicks, and boasted of plans for fame, according to supporters of
this theory. Recognizing talent in the young girl, Edwards promised to put
her up in a hotel in New Jersey for a few weeks while she launched her
career on the New York stage as a chorus girl or Broadway star. Even the
hometown paper had taken note of her talent, writing, "Lola is the belle of
Asheville, and Asheville is noted far and wide for its pretty girls." Still others implied theirs was purely a sexual and financial arrangement, wherein
Edwards would pay Lola's expenses as long as she lodged with him as his
paid mistress. Witnesses claimed Walker bragged about already having
been onstage before coming to Asheville. They said she showed off her
dancer's legs in person and in suggestive photographs that she aimed to
distribute to any man who might further her career.[41]

In any case, the relationship soured. Walker left New York City by joining a series of traveling theater troupes, the Bizzy Izzy, the Mr. Jolly of Joliet Company, and the Louisiann show at the St. Louis World's Fair (the very fair at which Julia Wolfe ran a boardinghouse). Tours took her to Texas, California, Chicago, St. Louis, and places in between. Edwards resumed his previous life, though some of the claims in court suggested he still was in contact with Walker, sending money and cards as she was on tour. In October 1904, Edwards married Lulie Campbell Gibbs, a woman "belonging to a prominent family," although how long they were engaged is unclear. By 1905, Cullen had joined her sister Annie Bauer, of Chicago, to persuade Walker to leave the theater and return to the family. They decided to sue Edwards for breach of promise, seduction, and damages. After a first attempt in North Carolina, the suit was moved to Union City, in Obion County, Tennessee, in the far western part of the state, north of Memphis.[42] A year of furious work to gather depositions near and far ensued.

Union City was Edwards's home community, and Edwards was alleged to have threatened Lola that he knew all the judges and all the juries there. He bragged they would never rule against him. But Walker's aunts refused to back down, so in the summer of 1906 the trial began. The case drew attention much farther afield than the county seat. The *Nashville American* devoted a daily feature to the trial, giving blow-by-blow accounts of the proceedings. Asheville and Charlotte newspapers followed closely, as did regional and national newspapers such as the *Louisville Courier-Journal*, the *Chicago Daily Tribune*, and the *New York Times*. Before it ended, a hot summer of witnesses, counter-witnesses, objections, and sustained evidence were presented. Lawyers spoke for the rafters. Lola dressed in demure white. Edwards cracked jokes from the stand. Reputations of Walker, Cullen, and Bauer were picked apart. The trustworthiness of Weaver's and Edwards's other male friends were examined. Courthouse crowds fought each other for the best seats to see the spectacle.[43] For the story of southern boardinghouses, the trial pulled back the curtains on society. It revealed how central drinking cultures could be to boardinghouses. It drew distinctions between locals and visitors—in this case, Appalachians and wealthy vacationers. It traced lines between wealthier establishments and more fleeting ones. And it outlined the risks and rewards for young women involved on the fringes of boardinghouse life.

Nine years earlier, an 1897 newspaper story in the *Nashville American* (the same paper that would devote so many column inches to the Walker trial) humorously argued that boardinghouse keepers looked forward to spring because of the outbreak of love among their residents. Written by a "newspaper man" named Will Beard, the story began with boardinghouse keeper Mrs. Butterine sighing, "With flour as high as it is now . . . and board so low, and young gentlemen so forgetful of the first of the month, it would be hard on us unless some of the boarders occasionally fell in love and lost their appetites." Beard asked for more specifics: "What kind of food do you find that young people in love like best?" The keeper replied, "Just any old thing will do. When young people are in love they eat so little of anything that it really does not matter; generally, though, they don't like anything heavy." She specified a spring lovers' menu: "Cabbage and turnips would sit on the table a year and a day before they would be touched. Pickle and cold slaw, though, are mighty pleasing to their palates." Mr. Smith, who ate "six biscuits as regular as a meal comes," ate only "one-third as many and only one of them buttered. No molasses either" when he was in love. Beard concluded that many keepers, real and fictional, had incentive to cultivate love in their lodgers because of the money they could save.[44]

Like Mrs. Butterine, Lynn Cullen balanced respectability, profit margins, and resort-town relaxation in her boardinghouse. Summer flirtations, while not explicitly on her menu, could be helpful if they stayed on the near side of the line of appropriate romance. Dick Weaver, a liveryman running one of Asheville's stables (essentially the early-century version of a taxi company owner), had no such scruples. He was the person responsible for connecting Edwards and Walker; he provided them transportation; he went along on many of their public adventures. Weaver seemed to specialize in matching young women to male boarders for the purposes of spring and summer flings.[45] Those flings saved keepers like Cullen in the same way that Mrs. Butterine so appreciated. The nights Edwards and Walker and members of their parties spent dining and drinking at other area hotels and the days spent roaming the town, as described in the trial, meant meals that Cullen and other boardinghouse keepers like her did not have to provide.

We do not know for certain what was served at Lynnoaks. But we do know that Cullen employed at least one cook, Hattie Morgan. On July 24, 1906, Morgan was sworn in and testified from the stand. The reporter from the *Nashville American* described her testimony as "the most spicy deposition." Part food joke, part racist dismissal typical of the era, nonetheless, the reporter treated Morgan's testimony seriously in his coverage. Our archives do not contain many voices of southern boardinghouse cooks from when they were actively employed (what voices remain tend to be those of keepers who also cooked or of cooks being asked later to remember their boardinghouse days).[46] Morgan and Walker had interacted in the corridors, kitchen, and working spaces of Lynnoaks.

Morgan recalled that she had "found Lola crying at the head of the stairs once." When asked, Walker said "her aunt had been scolding her" over a Mr. Cooper whom Cullen thought was calling too frequently. Morgan said Walker had confided in her on at least two other occasions about plans to run away. Morgan further said Walker had bragged about being on the stage, and she demonstrated she could "shore kick high, like show folks, and could kick straight out." Whether the stories Walker told Morgan were serious or just talk from a young girl blowing off steam was not clarified; Edwards's lawyers wanted merely to plant the thought in jurors' minds that Walker herself initiated the New York scheme.[47] Hattie Morgan's testimony revealed a working boardinghouse in which girls and women found time to dream between meals and laundry and public spaces.

Morgan was not the only boardinghouse employee to take the stand. Mary Willis was described by an *Asheville Citizen-Times* reporter as having been "at one time a servant in the Cullen boarding house at Asheville." The Nashville journalist did not specify Willis's role, but both agreed she ran errands around the house and for its residents. Willis testified that Cullen "conducted herself as decorously as she ever saw a lady in her life." Willis also testified that the other boarders in the house were respectable, "the very best of people." Working-class women's activist Jennie Collins argued forcefully in the late nineteenth century that employees in households like Willis and Morgan were key to listen to if one wanted to know the values of an establishment because they were positioned to hear what people needed and see how the household responded.[48] Morgan and Willis, then, should have had a privileged perspective on Lynnoaks and its respectability. Whether they felt they could speak that truth on the stand cannot be known.

Much of the trial's focus questioned or defended Cullen's morality based on whether she served and drank alcohol in her house. If she did, the logic suggested, then her niece's character was corrupted long before Edwards came along, and the case would fall apart. Miss Dora Meadows and Mrs. Ellis Sharpe, former boarders at Lynnoaks, said Cullen had a good character, but W. C. Brown, a lawyer in town, said he "considered the reputation of Mrs. Cullen bad." A. B. Freeman, a banker from nearby Hendersonville, and W. A. Howards, a dairyman, had taken regular meals with Cullen's boarders at the house; both testified that it was a respectable house. A parade of salespeople and other Montford Avenue boardinghouse keepers, merchants, and friends agreed. However, John O'Gillen, a newspaper editor, and a Mrs. Humphrey claimed whiskey and "illicit cohabitation" might have been present at Lynnoaks. Dick Weaver testified he had imbibed with Cullen on some outings but under cross-examination was forced to admit that he himself had drunk so much on those occasions that he could not recall precisely who was in the carriages.[49] Lawyers traced a straight line from alcohol to sex to lies; the beverage in one's hand was a high-stakes indicator of the value and merit of participants in the story.

Temperance was on the horizon while Edwards defended himself in court. People on the stand in the case used beverages to signal their distance from or closeness to the revelries they witnessed. For example, Dr. Carl Reynolds testified he had been hanging out with a group of men in front of Sawyer's Store when Edwards, Walker, and others in their party drove up. But Reynolds carefully noted he had been "drinking lemonade." By so doing, he implied his character was upright and his memories were clear. Perhaps less obvious to readers today, in the late nineteenth and early twentieth centuries, lemonade signaled allegiance to temperance. First Lady Lucy Hayes, wife of President Rutherford B. Hayes, had acquired the nickname Lemonade Lucy for her support of temperance. Songs and recipe books pushed substituting lemonade for liquor. Temperance pledges and clubs advocated strongly for the public renouncement of alcoholic drinks.[50] The doctor deliberately mentioned his mild beverage while witnessing the wild behavior outside a general store.

Witnesses for the plaintiff emphasized they never saw intoxicating beverages at 103 Montford. Cullen herself claimed she had drunk only soft drinks while chaperoning her niece early in the affair. But no one doubted cocktails were imbibed both in the various wine rooms and dining rooms at hotels in which Walker and Edwards's group partied and on mountain roads in containers stashed in the back of buggies or in flasks in the pockets of their occupants. Beer in bottles was tucked by the case in the back of carriages. Wine was imbibed at the hotels, including sweet wines and port. A witness suggested that he was most surprised when Walker had drained the glass out of which she was drinking beer and had him fill it to the brim with the cocktail others were drinking.[51]

Edwards described his highballs as primarily composed of whiskey and seltzer. That marked him as typical of his time, a "golden age of whiskey" in the US South. Sales of whiskey were in transition, with some brands insisting on bonded sales, in bottles designed to highlight distinctive labels, and others still offering wholesale barrels so that individual bars or stores could resell in whatever containers they chose. A menu from the Battery Park Hotel from 1900 reflected exactly that: the menu offered eleven different "whiskies." A glass of Wagner's No. 3 cost $1.50 and one of Jas. E. Pepper original was $1.25. However, a patron could also choose either "Battery Park Hotel, Old Rye" or "Pure Corn, North Carolina 1890" for $0.75 a glass. If a glass was not enough for the evening, any of the eleven whiskey choices could be purchased by quart from the menu, with prices ranging from $3.00 to $1.50.[52] Dick Weaver likely purchased the flasks of whiskey he bought for the summer tallyho and stage rides from one of the wine rooms or stores through which the Walker-Edwards party circulated.

Precise types of alcohol and amounts Lola and her aunt drank in the summer of 1903 were hidden behind competing testimony in the trial. However, no one disputed that Lola was around cultures of drinking that summer, many of which took place in the boardinghouses and hotels of Asheville. After the notorious summer of 1903 in Asheville, that proximity continued as Lola joined various touring theater troupes as a chorus girl. Because the trial centered on whether Walker had suffered injury from Edwards's behavior, chorus girls who had traveled the nation with Lola testified to her character and life conditions from 1903 until 1906 in the latter half of the trial. Chorus life brought boardinghouses, brothels, and alcohol into the late-night life of many young women in these careers. Mary Barrel, who had worked with Lola in the Mr. Jolly of Joliet Company, called it "hopping down the line"—after curtains fell on evening shows, troupes visited "immoral houses" to drink and wind down after their performances. They would then pile back onto the train cars they used as "sleeping quarters" and be carried to the next town on the line for the next night's shows. One of the troupes Lola joined even had a cocktail named after it, the Bizzy Izzy.[53]

Lola Walker's story was inextricable from Dick Edwards's story. In turn, Edwards's life was the story of bachelors and clubmen at the turn of the century. The flourishing of bachelor culture—single men shaped by urban living finding each other through identifying themselves as such and joining clubs devoted to the life—not only affected the men in question but also triggered longer term changes in social life in the United States. Chicago-based social worker and activist Jane Addams worried about bachelor men and the "boarder problem" specifically because "these individuals threatened sexual propriety, especially that of the girls and young women living in households that rented rooms to boarders."[54] Edwards had friends in Asheville, but he did not have family; Cullen, trying to suss out his reputation, had access only to other bachelors and clubmen vacationing with him. While Cullen was trying to chase down her eloping niece, she might be forgiven for thinking disorganization reigned. But for girls like Lola, the chance to have a life free of family scrutiny may well have looked like a welcome reorganization.

The specific club or clubs to which Edwards belonged were not named in trial coverage. Yet newspapers from Washington, DC, to Nashville all agreed that he was "a clubman." The moniker denoted class privilege transferrable across the United States. One newspaper piece listed his net worth at $300,000. To critics, being a clubman could also signal "dissipated habits" supported and encouraged by the all-male cohort with which bachelors surrounded themselves. It could lead men to seek out, for the purposes of pleasure, women they had no intention of marrying. Variously described as "chippies" or "The Kind of Girl One Doesn't Marry," some women entered relationships with their eyes wide open. Some women sought fun and leisure after long days at work; some worked as professional prostitutes. And some were unwilling girls who thought they had found romance with a wealthy, serious suitor. Where Lola fell in this continuum became the business of the trial. Edwards made no apologies for coming to Asheville seeking "kissing and hugging" for the summer from a girl he had no intention of marrying.[55] He was sure he would find one in Asheville's boardinghouse culture.

Martha Hinton's later fear that a pack of cards was a slippery slope to her boardinghouse becoming a den of gambling and a house of vice was related to Alice Lee Larkins's earlier careful choice of location so as not to attract the "wrong" class of boarders. Mary Ellen Pleasant's decorations and menus allowed boarders to fill in their own fantasies while still attracting respectable boarders. The more charitable read of popular culture portraits of humorless boardinghouse keepers with rigid rules and eagle eyes was that they knew how thin the line was between an upstanding house and a suspicious one. One of the punishments that a boardinghouse keeper could face was having her establishment labeled a "disorderly house." A legal term, the designation also points to how quickly a house could lose its footing. Some keepers, however, had fewer scruples or more disregard for societal pressure and instead worked that line to offer both room and board and sex for hire. When was a house a boardinghouse, and when was it a brothel? How did prospective residents know? And what happened when a location offered both? The house at 103 Montford Avenue, where Cullen presided, rented rooms and served meals to respectable married couples; traveling salesmen, some of whom drank and some not; and single girls like Lola who were navigating a changing world of acceptable behavior and permissible desires.[56]

By their very nature, stories of southern brothels can be hard to see. They trade in privacy, closed doors, pseudonyms, and erasures. Communities often want to exclude brothels and the people who worked in them from their official histories and memories.[57] Police records and town directories often obscured activities with coded language. Researchers have had to be resourceful to unearth histories of even famous brothels. Towns large and small had men and women who paid or were paid for sex acts— whether on the "wrong side of the tracks" or in luxurious back parlors or in arrangements that police overlooked. Southern port cities had long histories of lodging houses offering sailors on leave pleasure as well as food and sleep. Establishments and the women owning, managing, and working in them were present—and they were present all over the South, in communities large and small, targeting customers of varied races, classes, and life courses. To be clear, sex work, when freely chosen and consented to, can be a viable career; making moral judgments, leaving unpunished violent encounters, and enforcing laws to target sex workers but not their clients are choices that society makes.

The Jim Crow South (and before that the slave system South) ensured bodies of Black women and some Black men were always vulnerable to exploitation. Expansion of travel and density of population across the century increased the sheer number of locations where sex as exchange or transaction happened. That sometimes meant that boardinghouses for privileged white lodgers were assumed to allow sexual encounters with Black workers by white men who cared little about consent or propriety. An African American girl, Jane Hunter, who worked "as a waitress and chambermaid in a boarding house" in rural Pickens County, South Carolina, and who lived in the free Black community of Liberia, South Carolina, had to "battle against unwanted advances" in her otherwise respectable workplace.[58] From a distance, lines between rape, violent coercion, choice, and free exchange can be very thin. Jurors in the Walker-Edwards trial had a complex task before them to decide who was consenting, in what type of place, and when profits were involved.

Along with his knowledge of Asheville's boardinghouses, Dick Weaver had connections in Asheville's brothels as well. Thomas Wolfe described the "easy women" who passed through Eliza Gant's boardinghouse: "They floated casually in—the semipublic, clandestine prostitutes of a tourist town." On the stand, Weaver admitted to visiting "questionable resorts" in his youth and "houses of ill-repute while in Memphis last week." He was asked about being arrested in Asheville in 1905 "on the charge of aiding and abetting a negro woman named Sarah Jane Lightle in running an assignation house." He answered only that he had been frequently "pretty boozy" and arrested and fined for gambling.[59] Asheville's activists railed against such behaviors, but its economy meant they continued.

Asheville was no different from other southern cities and towns in terms of its "assignation houses." At 59 Megowan Street in Lexington, Kentucky, on any night in the 1890s and the first years of the 1900s, Belle Brezing welcomed wealthy travelers, men flush with profits from horse racing, civic leaders, and regular customers to her brothel. Hers was one of many establishments in Lexington's red-light district. Likewise, New Orleans allowed but confined its district, concentrating brothels, bars, and gambling to a single Storyville neighborhood. Because its era overlapped with that of cameras and cheap printing technologies, New Orleans's madams and working women were photographed, visited, and now can have their stories at least partially told. From this historical remove, we can appreciate the creative energy such places generated—jazz musicians like Jelly Roll Morton credited Storyville for the start of their careers. Just as boardinghouse keepers acquired business skills, so could brothel owners and operators. Peter Guralnick wrote of legendary soul singer Sam Phillips's debt to an Alabama "whorehouse" operator, Kate Nelson, "the best businessperson I ever met in my life," who taught him her business skills and how to manage people even as she also let him pay for her "girls'" services.[60] For all their strengths, though, southern brothels also could be difficult places to escape, if a person was thought to work in one.

Sometimes brothels and the sex workers associated with them were mixed with mansions and respectable households in neighborhoods. Visitors to Charleston described as much in that port city: "White visitors . . . found themselves alternately fascinated, shocked, perplexed, and repulsed. . . . Heading up Meeting [Street], away from the water and toward the center of town, they walked by prostitutes of all colors who worked in the brothels along French Alley, between Meeting and Anson Streets." Further, visitors found "brothels and boardinghouses lay just steps from the elegant mansions on East Bay." In post–Civil War Natchez, Mississippi, Luke and Margaret O'Conner's divorce devolved into accusations that he frequented brothels (exposing her to sexually transmitted infections he picked up there) and that she "rented rooms to whores who serviced rough-edged male lodgers." Across the South, widowed, abandoned, or, in scholar Joyce Linda Broussard's term, "not-married" women like Margaret ran brothels as a way to acquire real estate and then legitimate footholds in the postwar economy, in a range of neighborhoods.[61]

Some brothels deliberately posed as boardinghouses. Hairdresser Eliza Potter, a free Black woman whose memoir provided a glimpse into high society in Cincinnati, Ohio, a city with proponents of both slavery and abolition in the 1850s, described once being "fooled" by an invitation to dress hair in a purported boardinghouse. Potter said, "I asked if this was a dress-making establishment or a boarding house. She said neither, it was a private house; but I had my doubts." Brothels could pose as boardinghouses full of women sewing or otherwise employed in piecework—such work required women to live and work in the same location; a houseful of single women working thus could acquire a veneer of plausible respectability.[62] But they did not need regular visits from the city's most sought-after, expensive fancy hairdresser. Potter was right to be suspicious.

Practically, the lines between brothels and boardinghouses *were* blurry. Women who worked in brothels often had their laundry done (or did laundry for each other); they ate some number of communal meals provided and often cooked in-house; and they slept and relaxed during their time off in the houses. That the homes were also their workplaces did not negate the underlying similarities to boardinghouses proper. Lexington's Brezing, for instance, kept ledgers that showed the rent she charged the women working as prostitutes in her house. In the 1880s, five women lived in the location of the business (then at 194 North Upper Street). Out of the $320 per month in rent Brezing collected, she subtracted the cost of hiring a cook, buying coal oil, and replacing bedsheets and towels. The food and drink she purchased for the house went to the women living there in addition to the customers spending evenings in their company.[63] For the five women and Belle, the house *was* a boardinghouse. Sex workers and brothels were, in other words, everywhere. Lola Walker's aunts and Sarah Hinton's grandmother knew the stakes. Lola's trial turned on them.

AFTER A THIRTY-TWO-DAY trial and three and a half hours of deliberations, the jury decided Lola was the innocent victim, not a schemer. Her aunts were judged not to be running houses of ill repute. In short, the jury awarded Walker $21,000 in damages. Attendees in the courtroom, "packed like sardines in a box," cheered. It was a major win for the chorus girl and her boardinghouse keeper aunts. Jurors donated cold watermelons and hosted a party for Walker, Bauer, and Cullen at a nearby home. They posed for pictures with her; they requested she give them copies of the salacious photos entered as evidence in the trial. She, in turn, gave the jurors flowers from a large bouquet a female admirer had sent. The *Nashville American* reporter concluded, "Never before in Obion County, and probably not in West Tennessee, has such a scene been witnessed."[64] It seemed that Walker and her extended family would start new lives with their case made and story endorsed.

In today's dollars the judgment would have been more than half a million dollars. Perhaps one of the reporters summed it up best: "Such a sum is calculated to impress Col. Dick with a painful sense of his eligibility, while rendering him by that much ineligible. And there now remains to him, not even the lady."[65] But, in the end, this was not the case. As Edwards had predicted, Walker could not win in his county. The judge overturned the jurors' findings.

Two days later, Judge Maiden agreed with Edwards's lawyers, ruling "the verdict of the jury is not sustained and supported by the evidence in the case. It is therefore ordered and adjudged that the verdict of the jury heretofore rendered and entered in this case be and the same is set aside and vacated and for nothing held." The judge allowed a new trial but increased the dollar value of the bonds Walker was required to file to take the case forward; she already owed $1,000 for the first trial. Reeling, Walker initially announced she would appeal, and, in fact, her legal team filed paperwork attesting as much. With already hefty lawyers' bills from the first trial, a new $750 bond to raise, and, frankly, three years of her life already tied up in unsuccessful litigation, Walker did not see the second trial through. Edwards never faced the "pain" of judgment by courts. Yet he was not destined for long life; Edwards died at age forty-one, from a car accident in 1914. Lulie, his wife, passed away two years later.[66] Whether his boardinghouse trial contributed to their early deaths is unknown.

By January 1907, the case was officially dropped. In the intervening months, newspapers turned their attention back to Lola Walker one last time to breathlessly announce, "Jilted Actress Won by a Printer." Another declared, "Chorus Girl Marries Star Witness." The Asheville papers were a bit calmer, with one headline noting Walker "Weds Man Who Testified for Her." George Lieferman had been present throughout the depositions and trials. He had testified "on behalf of Miss Lola Walker" and "under cross-examination [was] made to admit some very ugly things about himself," as one newspaper proclaimed. Lieferman admitted to gambling and drinking, but he also had boarded at Walker's aunt Annie Bauer's Chicago boarding-house during Lola's chorus days. He knew Lola from childhood, long before her fateful summer in Asheville. Had they been in a long-term relationship, or did they fall in love over the course of the trial? The records do not tell. Charlotte papers summarized the case and its financial impact on Walker before announcing her marriage. It concluded, "Everybody here, regardless of opinion, seems to be glad the odious case will not again be brought up." Walker and Lieferman settled in Chicago; she did not make the papers again, but the final newspaper coverage for her described her as "'milady' milliner," as well as a "chorus girl, artists' model, and church worker."[67]

Sarah Hinton's story, somewhat miraculously, had a happy ending to modern eyes, even if Martha strongly disagreed. Sarah managed to escape from the institution her grandmother had put her in and got a job in a college town taking care of the children of a professor's wife. Martha in the Federal Writers' Project interview gave no further hints as to how this came about, except to say Sarah finished high school and trained as a librarian. Did the professor's wife help pay for her schooling? Did she aspire to a life of the mind once she escaped from her grandmother's narrow world? At the time of the interview, Martha said Sarah had a job in a city library. Martha, however, insisted, "But, nothing will ever make me think Sarah is any good; she'll never amount to anything, she's vain and determined to have her own way, loving the pleasures of this world. If she had listened to my teachings and walked the path I have trod, she would have been a good woman."[68] It is hard not to notice the similarities between what Sarah's life must have been—surrounded by books, employed by the government, and supporting herself through education—and the life of Travis Tuck Jordan, interviewer, poet, and Federal Writers' Project employee.

Walker's aunt Lynn Cullen stayed in Asheville another five years. City directories in 1909 and 1911 list her on North French Broad Avenue, at one point as the "proprietor" of the "Richelieu Hotel." After 1911, she relocated to Florida. She continued in the career she knew best, running boarding-houses and hotels (and occasionally living in them with family members, including, at one point, her ninety-year-old mother, Abbie Overton) in Jacksonville and Miami. In Florida directories, she still identified as the widow of C. J. Cullen, and as late as 1939, when Jordan had completed her interview with Martha Hinton, Cullen still ran hotels and had boarders. Lynn M. Cullen died in Miami, Florida in 1941.[69]

In trial evidence given over the course of the Lola Walker case, her aunt's boardinghouse "piazza" and arbor played a crucial role. Nights spent roving from hotel to boardinghouse to inn, with drinks, dancing, kissing, and hugging, offered revelry and release. Susan Hinton, Lola Walker, and fictional Carrie and May Thornton all rode out on adventures from their boardinghouses with bachelor men. Carrie, May, and their boarders spent evenings in respectable and socially acceptable gentle flirtation, successfully navigating a new world of relations between single men and women. We know about Susan's marriage only from her judgmental mother, but even Martha admitted Susan's husband was there to hold her hand as she died; perhaps it was a loving, if short, relationship. Lola and Colonel Edwards's evenings led to social ruin and public censure, especially for the teenage girl with dreams of fame and fortune. Colonel Edwards proved to be no Mr. Ross, and Lola's dreams did not have the happy ending of Carrie Thornton. Asheville, the location of both boardinghouses (the fictional and the real), represented complicated fantasies and realities for women and men thrown into boardinghouse cultures there. Durham, the site of the Hinton family's life, brought religion, morality, and social change crashing into each other—but somehow Sarah managed to find a path into education and middle-class employment. Drinks and delicacies, sitting on the edges of the boardinghouse menus, reveal possibilities for new standards of behavior within the cultures of southern, boarding, and vacation life.

Did Jordan have a lot of motivation to erase moments of kindness and emphasize the harshness of Martha Hinton's worldview? Standing as it does relatively by itself in the historical record (as it has a pseudonym and no interview notes, I can do little as a researcher to confirm or contextualize Hinton's life), the interview serves as a cautionary tale. Was Sarah Hinton truly rebellious and incorrigible, or did she just long for a career in the new South world? Was Lola Walker the innocent waif, or did she and her family use hidden spaces of resort town boardinghouses to scheme an almost successful plan to profit from a wealthy playboy? Was Lola an unapologetic schemer, or was she just part of the first wave of girls embracing their sexuality and insisting on freedom of career choice? Was Lynn Cullen a heartbroken aunt struggling to make things right for her own sister, who had entrusted her daughter to her? Or was she a blackmailer cloaking her schemes in a resort town's need for boardinghouses? We must check our romanticism at the door of boardinghouses and then be open to the range of human experiences found inside. Sometimes kind and loving women opened their doors. Sometimes women with "relentless and stoic" faces stood there. Some women were hardened by the difficult work of running a boardinghouse. But still others, like Martha Hinton, might have been that way long they began taking in boarders. Women like her did not want compassion or romantic notions coming into their spaces. Hinton "closed the door without saying good bye" and Jordan "heard the key turn in the lock," her story at an end.[70]

With birth control, civil rights, and feminist movements all on the horizon, girls like Lola and Sarah demanded different endings for their own stories. The changes they pushed for over time nudged American culture into greater freedom and flexibility for girls' lives—whether they sought romance or sex on their own terms or education or relaxation without gender-based expectations. Other people used the in-between spaces of boardinghouses to create freedom to travel, live, and thrive in the face of violence or hatred. Boardinghouses and networks between them could offer safety for non-white, non-Christian, nonmainstream travelers. Boardinghouses and the women running them also facilitated transformations of a different sort—those of selves across fluid boundaries of class, race, gender, or religion.

SAFE PASSAGE IN JIM CROW'S BOARDINGHOUSES

Jackie Mabley and Frank Gibert

IN 1948 ON a busy movie set, actors sat down at a table to film a scene about a surprise meal at a down-and-out boardinghouse. In the movie's plot, boarders have financed the meal. Pawning clothing, jewelry, and other incidentals, they have used the money to buy food to treat the broke boardinghouse keeper on her birthday. It is a kind gesture, and the film meal is joyous. Real life intruded on the set of the fictional story. The director called for a second take, but the actors, themselves hungry and without much money in their pockets, had emptied all the dishes on set during the first take. Gig workers, uncertain about their next paycheck, these actors did not let the opportunity to fill their bellies pass. There was nothing left to film. At the head of the fictional table for the all-Black cast feature film *Boarding House Blues* was Jackie "Moms" Mabley (1897–1975).[1] The film's boardinghouse table was in Harlem, but for Mabley the scene may well have recalled her childhood in Brevard, North Carolina, at her mother's boardinghouse. Equally, it could have brought to mind the many boardinghouses she saw during her years touring on the performance circuit around the Jim Crow South or the various boardinghouses full of fellow theater performers at which Mabley stayed in off-seasons. A queer Black woman, Mabley needed the safety of welcoming boardinghouses when the world was not open to her full self. When they did not exist, she created them.

A few decades earlier, in 1902, aspiring writer Frank Gibert (b. ca. 1870) left behind a successful saloon in Danville, Virginia, packed a trunk, and traveled with his companion, Cora Douglas, to Washington, DC. They booked themselves into a boardinghouse in the Tenderloin district and began unpacking, intending to settle into life in the capital city. Having brought money, assets, and references, Frank and Cora seemed poised to make an easy transition to city life. Someone in the boardinghouse had suspicions, though. Was it a maid, going through a trunk in a stolen moment? Was it a dropped handkerchief or an inexpertly set collar? Was it a fellow traveler who had heard stories in Virginia? Was it a shot in the dark that happened to hit true? It is a detail we will never know. Regardless, the police came to the boardinghouse. When they arrived, Frank had changed into a gown and admitted to having been called Frances Harris in the past. Newspapers covered the story with the headline "Woman in Guise of a Man."[2]

Some people stepped into boardinghouses with one identity intending to emerge with another. Jackie Mabley found her way from a life in a small mountain town to an international career. Frank Gibert shed his past as Frances. Elsewhere, a man named William Ward became white. Former brothel keepers presented themselves as heiresses. Men in Tennessee Williams's two-act play *Vieux Carré*, which he began writing in the 1930s and did not finish until the 1970s, found in boardinghouses the freedom to form relationships and express sexualities with each other with less risk.[3] When boardinghouses were in the US South, the stakes of who interacted with whom could carry a high risk of violence, especially if boundaries of race were involved. Travelers turned to guidebooks sensitive to the challenges they faced. Structures of segregation also meant that boardinghouses persisted in southern communities well into the twentieth century. Some keepers and lodgers policed and entrenched systemic inequalities to keep people apart. Others resisted Jim Crow and other segregationist impulses and made space for individual travel or reinvention despite social structures. Inside some boardinghouses, in-between spaces offered individuals opportunities to rest, reinvent, regroup, or alter their path going forward—all of which could be key strategies in the face of external systems of oppression.

Knowing which fork to use, understanding how to navigate the codes of the parlor, and being accepted into the right houses unlocked surviving and thriving in a new town or city. If you wished to reinvent yourself, change your race, practice your religion outside the mainstream, embrace your gender even if that required a transition, love or marry or remain single in same-sex spaces, jump over economic class divides, simply shed your past, or travel safely regardless of who people thought you were, successfully navigating a boardinghouse could help you do so. Some boardinghouse women consciously cultivated houses in which moments of safety were offered. Other lodgers seized moments regardless of the keeper's intention. In all these houses, boardinghouse women challenged and broadened who counted in American culture. That work is unfinished, but it is work we build on today.

From Loretta to Jackie: Becoming Moms

Loretta Mary Aiken was born in Brevard, North Carolina, in 1897. A small town in the western North Carolina mountains, Brevard was already a stopover for tourists sightseeing—for instance, characters in S. S. Tennent's story "Among the Mountains" stopped for a meal in Brevard before continuing on an overnight trip from Asheville to Buck Forest and Caesar's Head in South Carolina. The group of Asheville-based city residents and tourists found Brevard to be "the merest village with its store, post-office, court-house and jail," but they were "made very comfortable at the hotel in the little town, which in the Summer is quite filled with persons from the 'low country,' seeking health and coolness amongst the mountains." Outside of fictional portraits, long-term residents conducted and supported county business in the "little" town, since it was Transylvania County's seat. Merchants, small factory owners, and brokers of raw materials such as timber and tannin conducted business from the town. An infrastructure to manage tourists was centered in Brevard as well, with businesses from which to rent conveyances or purchase picnic supplies. A school, which would become Brevard Institute and then today's Brevard College, had been founded two years earlier for white students. African American youth were educated at three different "colored schools" in 1897, and their parents were hard at work on a more permanent, consolidated school for their children. They would soon find success in that effort by partnering with the Rosenwald Foundation on a school building.[4]

Aiken was one of sixteen children between her parents, James Aiken and Mary Smith. Brevard's Black population was relatively small (especially compared with nearby Hendersonville and Asheville); its group of middle-class Black residents was even smaller, but they were organized and prominent. James was one of them. He was an integral member of the community. He owned businesses around the rural mountain downtown—a general store that also sold caskets, a common practice during the era; a bakery; a barbershop catering to wealthy white male residents and tourists; a drayage service responsible for mail and cargo; and a restaurant. Meetings of groups like the Odd Fellows, the Masons, and the women's auxiliary Eastern Star took place in Aiken buildings. He was on school oversight committees, including those working to establish the permanent school; he was a prominent member of a Baptist church; and he was the only African American to be part of the town's volunteer firefighting crew. He amassed real estate in town and, more importantly, a solid reputation for helping to make "the world better than he found it," according to M. L. Shipman, editor of the *French Broad Hustler*, a white-owned newspaper from Hendersonville, the next town over. As is often the case, the family's economic security was a team effort: Loretta's mother, Mary, likely staffed the general store, and her grandmother baked gingerbread and other pastries to sell with apple cider in the store.[5]

Prosperity and shelter did not last, however. At seven o'clock on Wednesday morning, August 25, 1909, the family's anchor gave way. Brevard's new "chemical engine"—a chemical-reaction-powered, pressure-valve firefighting machine—rushed down a hill to Jim Axum's burning house with the volunteer firefighting team aboard. Unbeknownst to firefighters riding along, dangerous levels of gas and pressure were building in the engine. Exacerbated either by the downhill dash or (more likely) by a faulty or wrongly set release valve, the danger grew. In the process of unwinding the hose to approach the fire, the tank exploded. Several men on the crew were hurt, with injuries ranging from broken bones to cuts and bruises. But the man standing closest to where the hose connected to the tank bore the brunt of the damage. James Aiken was thrown twelve feet into the air by the explosion. He suffered a broken neck and nearly severed arm—injuries that killed him instantly.[6]

According to local newspaper coverage, Aiken's death was "a distinct loss to the town." It continued, "He was the most widely known colored man in western North Carolina; was a successful and enterprising business man whose store on Main Street is well patronized." Further, the *Brevard News* article went out of its way to emphasize that Aiken was a trained and experienced firefighter—this was not a case of human error. Not only was Aiken on the crew, the article insisted, but he "was always among the first to respond to the call of the fire-bell and one of the hardest workers at every fire in the history of the town." Listing his volunteer associations, religious affiliation, and influence with both Black and white mountain residents, the article concluded he would be missed by all Brevard's residents. The editor of the *French Broad Hustler* aimed even higher in his praise, even as it was tempered by a hefty dose of paternalism. Saying he had known Aiken well for at least fifteen years, Shipman wrote, "In the opinion of the editor of this newspaper, 'Jim' Aiken was the best negro in the United States." Shipman continued, "He was ever ready to assist those in distress and here is one colored man who left the world better than he found it." More tellingly, Shipman noted that Aiken's funeral was integrated and "the business houses of the town were closed during the hours of his service."[7] James Aiken's death rippled through western North Carolina.

Likely, none felt his absence as much as his family. Loretta's mother assumed proprietorship of the family general store and took in lodgers while also working to settle his estate as executor of his will. Estate records show this involved inventorying the store, assessing personal property that ranged from parcels of city lots to hogs to a piano to stockpiled lumber, and settling outstanding accounts, including those of lawyers helping her to resolve her husband's business affairs. On behalf of the whole family, Mary placed a "Card of Thanks" in the *Brevard News* "to the many friends, both white and colored, who so kindly came to our assistance after the calamity which deprived us of husband and father." In subsequent months, she advertised in the newspaper to assure customers the general store and restaurant would continue to offer the same service and quality. One ad asserted, "The business established by my late husband will be continued at the old stand to the best of my ability, and I would most respectfully ask for your continued patronage and support." By the 1910 Federal Census, Mary was listed as head of household. Seven of her children, including Loretta, lived with her in the home she owned free and clear on Oakland Avenue (today's Oaklawn Avenue; possibly misinterpreting western North Carolina accents, the census taker also heard and wrote "Loretter"). Alfred and Lula Bowen, with their two adult and two young relatives, were lodging with Mary at the time. Alfred gave his profession as restaurant proprietor,

Lula listed hers as a laundrywoman, and twenty-three-year-old Daniel was a waiter in a boardinghouse (it is unclear whether there in Mary's home or elsewhere in town). The home must have been bustling.[8]

Alice Lee Larkins, Mary Surratt, and Malinda Russell would all recognize Mary Aiken's life after Jim died as similar to their own boardinghouse stories. Mary was most likely cash-poor after settling her husband's estate. But she was property-rich and had skills, so she opened her doors to boarders. Did Loretta help cook or do laundry for the family? She was certainly of an age that she might have. Was she busy with school and employed outside the house? How much time did Loretta spend with her grandmother? The family faced many adjustments with one of their two primary breadwinners gone.

Mary listed her occupation to the census taker not as boardinghouse keeper but as general store merchant. The relationship with the Bowens extended beyond living arrangements and into Aiken's other business endeavors. In the census, Alfred Bowen gave his occupation as restaurant proprietor, and an ad in the *Brevard News* from that year described his "New Hygienic Restaurant" accessible from the side entrance at the rear of "Mrs. Mary P. Aiken's store." Another notice in the paper described its "quick lunches and meals on short notice" and deemed it an "up-to-date restaurant." Eventually, Bowen opened his own general store down the street, in partnership with his son. In the meantime, ads for Mary's store soon revealed her remarriage. By January 20, 1911, she had gained her feet as proprietor, confidently asking in print, "What are you looking for?" and answering, "If it is a nice Hat, If it is a nice pair of Shoes, If it is a nice Shirt of any kind, If it is a nice warm meal when you are hungry, This Is the Place to Come." After discussing the goods for sale, she added, "I also have Fish and Oysters each Wednesday and Saturday." She signed the ad "Mary Aiken Parton."[9] Her mother's new partnership with George Parton augured changes for young Loretta.

Loretta was only twelve when her father died. What happened next in Loretta's story is difficult to parse in the historical record. Elsie Williams's recent monograph on Mabley's humor tells some of the story, as does the careful history of Brevard's Black community written by Nathaniel B. Hall for Mary Jane McCrary's *Transylvania Beginnings: A History*, published by the local historical society. Oral histories in Betty Jamerson Reed's *Brevard Rosenwald School* add details from relatives. But as with Mary Ellen Pleasant, Malinda Russell, and others, personal biography can be obscured by public institutional systems disinclined to document a young

Black woman's life. Women themselves could choose to obscure stories out of doubt that they would be treated with respect or justice, what Darlene Clark Hine has called a protective "culture of dissemblance." Williams noted that while Mabley "on occasion" discussed personal details in performances, "she characteristically avoided revealing specific, intimate details of her life to interviewers." Mabley gave multiple versions of stories (such as how she got her stage name, her birthdate, and the details of her children's backgrounds).[10] She did not talk at length on the record about her teenage years in Brevard.

This is not a work of investigative journalism, so I have chosen to follow the already published pieces rather than, for instance, interviewing figures in Brevard. What can be said is that the years following her father's death were difficult for Loretta. More broadly, life for many if not most young Black girls at the height of the Jim Crow era was fraught. Community histories shared orally suggest that Loretta was raped not once but twice, and at least one of the attacks may have been by a white sheriff. The rapes may have resulted in pregnancies. Mabley said only that she had been "raped and everything else." Fragmentary news and court evidence gave glimpses of what she faced. Around the same time, her stepfather (according to her later accounts) pressured her to marry an older man he had chosen for her. Loretta resisted. The same grandmother who specialized in selling baked goods through the family café in the back of the general store encouraged Loretta to seize her own destiny. Whatever horrors happened, they were enough for Loretta's grandmother to urge her to "leave Brevard, see the world, and go make something of herself." By about age fifteen, Loretta did just that.[11]

She still lived in boardinghouses. But now they were ones on the road. Like Lola Walker during her chorus girl days but with the added complication of being an African American traveling through the segregated South, Loretta ran away—as far as she could. She joined touring companies. She traveled with the Theater Owners Booking Association (TOBA, nicknamed by the performers "Tough on Black Asses"). She changed her whole name, first and last. In Houston, Texas, performers Butterbeans and Susie took Mabley under their wing. One of the most successful acts on the circuit, Butterbeans and Susie gave Mabley the launching pad she needed for a career in comedy. She performed for the rest of her life. Her most recognized stage persona was a lusty older woman talking about younger men; wearing a floppy hat and loose clothing, she fearlessly joked about racism, Black life, and women's experiences without having to reveal much of her own life offstage. She explicitly challenged stereotyped options for Black women, southerners, and Appalachians, saying, for instance,

No *damn* MAMMY, *Moms*
I don't know nothin'
'bout no log cabin;
I ain't never seen
No log cabin . . .
Split level in the suburbs, *Baby*!

The claim from later in her career carried a rejection of popular culture's racist nostalgia circling around Black women (the very ones about hospitality, mothering, and cooking that Mary Ellen Pleasant had worked to her advantage after she was unable to counter them). Mabley signaled she was never going home to her small southern mountain town, except as a visitor. For those who knew Brevard, it contained an insider's nod to the sophistication of the town—there were no isolated log cabins on Oaklawn Avenue when she was a child. In six short lines, Mabley clearly signaled her career and life choices would not be limited by ideas of appropriate gender roles, place of origin, or age. It worked.[12]

So successful was her distancing of herself from her childhood, hardly anyone outside Brevard remembers Mabley as especially southern or at all Appalachian or mountain. Few could know she was from a boardinghouse table in the western North Carolina mountains.[13] "Moms" Mabley is remembered today as one of the most successful comedians—male or female—from the heyday of Harlem's Apollo Theater, despite comedy being a highly male-dominated business. That achievement was helped by fellow travelers making it acceptable to expect safety and care while far from home.

In her 2016 book, *Colored Travelers*, Elizabeth Stordeur Pryor examined why freedom of travel has been key to civil rights—whether that be for people of color, people with disabilities, women, the elderly, or immigrants—since well before the Civil War. She argued that "colored travelers" from the earliest decades of the nineteenth century recognized that "being able to travel freely was a crucial component of U.S. citizenship." In letters, diaries, speeches, and memoirs, "they insisted that, outside of slavery, there was no better way to understand the oppressive nature of white supremacy in the so-called free states of the United States than to take a good hard look at travel."[14] Boardinghouses persisted in the US South as long as freedom to travel was threatened for a substantial number of people. Under

Jim Crow, citizens were nominally free, but people of color were not free to move about as they wished. Women and men who ran boardinghouses were connected across centuries in their efforts to create pockets of safety and freedom. Beyond the food, conversation, or welcoming spaces, this, then, is why boardinghouses matter.

Former New York postman Victor Hugo Green, some twenty-five years after Mabley first left home, still saw a need to make travel easier. Beginning in 1936, he compiled a yearly motor guide to help people of color find such spaces, especially when traveling the US South during segregation. By 1937 he expanded to feature as many states as he could, growing steadily in coverage and reach and ultimately including vacation locations as far afield as Bermuda and encompassing international air travel advice as well. Over time, the titles were tweaked to reflect travel and vacationing more broadly. In compiling and releasing his *Negro Motorist Green Books* (often colloquially called "Green Books"), Green helped Black travelers move safely through the Jim Crow South. Twelve years into the project, he looked back to his first publication and wrote, "It has been our idea to give the Negro traveler information that will keep him from running into difficulties, embarrassments and to make his trips more enjoyable."[15]

Green credited another group that had difficulties traveling in the United States for inspiration: "The Jewish press has published information about places that are restricted" to Jewish travelers. Jewish travelers often needed to know where kosher kitchens and synagogues were located and where Jews could shop, stay, and relax. S. M. Fleischman, writing in the *Jewish Exponent*, for instance, gave his "Impressions of Asheville." The piece compared vacationing in Asheville, North Carolina, and Aiken, South Carolina, and came down solidly on the side of Asheville. Having stayed a month, Fleischman felt qualified to speak authoritatively about the "town of about ten thousand inhabitants, containing a fair share of progressive citizens, who, recognizing the advantages of the place as an all-the-year-round health resort, are busy enhancing its beauty and increasing its facilities." He detailed the seventy-five-member Jewish community and its congregation. He also noted that "some of the nicest stores" in the city were "in the hands of our co-religionists." He waxed poetic about the care he received in the Oakland Heights Sanatorium where he stayed and the views of mountains, rivers, and clouds it afforded him.[16]

Among nearby Hendersonville's five Jewish boardinghouses in 1926, three operated kosher kitchens (and shared a shohet full-time for the busy summer months). Having such capacity meant that Jews from around the region felt supported in taking vacations of some length in the mountain town. (The robustness of Camp Blue Star, founded in 1948, continues the traditions of Hendersonville as a summer destination into the present day.) Elsewhere, Mrs. R. J. Slager advertised her "First Class Jewish Boarding House" in Jacksonville, Florida, in 1878; as Florida established itself as a vacation and resort destination, enterprising members of marginalized groups took a chance on expanding travel opportunities for others as well.[17] For travelers keeping kosher and facing religious prejudice and for people shut out of businesses because of the color of their skin, guides helped not only with finding welcoming places to sleep but also with securing meals, gas, and even haircuts or clothing alteration and repair—or boarding-houses, which could offer almost all those services under one roof. Green built off the model to create his guides.

For musicians, comedians, singers, or actors in the late nineteenth and early twentieth centuries who were African American, like Mabley, or taken to be, tours especially through the US South were high-risk, high-reward. Black communities were concentrated and segregated. As a result, audiences were appreciative and large, and, because of Jim Crow, a trail of dedicated venues had been formalized. Getting from place to place safely, however, could be tricky. In midcentury years, once musicians dominated the traveling entertainment circuits, the southern route came to be known as the "chitlin' circuit." A network of performance spaces (ranging from full-blown theaters to juke joints, barns, and outdoor tents), advertisers, and audiences, the circuit in both early and later forms provided entertainers some safety and stability even while traveling through towns and cities hostile to strangers, especially strangers of color.[18] The food reference is evocative—a delicacy to some, needing skill to prepare well, shunned by others, and cheap and often discarded parts of the hog, chitlins are quintessential scrappy, hardworking foods.

The comedians' booking association and later musicians' circuits were not just made up of performance venues. Less discussed but just as crucial, touring performers and their managers built a network of boardinghouses, restaurants, and hotels for performers and troupes to eat and stay at. Moms Mabley's *Boarding House Blues* was set in Harlem, but its characters could well have come straight off the southern tour to land in New York. Performers in the film included Dusty Fletcher, a vaudeville comedian; the Berry Brothers, a trio of dancers; Lucky Millinder, a bandleader; Una Mae Carlisle, a singer; and Henry Heard, a one-armed, one-legged dancer. Slappy White, who told the story of the vanished meal, was a dancer and comedian who visited the set. Temporarily off the road, staying in the titular boarding-house, the film's characters used their downtime to practice acts, audition for new shows, and prepare for the next season. While the characters had long relationships with Moms, who played the keeper, viewers understand that they came and went as jobs opened up. A plot in the film turned on a plan by residents to create a show that, if a hit, would help everyone pay the next month's rent. The boardinghouse in the film was a safe landing spot, an individual establishment but one necessary to the larger networks that circulated people, ideas, and cultures.[19]

Whether in the fictional world of film or in real life, when performers went on the road, they had a range of published automobile-based travel guides like Green's from which to choose. Guidebooks were part of a long tradition of trusted voices picking out routes for others. For European tour-ists, Baedeker guides predated automobile travel, having debuted in 1861. They emphasized rail and stagecoach travel, with recommendations about how to pace a long trip. Twentieth-century guides' narrative structures— the descriptions and scene-painting details—built off practices worked out in nineteenth-century books, such as Anne Royall's *Black Books* (when she wasn't marrying off the keepers she met), as well as a larger genre of travel writing, from Frances Trollope to Frederick Law Olmsted. Whereas Trollope and Olmsted did not explicitly intend for readers to follow them, Royall, with her detailed and frank advice about location, proprietor, and costs, did. She encapsulated the spirit of the later guides, including her advice for travelers in areas hostile to the author (in her case, a woman traveling alone). By the twentieth century, choices for guidebooks prolifer-ated; people traveled farther with fewer connections in communities they visited. Packing a guide to help navigate food, lodging, and supplies only made sense. The Michelin star rating system, still coveted today, initially was a promotion by the tire company to encourage longer road trips that might necessitate more tire purchases. The American Automobile Associa-tion was formed in 1902; it published its first maps in 1905 and first hotel guide in 1917. Duncan Hines, discussed more fully below, began traveling as a salesman in 1905. His first guides were distributed to friends and col-leagues as early as 1910. He began selling them in 1936, the same year as Victor Hugo Green's first. *Negro Motorist Green Books* lasted through the period of formal Jim Crow in the United States, ceasing publication after 1966; Hines ended his yearly guides in 1962.[20]

Green's guides have caught the cultural eye recently, with documentaries and feature films as well as major museum and digital exhibits available.

Over time, Green used more green ink on his covers, merging color and name. They were inexpensive: for instance, in 1935 gas cost ten cents a gallon, and that year's guide cost a quarter. Ten years later, the book cost seventy-five cents. Guides were divided alphabetically by state and then by cities within the states. For each city, listings could include hotels, taverns, roadhouses, restaurants, gas stations, barbershops, beauty parlors, and the term Green used for boardinghouses: "tourist homes." The 1947 edition listed historically Black colleges and universities in each state and urged travelers to make short detours to see as many campuses as possible. The volume from 1948 reprinted letters from cabin and camp operators out west (with some frustration regarding how segregated or hostile such locations were). The 1952 edition detailed national parks that might be friendly to Black travelers. The book from 1956 focused on options for ski vacations. In later editions, air travel and world cities were discussed.[21]

Hines, better known today as a logo on cake mixes, published his guidebooks contemporaneously with Green. They were useful for seeing inside the doors of boardinghouses, albeit ones catering primarily to white customers. Green's lists were more thorough, but the details were sparse. Hines's guides began as quirky yet reliable restaurant reviews for readers who were less used to finding good food when in unfamiliar towns. From the beginning, he included "the wayside tavern and roadside home receiving guests," not just "ostentatious and formal" hotels and restaurants. For instance, in Paris, Arkansas, he found Mary Rowton's restaurant, operating out of her boardinghouse, serving "radishes, onions, chicken, country ham, whipped potatoes, candied sweets, macaroni, baked beans, spinach, rice, Southern cabbage, stuffed eggs, cottage cheese, three kinds of pickles, homemade relish, coleslaw, two kinds of cake, mince pie, grape pie, custard pie, [and] ice cream." He championed tearooms and taverns, urging men in particular to stop avoiding places decorated with "spinning wheels and quilt designs" because therein could often be found cooks to rival any. Bertha Hinshaw's Chalet Suzanne, decorated in Florida's finest exuberant pink paint, was another such location celebrated by Hines. When Hinshaw was unexpectedly widowed, she began her "restaurant and guest house" in 1931, the height of the Great Depression. Hines celebrated her "baked grapefruit and steaks with mint ice" as well as her "orange soufflé." Hines added recommendations about where one could stay later in his run, with *Lodging for a Night* (first published in 1938) coming on the heels of his *Adventures in Good Eating*.[22]

Hines's most recent biographer, Louis Hatchett, noted that Hines's guides stood out from others because he did not confine his recommendations to big cities, offering opinions on small-town establishments. He wrote in a folksy and chatty—and, to most readers, an eminently trustworthy—style.[23] Hines emphasized cleanliness and freshness, useful since food safety and health inspectors were inadequately funded throughout most of the twentieth century. Cleanliness was a fraught, racialized concept, but more immediate and systemic dangers faced women and travelers of color, dangers to which Hines was immune.

Would the boardinghouses that Hines profiled as good places to eat or to stay have helped a traveler like Olive Ruth Neal from Maryland had they been available ten years earlier? In 1926, Neal and seven other young women, presumably white, arrived in Durham, North Carolina. They had been hired by the Calumet Baking Powder Company to tour the US South and convince southern women to start purchasing Calumet for their baking. Calumet Baking Powder Girls represented the company's latest advertising strategy to increase bottom-line profits. Neal's companions signed her autograph book, "Blessed be those who have tasted of the fruit of travel with calumet and have not fallen by the wayside with homesickness." Their words spoke to the benefits and costs of work travel for women. Unfortunately, the company prioritized profits over taking care of their spokespeople. Neal recorded on stenographer pages tucked in the back of her autograph book an unofficial diary of the trip. She said, "The first night and day in Durham the company paid our expenses at a beautiful hotel but the next day we had to go find a place to stay on our own." Neal and the other "Girls" managed to find a boardinghouse with congenial (if strict) keepers. The Tews instituted a curfew on the girls and generally provided security and chaperonage for them while they were in an unfamiliar state whose codes they did not know. From that safe landing, Neal toured Durham's tobacco factories, hosiery plants, cotton gins, and houses of women who one presumes were prospective customers. Although Neal did not report any success in changing North Carolina's baking patterns, she concluded, "Any how I enjoyed my experience. Nothing like it, give me the South."[24] Traveling for work, Neal could not rely on her employer to guarantee safe and organized lodging, but she found it through her choice of the right boardinghouse.

Green Books were not coy about the added political and social dangers they sought to mitigate for Black travelers. In 1939 (and for several subsequent years), Green printed a letter from a man named William Smith who called the guides "badly needed" and enthused, "We earnestly believe 'The Negro Motorist Green Book' will mean as much if not more to our race as the A. A. A. means to the white race." Later editions included an interview with Wendall P. Alston, a traveling representative of the Esso oil company, whose career had also featured traveling for the US Department of Commerce and with the theatrical magazine *Billboard* (giving him experience with the industry in which Jackie Mabley worked). He commented on the challenges of navigating physical comfort and social class codes in towns new to him. Lacking personal connections, Alston commented, "When I started jumping from place to place, just like the white commercial travellers have been doing from time immemorial, . . . the folk in many, many places looked with fear and doubt upon the traveling man from beyond the borders of their own county." He confessed to worrying himself, wondering "if my bags were safe, and if the bed I acquired for the night would be mine alone; or if I would have the night companions such as those for which D. D. T. has been created." Alston concluded, "I would have missed a lot of anxieties, worries, and saved a lot of mental energy which, had it been conserved and used solely to the advancement of the business interests for which I traveled, my years 'on the road' might have been concluded long ago, with enough saving to permit my living a life of peace and quiet, now that I am becoming an old codger." In other words, Alston (and Green, by extension) calculated a direct financial cost to the additional burdens Black travelers bore due to the violence at worst and worry at best of navigating Jim Crow social divisions in every new community to which work brought them. Guides could mitigate the cost.[25]

For people likely to be unsafe in the US South—strangers of color, immigrants, radical activists, recognizably queer people, anyone resisting or targeted by the system of Jim Crow segregation—knowledge passed through family networks, word of mouth, and other informal systems. Boardinghouse women were key to the networks. At this historical distance, ephemeral and underground exchanges of information are hard to reconstruct. That is what makes Victor Green's guides, articles from the Jewish press, African American movies, and theater troupe and later "chitlin' circuit" records crucial. Sometimes, though, the secrecy and transitory nature of interactions was precisely the point.

Frank Gibert: Reinvention and Passing

Some travelers were not looking for boardinghouses full of people who knew them or who shared challenges to safe travel. Instead, they were seeking a boardinghouse where no one knew them or their past lives. Such people took advantage of a different story told about boardinghouses—that they could be bastions of manners, neighborhood or community tradition, and strongly enforced social boundaries. Boardinghouses could be useful in-between spaces where, if persons entered as an unknown quantity and were later accepted as members of the place, they could shed their past and rein-vent their present. Simply put, there is no way to know how many people did this successfully. In the historical record, we get glimpses of figures like Frank Gibert who almost, but not quite, succeeded. Their stories, however, strongly suggest that others did smoothly transform their self-presentation to better fit their identities. While many things could challenge individuals' ability to tell their own past and create their own future (and indeed, the not-quite-successful cases garnering newspaper coverage illustrated some of the hazards), people had a chance to introduce themselves anew. As inti-mate as boardinghouse space could be, if it was in a community to which new tenants were strangers, their life before they walked in the door was theirs to narrate.

Gibert and Douglas arrived in Washington, DC, with their trunks, which held outfits appropriate to "the height of fashion." Gibert's wardrobe included "new suits, shirts, collars, cuffs, extension-sole shoes, hats, razor—and a handsome revolver." Gibert was described by the reporter covering the story as having "short hair, a round, full masculine face, large hands and feet, and mannish ways." While we do not know his race, he also had pictures of himself with other male friends, in some of which he was sport-ing a mustache, and a collection of letters he had received. When asked, he explained his travel was ongoing, part of an effort to gather material for the book he was writing.[26]

The *Washington Post* reporter did not get a byline, but the story did list a location: the "Tenderloin District." For regular readers of the paper, the address sent a message. While the original New York Tenderloin district and San Francisco's well-established one were better known, other towns and cities around the United States also called neighborhoods well known for vice arrests and crime "Tenderloin."[27] Newspaper readers were poised for a salacious story as soon as the address was mentioned.

The newspaper account does not reveal what tipped off the police to investigate and caused Gibert's plans to be interrupted. Gibert and Douglas may have received advance notice: when police knocked on the door of the boardinghouse, Gibert was already wearing a dress and gave his name as Miss Frances Harris. (The newspaper reporter and the police used female pronouns for Gibert/Harris throughout; I am using he/him, following

Gibert's lead.) He originally denied having arrived as a man. Arrested and taken to the station, both Gibert and Douglas told more of their story to the police. Gibert said he and Douglas had arrived in Washington, DC, from Danville, Virginia, where Gibert had been "engaged in the saloon business." Successful at it, Gibert explained that "she assumed male attire, because a license would not be issued to a woman in Virginia." That strategic explanation hinted that Gibert embraced his identity, "associated with men, drank with them, traveled with them, and did everything in a mannish way." The mustache, Gibert said, was fake, but the photographs were of genuine moments between men. Between the lines, it was a tale of friends, fun evenings, and a successful business with a charismatic head. Upon licenses becoming more expensive, Gibert gave up the saloon and traveled with Douglas to DC. Gibert had resources with him: police found "money, diamonds, and jewelry" in his trunk.[28]

Writing in 1930, Jefferson Williamson looked back on what he saw as the glory days of the American hotel and waxed rhapsodic about diamonds worn by men, both hotel clerks and customers, throughout the second half of the nineteenth century. Williamson swore some lived in "an incessant blinding glare of these precious stones" that could be "diamond shirt-studs, and diamond sleeve-links," as well as rings and scarf pins. An English commenter, Lady Blanche Murphy, penning "American Boarding-House Sketches" in 1885, agreed, saying, "Diamonds, in America, have a special significance in costume; in fact, they are a pretty correct standard of the social and intellectual status of the individual, male or female, who wears them."[29] The presence of diamonds and jewels in the Gibert story may have been a convenient way to transport assets, a savings account set into wearable form. They spoke to his preparation for the trip, as well as to his resources to stay for a while.

In some ways, Gibert's was a boring story about taxes, licensing, and career change, told in sensational ways. The boardinghouse in the story facilitated an often hidden but by no means uncommon desire to live one's truest life by matching outward gender performances to inner self regardless of sex assigned at birth. That Gibert and Douglas ended up in the newspaper did not mean they were not later successful in another town.

While Gibert was a boarder, other newspaper evidence showed boardinghouse keepers using their boarders' trunks for their own transformations. In Atlanta, Mrs. Nancy Ware countersued two of her male boarders because they accused her of taking trousers from them. The reporter observing the court proceedings commented, "The charge carried the imputation that she may have worn the breeches, because she was not charged with stealing them." Indeed, Mrs. Ware heard the same threat from her intoxicated boarders: "'Did he intimate that you took them to wear?' the recorder asked Mrs. Ware. 'No, but it might have sounded that way,' replied Mrs. Ware." Perhaps Mrs. Ware did not in fact sometimes don men's clothing to walk around her boardinghouse or Atlanta. Perhaps she did. The official fined the two men $5.75 each and told them not to hassle an "elderly woman" again.[30] If individuals wished to change their presentation in a new community, they could hardly choose a better place to begin than in a boardinghouse.

Perhaps the most interesting part of Gibert's story, however, happened when Washington, DC, police contacted their counterparts in Danville. Virginia authorities replied, "The women were as they represented themselves to be, and were not wanted there." Virginia officials continued, "The principal was known in Danville as Frank Gibert." This suggests that at least some members of the power structure in Danville supported Gibert living as a man in their community. A final mystery arose when some in Danville reported that Gibert may have lived previously in Greenville, South Carolina, as "Mattie A. Hughes." About this portion of life, Gibert simply refused comment. Instead he mentioned parents in Denver, Colorado, but did not suggest any interest in going west to them. The final paragraph of the story read, "The women were held until late last night, when they were released. There was no charge upon which they could be held, but the Harris woman was warned that masquerading in male attire would not be tolerated by the police in Washington." Gibert and Douglas disappeared from the historical record after their brief moment in the pages of the *Washington Post*.[31]

So few details of Gibert and Douglas's stories remain. Here, I am assuming Frank wanted to live as Frank. Could this story be read in the opposite direction? After years of living as a man because of economic necessity, did Gibert wish to shed that performance and return to living life as Frances Harris? The relationship between Gibert and Douglas is unclear too. Were they friends? Lovers? Conspirators? Were the diamonds and jewels mere assets, or were they set into tiepins to augment Frank's cravat? Were they necklaces for Cora's décolletage? Earrings or cufflinks? Both? The suits were new; the trunk contained more than one hat. Even through the awkward language of the sensational journalist, Gibert seemed most comfortable as Gibert rather than as Harris—and he certainly did not want to be Hughes. Traveling with both sets of clothing, perhaps Gibert wanted options—rather than either/or, the ability to choose both/and. Trunks could hold outfits of choice; boardinghouses could allow for mobility of person and identity.

Trunks were crucial currency in boardinghouse economies. Sold by companies across the United States, trunks were sometimes the only large object owned by people without permanent homes. Confiscating a boarder's trunk was often a last-ditch effort by boardinghouse keepers to collect past-due rent or bills. It could also be leverage to get the boarder to do what the keeper wanted. Dixie Medcalf found herself separated from her trunk when she tried to leave Mr. King's boardinghouse in Atlanta in September 1899. King claimed she owed him $2.05 and he was holding her trunk until she paid; Medcalf said her bills were fully paid but that he was holding it for "spite" because she refused the married King's flirtations. The incident made the Atlanta newspapers because Medcalf pulled a pistol on King to demand her trunk's return. For people without family or permanent homes, a single trunk could hold their past, present, and future—all one's worldly goods in a single package. Having a place to safely store one's trunk was more than a convenience. It translated to personal safety, belonging, and even connection to a place. As Gibert's story shows, however, a trunk could also be deeply private, especially when there was a disconnect between a person's past and future.[32]

Inside the trunk could nestle evidence of that past or toward a desired future. Sometimes passing—including gender, but also involving race, place, and social class—was motivated by strategic decision-making to simplify employment or survival. The stakes were not lower in those cases, just different. In Louisville, Kentucky, William Ward rented a room from Mrs. Bond. Presenting himself as gainfully employed and respectable, Ward worked at an ax-handle factory in the town. Suspicious from the beginning, Mrs. Bond "noticed that his skin was of a peculiar color, and asked him 'if he was not a negro.'" Ward emphatically denied it, saying he was "as white as anybody" and explaining that "he had been ill with jaundice, and the disease caused the odd color on his countenance."[33] Bond was satisfied. Ward moved in; all seemed well.

Soon, though, "a report was started" that Ward worked in the section of the ax-handle factory staffed by African American workers. The rest of Bond's boarders held what the newspaper evocatively termed "an indignation meeting." They resolved as a group to leave because Bond had "compelled" them to "associate with a negro as their equal." Making good on their threat, the boarders left, and Bond found herself without income. However, when she tried to prosecute Ward, both the officer and a judge found "no law by which Ward can be punished for his imposition and malicious conduct, except by a damage suit, and as he has no property, he escapes." Again, the fragmentary source—a newspaper report—does not reveal what gave Ward away (rather dubiously, the newspaper suggested perhaps Ward's reputation as a magician was relevant). While his passing was unquestioned, he established a reputation as a collegial boarder, fitting into the social environment of Bond's "large number of boarders."[34] Racism of the time meant that collegiality was not enough—Ward was found out.

Had he not been discovered, Ward could well have used Bond's reference for future keepers. Her letter of recommendation, the good name of his friends with whom he boarded, and the neighborhood in which he boarded together would have worked to ensure his new reputation as a white man. Secure in his combination of light skin, story of jaundice, and record of boarding in segregated, white houses, Ward could have rested on his new identity. During the later twentieth-century civil rights battles, housing, restaurants, and swimming and bathing facilities were three of the most explosive grounds for struggle. Each had an intimate exchange at its center—sleeping and dressing in bedrooms and baths; sharing food, smells, and tastes over meals at all times of day; and stripping down to exercise or sleep. A fourth locus of civil rights legislation and struggle was travel and transportation. Free movement of strangers from one place to another without the preclearance of people holding power was equally high-stakes.[35] Boardinghouses—where people slept close to each other, ate together, and bathed, and which facilitated their travel between places—managed to combine all the flash points. When people like William Ward were successful, structures built to keep people separated faltered. They did not fail, of course, until the whole edifice was taken on—beyond the individual to the societal. Ward and people like him may not have been seeking wholesale social change. He and others who were not caught used what they had at hand to integrate southern spaces, even if by hiding their own complicated racial backgrounds from their boardinghouse keepers.

Other times, boarders assumed a mantle of place of origin, bringing with it ideas of social and economic class. When simply participating in a long American tradition of what scholar Karen Halttunen has called "confidence men and painted women," the gamble was great, but the personal risk—specifically, the risk of violence—was much lower. The schemes are worth discussing here, though, because the accumulation of people posing as something other than their previous selves created the atmosphere in which higher-stakes transformations were possible. In other words,

William Ward could have faced a lynch mob when found out, but he may have found the courage to try on a new identity amid stories like the one told in a fictional 1834 piece published in Washington, DC's *United States' Telegraph* and pulled from the pages of *Knickerbocker*. Mr. Clarence Gower successfully passed himself off as an "eminent English nobleman, with the most exquisite manners, and the best blood in his veins," at the "genteel boardinghouse" at "number seven Lambkin street"—until he was recognized as humble Mr. Flipkins, a local hairdresser whose customers were merchants in town. After being found out, Flipkins unceremoniously left the boardinghouse and afterward was only seen "dodging around some adjacent corner," a footnote to the tea table conversations and, of course, a fictional cautionary tale in the annals of boardinghouse stories.[36]

Frank Gibert may have been inspired by stories like "Flare Up at a Fashionable Boarding House" from 1849. The *New York Star* piece, picked up in the Baltimore papers, concerned a woman who introduced herself as "the wife of a wealthy planter of the South." She was given every luxury the house afforded until a day later when she was recognized instead as "the keeper of a house of ill-fame, at Augusta, Georgia."[37] Before police arrived, the woman and her many trunks quietly departed—a quiet resolution, without personal harm, and of minimal financial impact. The former customer who recognized her, unsurprisingly, seemed not to face any censure.

Other stories followed out the consequences of burgeoning love when people at boardinghouses were presenting themselves as something other than their previous lives suggested. In 1885's "Duplicity Punished," a boardinghouse "true story" published in Alabama's *Huntsville Gazette*, the two main figures were neither boarders nor keepers but instead employees. Still, they were not entirely who they said they were. Hannah Hodges was "a model cook, so far as culinary skill, cleanliness and management go," but rumor had it that she had "in a long course of earning wages and husbanding perquisites, saved one thousand dollars." Seth Strawn was a drayman who showed off his "elegant truck with two enormous horses," thereby winning her hand in marriage. Both had convinced the other they were more economically secure than they were—Hannah had no savings; Seth had borrowed the truck. This story had a happy ending: post-marriage they remained in love but also at work since neither could finance the other's leisure.[38] Indeed, the promise of intimate boardinghouse spaces could be the successful transformations of self. If done right, it could result in love, romance, and physical intimacy available to others, sometimes for the first time ever.

Gibert, Ward, Flipkins, the brothel keeper, Hannah, and Seth were only a few of the many people featured in magazine and newspaper stories in the nineteenth and twentieth centuries who were not what they seemed in boardinghouse settings. The widespread expectation that people could differ from how they first presented themselves in fictional or newspaper or magazine boardinghouses reflected boardinghouse life on the ground and was a tool for readers across the United States to plot their own transformations, introductions of their truest selves, or beginnings of new life stories.

Like Gibert, Jackie Mabley resisted expectations of gender roles in her offstage personal presentation. She dressed neither as her character, an elderly Black woman, nor as the girl who grew up in Brevard. Instead, "offstage she shed the ill-fitting costume for tailored slacks, silk blouses, Italian shoes, and—at Sunday's church service—stylish hats." She preferred clothes, in other words, fit to her and suitable for a successful performer. In addition, and especially when out touring on the road, "Moms often donned men's attire," according to her biographer Williams. That could include differently cut slacks and added suitcoats, jaunty hats, ties, and handkerchiefs. Surviving pictures of Mabley show this range of self-presentation, what today we might term gender-fluid dressing. Forthcoming about being lesbian in the early twentieth century, she also stands as one of the most important queer comedians in US history.[39] When she came off the road, Mabley settled for longer stays in places where she and her friends could be their whole selves. When she could not find them, she made them.

Early in her career, Mabley paid for her rent and food in a Buffalo, New York, boardinghouse using money from her mother (perhaps from the Brevard boardinghouse). The New York house was full of other theater hopefuls. The trope of a theater boardinghouse lingered in American popular culture well past the heyday of boardinghouses in general. While not all southern, films and novels featured actors in shared homes throughout the century. As early as 1915, the short film *The Actor's Boarding House* was made. Writing in the *Ladies' Home Journal* in 1917, Catherine Van Dyke characterized a Philadelphia actors' boardinghouse keeper as "one of the greatest patrons of the arts, in its realest sense, in America" because of the space, joy, and constant encouragement she gave her boarders. The film version of *Stage Door* (1937) starred Katharine Hepburn, Ginger Rogers, Lucille Ball, and others and was based on a similarly fondly recalled place, New York's Rehearsal Club, where Carol Burnett was a later resident. A 1980s slasher film, *The Boarding House*, featured a Los Angeles boardinghouse for actors. And, of course, Mabley's own vehicle, *Boarding House*

Blues, was full of aspiring actors and vaudeville performers. For early career performers, trying to break into a notoriously hard business, the chance to share rent and expenses and the ability to practice—sing, dance, play instruments, run lines, and keep late hours—among others doing the same was a persistent draw. Behind closed doors, actors' boardinghouses provided shelter for those needing to drop public personas and relax in whatever way felt right.[40]

In some southern spaces, boardinghouses were discreet places for men and women who for whatever reason chose nonmainstream paths. For Tennessee Williams, a boardinghouse in New Orleans was such a spot. He wrote about it in detail in his play *Vieux Carré*. While there were no actors in the play's boardinghouse, there were artists, writers, and musicians. In Williams's memories, as well as in Mabley's, the scene behind closed doors of off-season boardinghouses could be delightfully domestic, regardless of who was in residence. They were queer spaces of possibility. Bachelor houses, maiden aunt proprietors, and long-term living arrangements gave cover to nontraditional relationships and contributed to the boardinghouse story. Finding the contours of such queer spaces requires that we pay attention to fragments and quiet voices. Proof is elusive, but suggestion is the point.

Mrs. Emma Bell ran "the most select boarding house" in Atlanta for twenty-five years. When she closed her doors in 1897, the *Atlanta Constitution* published a long retrospective of her career and her boarders, all of whom were "prominent men only." The author meant "only" to modify both words: social prominence was a prerequisite to stay, but so also was gender. Mrs. Bell accepted only male boarders. Sixty-four men remained when she closed, but over the life of her house, the article claimed, dozens more had stayed with her. The home acquired the nickname "The Bachelor's Home," and for long stretches her residents refused marriage. Some men lived in the house for its full twenty-five-year run. Fifty former residents came to the closing party. Were the men career-focused? Were some uninterested in heterosexual romance and heteronormative domestic arrangements? The article gave no firm answers; as such, it raised the possibility that in her homosocial space at least some of Mrs. Bell's bachelors enjoyed the "magic charm" that allowed men to live together without accompaniment of women. Mrs. Bell herself attributed success to "let[ting] my boarders do as they please."[41] As she set off into retirement, the newspaper mourned the closing of the house and the dispersal of its company.

Judging from the loyalty that drew fifty men to the final gathering, Bell had clearly created a memorable community. For her boarders, the house may have been as important as the boardinghouse Tennessee Williams memorialized in *Vieux Carré*. In the words of one Williams scholar, "Even though he roomed there just longer than a month, the boarding house remained a fixture in his imagination for decades, a creative well from which he would draw one-acts, stories, poems, and the full length *Vieux Carré*."[42] Today the building where he stayed is part of the Historic New Orleans compound; Williams is remembered for his other writing; and the French Quarter maintains its delicate balance between permanent residents, transient visitors, and commercial and intimate spaces.

Williams came to New Orleans in 1938 seeking work with the same Federal Writers' Project that brought Travis Tuck Jordan to Martha Hinton's front door. He lived in the French Quarter, also known as the Vieux Carré, in a boardinghouse run by Mrs. Anderson at 722 Rue Toulouse. The house was located three blocks away from the Storyville neighborhood of bars and brothels, although Storyville had been shut down by authorities in 1917. By the time Williams moved in, madams and workers had scattered; New Orleans was trying to forget its experiment in concentrating sex work into a single district. But behind closed doors, in inner recesses of the boardinghouse, Williams's desire for romance and stability perhaps did not have to pretend to match popular culture's heterosexual imaginings. The play had its formal Broadway debut in 1977, but Williams had been working on drafts of it since the 1930s.[43]

The two-act play directed set designers to create "a poetic evocation of all the cheap rooming houses of the world" for the stage. Narrated by the Writer, all scenes except one take place in the boardinghouse. Residents include the landlady, Mrs. Wire (who feels akin to Mrs. Sad from some hundred years earlier); a couple of starving, elderly sisters who go through restaurant trash bins to feed themselves; a woman working as domestic laborer in the home; a violent man and former college woman living together; a photographer squatting in a basement room; and the Nightingale, a gay artist dying of consumption in the attic. Mrs. Wire is sure she is being ripped off by tenants; she tries to enlist the Writer in a scheme to open a lunchroom in addition to the boardinghouse in order to get back some money she feels she had lost. By the play's end, Mrs. Wire has been fined for pouring boiling water through a hole in the floor to try to force the photographer to leave, the Nightingale has been taken away to die, and the

Writer leaves with a musician who drew him out by playing clarinet in the yard. Planning to wander west rather than stay in New Orleans, they flee the cloying walls of the home.[44]

During its two acts, interplay between cultural expectations outside the boardinghouse rooms and the desire and longing expressed inside them is complex. Characters bring cultural associations with them, along with the self-hatred and convoluted emotional responses such associations create. At the same time, when the doors shut, leaving the men alone, meaningful connections happen. Williams made it clear that the Nightingale and the Writer had sex (critic Robert Bray called it "the first unambiguous homosexual liaison Williams ever staged"). They shared physical intimacy, and they shared emotional intimacy. In their first conversation, the Nightingale says, "I know the sound of loneliness, heard it through the partition . . . trying not to, but crying . . . why try not to?" He urges the Writer to believe that crying was a release, not something "unmanly." When the Writer says he was "taught not to cry because it's . . . humiliating," his new companion replies, "You're a victim of conventional teaching, which you'd better forget." Reflecting back, the Writer concludes, "Instinct it must have been" that brought him to the Vieux Carré; "I couldn't have consciously, deliberately, selected a better place than here to discover—to encounter—my true nature."[45] However fleeting, the moment was touching. While the play was not a success in its debut (closing after only a week), it clearly mattered to Williams himself, given how long he worked on it. The play gave voice to a moment of connection in the only setting—a boardinghouse—he created that could hold it.

Queer southern life can be hard to excavate from historical and literary sources. But as scholars such as Jamie Harker, E. Patrick Johnson, and Michael P. Bibler have shown in print, and as common sense and people's lived experiences tell us, it was present and vibrant even if we must work to document it.[46] Much as southern food could come into existence in the public-private domestic spaces of the southern boardinghouse, new southern identities could be nurtured and grown as well.

LIKE TENNESSEE WILLIAMS working for the Federal Writers' Project and staying in a loft in a New Orleans boardinghouse, Jackie Mabley had to pay her dues before she could abandon life in boardinghouses and get to the "split level in the suburbs" she celebrated. For her, though, the institutionalized threats of Jim Crow racism added layers of difficulty to her ability to find her own identity. Performers on the TOBA circuit reported brutal trips, with few luxuries and intense time pressures. Most every night saw a new town with a new boardinghouse, hotel, railcar, backseat of the touring car, or even a cot behind the stage. New mornings meant repacking bags yet again. Mabley kept at it, as more and more people wanted to see her, either with Butterbeans and Susie or, later, as a reliable solo act. Her grandmother's prediction, that she needed to leave Brevard to make it, proved true.

Still, recognition and success did not translate immediately into economic wealth for performers like Mabley. Even when she became a top-dollar headliner, conditions of travel in the United States and especially in the Jim Crow South, where so many potential fans lived, meant that luxury hotels still were frequently off limits.[47] Boardinghouses filled in.

Judging from her later practice, perhaps the collective living arrangements of boardinghouses were not just necessity. After the 1940s, Mabley took up more permanent residences rather than grueling life on the road. She had bases in Washington, DC, and in New York City. By the peak of her career, she was a fixture at Harlem's Apollo Theater, played Carnegie Hall, and appeared regularly on several television shows, including the highly popular *Smothers Brothers Comedy Hour*. She continued working in film; she also released more than two dozen comedy albums. She did not have to be on the road to support herself. Biographers note that when she was past her touring years and settling into a performance life on the East Coast, Mabley continued to live with others as she had in the theatrical boardinghouses of her early career. She drew around her friends and family and helped newer performers find their own footing. Dressed in fine menswear, she embraced the social and cultural freedoms of the Harlem Renaissance, including the female lovers with whom she found romance.[48]

The scene in *Boarding House Blues*, while played for exaggerated laughs, nonetheless showed the care and community that performers' boardinghouses engendered. Boardinghouses for actors, musicians, artists, and others in the theater were staples of comedies and dramas well past the era of peak northern, urban boardinghouse culture, and they still function today. My campus's theater company puts visiting actors up in a house near campus; summer stock companies, music festivals, and artists' retreats all deploy versions of communal living. The combination of performers and southern tours—where lodgers needed spaces to spend the night, support each other, and make art—contributed to the persistence of boardinghouses long past century's midpoint.

The performance persona of Moms (upside down, "wow," she would say) allowed Mabley to dance around and often shed stereotypical roles for

Black women onstage—she did not have to play young and sexy, nor did she play nurturing and conciliatory. But that does not mean that she did not have love, intimacy, and family of choice. In her private life, the nickname, especially with the extra *s*, was more about respect than traditional gender roles of mothering. Other performers called Mabley "a giving person" as on and off the road she constructed a supportive circle around her. Boardinghouses and communal living made it possible. Foods, ideas of hospitality, and shared living, forged from years on the road, followed Mabley as she moved her home base to northern cities.[49]

While Jim Crow remained in place and freedom of movement was constrained by the color of one's skin, boardinghouses served a role in the US South. African American and Jewish travelers relied on guidebooks written by fellow adventurers. Networks of knowledge helped marginalized folks travel safely across the region. People like Frank Gibert, William Ward, and Dixie Medcalf dropped out of the historical record. Tennessee Williams returned repeatedly in his writing career to the New Orleans boardinghouse of his memories and creative expression. Traces left by Mabley, Green, Gibert, Ward, Medcalf, and Williams, however faint or obscured, remind us that boardinghouse reinventions were possible. For some people, they were also necessary.

Behind boardinghouses' closed doors, what otherwise was hidden or taboo could be explored. Mary Ellen Pleasant amassed a fortune to finance abolition nationally and push for civil rights in her home community, because people could not see beyond their own expectations of Black boardinghouse keepers. Mary Surratt committed treason from her boardinghouse parlor, hidden behind some of the same expectations of what a woman could not do in American politics. Ideas about southern hospitality and manners obscured women's political ambitions and facilitated them as well. Sarah Hinton and Lola Walker grew up in boardinghouses where older women worried over their desires, sexual encounters, and ability to take control of their own romances. Southern girls and women like them ultimately dislodged the most restrictive definitions of sex and gender in mainstream US communities. When Moms Mabley set the table for actors and other performers, she cleared space for fellow travelers who were leaving their past and writing themselves into new futures. Queer and gender nonconforming boardinghouse residents, as well as boarders who sought to obscure their race and class identities, knew keepers could be keys to safety and freedom.

Boardinghouses were powerful for women at moments of rapid transformation of American society. Southern boardinghouse keepers and the people who lodged with them played key roles as media and communication structures exploded, industrialization and workplaces expanded, and restaurants changed the landscape of cities and towns. Boardinghouses and the women who ran and lodged in them together helped broaden the possibilities of who was able to support themselves by the pen. Writers Anne Royall and Ida May Beard were two women who discovered how boardinghouses allowed them to participate in a rapidly expanding media culture of the United States. Southern routes offered long months of the year for travel and solo writing and expanded opportunities for women that remain today.

CHAPTER 7

BOARDINGHOUSE ROOMS OF THEIR OWN

Anne Royall and Ida May Beard

ALTHOUGH SEPARATED by decades, Anne Royall and Ida May Beard found themselves at similar crossroads in their lives, unexpectedly on their own in a hostile world. Both used boardinghouses to find a way out of trouble. Neither Beard nor Royall had the aunts whom Lola Walker was surrounded by to rally on their behalf. Neither found a kindly professor's wife to take them in and put them through library school like Sarah Hinton did. Malinda Russell, fleeing with her son from Tennessee's racial violence, may have nodded in sympathy, even though she hopefully had comfort from family left behind during her exile. I hope Frank Gibert found rooms like Royall's and Beard's, with space to write and imagine, free of constraint, but the historical record does not speak of his life after the sensational headline that drove him from his Washington, DC, boardinghouse.

For female-presenting nineteenth-century Americans, divorce, abandonment, and widowhood with contested estates all proved especially challenging in societies set up to privilege marriage and extended family support. The US South, particularly for white residents, was structured in precisely that way. Women without partners or supportive family had to find their own resources. Peering into boardinghouses through their eyes reveals the challenges they faced. The same boardinghouses, though, were poised to help enterprising women reinvent themselves, especially through writing and publishing. It is perhaps the most persistent function of boardinghouses, crossing centuries and locations.

Anne Royall (1769–1854) was not an established boardinghouse keeper. She did have opinions about them, just like she had opinions on most things. She recorded them in detail as she embarked on a tour around the US South almost 100 years before Jackie Mabley took her grandmother's advice and left on her own tour. Before Duncan Hines began his reviews of restaurants and motor lodges, before the Michelin Guides reached across the world to rate hospitality, before the *Negro Motorist Green Books* addressed safety and shelter for specific travelers, and long before Yelp and Eater with their legions of sarcastic and flaming commenters were even imagined, Royall in her notorious *Black Books* reviewed and rated places to stay when traveling. The opposite of a tactful or polite reviewer, Royall packed her trunks and cut a swath through the early United States and its taverns, stagecoach stops, hotels, and boardinghouses. Readers subscribed to the volumes of her travel writing and read their pages eagerly. While some must have planned trips by following her recommendations, most reveled in the gossip, praise, and pointed criticisms she provided about towns she visited and lodging she found.

If you know Anne Royall today, it is probably as the first woman in the United States (or colonies before that) to edit and run her own newspapers or as the last woman in the country to be formally tried and convicted as a "common scold." Issues of both *Paul Pry* (1831–36) and *The Huntress* (1836–54) survive, so we can read Royall's public, political newspaper voice accompanying her similarly public but more personal *Black Book* writings. Her trial took place in Washington in the summer of 1829 and was covered avidly by all her competitors' newspapers. An apocryphal tale of stealing President John Quincy Adams's clothes while he bathed in the Potomac and sitting on them until he agreed to grant her an interview (again, the first to a female journalist) testified to her journalistic fearlessness and willingness to surprise, even if the event's details have been mythologized through the centuries.[1] That spirit, applied to towns and cities on her tours, made Royall an especially valuable tonic to romantic tales of southern hospitality or welcoming tables. Her boardinghouse story allowed a woman to pick up her pen, grow as a writer and journalist, and ultimately live independently and support herself.

Born ninety-three years after Anne Royall, Ida May Crumpler Beard (1862–1951) was at pains to present herself as the calm, clear-eyed heroine of her story. She wanted readers' understanding and compassion. Pity was welcome, if it meant a purchase of her book, *My Own Life; or, A Deserted Wife*. Go ahead and dislike her husband, he who caused her to write her life story and travel the region selling it. Beard helped readers out in that last task by printing a photograph of her former husband on the frontispiece of her book when she published it in the late 1890s.[2] She wanted readers to know John Beard: for women to be on alert about his methods of seduction, for law officials to recognize his many cons, and for hotel managers and boardinghouse keepers to know the trail of unpaid bills strewn behind him. She desperately wanted to separate her future and that of her children from his deadbeat past.

Before she settled on being an author to support her children off the proceeds of book sales, Ida Beard tried out a range of other careers. She presented herself as a medical expert for hire, wielding a folk medicine remedy.[3] She pawned the last of her jewelry and furniture. She threw herself on the mercy of strangers. And she opened a boardinghouse. Ida Beard, though, was not a very good boardinghouse keeper. Her venture quickly failed. Beard's story of it and all the other houses from which she and her husband fled survive in the pages of *My Own Life*. Boardinghouses helped women like Royall and Beard find their public voices through words written in rented rooms on travels across the South.

Boardinghouses provided women ways to travel, write, and otherwise resist pressures to marry and stay home if they did not want to or were not able to. Southern states offered longer warm seasons, better weather, and burgeoning tourist industries. Travel writers and memoirists documented boardinghouses in towns large and small, in good neighborhoods and bad, and taking a surprising variety of forms. Finalizing divorces, gaining new careers, even just relaxing in a space without fraught family arguments, women in boardinghouses found new energy and resources for engaging the wider world. Boardinghouse women, keepers and lodgers, even at low points in their lives, used the possibilities of southern boarding "rooms of their own" to ingeniously change their circumstances. The example and the trope so famously explored by British writer Virginia Woolf found purchase in twentieth-century American feminism as well as twenty-first-century women's publishing and career counseling. It works as a metaphor illustrating earlier women's choices too.

Women like Anne Royall. Her life story was made possible by the escape she found in travel. That she traveled so frequently late in life illustrated how reinvention could occur at any age for women—and how boardinghouses were useful across the life span. Ida Beard's struggles over her marriage's end also took placed in rented rooms. Divorce and boardinghouses have long and unexplored histories with each other. Both Royall and Beard turned to the pen to complete their new selves. When Virginia Woolf imagined *A Room of Her Own* for Shakespeare's lost sister, women writers across the South had already checked in. Along with Royall and Beard, writers like Carson McCullers, Grace MacGowan Cooke, and Tennessee Williams found rooms in boardinghouses, tucked into communities of lodgers and keepers, and wrote their way into independence in rooms of their own.

Anne Royall: Boardinghouses for Survival

Born in 1769, likely in rural Maryland, Royall was the white daughter of a farming woman who later became a housekeeper for wealthier families. Her parents migrated to the western Pennsylvania frontier during Anne's youth. Having a "frontier childhood" became an important biographical detail Royall shared about herself. Caught in the violence of the pre-Revolution "Indian Wars," Anne's father died.[4] Her widowed mother split up the remaining family to increase their chances of survival. Anne spent the rest of her childhood near Staunton, Virginia, and Sweet Springs, (now West) Virginia.

Royall's recent biographer Elizabeth Clapp speculated that during her late adolescence and early adulthood, Anne worked in a succession of jobs such as domestic service, serving in taverns or shops, nursing, or sewing, perhaps supporting the early growth of Sweet Springs's resort economy.[5] When she wrote of how a boardinghouse should function or how a private house that took in travelers from stagecoaches should manage, glimpses of her early work informed adult Anne's thoughts.

In 1797, at the age of twenty-eight, Anne married Major William Royall, a veteran of the Revolutionary War, many years her senior. They had been together perhaps ten years before that. He was in his forties when they first started their relationship, wealthier, educated, and from a socially established family. By all accounts it was a successful fifteen-year marriage. Anne and William entertained and lived in material comfort in their Virginia community. Some of Anne's extended family, including her mother, lived with them for a while, and Anne educated herself by reading her way through William's extensive library, under his tutelage. William drank too much, too often; he ran up debts and neglected to manage his lands. Anne was criticized by neighbors for her lower-class background and family; she had too few allies in the community. When William died, gossip that had simmered in the town came to the surface. According to his will and to common practice, Anne as his widow should have received assets. But his family contested the will, no one spoke up for her, and ultimately Anne was left without resources.[6]

Court cases over the legitimacy of the will and eventually over Anne's reputation and rights took years to work their way through the system. The back-and-forth wrangling was contentious on all sides and cost participants dearly. In the initial stages of settling the estate, Royall moved to more bustling Charleston (now in West Virginia). Once there, she initiated several investments in hopes of stabilizing her income—in the burgeoning salt industry, for instance. She was also involved in building and equipping a house to be a tavern in the center of commercial Charleston. It is unclear whether the tavern ever opened. Did Royall intend to hire someone to run it, or was she going to be the keeper herself? Her time in Charleston was short. Royall was soon drawn back to Sweet Springs as William's extended family, with an openly biased judge, overturned the will. Royall then appealed, but she absented herself from the whole state while doing so, as it was increasingly hostile. Between 1817 and 1823 she lived in Alabama, traveling back only when necessary for legal appearances. It was the beginning of a new career for her, although she may not have recognized it as such at the time. By 1819, the case was over, and in Clapp's words, at best Royall was poorly served by Virginia's courts and at worst was outright defrauded by the family and their allies in the legal system. A widowed woman in her fifties without family to support her, Royall launched a new plan. She wrote a friend back in the mountains, "I have some notion of turning author some of these days."[7] What form that would take was still up in the air, but Anne Royall had decided on a career in the public eye.

While moving between Virginia and Alabama, Royall carefully shaped her correspondence; she later published it as *Letters from Alabama*. She experimented with writing and published a novel about frontier life (*The*

Tennessean) but soon settled on sketches and travel writing she had begun in the Alabama letters and continued through the pseudonymous *Sketches of History, Life, and Manners, in the United States.* Her model reached full expression in the *Black Books*, including the three *Southern Tour* volumes, which she published under her own name.[8]

Royall traveled down the Atlantic coast, into interior southern states, up the Mississippi River, and across the Allegheny Mountains. For the decade of the 1820s, she traveled avidly and continually. During these years, her home really was the road; she sold books, sought new adventures, wrote new volumes, and used money from previous trips to finance next ones. Travel was her life. She took boats, ferries, stagecoaches, and wagons, which broke down, were late, involved passengers sharing berths with mail bags and freight, and relied on a community of strangers to travel safely.

Throughout, Royall was never without a notebook. She recorded names, jotted down distinguishing features of fellow travelers and the towns and cities they saw, made up nicknames to help her memory, and meticulously tallied who charged her for their services and who gave her free accommodations. She had an eagle eye for what she determined to be religious hypocrisy and corruptions. She did not mind exaggerating adventures in the service of a good tale. She hated bad food, poor service, and spaces where bar drinking blurred with parlor talk. People began to give her free rooms, entertain her by showing her around town or inviting people over for the evening, and help her find the fastest conveyance out of town. For instance, John Tyler, from Richmond, Virginia (likely the future president of the United States), wrote his daughter that Mrs. Royall's book had arrived and "she speaks highly of all of us, particularly of yourself." But he cautioned they should "not to be rendered vain" by this moment of praise from notoriously difficult Royall. People like Tyler crossed their fingers that subsequent volumes of writings would look kindly upon the society, lodgings, and travel resources they offered. One enterprising keeper, knowing Royall was sharpening her pencil to give him a negative review, snuck into her room and tore his name from her notebook. Royall could not help but "give him credit" for the strategy when she discovered his subterfuge, but it did not stop her from writing about the Mobile, Alabama, boardinghouse: "This is a dangerous house, and my friends the contractors had better move their stage office to some other place before they incur my pen."[9]

Readers in the United States were eager for writers like Anne Royall. In the 1830s, Harriet Martineau, Frances Wright, Alexis de Tocqueville, and the previously discussed Frances Trollope wrote travelogues from their perspectives as Europeans encountering US cities; as outsiders, they claimed to see clearly what residents did not.[10] Royall also positioned herself as an outsider, but of a different sort. She was a solo, older female traveler, one who came from the outskirts of society both geographically and in terms of social class. She promised to tell truths people in communities would or could not.

Systems of travel and population in the United States were poised for expansion. The *Black Books* spoke directly to readers with provocative, pointed, and occasionally near slanderous diatribes against anything and everything difficult along the new routes. Royall drew from a similar wellspring that birthed salacious nineteenth-century city mystery novels. City mystery novels, largely authored by men, featured white narrators describing Philadelphia's, New Orleans's, Paris's, or New York's poverty, urban density, and violence to economically secure and innocent readers assumed safely home in armchairs. Royall witnessed prostitutes visiting the captain of her steamboat from Augusta to Savannah. An unscrupulous guide abandoned her at a house in Bayou Sarah, Louisiana, that proved to be a brothel (an "infamous house," Royall called it). Royall and city mystery authors flirted with dark undersides of travel, lodging, city streets, and town secrets.[11] For a female author to tell such stories without being tarnished by them, Royall had to strike a delicate balance.

Through her publishing career, Royall clung to many things, but none tighter than her own respectability; her preference for private homes or boardinghouses rather than taverns or stagecoach inns was part of her efforts. In Sparta, Georgia, she was mistakenly shown to a public lounge where women received men in a combination bar and boardinghouse. She demanded the drunken barkeeper, who she thought was the landlord, take her to a private room: "Lead on sir, I will not stay here." Her loud protestations brought the actual keeper, a widowed lady who immediately apologized and greeted Royall as the respectable lady she was. Royall said, "The lady like appearance and subsequent attention of this mistress of the tavern, acted as a cordial upon my fainting spirits." Losing respectability was not an option if she was to maintain a public, acceptable career.[12]

Royall had strong opinions about food on the road as well. She used quality and types of food offered to gauge the merit of people and places. Food was simultaneously marked by gender and class; what she was offered was a direct comment on others as well as on herself. Rough and greasy food indicated rough manners that did not respect either gentlemen or ladies, as she found in a Warrenton, Virginia, boardinghouse in which "I did not envy the gentlemen the room, as it smoked sufficiently to have smoked all the madam's bacon, and from the grease on the floor I should think she had used it in that way." She was especially bothered by places that did not have more feminine or dignified coffee or tea ready for road-weary stage travelers. In Winchester, Virginia, she put up at Stage House, owned by a German American man named Massie and attended by a barkeeper and a landlady. Before the landlady arrived to care for Royall, she fussed at Massie: "Being very cold, and the fire low in the stove, no supper ready, I told friend M. he ought to keep up a good fire when he looked for the stage, and coffee ready hot on the stove." Massie's landlady made Royall, the lone woman traveler, comfortable, and Royall admitted that perhaps his business model relied on male travelers warming themselves by purchasing alcohol from the bartender, certainly more profitable than her request for fire and coffee.[13]

Facing cold turnips ("who ever heard of cold turnips for dinner," she fumed), Royall found the same scheme in Amherst County, Virginia. The landlord there employed a waiter (likely an enslaved man), but the gesture to hospitality did not fool Royall: "I asked his shriveled-ship if he could not warm the turnips, he showed his teeth, and said 'no missee, no fire.' . . . I paid 37 ½ cents for the dinner! I think it is a trick of these Tavern-keepers to keep bad fires, that people may warm themselves by drinking." Near Hillsborough, North Carolina, the bad food blurred with the politics of the owner with which Royall strongly disagreed. Together they made an establishment beneath Royall's standards. It offered "the worst fare I met with in my travels; it was worse than the frozen hominy in Virginia. The bread was black and raw, the cheese and butter had all the colors of the rainbow, and the smell would attract all the turkey buzzards in Charleston—the coffee, I must stop; it was beyond my pen." She concluded, "There was some meat on the table, but from the manner it made its debut, it was impossible to tell to what species of animals it belonged." For some particularly remote stretches of road, she recommended packing one's own bread and cheese to supplement the insufficient dining facilities on the way.[14]

By contrast, the keeper of the Franklin Hotel in Lynchburg, Virginia, kept "a good house, has very attentive servants, and richly merits the patronage of the public. I find too, I have noticed a worthy and respectable colored man, a Barber, Clayburn Gladman[.] I am under particular obligations to his polite attention, as a servant: he lives at the house, is a gentleman in his manners, and deserves the patronage of the public." In the Milton boardinghouse where Royall dined on guinea fowl for the first time in her life, food was further evidence of the gentility of the widowed keeper.

Royall concluded she too deserved public patronage. It truly was not a matter of luxury for Royall; if the food was appropriate and she was treated well, she would endorse it. At a poor family's makeshift boardinghouse in Mississippi, Royall nonetheless found that "we had stewed chicken for dinner, sweet potatoes, and delicious buttermilk and sweet milk, with butter, corn-bread, and a cup of tea for myself, and all so cool and neat. It wanted nothing but a pebble brook to render it another Eden. . . . Heaven knows how they procure bread, for the land was very poor." Similarly, outside of Camden, South Carolina, Royall noted, "We reached our quarters, which some of your very particular folks would have reckoned bad—but if it be anything in the shape of a house, I care nothing about the balance. It was old, empty, and dreary, and the worst of it was, there was no tea." But Royall was reassured when "the lady of the house, or rather the cook, had me a hot cup of coffee by times, and we were early on the road"; she did not hesitate to recommend it.[15]

For Royall, class and gender could sometimes trump her assumptions about race. If she felt she was treated like a lady, Royall gave good reviews regardless of the race or ethnicity of proprietors. Outside Fort Mitchell, Alabama, Royall described a boardinghouse with a white landlord, constructed by Jewish builders, and run by Native American landladies and cooks. She found it "a most delightful cool, roomy house, with several pleasant cottages in the rear, completely shaded with trees" that "fairly restored me to youth, it was so consonant to my feelings and taste." That taste was further fulfilled by food prepared in the house, delicious tea, and all the candles and writing materials she needed. In Macon, she met a Black man named Frank who had used profits from his "small eating shop" to start his current "mercantile business"—Royall detailed his successes at length, and she dined with his family. Royall was not free of racism; she was a product of her time, and an especially inconsistent one as well.[16] But she ate with Frank and his family, finding boardinghouses, lodgings, and restaurants like his to be places where she could invent her new career and life by traveling—and by seeking shelter despite preexisting assumptions.

Some readers thought Royall must have been rich or profiting greatly from her trips. She vociferously protested that the opposite was true. Pausing her travelogue, Royall said, "A report is rung from one end of the United States to the other, that I am amassing vast sums of *money*." She continued, "On all the works I have published, I have *not* been able from sales to pay for the paper, much less the printing." She listed fraudulent agents, losses of books on sea and through the mail, and, her pet peeve, unfair postage applied to her works because they were not religious. She ended her rant by focusing on the lack of furniture in poor rooms that people charitably offered her when she could not pay.[17] Grumpy as she was, Royall used her writing and her willingness to move from boardinghouse to boardinghouse to finance adventures that other readers were only beginning to contemplate.

Quieter but nonetheless adventuresome, Abbie Brooks did not stop at reading about other women's travels. She walked in Royall's footsteps forty years later. Brooks was born in the 1830s in Pennsylvania. She never married but had a child whom an aunt raised in Ohio. Disowned by her family, Brooks briefly worked as a schoolteacher in Tennessee before embarking on a life touring the US South. On the frontispiece of her 1865 diary, she wrote "Miss Brooks, Journalist," as if calling that role into being. In unpublished diaries stretching to 1876, she chronicled boardinghouse experiences while working to support herself as a bookseller. She later found publishing success as an author, the diaries having helped her practice. Brooks seems to have been the same Abbie M. Brooks who wrote under the pen name Sylvia Sunshine and published *Petals Plucked from Sunny Climes* in 1879, a nearly 500-page tome on Florida and Cuba based on her later-in-life travels to both. In the diaries and the preface to the book she complained about being frequently ill and relying on a string of boardinghouses to recover. Travel was a little easier for Brooks than it was for Royall in Alabama, Georgia, and Tennessee by the time Brooks was on the road, but that did not mean she, like Royall, turned away from boardinghouses. Brooks wrote in her diary in the fall of 1870, "Hotel stopping does not answer my purse very well, consequently I commenced looking for cheaper quarters." She found them in boardinghouses.[18]

But why? Why did women like Royall and Brooks embark on such dangerous, uncertain lives? Transportation was still unreliable in the United States. Royall endured many near-misses on the road in untrustworthy stagecoaches. Brooks faced late or never-arriving trains and ferries. In Alabama, Royall fumed about a house that looked respectable but was filled with "Gamblers, Pickpockets, Shavers, Sharpers, Pirates, Robbers," one of whom broke into her room and then into her locked trunk to steal "five or seven dollars." In Georgia at Mr. Linton's house, Brooks was supposed to have a private room but ended up having "some girls placed in my room which talked out of the night. I slept but little." More than that, the room was directly over a sitting room where men talked "until nearly midnight and all day beside." Brooks resolved to leave. The next day she noted in her journal, "Extortion is the order of exercises now upon all sides. I remonstrated in consideration of my being a lone lady but all to no purpose—he was incorrigible to the last. I ordered my baggage to the depot and bade farewell to Linton's boarding house."[19] Both women exposed false promises and unscrupulous behavior in warmly recommended boardinghouses on their paths. But they continued to travel.

Brooks gave one answer in the pages of her diary, writing, "It is pleasant for me to live among strangers where no sad memory lingers, where no harrowing associations brings [*sic*] up memories from the past with their visages to haunt harass and destroy my happiness here and hereafter." Whatever happened to Brooks that led to her being disowned by family and separated from her child, boardinghouses gave her a chance to rebuild and move forward. Royall simply avoided places with sad memories, saying, "I have suffered too much amongst mountains; they are splendid objects to look at, and sound well in theories, but nothing wears worse than mountains when you take up your abode amongst them." Royall answered a critic who told her to "go home" with her strongest statement of the power of boardinghouses: "My country is my home."[20] Boardinghouses and life on the road afforded women like Royall and Brooks the opportunity to escape their past and create a future in the wider United States.

Royall, Brooks, and Ida Beard lived in southern boardinghouses in three distinct eras of the nineteenth century, but they shared a strategy to support themselves. Whether in the 1830s, the 1870s, or the 1890s, all three sold books from their boardinghouse lodgings. It was a viable career option for women across the century. Julia Wolfe, before she married and began her boardinghouse-fueled real estate expansion in Asheville, had been a bookseller. Offering a catalog of books by other people, she met her future husband, W. O., on a sales visit. Royall exclusively sold her own writing, and she admitted to destroying materials by competitors, dumping them overboard or quietly whisking them away from displays. Brooks sold others' books as a traveling saleswoman. The part of her diary that connected her sales experience with her decision to write no longer exists; she seemed to have stopped selling books before becoming a published author of her own stories. As her marriage was failing, Beard sold many products before settling on books: furniture, ribbons, and so-called madstone treatments, reputed to draw out infection and cure rabies. By the time she turned to book sales, she was accustomed to needing a range of offerings, her own writings and others'.[21]

A guide from the 1860s claimed, "The whole country, from one end to the other, is a Book Market, full of Book Buyers; and the reading of one book, so far from satiating, only gives thirst and appetite for another and another."

While the guide did not specifically address book selling as a job for women, many staked their finances on it. It was not an easy life. Brooks described the reputation she and women like her acquired, saying, "Book agents are not looked upon as ministers of grace or messengers of mercy. There are no rapturous receptions to be expected or received by them, no exhibitions of extended friendships or flattering encomiums." She took comfort that "their reputation is unsullied with the memory of wrongs to the widow and orphan, undisturbed by injustice and punishment meted out to the innocent." Brooks contrasted the clean consciences of female booksellers with the guilt experienced by other traveling salespeople such as "light weight dealers, whiskey diluters, [and] sugar sanding chicken cholera venders." It was not glamorous, but it had dignity, in Brooks's mind. Selling books honed women's senses of what stories people wanted to read. Readers and audiences became vividly real. Beard used her first book tour as writing material for her second book—which she then also toured to sell.[22] Key to the career were boardinghouses, as women fanned out across markets, seeking entrance into parlors, private rooms, and imaginations of potential readers. Surrounded by books in rented rooms, women booksellers gained insiders' knowledge that helped when they picked up their own pens later.

Ida May Beard: Unhappy Boarder, Desperate Keeper

First, though, women who would be booksellers and women who would choose to carve out their own freedom had to decide to live away from home. Unhappy memories, unsustainable home lives, and difficult conditions pushed women like Royall or Brooks out onto the road. For Ida, events started when she was a teenager. Born in Salem, North Carolina, in 1862 to a financially comfortable white family with status and respectability, Ida May Crumpler had what she called a charmed childhood. Her father and mother loved her dearly, her siblings shared children's dreams, their community valued the good family name, and her ancestors brought recognition to the family beyond the confines of their small town as lawyers and state opinion makers.[23]

Unfortunately, that changed when as a young girl Ida May Crumpler met John Beard, a handsome boy from a less prosperous part of town. Her family offered all kinds of warnings about him—including repeating rumors that he was not white enough and maybe was part African or Native American (and making negative value judgments about that). Their efforts to keep Ida and John apart only strengthened the young couple's resolution to marry, which, indeed, they eloped and did just as soon as she was eighteen years old.[24]

By all measures it was a bad marriage. They fought. He was unfaithful to her almost from the beginning, but with rising audacity as their marriage dissolved. He was violent to her (physically as well as emotionally)—one horrifying passage described him pushing her down a staircase and then beating her with a length of rope.[25] Another offhand remark from Ida noted scars she carried from his abuse. He tried very hard to get whatever family money from her he could. He schemed to ensnare Ida in lawbreaking (hoping, it seemed, to deflect blame from himself or at least make it impossible for her to testify against him). He tried to trick her into looking unfaithful and thereby get a divorce without penalty to him. From Ida's perspective, John was a drug-addicted, violent con man who did not hesitate to take advantage of anyone and everyone with whom he came in contact. She wrote, "John was past all redemption, and spent many of his leisure hours in reading Tom Paine's works, eating opium and drinking bromo-seltzer." Recounting one of their fights, Beard recalled saying,

How about your bicycles, guns, dogs, etc.? I suppose I was the sole cause of your having them also, was I not? You know that it has cost you no little sum to board your lovely little canine family here and elsewhere for the last six years, and I think it's high time you cease your everlasting hunting expeditions, when they cost you ten dollars or more, on account of your paying railroad fare for dogs and friends who accompanied you. Then, every time there is a bicycle race, ten dollars more must come out of your pocket, so that you will be in the swim with the rest of the boys. The very idea of your having two $150 bicycles and two $35 guns in your possesion [*sic*] at one time, not mentioning your $9 watch chain, $10 ring, $5 silver-headed cane, and a thousand other things. I think it perfectly awful that you paid $25 for one of your bird dogs. Then, you remember, you paid $24 more for a hair tonic, which never did your bald head a particle of good.

It was not a salvageable relationship; Ida almost did not survive it. Before the marriage ended, Ida and John had two children together. Ida's mother passed away and her stepmother cut Ida off from her father, drove a younger sister away, possibly into prostitution, and callously disposed of all traces of family mementos. John sued her for divorce a year after abandoning her.[26] Ida found herself quite alone.

But Beard was educated and entrepreneurial. She wrote and self-published her life story; then she toured the South selling it and other books. Her book was pocket-size, just the thing for reading on a train or in spare moments. She priced it to move and quickly went through more than eighteen editions. Selling books netted her much-needed money to settle bills and support her sons. Much like Anne Royall and Abbie Brooks, Ida Beard embarked on tours and acted as a book agent for her own writing. She traveled to military outposts, major cities, and small towns across the length and breadth of the South; in her second publication, she said she toured twenty states with *My Own Life*.[27] She presented herself as a respectable woman, but she also made sure people knew she had a salacious story to tell. She laid out as many details of John's cons and schemes that she knew, hoping he would eventually be prosecuted—but also counting on readers' appetite for page-turning action and voyeuristic enjoyment of conspicuous consumption.

Not only was Ida Beard's memoir a product that she carried from boardinghouse to boardinghouse as a saleswoman, but its pages also documented the role boardinghouses played for economically vulnerable women at the turn of the twentieth century in the Piedmont South. Her path to self-support was not easy; she had to make her way through a series of uncomfortable and unfriendly lodgings on her way to independence. Failures of her marriage and loss of family and home came into focus as she and John moved through a variety of living situations. Her father helped the young couple as they built a house at the beginning of their marriage, but soon John "insisted that we dispose of our residence in order that he might go into business for himself." To do this, he told Ida, "I want you to say" to friends and family that "you are anxious to break up housekeeping and try boarding for awhile, as you are not very strong and think a little rest would do you good."[28] Reluctantly, she did. Their finances never recovered from this decision. For the rest of her memoir, Ida applied her careful accounting, which clearly took stock of their outlays on luxuries (his bicycles, canes, and hair tonics), to her housing budget.

Beard detailed for readers the range of options for boarding—including specific costs and relative merits of neighborhoods in small towns and cities across piedmont North Carolina and its neighboring states. Over the course of the book's short 212 pages and her fifteen-year marriage, she described nineteen different boarding situations (most in and around

Winston-Salem) she and John experienced. The most expensive, in which they lived during flush times, went for at least fifty dollars per month; when at her most destitute, Beard was in rooms that cost only three dollars per month—seven dollars less than what boarding John's dogs cost in flush times. She recounted paying outstanding bills by leaving furniture behind, offering cash up front, pawning her wedding ring, and promising future earnings to various keepers. Mrs. Rose Williams offered rooms in the City Hotel on Main Street over Jacobs' clothing store for the heady fifty dollars per month. Mrs. Elizabeth Rierson's rates were cheaper for her rooms in the less desirable Buxton Block of Liberty Street, so Ida and John moved and stayed for almost two years. At the Jones House, rooms in the main building were full, but they boarded in "a little brick structure formerly known as Judge Wilson's law office" out back. Jones left to take over the "Merchants Hotel," and Mrs. Hanes took over the Jones House. Ida wanted to stay with Hanes, but John insisted they move with Jones. It turned out to be too expensive, so they returned to Hanes House with unpaid bills owed to Jones. Debts accrued again, and after sixteen months, they fled, leaving furniture as partial payment with Mrs. Hanes. Short stays in Greensboro's Benbow House and Roanoke's Hotel Roanoke and an unnamed place in Wilkesboro, North Carolina, followed as John chased jobs and ran from scams. Back in Winston, they were reduced to one room in H. Montague's building over a telegraph office and, later, two rooms in James Dunn's Grubbs Building back on Liberty Street.[29]

For Beard, L. D. Kingsbury's boardinghouse in Bluefield, West Virginia, marked the lowest point of her married life. On first sight, she found it "a miserable looking place." Even before going inside, she "caught a glimpse of about seventy-five men and women who were playing pool in the lower part of the building." As Ida recalled it, "There I was standing in the mud and water up to my shoe tops in front of a gambling den at 11 o'clock in the night." John had arrived months earlier and established himself in the community. He sent for Ida but introduced her as his sister rather than his wife. She also discovered he changed their last name to Bird for the stay (likely to avoid creditors or to anticipate needing to disappear quickly later). Before finding temporary shelter with a Baptist minister and wife in Bluefield, Ida took meals with the thirty-five "miners and machinists" in the pool hall repurposed as dining room during the day. To her horror, she learned from diners that John had engaged himself to three women in the town. Before she managed to leave, John stole money and goods from the store employing him and ramped up violent outbursts toward Ida and others—which were easily overhead through the flimsy walls of the make-shift boardinghouse sleeping areas.[30] Much like the scene of Lola Walker's summer of seduction, boardinghouses could be spaces where domestic contracts gave way to illicit sex and seduction, drinking, gambling, and broken promises. Ida eluded John's attempts to get the last of her money, hurriedly returning to Winston with him in rapid pursuit.

The marriage soon effectively dissolved, and John lived elsewhere before finally filing for divorce and moving back to West Virginia. Ida moved with her two sons through a series of very cheap boardinghouses, some unfurnished, some in dangerous parts of town, and some secured through past friendship much more than through her current ability to pay. The Hardy House, Mrs. E. Starbuck's block, a repeat stay in Mr. Dunn's residences, the Grubbs Building, the Bitting block, a cottage near a grade school in North Winston, the Tise flat, and others made up the parade of places Beard tried to make a home for herself and her sons.[31]

Beard's housing shifts created a vivid map of southern boardinghouses in cities, towns, and rural locations across the South. Lines between boardinghouses and hotels were so fine as to be almost nonexistent. Some hotels were more luxurious than some situations she described as boardinghouses, but just as often hotels were rough while boardinghouses were better. Physically, some of the boardinghouses took expected form, in a single house or building such that boarders' rooms shared walls with each other. Even when the Beards rented cabins or cottages on the property, they still called themselves boarders (presumably, even if their room was a stand-alone building, they could eat communal meals with fellow boarders if they could afford them). Occasionally, within the same hotel, according to Beard, some rooms were designated as part of a boardinghouse, while adjacent ones were listed as mere hotel rooms (in these cases, the manager apparently contracted with women to be keepers for wings or sections of the facility). Beard herself briefly contracted a few rooms in Mrs. Starbuck's building to run her own boardinghouse, but elsewhere in the same building Mrs. Holish and her "companion" Phillips had their own rooms, as did "several young gentlemen."[32] Beard's descriptions here are unique in the written record, and they raise so many questions; I have not found evidence anywhere else of a hotel containing individual boardinghouses within it. Keepers were in and out of each other's kitchen and bath spaces regularly, so the distinctions seem largely understood, not a matter of physical, architectural separation.

Beard's first attempt at running a boardinghouse was brief. Historian David Silkenat describes the location as being "Winston-Salem's notoriously squalid Starbuck Block." Beard had to scrub the rooms and scrounge to make them habitable before she could even begin.[33] Her vivid descriptions revealed cultural assumptions about how to be a keeper. They also showed the space between assumptions and reality, as Beard quickly failed. As rare as copies of Beard's books are today, even more precious is her record of what it looks like to *fail* at keeping a boardinghouse.

Beard did not want to be a boardinghouse keeper. She first made "a thorough canvass of the city in order to obtain employment," but finding nothing, "at last decided upon opening up a boarding house." Her first problem was finding capital to begin. Even if she rented rooms unfurnished (something she and John had been forced to accept several times), she needed food and serving dishes, and she wanted table linens. She said, "I studied over the matter for a day or two, then concluded to make the attempt, fail or succeed—one or the other I was sure to do." Rather than taking a hard-eyed look at the business of keeping boarders, Beard began with a romanticized image of it. She reported, "While in this state of mind, I began keeping boarders. I will always remember the first table I spread for the boarders. It was really amusing to see me arranging viands and the few pieces of ware aunt had given me. I was so afraid that something would be wrong, and that it wouldn't seem like a boarding house." Focusing almost entirely on appearances, she continued, "I prepared for my boarders as though they were guests coming to tea, and on leaving the dining room, they each declared themselves highly pleased with their first meal. In the center of the table I had placed a lovely pyramid of flowers; the napkins were arranged in the shape of a lily, and the viands consisted of fried chicken, fresh butter, pickles, honey, banana cake, strawberries and cream, lightbread, milk, and tea."[34] The first meal, however, did not augur ongoing success. The boardinghouse closed quickly.

Beard claimed she failed because one of her sons fell ill and time spent nursing him forced her to close. Perhaps. We do not know whether Beard hired a cook (it is hard to believe she had the resources), purchased ingredients and cooked herself (a possibility, though she rarely discussed cooking elsewhere in the text), or found a grocery or restaurant to order prepared food on credit. Serving baked goods and so many delicate, less-filling foods meant high grocery expenses. Beyond the food, Beard's boardinghouse also required fitting up the lodgings. How much credit did she get to furnish rooms and supply linens and bedding? What terms did merchants force on her to set up accounts for daily needs? Did she have a business plan, and was it practical? Her memoir doesn't say.

A newspaper article titled "Keeping Boarding-House" from 1870 written by "Uriah Slipskin" for the *Louisville Courier-Journal* told the "Sad Experience of One Who Tried It." Much like Beard, the humorist recounted a string of naive assumptions about how easy it would be to open a successful boardinghouse. Slipskin and his wife decided "to fix up a small house of eighteen or twenty rooms" and take in some friends—not small at all. They were sure they would "make a small fortune." They took a house on Vegetable Street, near Bull-eye and Mutton-head Avenues (humorous names foreshadowing trouble ahead in food costs and procurement). The house cost $1,800 per year, and they furnished it on credit for $2,500 more. They paid an employment agency to hire "two cooks, five dining-room servants, [and] four house servants," and they inherited "about eight relations" in addition who had to be fed. Slipskin gamely set up merchant accounts—greengrocers, flour merchants, bacon providers, confectioneries, and ice suppliers. He optimistically calculated nearly $4,000 profit per year that would roll in.[35]

Reality arrived with a jolt. Boarders disappeared without paying, much as the Beards did several times to Ida's horror. Bills came due. Remaining boarders were dissatisfied with the food and demanded special meals, and the doorbell wore out from ringing, which necessitated costly home repairs. Soon, "I was turned out for non-payment of rent the eighth week, and find myself just $3865.74 in debt—all done in about sixty days—and haven't a friend in the world." Slipskin concluded, "I never lie down to sleep at night without sending up three well-grown prayers for boarding-house keepers. They are the world's martyrs." The piece ended with a curse: "Reader, are you a boarder? If you are, may all the torments of bed-bugs and caterpillars follow you through this life. May you suffer from toothache and tight boots till all the inflictions you are putting upon your helpless host are fully, thoroughly, fearfully avenged."[36] Whether Beard would have read along with Slipskin and laughed ruefully or instead have stuck to her story that only her son's illness prevented her success, we cannot know.

Beard's boardinghouse experiences were not over. Once John left, she wrote her memoir and hit the road to sell it. Now she toured hotels and boardinghouses as a woman alone—divorced, more worldly, and financially independent. She wrote a second book, *The Mississippi Lawyer; or, Was It All a Dream?*, also a memoir, carrying her life story forward. Publishing some ten years later, Beard chronicled another danger in hotels and boardinghouses, that the people one met might not be who they said they were. The freedom Abbie Brooks celebrated of reinventing oneself among strangers had another face for Beard. A man introduced to her as a prominent bachelor and lawyer admired her writing and loved her cat but proved to be a bankrupt bigamist who had abandoned his existing family to scam widows and finance his drug addiction. Beard did not fall for his scams. She woke up from her "Mississippi dream" and settled down in Winston, North Carolina. Census records and city directories until about 1915 called her an "authorist" and boardinghouse keeper. Her adult sons boarded with her, as did clerks and merchants.[37] Presumably Beard had learned by then how better to manage a house, the food, and the business, no longer in need of Slipskin's curses on her boarders.

By the time John Beard initiated the divorce from Ida, she was ready to accept it. The situation was trickier when it was the wife who wanted a divorce, especially if the husband was in the public eye. States with lighter residency requirements and less draconian laws gave refuge to women with economic or social privilege who traveled to find divorces or wait out unwanted pregnancies. One boardinghouse keeper in Alexandria, Virginia, near the differently regulated Washington, DC, stepped in to help women who could not go all the way to Nevada, site of the most famous getaway. The resulting scandal, when she was found out, led to Alexandria being dubbed the "Super-Reno" of divorces by sensational newspaper headlines in the area.[38] Royall's husband died; Beard's ran off; Brooks and the father of her child did not marry; other women needed divorces from husbands when relationships failed. Boardinghouses helped.

In February 1922, newspapers reported that Alexandria, Virginia, resident Mary Baggett was one of a group dubbed the "divorce mothers." Boardinghouse keepers all, Baggett and fellow Alexandrians had created a profitable "divorce mill" using their boardinghouses that one reporter suggested followed best American business practices: "big production—low unit costs."[39] Newspaper coverage began on Baggett's arrest. It continued through investigations of her, other keepers, a judge, and several lawyers accused of conspiring in the ring.

For a small fee, DC women wishing to secure a divorce in Virginia's more lenient and less gossipy environments could pay for "the hanging of a nightgown in a closet" in Baggett's boardinghouse. After a year of prompt payment, Baggett would testify that not only the nightgowns but the women who owned them had been in residence the legally required length of time to file for divorce. Baggett's boardinghouse was located next to the court where cases were heard. One newspaper suggested a petitioner could conduct the whole business from boardinghouse to courtroom to decree without ever coming out of the shade: "On the brightest days of the year when the sunshine flooded the streets one could establish residence, join in conference with the lawyers and attend the court hearing without once stepping out of the shade." Baggett denied the charges, saying that "in all the years I have run this boarding house I have never knowingly done anything irregular or contrary to the law." Investigative journalists followed by lawyers researching on behalf of the bar association discovered that Baggett's name was on an extraordinary percentage of cases heard by one judge, Robinson Moncure.[40] They vowed to uncover the scheme turning Alexandria into the East Coast's Reno, Nevada.

Newspapers reported their calculation that the number of people in the court records "who gave the residence of Mrs. Baggett as their domicile showed that during the two years from November, 1919, to October, 1921, the maximum number claiming such residence during any one month was 115 (in August, 1920)." The average monthly number of residents in her modest house was an astounding 78. Baggett did not have 78 rooms. She did have closets that could hold 78 or 115 hangers. Boardinghouse keepers charged a modest sum to each woman, but in aggregate they made a hefty profit because lots of nightgowns took little outlay from the keepers. No cleaning, cooking, food, or laundry were required. Further, because nightgowns were not accompanied by husbands' nightcaps, in 709 out of 807 cases, grounds for divorces were simple desertion.[41] In one neat package, a path to quick and favorable separation was on offer.

On March 7, 1922, after a police hearing, Mary Baggett was set free and the warrant against her dismissed. Before that denouement, papers and letters relevant to the case mysteriously vanished, witnesses failed to show, and proceedings were delayed because Baggett fainted when standing before a judge. It looked corrupt to reporters. After the hearing, investigation of Judge Moncure was given over to Alexandria's bar association. At issue was whether judge and boardinghouse keeper solicited clients for and gave kickbacks to each other.[42] Coverage in newspapers dropped away, and presumably, boardinghouses returned to daily cooking and laundry for actual residents who stored whole outfits in closets and slept whole nights in Alexandria beds. But what happened to women who had successfully obtained divorces with Baggett's help? Did they pick up pens like Royall, Beard, and Brooks? Did they relocate and begin new lives? In other words, did they leverage Baggett's closets and corners to purchase rooms of their own?

A Room of One's Own: Boardinghouse Writers' Retreats

As early as 1821, when Anne Royall lodged in small towns across Alabama, she found herself, in biographer Jeff Biggers's words, "unfettered from domestic duties" and "seeking to clear her mind." Biggers concluded Royall had "begun the process of reinventing herself in the relatively anonymous and transient quarters of Alabama."[43] Royall had created a room of *her* own, and she nurtured her subsequent writing career inside boardinghouses across the US South on her epic travels. Abbie Brooks wrote her Florida book, staying in boardinghouses around the state, finally finding the peace and quiet she sought. She washed dishes for no one in the family that rejected her; instead, she wrote of a new, loosely connected community, made across the length and breadth of her adopted state. Ida Beard remade her identity as "authorist," no longer simply an abandoned woman, and she did it in others' boardinghouses and her own where she set up her desk to write.

To Carson McCullers, the room was in a quiet Charlotte, North Carolina, neighborhood in 1937. McCullers began drafting her masterpiece, *The Heart Is a Lonely Hunter*, in a boardinghouse at 311 East Boulevard in the Historic South End neighborhood. Today a historical marker commemorates the site, its boardinghouse, and McCullers. She wrote a friend about the rooms she and her husband rented: the refrigerator was in the bedroom; there were no lamps; overstuffed furniture abounded but bookshelves were scarce; and the couple had to work at the same small table. The rooms were cold, but during the day while her husband was out, they were entirely McCullers's own. Travis Tuck Jordan wrote her poetry about the inner lives of women like Martha Hinton and her granddaughter while living in Raleigh's Bland Hotel. Long-term residents like Jordan balanced short-term tourists in the building—but within the walls of her rooms, she created worlds. Tennessee Williams used his New Orleans boardinghouse to do the same. Grace MacGowan Cooke dissolved her marriage to find her own utopian rooms—and wrote about Aunt Huldah's Texas boardinghouse respites.[44] Boundary-crossing, brave, financially lucrative, and award-winning works of fiction, journalism, poetry, and scholarship were made possible by boardinghouses. We just haven't bothered to tally all the works with boardinghouse roots before.

When Virginia Woolf wrote *A Room of One's Own*, she had in mind lost works of women's genius that never came into the world because the writer was interrupted by tasks of daily life or noise of family and household clamor. She mourned women who never realized they could be writers, who never imagined poems, novels, and essays they were uniquely positioned to write, because the busy-ness of everyday life kept them from creating in the first place.

Woolf's classic essays began as a series of talks she was commissioned to give in October 1928 about women and fiction. She acknowledged she could just write about Jane Austen, the Brontës, and George Eliot; collect her money; and go home. But Woolf set herself a harder task. Instead, she imagined a woman named Judith, William Shakespeare's fictional sister, equally gifted but unable to spend hours in a library or school, barred from moving on her own to London to immerse herself in a creative life, expected to pick up household tasks before and after marriage, never free to live on her own. Woolf's Judith Shakespeare died without ever picking up a pen. Woolf identified myriad explanations in the six connected essays, but she distilled them into a central metaphor, to which she returned on the final page. Woolf concluded, "This poet who never wrote a word and was buried at the crossroads still lives. She lives in you and in me, and in many other women who are not here tonight, for they are washing up the dishes and putting the children to bed." Woolf clung to hope that if women could gain "five hundred a year each of us and rooms of our own," then great works of art and great women writing them would emerge.[45]

ANNE ROYALL LEFT the road in the late 1840s. She committed to her newspapers and to lobbying for pensions for Revolutionary War widows like herself. She did not leave boardinghouses behind when she settled down; a woman named Sally Stack allowed a penniless Royall to stay for free for six months in her DC boardinghouse. Royall returned the favor when Stack faced financial setbacks; eventually the two women decided to combine households and share expenses.[46] Stack took on more work for Royall, even traveling with letters of introduction to represent her when needed. Royall embraced her conviction as a "scold," though one suspects she never would have accepted the adjective "common." She felt it was crucial for the body politic to have irritants—people calling out hypocrisy or corruption, people fearlessly defying prevailing winds. She strongly believed that religion had no role in civil society and political life. She championed not only a free press but an equally taxed one. If one publication shipped without charge through the mail, to her mind all should. Even as she settled down, Royall never wavered in her belief that women traveling alone had just as much right to roads and lodgings as men. She demanded respect and courtesy equal to that given any other traveler—and if you wanted to give her even more, because of her writing achievements, you were welcome to. By the time Royall passed away in 1854, her reputation was enmeshed in Washington's political life.

Boardinghouses provided safe landing spots for women with few resources. Finalizing divorces, gaining new careers, or relaxing in a space without fraught family arguments, women in boardinghouses found new energy and resources to engage the larger world. Sometimes the boardinghouses made space for women to start new, creative careers, plugging into structures for selling books, taking advantage of new media and communication. After Ida Beard returned to Winston-Salem, her lodgers were her sons, Basil and Rebah. The boys ran a shoe business, and they all three lived above it. Eventually, one son married. The other traveled to Texas as a salesman but fell ill and died there. Beard herself died in 1951, but she left behind two books and documentation of how even failing at boardinghouse living and keeping could lead to succeeding at writing and traveling. The independence gained in boardinghouses mattered for whole generations of women.

Not all people in the South had equal access to boardinghouse rooms of their own like Anne Royall and Ida Beard while media and communication structures of the nation expanded. More men and women were swept up in another fast-growing aspect of the southern economy. Factories, mills, mines, and other resource-extractive industries, as well as government, banking, transportation, education, and support structures that accompanied them, spread across the New South in the twentieth century. Industries needed workers. And workers needed places to live, eat, and relax. Specifically, they needed lunches. Boardinghouses were there. Mary Hamilton in remote logging camps in the Mississippi Delta and Della McCullers in the crash and noise of Raleigh's state capital neighborhoods both used boardinghouses to expand opportunities for women in American cultures. Along the way, they helped bring a new southern meal into existence.

CREATING MODERN SOUTHERN LUNCHES

Mary Hamilton and Della McCullers

FIRST, THEY CAME to the end of the railroad line and had to board a slow-moving river barge. Then, the barge let them out at a remote dock with only a wagon waiting for them. Soon, even the road ended, and they had to walk the final miles. Mules plodded alongside them to haul in supplies— flour, salt, beans, precious canned goods, and dried foods. After a few weeks of open-fire cooking, all the parts of a stove had been slowly walked in and could be assembled. Still, men slept in tents, and her kitchen was in an open shelter. Occasionally, when they were lucky, a worker killed a bear or a deer in his off hours and brought her the carcass. Rich stews and luxurious pies followed. At other times, the boat could not forge the high water or other accidents met their supplies, and she had to improvise with thin soups and repetitive, ingredient-light dishes. One terrible day, the floods came, and she ended up on top of a roof holding tight to her children, wondering if death faced her. Mary Hamilton (1866–ca. 1936) and her husband lived and worked in the Mississippi Delta in the late nineteenth century in remote logging camps before roads, railroads, and supply lines were established for industry. Hamilton cooked three meals a day in extreme conditions for as many as 115 hardworking men, sometimes not seeing another woman for upwards of a year at a time. It was a boardinghouse without walls. But Hamilton was not anachronistic in the twentieth-century South; instead, she was on the cutting edge of eating in the modern South. She created a system for customized lunch pails so that men who could not get back to camp for midday break could still eat the foods they craved.[1]

Della McCullers (1874–1954) charged twenty-five cents in 1939 to eat lunch at her establishment in Raleigh, North Carolina. For that price, customers received a hearty plate of nourishing food. They relaxed at tables inside or outside, where they listened to the latest music, heard neighborhood news, and caught up on national celebrities. Around the corner from Shaw University, McCullers's business was close enough that students, faculty, and staff were potential customers. Raleigh had a robust Black business district at the height of Jim Crow segregation, filled with banks, car dealerships, stores, doctors, hotels, and restaurants. McCullers was one of those African American businesspeople in the heart of Black Raleigh. She served lunches and fast meals to workers on the go—and she helped them wind down after a hard day's labor. Her customers lived in urban Raleigh, but they worked hard, like Hamilton's backcountry timbermen. McCullers's approach to the changes in Americans' midday meals, however, showed the meandering paths that creative Black businesswomen had to forge in southern towns and cities. Della McCullers was running a boardinghouse when she was interviewed by Robert O. King in 1939 as part of the Federal Writers' Project. More precisely, she ran a restaurant with a few beds in the back (primarily for extended family) that passed as a boardinghouse. King explained the arrangement in his opening paragraph: "A license, costing several dollars, is required to do a restaurant business in Raleigh, and that is why she prefers her eating house to be known as a boarding house."[2]

I began this book with a focus on the food in boardinghouses, arguing it was no coincidence that our earliest southern cookbooks were written by boardinghouse keepers. From Mary Randolph to Malinda Russell to countless other keepers, women responded when guests asked for food they recognized; southern food—as a coherent, recognizable collection of tastes, flavors, and techniques—cohered around boardinghouse tables.

Food has come with us as we moved across centuries, though it has often been a means to an end for the various themes each subsequent chapter has explored. Texie Gordon taught fellow boardinghouse keepers an ethic of nurturing and care through business lessons in her dining room. Presumed competence with southern food allowed Mary Ellen Pleasant to achieve financial success while funding abolitionist and civil rights projects. Ida Beard and Anne Royall used the quality of food to judge whether an establishment would allow them the freedom they needed to write in rooms of their own. Later boardinghouse keepers like Gordon, McCullers, and Hamilton contributed one more innovation to what we know as southern food today: they helped invent the modern lunch.

It is hard to imagine the dense, dark, overgrown, and wet landscape Hamilton and her husband faced. Workers in logging camps, railroad work sites, mines, textile factories, furniture factories, food processors, and other industries shared the experiences of harsh working conditions. Hamilton's camp cooking initially feels distanced from the promise of consumer goods and laborsaving innovations in the homes run as boardinghouses in the South's bustling cities like Raleigh where banking, government work, and pink-, blue-, and white-collar work all expanded. Spoken and unspoken racial codes that businesswomen like McCullers had to navigate to use cooking and business skills to support herself and her family were strict; violating them could bring devastating consequences. Yet in both types of locations, workplaces brought tired and hungry workers needing food away from their family homes. Boardinghouse keepers were still there to feed them, with lines of lunch pails, take-out food, grab-and-go meals, and economical lunch options.

Mary Hamilton's Boardinghouse Kitchen

Coal and cotton left outsize footprints across the industrializing South. Mining company towns and textile mill towns hold boardinghouse stories large and small. Less remembered, timber and its associated industries— tanneries, paper mills, and shingle manufacturing—cleared agricultural land for future cotton crops, built ships and rail lines that opened markets, and transformed where and how people extracted and then used coal's power. Later mill villages that ran on electricity, had steel equipment, needed cooking and heating technologies, and processed cotton (and raw material imported from overseas as well) had to be built from something, and many of the answers began with timber. Mary Hamilton's life cannot be separated from the interconnections of timber and southern industry. Born in 1866, Hamilton wrote her autobiography, *Trials of the Earth*, in the 1930s at the urging of Helen Dick Davis, her friend and a novelist, who served as editor for the manuscript.[3] Hamilton's matter-of-fact narration of her extraordinary life experiences brought industrial boardinghouses of the late nineteenth and early twentieth centuries to vivid life. *Trials of the Earth* is a story of love, marriage, children, heartbreak, illness, and triumph for Hamilton, her family, and her community; boardinghouses were central to each.

Hamilton's boardinghouse experience began on the first page of her autobiography; early boardinghouses in her life looked a lot like the ones we have seen already. "In the early 1880s," she wrote, her father brought the whole family "from Missouri down in to the wild country of Arkansas" pursuing jobs and land. Unfortunately, he contracted pneumonia almost as soon as they reached Arkansas and died three days later in the end-of-the-railroad town of Sedgwick. Hamilton's mother was left a widow with six children to raise in a completely unfamiliar community. Hamilton said, "As we had the only livable house in town, we took a few boarders." Hamilton was seventeen, but she and her thirteen-year-old sister, assisted by an unnamed Black woman, took on "all the cooking." The fractured family started to recover. Standing in the kitchen only a few weeks later, with flour on her hands and sleeves rolled up, Mary met Frank Hamilton, her future husband and partner in life and work. Frank was an Englishman, with no small number of mysteries in his past. His skills included logging, supervising men in camps, bookkeeping, and supporting the boardinghouses he and Mary ran during their working years. Mary and Frank had nine children together, five of whom survived to adulthood. They raised and supported their family in jobs around the Delta.[4]

But when they first entered the remote camps, Hamilton had to expand her skills as a boardinghouse cook and keeper. On a "cold gloomy morning in January 1896," Mary got her first glimpse of "to us a new world, the Mississippi Delta." The landscape was densely filled with hardwoods and fringe trees, "oak, gum, ash, hackberry, and poplar"; blue cane growing up to the lowest branches of the trees; a thick black mud everyone called "gumbo"; some black sand; and, of course, the Mississippi River, lined with sycamores and cottonwoods. They battled gnats, mosquitoes, and weather. Wolves, bears, and other wild animals circled close to the settlements when night fell. The first camp combined clapboard shanties with tent living. The company employed local white and Black men. Later camps had even more diversity, with Jewish men, Croatians from the Slavonian region of the country, and other eastern European timbermen joining Black and white southern male workers. Ethnic and racial diversity in rural and isolated work sites across the South was not uncommon. An article in the professional industry journal *Timberman* described a Texas sawmill community filled with "Finlanders" in 1888. Suronda Gonzalez wrote movingly of her ancestors' emigration from the Galicia region of Spain to aluminum smelting factories of West Virginia, where they lived and worked with Black and longer-settled white Europeans. Mary Hamilton and her family members were consistently the only women in camp. She suspected she was the first white woman to go to that part of the Delta before it was cleared, much less live there.[5]

The Hamiltons lived both in other people's boardinghouses and in their own. Not until late in her life was Mary finally free from the added expectation of other people's laundry, food, and work schedules. She and her children traded one kind of hard work for another, and she ended her career in the 1930s planting and picking cotton on rented land. She outlived her husband and did not start writing her life story until her late sixties. *Trials of the Earth* can be read for many different purposes: to learn of the environmental transformation in the Delta, to appreciate the story of a marriage featuring love and mystery, or to respect the artistry of an accomplished but untrained autobiographer who pulled readers in on every page. Across all, however, ran a narrative of food, gender, labor, and boardinghouses.

Six months after their marriage, Mary took over "general cooking" with her sister for an eighty-man boardinghouse Frank had opened. She asked for a pastry cook to help; they had a "boy and girl" to wait tables, but the rest of the work fell to Mary. A month later, the pastry cook left, and Mary quietly picked up the pieces and did his work too. It was a harbinger of her character and work experiences she collected over time. In the busy season, Hamilton said, "we had 115 men at the boardinghouse, besides the six helpers and Frank and me." She detailed ingredients such industrial-scale cooking entailed: "I have been laughed at for saying we used a barrel of flour a day; but you bake 115 loaves of bread a day, biscuits or flapjacks for breakfast, at least thirty pies for dinner, and always tea cakes for supper, as I did, and you will see. Then we had to make our own yeast, and that took lots of flour. We made a five-gallon churn full every two days."[6] To satisfy the caloric needs and palates of workers, Hamilton's work was never-ending.

Hamilton also detailed how she stretched leftovers to satisfy boarders. She made good use of what she could, saying, "The only leftovers of anything we could use were bits of beef roast or soup meat and boiled ham, run through the food chopper. To this we would add cold potatoes and onions, mix well, thin with soup stock, season with pepper, sage and salt, press in a pan, and bake brown. We served this hot for supper." She editorialized, "It is boardinghouse hash, older I think than boardinghouses themselves. I don't believe there is a timber man in America that hasn't eaten it." Unlike keepers who were the butts of songs and jokes, as mentioned in chapter 1, Hamilton did not get complaints over her hash, perhaps because she did not economize to the detriment of flavor. As she said, "Bread, cakes, or pieces of pie we would never put on the table a second time. It didn't make any difference how much we had left over, but God help us if we didn't have enough."[7] Hamilton's graceful writing made food sound delicious and dining easy, but the passage also hinted at the relentless work required to produce such pleasures. Breaks between meals for Hamilton and employees were filled with cleaning from previous meals and prepping ingredients for next ones, from the careful artistry of replenishing yeast starters to less-skilled but still necessary potato peeling, stewing, and roasting.

Hamilton had to track supplies carefully, because ordering required coordinating with Frank's schedule to trek back out to the river or railroad access points, not something that could happen frequently. Although she did not name it, Hamilton must have had as much a plan as the women in Mary Randolph's kitchen did, some seventy years earlier. In Hamilton's case, one could not run out for forgotten ingredients or whip up something on a whim. Because it was up to Frank and Mary to create profit out of the successful running of the camp, she had to balance special dishes with the everyday.

Preachy advice columns in newspapers for actual and potential boardinghouse keepers, mostly written by the cooking school experts, warned sternly there was no reason to miscalculate supplies needed for a week's or even a month's worth of cooking. "Mrs. Stayclose" suggested "Daily, Weekly, Quarterly, and Annual employments." Domestic scientist Sarah Tyson Rorer acknowledged that boarders might need to be understanding but strongly urged keepers to plan well ahead and "give variety; do not allow the same dishes to come and go upon your table day in and day out." Laurine Marion Krag, second-generation keeper, warned women only to "buy the freshest vegetables and best quality of meats" in precise amounts. Advice columnist and cookbook author Marion Harland, while admitting she never kept a boardinghouse, was nonetheless confident in her advice to keepers: "I do not say you must not economize, but it should not be in the meat and vegetable and grocery bills."[8] In remote camps in which Hamilton cooked, life was not nearly as predictable as well-meaning writers assumed.

Hamilton was unlikely to have the latest equipment advice that columnists felt was necessary for success. What equipment did she have in her open-air kitchens? Beyond the stove, which was carried in by hand in pieces, she mentioned a food chopper. She clearly had pots, pans, cooking spoons, and knives in daily rotation. But she mentioned little more. Did she have loaf pans for bread or pie tins for sweet and savory dishes? Did she have anything else?

The late nineteenth and early twentieth centuries saw an explosion of new patents issued by the US government for canning, baking, and kitchen time-saving of all types. By 1922, a book published by the American School of Home Economics, *Cooking for Profit*, suggested that to feed 100–200 people in a boardinghouse the female proprietor needed "a large double range, a bake oven with four or five shelves, cook's tables with rack overhead for utensils, large boilers of tin, copper or enamelware, large roasting pans that fit range ovens, agate pans for baking puddings, apples, etc., of size to fit bake oven shelves, food chopper, bread mixer, bread slicer and such other utensils as are found in home kitchens, but of larger size or in larger numbers." For large establishments, *Cooking for Profit*'s author, Alice Bradley, recommended a "steam table, steam kettle for vegetables, soups, etc., power ice cream freezer, power mixing machine, dish washer, bain marie, broiler, vegetable parer, meat slicer." Hamilton cooked for 115 men at a time, large by almost any measure, but she hardly had access to such tools.[9]

Once the Smith-Lever Act established land-grant universities and agricultural and home extension programs followed, Black and white demonstrators fanned out, urging consumers to purchase equipment. As mail-order catalogs filled trains and mailbags, so too did widgets, devices, and inventions. But they were, of course, unevenly distributed. Would a cook like Mary Hamilton have had access to the latest gear-assisted eggbeater or had the bain-marie set up? Looking back in the 1930s, as she penned her memoirs, her silences spoke volumes.

During the early years of their marriage, Frank and Mary moved frequently, faced the death of children, and were economically unsteady. At one point while Frank was away recovering from a mysterious illness, Mary saw "an advertisement in the paper for a good cook at a hotel in Imboden, Arkansas." She applied, but the owner worried she was too "little and look[ed] so frail" that she would not be able to do the work. The owner's husband called Mary "a little delicate girl about the size of a washing of soap" but then nicknamed her "Lady Grit" once he saw her work. Mary convinced them to give her a chance to prove she could "do as well as a man cook." She succeeded. More than that, as testament to her skills, she convinced the owners in Imboden to pay her "a man's wages" because she was doing so much work for them.[10] Boardinghouses did not have to be fancy to hold ambitious women who sought to develop their skills and improve their service for others. What they learned in turn pushed models of food service forward.

Hamilton's story showed blurred lines between hotels and boardinghouses, trained chefs and cooks like herself. Workers moved back and forth, from hotel kitchens and haute cuisine to camp setups with fast, efficient production. Soon after the birth of one of their children, Frank "went to Memphis and got a German cook by the name of Stine" to relieve Mary. This proved another opportunity for Mary to add to her education. She wrote, "He was good, but like all professional cooks, was cross. 'I know my business and don't want no woman telling me what to do.'"[11] Of course, Hamilton did not accept Stine's decree to stay out of his kitchen.

Watching him closely, she noticed, "He made a yeast that would have bread ready to bake in two and a half hours after making it up, and every time I could make an excuse to be in the kitchen, I was there trying to watch him." When he called her on it, she replied, "You say you are not going to stay but two months, and after you leave I will have all this work to do again. I am sure I have had at least twenty men cooks and from every one I have learned something that was such a help to me. . . . Let me be your pupil." He asked her, "Do you mean to tell me you have done all this cooking for this crew of thirty men and more?" She said yes. He proposed, "I am going to do for you what I never did for a woman before. I will take you, as you say, for my pupil." But he warned, "If you show signs of wanting to teach, I expel you."[12]

Because of a lack of good water in the Delta, Hamilton also wanted to learn Stine's recipe for a helpfully lower-alcohol beer using techniques with yeast like those he used for bread. As would any woman on her own in a mining camp, Hamilton hesitated to introduce a culture of liquor drinkers. But to keep employees for whom she was responsible healthy, Hamilton needed safe water supplies and hygienic food safety practices, as well as refreshing food and drink for tired, hard workers.[13] So she agreed to Stine's conditions.

Allowing Stine to "make out a bill for everything you need to make cakes and decorate them," she absorbed the expense, saying, "I have had to do the work alone so much I have never had time for much fancy cooking." Hamilton justified her desire for learning because it could increase her "pleasure of knowing how to cook." It would also improve her ability to "handle" the work in the "easiest way." For her, learning served a combination of quality of life, curiosity, and efficiency. They embarked together on her lessons: "light bread, rolls, French, plain, sweet, and fruit." Stine also improved dishes Hamilton had long served by teaching her speed and efficiency with recipes. Hamilton, even while apprenticing herself, was confident in her own abilities; this was simply a way to add to her options. She wrote, "I was as good on meats and fish as Stine was but knew nothing about cakes, fruit salads, or dozens of other things, compared to what he did." Hamilton concluded, "Stine was the finest cook I ever saw"; he may have thought she was a strong student in return, judging from his enthusiasm in teaching her as weeks wore on.[14] Stine did, indeed, leave after two months. But Mary had learned what he had to teach her.

In 1918, the US Bureau of Labor produced a manual designed to outline occupations in logging camps and the various names by which those jobs were called. According to the manual, bakers and bakers' assistants should have been able to produce pastries and baked goods for even large camps with only two or three people working. Bakers needed to be "able to make straight dough and sponges and also to use potato ferment for yeast making." Bakers managed stoves, whether fired by "coal, coke, or wood." Cakes, "baking powder and raised biscuits" were under the baker's purview, as was managing helpers, keeping an eye on budgeting and ordering ingredients, and "understand[ing] the fundamentals of camp sanitation." In order to advance to the position of baker in this apprenticeship system, one "should have had experience as a baker's assistant" but needed only "common school" education. In turn, assistants needed to want to learn and be willing to work, be neat "in appearance and habits," and be good at taking directions.[15] Four other food-related positions were discussed: commissary man, camp chief cook, cooks, and cookees. Cookees were scullery workers, in training for other positions. Commissary men needed to know some bookkeeping but also have food knowledge of ingredients, commodity price swings, and the like. All the cooks needed to be able to work in "temporary" kitchens; it helped for them to be in "good health and strength." The guide summarized: "The camp chief cook must be able to prepare meat and vegetables, bake biscuit[s] and bread, pies, and plain cakes, with a camp kitchen outfit; must be able to handle a coke, coal, or wood range, and select the proper kinds and amounts of food for the various meals of the day." More than that, the chief cook must "prepare lunches for men who have to go a distance from the camp. He must be prepared to serve hot drinks and soup with meals served at a distance from the central kitchen."[16] As was government practice for publications, the *Descriptions of Occupations* used all male pronouns. But we can read Mary Hamilton on the pages. Over her working years, Hamilton manufactured apprenticeships for herself and progressed through occupations one by one. By the end of her memoir, she had cleaned, cooked, baked, run the commissary, ordered food, and served as camp chief cook, sometimes fulfilling positions simultaneously.[17]

Hamilton had to deal with occasional deliveries gone awry—whether from miscommunication that caused missed connections between rail and ferry, natural disasters that resulted in overturned boats or impassable trails, or human frailty such as deliverymen who took off for new horizons or who drank too much and slept off hangovers rather than bring Hamilton her barrels, bags, and necessary equipment. She noted, "Camp life is always either a feast or a famine." One week, her husband killed a 250-pound bear, so Mary "cooked bear meat every way I could think of, and we sent the Minkus camp some. I didn't cook it every meal, as we got a beef or a hog from Lemaster every week and corned beef by the barrel from New Orleans." Her point was that "we treated our men so well through the feast days that when the famine days came on because of bad roads or high water or missent goods, they understood it wasn't our fault and never grumbled."[18] Around camp, men had few options. But even in remote situations, they could walk out on contracts, take jobs with rival companies or managers, or otherwise rebel against Hamilton's boardinghouse. That they did not was testimony to her skills.

While Hamilton was a white woman, in other industrial sites women of color were at the heads of the kitchens and boardinghouses and would have recognized the work. In Texas, pop-up immigrant restaurants and camps supported dam building and other cooperative projects between US and Mexican workers, engineers, and companies. Mexican American women created outdoor restaurants next to where workers slept that strongly resembled Mary Hamilton's open-walled timber camp kitchens. Tents, makeshift tables, and portable cooking techniques powered workers who then completed projects that powered the South. San Antonio's self-named chile queens, who served meals at open tables in the town square, and waiter carriers of Virginia who provided fried chicken to rail passengers may have avoided providing lodging to customers, but they still cooked and served in rugged conditions. West Virginia's mining camps brought Italian, Spanish, and eastern European Jewish workers looking for food and respite that reminded them of flavors of home. Ingredients were imported to general stores and groceries across the state, but someone still had to do the cooking. While fewer women were present in early camps, Chinese men built southern railroads and figured out their own ad hoc kitchens and lodging while doing so. Today working-class immigrants shop at flea markets for familiar ingredients and pool resources to share housing while establishing themselves in new communities—the model remains.[19]

Equipment and space meant little if unaccompanied by skill and responsiveness to evolving tastes and desires—and on this topic, Hamilton had more to say. She clearly learned cooking skills in her mother's kitchen, but she also educated herself over her career. Seeking mentors, learning skills, and adding to her professional capabilities, Hamilton did more than just make do in her wilderness kitchens. Like Malinda Russell, Hamilton modified, improved, and challenged her own cooking prowess—and she did so as boarders started to ask for a new type of midday meal.

Creating Modern Lunches

Hamilton customized lunch pails to meet demands of boarders who could not easily return even to her ad hoc dining rooms midday. In remote camps, Hamilton developed a system for personalizing each logger's to-go lunch. She built on skills she had acquired back in her early days cooking in Imboden. There, she learned significant additional cooking skills as the hotel kitchen worked primarily by providing what Hamilton described as "short-order meals"—food quick to cook, often fried, griddled, or assembled into portable stacks. Hamilton revisited the concept of cooking to order as she developed a system for lunches in work camps that both offered variety to the men and allowed her more free time in the day. Packed into lunch buckets, the meals emerged from a kitchen operating more as a sandwich shop, deli, or short-order diner.[20]

As logging expanded in timber camps, daily work pulled employees too far away to return to the dining room for the midday meal. Portable box lunches provided solutions. For the boardinghouse keeper, though, adding in the task of prepping meals ahead required reshaping strategies for time management and business structure. In Hamilton's case, prep started as she processed venison brought into the kitchen. After using some of the carcass for hams in her traditional dining room, Hamilton "dried the rest for the men's lunches." On days that box lunches were needed, Hamilton began the night before. She "had a long narrow table made like a counter in the dining room against the kitchen wall so the men could set their lunch buckets on it as they came in to supper the night before. We washed them, scalded them, and set them back." The day dawned with "four o'clock mornings" during which Mary cooked breakfasts for workers there. She then set her sister and husband to prep and serve tables for the morning meal so that she could pack up lunches while the men ate. Hamilton remembered, "I would slice my bread and meats and make sandwiches and pies. It is a lot of trouble to put up so many lunches and change them from day to day. Some liked one thing, some another; hardly any two buckets would be alike. Every man's name was on his bucket."[21]

Hamilton's experiences as a short-order cook in Arkansas prepared her to pack individualized meals efficiently and accurately. Even in the extreme environment of isolated wilderness industrial sites, Hamilton was at the cutting edge of the food world: take-out foods, European cooking techniques, wise economics and efficiencies in the business model. Again, boardinghouse keepers like her proved innovative as they reshaped modern southern food. Over the course of Mary Hamilton's time in Mississippi timber camps, the modern American lunch was invented. Ideas for sandwiches appeared in newspaper cooking columns and cookbooks.[22] Public food businesses experimented with faster, flexible midday options. Change took place in big cities, around factories, and especially among newer pink- and white-collar workers in American towns. However, this was not a change taking place elsewhere for Hamilton. She saw it firsthand in her remote industrial wilderness work sites—and responded with innovative solutions.

Abigail Carroll, in *Three Squares: The Invention of the American Meal*, examined the American lunch. Unlike breakfast and dinner, which were modified over time, lunch "was not a traditional meal forced to adapt to the changing social and work patterns wrought by industrialization." Instead, "it had not existed as a meal at all. It had to be invented." Although Carroll does not turn to them, boardinghouses in the South are perfect locations to study why lunch came into existence and progressively became "lighter, colder, cheaper, and quicker" from its invention in the "mid- to late-nineteenth century" to its blossoming in the twentieth. Hamilton's box lunches for workers were in this tradition. As Carroll argued, "The Industrial Revolution shifted work from the home and workshop to the factory and the office, and these new sites of production made returning home for a meal in the middle of the day increasingly impractical." Loggers could not afford the time it took to walk back to camp, hence Hamilton's clever, personalized solution.[23]

A few decades later, hungry midday customers in Raleigh turned up at the city's new hot dog stands for cheap food, fast. For the truly time-pressed, delays to warm food—or simply finding hot food quickly—remained challenging. Sandwiches came into fashion because they met all these requirements: portable, inexpensive, easy to gulp down without further prep. Many eaters, however, were not quite ready to give up the trappings of a family meal even if they needed to experience it quickly. Students, clerks, laborers, and office workers found a meal at Della McCullers's eating establishment instead.

Della McCullers: Daily Life in Black Raleigh

Born in 1874 on South Bloodworth Street, two blocks east from the location of her business in 1939, Della McCullers had prepared her whole life for the career she had when she sat down to talk to Robert O. King as part of the Federal Writers' Project. She had hard-won resilience, flexibility, and inventiveness. Daughter of Walter and Henrietta Harris, Della learned skills of laundering from her mother. McCullers told King that her parents had been enslaved in Wake County. By the time Della, their first child, was born, the Harrises had a home on Bloodworth Street, in the heart of Black Raleigh. McCullers said, "We lived in a two room house in the back yard of some white folks when I was a child. Ma took in washing and Pa did first one thing and then another." Henrietta taught her two daughters, Della and sister Lilly, how to do "washing and ironing" for hire. Even as a young child, Della took note of heavy labor versus small profit: "Ma got only 75 cents a week to do the washing for a family of six or seven and we washed not only the clothes but the bed linen." She continued, "I guess Ma made about two dollars a week from the work."[24]

Soon Della started working outside her childhood home: "When I got to be a good sized girl, I went to work in the home of some white folks." To her laundry skills, the new job added cooking and childcare experience, as she had responsibility for "all the cooking, washing, ironing and help look[ing] after the chillun for seventy-five cents a week." Her employers, as did many southern white families, allowed employees to take leftovers home. McCullers's father had died, so Henrietta needed help to feed the family. Della's sister married and left; one brother became a "delivery boy," and his wages helped clothe the family; another brother left for the Spanish American War and made a career in the army; the youngest brother, Jeems, worked in Norfolk for years before coming back late in life to live with Della in the boardinghouse.[25]

Armed with a work history of domestic and cooking skills, Della married John (Ruffin) McCullers in 1911. Henrietta lived in their home for a while but succumbed to pneumonia soon after McCullers's marriage. John was a brickmason; the couple had a comfortable income and soon welcomed five children into their lives. McCullers told King, "The first two died when they was babies." Death certificates confirm one baby died a few hours after birth as a "weak child." The other passed away at age eleven in 1929; the death certificate was hastily written, revealing only that Della's son contracted an illness while visiting a farm near Raleigh. He died at St. Agnes Hospital, the regional Black hospital. John also died young, passing away at age thirty-eight in January 1924 of pneumonia after being ill for a month; Della then had to raise her three daughters alone.[26]

McCullers at first continued as her mother had, washing and ironing for pay. But she was a keen observer of cultural and technological changes. In her words, "White folks don't have their washing done" by Black folks "like they used to, and I couldn't make ends meet to save me." Assessing the paucity of public dining options for African Americans, McCullers "decided to open a small cafe for them to eat in." City directories show Della as a "cook" as early as 1926 and a restaurant owner by 1931. She "did pretty good" in that endeavor, sending "her daughters through high school" and keeping them "pretty well clothed" on revenues from the café. Daughter Mary was listed as a student and then a schoolteacher in Raleigh directories through the 1930s.[27]

When an opportunity presented itself, McCullers closed her first café and opened a new one in a newly built eighteen-room hotel on Cabarrus Street that she leased from the owner, whom she described as a rich Black man. City directories tell us it was the Liberty Hotel at 218 East Cabarrus. The hotel offered a bigger clientele with more money to spend on food. McCullers told King, "I put a cafe in the hotel and with the rent from the rooms I got along all right until 1929 when the panic started." Along with Americans across the country, McCullers watched as people began losing their jobs. She said, "I lost my roomers and customers in the cafe. I held on to the hotel as long as I could, thinking things would get better, but they didn't." To hold on, McCullers spent her savings down and went into debt for "rent and groceries." She knew she had to make a change.[28]

McCullers "gave up the hotel and came over here in this little place and started my boardinghouse." Located a few blocks away, at 432 South Blount Street, the boardinghouse allowed her to get out of debt and support her brother, a grandson, and herself. At age sixty-four, she had worked as a laundress, a cook in private homes, a café cook, a hotel manager, and a boardinghouse/restaurant owner. Still keen to calculate the economics, McCullers told King, "I pay $20.00 monthly for the store building and the two rooms which adjoin it. My light bill runs around $3.50 a month and my water costs me about $1.00 a month." After clearing expenses, McCullers could still send her grandson to school and save the rest from the boardinghouse "to send him off to college and make a doctor out of him." Characteristically self-deprecating, McCullers told her interviewer she was independent (not "on charity") and happy.[29]

Having previously owned a café and run a hotel with associated restaurants, McCullers had specific and pointed reasons to call her new business a "boarding house." Robert King recognized and respected her preference as he wrote up the interview. The expense of the license, which he noted, was certainly part of it. Being a Black business owner in a complex, multiethnic New South city like Raleigh brought challenges beyond money; McCullers signaled as much in the interview with King. Boardinghouses like hers exposed both the lingering racial power structures in the growth of southern restaurants and the responses of savvy business owners of color to the changing palates of their customers as the ethnicities of the town multiplied.

Photographs and city directories from the early century show Blount Street, where Della's boardinghouse was located, as a neighborhood that could fulfill all one's needs—there was a general store, gas station, car repair shop, a church, and the impressive three-story brick Prince Hall Freemason building erected in 1907. Residents could get their hair done at the Bee Hive or by barber John Williams or from the men at Fuller's Barber Shop; Gill the Tailor could take care of their clothes, but so could Cumbo's Tailor Shop. If people did not want to eat at Della's, they could walk from 418 down to the Busy Bee Café at 410 or to Joseph Blacknall's restaurant at 407½. Lafayette Koonce was a veterinary surgeon next door. King mentioned him as "operat[ing] an animal hospital . . . where operations are frequently performed upon dogs and cats." It was not just pet care offered in the neighborhood: Harper Fleming was a dentist and Nelson Perry a physician, and all had offices on the same block as Della's. At the end of the block, the Masonic Lodge and its dance hall sat next to Roberts Drug Store. The blocks to either side had gas stations, service stations, and auto dealers, as well churches and homes. Shaw University, founded in 1865, making it the first historically Black higher education institution in the South, was (and still is) nearby. While Della lived on the property, King did not mention seeing other employees when he visited. However, Minnie Gooch was listed in the 1939 directory as "waitstaff," with 418 S. Blount Street as her only address; in 1940, William Waddell, living around the corner on Davie Street, was a "helper" at the boardinghouse.[30]

Businesses and services were concentrated on the street because Jim Crow meant that Black customers were not welcome elsewhere in the city. Passage of the federal Pure Food and Drug Act in 1906, which led to the formation of the modern Food and Drug Administration, came in response to widespread adulteration of food and accidental poisonings from unsanitary conditions in food production and food service across the nation. Lawmakers debated whether boardinghouses should be included in new inspection requirements, fearing that "the matter of getting evidence against the restaurants is easy, but for the inspectors to penetrate into the boarding houses is another and far more difficult undertaking." As Psyche Williams-Forson discovered, often the work of inspectors was less about potential food safety violations and more about enforcing preexisting prejudice and recreating the separations and differences between Black and white neighborhoods.[31] Did Della McCullers rightly judge licensing processes in Raleigh as something best sidestepped? Did her fellow restaurant proprietors on the street all pay for licenses? What precisely was McCullers saying about larger societal structures behind her decision to step out of the restaurant business in favor of the nudge-and-wink boardinghouse on the street?

Twenty-five years later, race politics were still high-stakes in southern restaurants. Waiter Booker Wright in Greenwood, Mississippi, took a risk and spoke to a national news crew that wanted to understand the burgeoning civil rights movement. Employed by Lusco's, an exclusive restaurant in town, Wright also owned a bar and juke joint. Like McCullers, Wright had experience with more than one side of the restaurant industry. Perhaps having his own source of income gave him the freedom to lift his mask and give viewers a peek behind the scenes. Whatever the reason, Wright listed indignities, disrespect, and hate that he faced daily in the white-owned, white-patronized restaurant.[32] With her experience doing laundry for white women in Raleigh and then running a hotel restaurant catering to Black customers, McCullers had seen the terrain of her midcentury city. There were many reasons for McCullers to have left the regular restaurant business and open a boardinghouse.

But Raleigh in 1939 was not simply a city of Black and white residents. For the restaurant business, Greek immigrants were influential entrants into a crowded field. Like some Jewish and Chinese store owners as well as Italian grocers and Syrian and Lebanese restaurateurs across the South, Raleigh's Greek restaurant entrepreneurs catered to both Black and white customer bases, especially for lunch meals. For McCullers, the effect on her boardinghouse was keen. McCullers outlined changes in Raleigh's demographics: "In a few years the Greeks started coming in to Raleigh and opening up hot dog stands." Savvy businesspeople themselves, hot dog stand owners soon "figure[d] out" what Black customers wanted to eat—"fish and things like that." It was part of what had made McCullers's café unsustainable, and it was a development she still was watching closely.[33]

Added pressure from the Great Depression's high unemployment numbers also affected clients' food choices. McCullers explained that her clientele wanted to eat differently when employed versus unemployed. She faced more competition from Greek restaurateurs when unemployment was high because people not working could eat "a hamburger and [have] a cup of coffee" and be "all right for several hours." When customers were doing manual labor, though, "swing[ing] a pick or shovel all day," then "that's where I can beat the Greeks, because they don't know how to fix vittles like collards, turnips, haslet stew and the other things" her customers loved.[34] Even as she came up with new lunch options, the Blount Street location also allowed McCullers to counter fast-food, grab-and-go models with a powerful tool at any time of day: community space.

McCullers's establishment, regardless of terminology, filled a role not only for the food she offered but also for the space she created. Her gathering space full of music, conversation, and food reflected the work schedules of her customers. She served food quickly and cheaply while providing both indoor and outdoor seating for customers. She had a "piccolo"—a nickel-fed jukebox—with "the very latest blues recordings" on it, a picture of Joe Lewis hanging on the walls, and outdoor benches. As a result, Della's was "the gathering place for Negroes during the evenings and on Sundays." King himself lingered during the Federal Writers' Project interview, and he was there in the daytime.[35] At night, laughter, music, and community fellowship must have bounced off the particle board walls and nourished many a soul as much as or more than the food nourished the body.

McCullers had made a wise decision for the 1930s. Formally or informally she had done the calculations that Alice Bradley in *Cooking for Profit* called for: "Divide the overhead and operating expense by the number of people that you serve or can easily accommodate. Add to this the cost of food material per person." She continued that if the math came out too high for the reader's market, then "consider that you are working hard for less money than you would get if you rented your furnished house and went to work for some one else."[36] Of course, Bradley's American School of Home Economics was an organization for white women. McCullers had to add in the "cost" of doing business in a Jim Crow southern city as a Black woman, no matter how skilled she was. Boardinghouses like McCullers's were places where both the exclusionary, racist Jim Crow enforcement policies played out and demographic changes toward multiracial and multiethnic residents wanting modern lunches were made visible.

While King sat at her table interviewing her, McCullers listed foods she served regularly. Breakfast offerings included "fried salt herrings, mullets, sausage, pork chops, biscuits, cornbread and baker's bread and coffee." She limited them to "one kind of fish or one kind of meat" in the morning. During the rest of the day, she offered "cabbage, collards, blackeyed peas, stew beef, haslet stew, pigtail stew, pig ears stew, and water." McCullers added, "I always have some kind of fresh fish for supper, pork chops, hog liver, coffee, and things like that. I fill their plates with as much food as I can get on them. [My customers] love cornbread and I give them plenty of it with their meals." A coal stove, "patched in several places with tin, and held together by wire," was the only kitchen equipment McCullers had to produce such a range of foods.[37] Along with quantity (and complexity—with multistep stews and long-simmering vegetable dishes that certainly upped the flavors), McCullers's list offered more.

First, McCullers had clearly developed an arsenal of economic recipes. Stew beef then and now was often a mix of leftover cuts bundled together and sold more cheaply than other beef. Pigs' tails, ears, and liver were all less desirable and thus less expensive parts of the hog. Haslet stew was made from hog liver and lungs (and sometimes heart), again, cheaper ingredients that took a skilled cook to process. Even the vegetables she described were available for long seasons (especially during the hard-to-shop winter months) and held better than other produce. In other words, McCullers shopped and cooked wisely while still pleasing her customers and giving them reason to return.

Second, McCullers's list was deeply responsive to the Piedmont food-ways in which she lived. Hogs are still plentiful today in eastern and central North Carolina, and they were foundational to foodways of the midcentury. Adding in regular fish dishes spoke to connections between Raleigh and coastal North Carolina. Collards were consumed all over North Carolina, but more so in central and eastern counties. The much-loved coffee was imported (as, likely, were beef, flour, and cornmeal), but all were foods firmly embedded in North Carolina food cultures.[38] When McCullers said she gave customers what they wanted, she knew what that truly meant.

McCullers offered both the cheap plates and customized meals to respond to her regulars and to answer both lunch norms and nourishing nighttime desires. Athens, Georgia, boardinghouse keeper Texie Gordon, whose nursing was a hallmark of her business, quietly slipped in a detail to her interview about profits from take-out meals that could be unappreciated if one did not see the math behind it. Gordon's business model met the changing needs of her customer base head-on. She shepherded working men and women into today's food world with her to-go lunch options.

To be clear, by the time Federal Writers' Project interviews took place, lunch options had grown from Mary Hamilton's earlier lunch boxes. In the 1930s, across the United States, diners could eat at lunchrooms, tea-rooms, automats, dope carts, company dining halls, cafeterias, and more. Some were segregated by sex; most by race. Many had clear class distinctions. Some of these existed in Raleigh and Athens, Georgia. Restaurant proprietor Jennie Favors also sat for interviews in Athens. Like Texie Gordon and McCullers, Favors witnessed changes in her clients' working lives and expectations. Sandwiches and demand for variety were not just facing boardinghouse keepers. Favors's café, a third of a mile away from Gordon's boardinghouse, catered to Black "working folks" who did not have time to wait. "Sandwiches and bottled soft drinks" were for sale, but so were "plate lunches" served on trays. Favors told interviewer Grace McCune, "The people of our race all want their vegetables and cornbread fresh cooked and warm at noon. Cold sandwiches and lunches wrapped before they go to work in the morning just don't suit 'em a bit." Favors's customers mostly grabbed the sandwiches and Cokes for snacks in between meals. Favors, like Gordon, also offered special meals to order for certain customers (in Favors's case, it was an elderly customer she went out of her way to accommodate).[39] Despite their many differences, the three women faced a shared challenge of offering profitable, desirable food fast for customers who still sought kindness and collegiality at a midday meal.

Gordon said she "sent out enough lunches last week to bring in between nine and ten dollars, and that is doing pretty good." Those take-out lunches—presumably sent to the offices and workplaces of white customers who could not afford to take an hour away to come to her—expanded Gordon's business model beyond typical boardinghouse offerings. Like McCullers's lunches, Gordon's in-house meals cost twenty-five cents each. If her take-out meals were the same, she prepared between thirty-five and forty of them per week. Not only did her take-out service add to her overall gross income, but it also represented a significant portion of her time and creativity. Gordon's "working class" clientele were moving into middle-class careers. White- and pink-collar workers joined blue-collar ones. Clerks, traveling salesmen, college students, and what she called "business girls" all took meals at her boardinghouse. Like in McCullers's case, boarding rooms were only part of what Gordon offered. But unlike the cots in the corner of McCullers's restaurant, Gordon's rooms were more formal, and lodgers stayed for longer durations. Along with the group of lodgers who could not get rooms with Gordon but instead stayed near enough to take meals with her, other customers came just for the food.[40]

Gordon's interview demonstrated how blurry and innovative food service even within typical boardinghouses could be. Breakfast started at six; dinner stretched from noon until two. Longer lunch hours were specifically set to accommodate student needs. If classes ran late or students were otherwise delayed, Gordon's cook (unnamed in the interview but rendered in African American dialect) "fixes their plates and puts them in the warming closet on the big old wood-burning range" for when they arrived. McCune, her interviewer, stayed for lunch. While she watched, "Several girls who work in the stores came together and discussed their work and the picture they were going to see that evening." At the same time, "a group of students was talking about tests they had had during the morning." Other diners were like the man who met his second wife at the boardinghouse. They both ate midday meals there because they "live[d] too far out to go home at noon"; they continued the practice even after their marriage. Finally, a well-loved traveling musical instrument salesman came in and was promptly served a meal of his own request, à la carte, ordered from Gordon herself. Once McCune stopped observing the people around her and started eating her own meal, she found "plenty to eat, almost anything that one could ask for, even two kinds of dessert. Never before had I bought such a lunch for as little as 25¢." For Gordon, dining room meals were enhanced by take-out boxes and special meals for late diners; all worked together in her profitable model.[41]

Celebrators of American hotels sometimes draw the line between hotels and boardinghouses most clearly around à la carte dining. The "European plan" adopted by hotels as early as 1835 in the United States allowed diners to order meals they wanted at times they wanted, paying for room and meals separately. This stood in contrast to expectations that everyone would eat the same thing at a fixed mealtime—often from common dishes placed in the center of the table from which diners would rush to serve themselves. If that sounds familiar, it is because it birthed a saying that has lasted even as boardinghouses faded from view: boardinghouse reach. Gordon, Hamilton, and McCullers likely occasionally used this serving technique. However, reality was more complex for all three. Susan Strasser, studying housework in the United States, found unexpected variety in boardinghouse service models even in the nineteenth century. She discovered records from northeastern boardinghouses in which "women who kept boarders with separate meat accounts often cooked separately for each person in the house; sometimes they fried different kinds of meat in one pan, 'each with a tag of some sort labeling the order.'" Strasser concluded, "These women, in other words, ran restaurants, and did not simply add people to a regular family mealtime routine; some boardinghouses actually functioned as restaurants, where nonlodgers ate along with the lodgers and the family."[42] Following Strasser's logic, Hamilton, McCullers, and Gordon all ran restaurants. Offering family-style boardinghouse dining; full service, à la carte ordering; and fast-food take-out meals to go, they catered to the South's new, important lunch customer base.

OUTSIDE OF ASHEVILLE, North Carolina, two public school teachers sat for their own Federal Writers' Project interview. This married white-collar couple found boardinghouses fit their chosen professions. They used boardinghouses to shape their forward-looking equal division of gender and rights. The couple worked apart, being "'modern' in their attitude toward marriage." Their schools were twenty miles apart in the county, so they "took, therefore, a small apartment at the county seat, and set up light housekeeping." George, the husband, fixed breakfast; the wife fixed supper unless either of them had to stay "at school directing extracurricular activities." (Since she "teaches English and French; has charge of the school library; coaches class plays and pageants; arranges class socials, receptions, and banquets; directs a literary society; coaches the girls basketball team; and accompanies the team as chaperon[e] when they take part in athletic contests at other schools," this was not an infrequent occurrence.) When that happened, they "went to dinner at a neighboring boardinghouse or at a cafeteria." Like Hamilton's men who wanted to take lunch to go and McCullers's customers who ate cheaply when underemployed and ordered when flush, Asheville's teachers found the flexibility they needed between the city's apartments, boardinghouses, and cafeterias. Perhaps not surprisingly, at the time of the interview, the couple had recently decided to give up their apartment and move into a boardinghouse closer to her school for the time-saving quality of life it afforded.[43]

As useful as boardinghouse keepers' and diners' memories are, they can inadvertently erase the diversity of meals present underneath the weight of finding common language. In a rush to describe the boardinghouse reach around tables serving communal meals, it can seem like only one model of food service and one group of boarders were present. However, in written texts, account ledgers, and behind-the-scenes memoirs of such houses, we see over and over that short-order meals, à la carte dining, take-out lunches, and special private dishes to fit the range of boarders and customers emerged from boardinghouse kitchens. As much as Malinda Russell and Mary Randolph helped create southern food through their innovative cookbooks and the boardinghouse experiences behind them, keepers like Mary Hamilton and Della McCullers helped create modern southern lunches out of their boardinghouse kitchens. During the rapid transformation of southern cities and towns, boardinghouse kitchens were poised to offer flexible and modern answers to changing consumer demands. We live with the changes every day.

Cooking for Profit not only outlined how to make money with a boardinghouse but also surveyed food-based jobs viable to its readers. They included selling from home "something that people want, made especially well"; cooking for a "Woman's Exchange" or other pop-up market; "prepar[ing] and pack[ing] lunches" for railroad stations, resorts, automobile routes, offices, or schools; catering; opening a shop; managing a kitchen for a hotel, institution, or summer camp; or managing a full-service guest house, camp, or hotel. *Cooking for Profit* said in no uncertain terms, "Variety with a big V is of the greatest importance when you are catering for the same group of people day after day."[44] Over the course of their careers, Mary Hamilton and Della McCullers gave their customers that variety by offering a surprising number of these options. When they retired, their boardinghouses had helped stabilize their families and support the next generation.

Mary Hamilton was living with her daughter when Helen Dick Davis met her. Davis would "beg her to write down the account of her life" and, after she did, shepherded the manuscript until it was published. Hamilton aimed simply to "writ[e] down for you the true happenings of my life." She passed away sometime around 1936. Davis tried to get *Trials of the Earth* published by submitting it to a contest, but it did not win and remained only in manuscript form. The book did not appear in print until almost sixty years later and only then because a friend of Davis's family found the dusty manuscript under a bed. Davis was able to fulfill her promise and have Mary Hamilton's extraordinary memoir published.[45]

McCullers's daughters had steady, good government jobs in Washington, DC, and wanted their mother to retire and come live with them. McCullers's health was not great for the hard work that running a restaurant required (she told King her doctor said she had diabetes and should change her diet and take it easier). Her daughters persuaded her; soon after King's interview, McCullers disappeared from the Raleigh city directory. She reappeared in suburban Maryland and, in fact, later died there. McCullers's family story can be read as an arc of success. McCullers said she had only a few months of formal education and that she taught herself to read and write in homes of white employers. Yet she was able to send her daughter Mary to school; Mary worked as a schoolteacher in Raleigh before moving to Washington, DC. At the time of the interview, the family was saving for grandson Theodore to go to college. Education helped families like McCullers's thrive. Participants in the Great Migration, they found homes in DC, feasibly an escape from the worst soul-crushing effects of life in Jim Crow states. Not that DC was free of institutional and structural racism, but just perhaps it afforded more stable employment and less constriction on daily life. McCullers seems to have met the goals she shared with Robert King: "As long as I can keep Jeems, Theodore and me off of charity I'll be happy."[46]

Just as they were in the eighteenth and nineteenth centuries, twentieth-century boardinghouses were largely unsupported by the US banking system. Keepers still used skills they carried and the labor of their bodies to start businesses. If they owned or rented property, they modified it to accommodate lodgers, staff, and supplies they needed—sometimes all at once and sometimes bit by bit as each year's profit allowed. They worked to find market niches that would bring steady customers—near work sites, as part of resort communities, in bustling neighborhoods, or close to transportation. Unlike in earlier decades, later boardinghouse keepers did not feel they needed to be coy about their employment. They apprenticed, studied, responded to new trends, and advertised. Hamilton and McCullers were unapologetic about their skills, capabilities, and successes in the world of business in the twentieth-century United States. Boardinghouses they ran and lunches they served stood shoulder-to-shoulder with other developments in food and hospitality in the South. Here in the twenty-first century, our culture has benefited from the inventions and models of southern boardinghouse keepers who have come before us.

BOARDINGHOUSE FUTURES

Airbnb, Assisted Living, and Side Hustling

⁓

WHEN I TALK to people about southern boardinghouses, conversation often turns to the question "Where did they go?" Oh, they survive in today's bed-and-breakfasts, people will sometimes say. It's often followed by "My aunt and uncle love staying in such places." Boardinghouses and legacies of their keepers absolutely can be seen in today's South—and larger American culture too. But I disagree that bed-and-breakfasts are the best place to look to trace their influence.

In 2007, David Sedaris wrote an essay in the *New Yorker* magazine titled "This Old House" about a year he spent in the mid-1970s in one of the last boardinghouses in Chapel Hill, North Carolina. Run by an eccentric woman who collected antiques and listened to vintage recordings on a Victrola in the parlor, the house "on the lip of a student parking lot" was a refuge for Sedaris. He described the house and its residents as "if you'd taken a Carson McCullers novel, mixed it with a Tennessee Williams play, and dumped all the sets and characters into a single box." But it proved to be the final year of the home's "Rooms to Rent" as the university's offers to buy the property for its land were too hard to resist any longer for aging Rosemary Dowd, the boardinghouse keeper. She sold, signing the deed over with a vintage fountain pen, of course. With its passing, a valuable space for thrift-store-clad, underemployed future writers trying to create their own identities separate from their childhoods also passed away.[1] Indeed, in our built landscape, few architecturally obvious boardinghouses survive. As I have argued across these pages, that is in large part because such buildings were by far the minority of southern boardinghouses; southern communities instead favored making do, making boardinghouses out of existing spaces of all types. More formal ones like Rosemary Dowd's college boardinghouse or those created to support managers and salespeople associated with textile or furniture industries have been subsumed by the growth of the towns and cities around the sites. But it would be a mistake to assume that no such boardinghouse spaces exist today. Instead, Sedaris's essay serves as a reminder that we should look for the *spirit* of boardinghouse women, the functions they performed, and the reconstitution of their flexible cultural and business model in present-day forms.

The legacy of boardinghouse women we live with today in southern communities can be found in retirement and care communities, amid Airbnb and similar property owners, among pop-up restaurateurs, and in ubiquitous side hustles. All owe debts to boardinghouses of the past. Their possibilities for reinvention by proprietors and customers alike remain today. The creation of southern food, with which this project began, continues as well. Ongoing intersections of food, gender, and innovative living are embraced by many of us today.

Grace MacGowan Cooke ended her 1909 novel about industrial mill villages, *The Power and the Glory*, with a dream of a utopian boardinghouse. It had roots in her own life story that included the cooperative kitchens in Upton Sinclair's Helicon Hall and the artists' colony on the beach at Carmel-by-the-Sea, where she lived out her days. On the beach, meals were often picnics of beans and abalone with friends like Mary Austin, Henry Miller, and Sinclair Lewis as an answer to domestic pressures of everyday life. In *The Power and the Glory*, Johnnie rescued Gray, her love interest, by outdriving kidnappers while dodging bullets. Fittingly, then, the final chapter is titled "The Future." Johnnie and Gray stayed in Cottonville, and

"Johnnie immediately set about seeing that Mavity Bence and Mandy Beacham were comfortably provided for in the old boarding-house, where she assured Gray they could do more good than many Uplift Clubs." Mavity and Mandy were tired from their work in mills; Johnnie was escaping that life, and she wanted to help her fellow workers do so also. Johnnie's vision for the boardinghouse was expansive: "We'll have a truck-patch there, and a couple of cows and some chickens." That would be "good for the table, and it'll give Mandy the work she loves to do. Aunt Mavity can have some help in the house—there's always a girl or two breaking down in the mills, who would be glad to have a chance at housework for a while."[2] Johnnie's plan reworked the boardinghouse idea to focus on health and well-being for female residents. Where previously married men (dismissively called "mill daddies") sat on boardinghouse porches and prospered while women collapsed under hard work, now wives, daughters, and single women used the space to restore their own health, take care of their physical and spiritual needs, and "uplift" communities beyond grinding poverty, very much a model our own community justice–focused present embodies.

Sometimes that need for care is most acute at the end of a person's life. From Shanghai to Sedona, central Florida to the Upper West Side, and the mountains of North Carolina to ocean views in California, luxury retirement communities compete for residents. Private rooms, on-call chefs, inclusive home repair and daily cleaning, shared conversation spaces, and organized activities make aging more comfortable for those who have economic resources to buy in. When residents need around-the-clock care or more advanced medical interventions, such communities can provide state-of-the-art nursing as well.[3] The good weather and low-tax ethos of towns in the US South mean that many such communities are in southern places.

For people with fewer economic resources and families at the edge of their care abilities, homes for elders are tucked into communities large and small. Some accept Medicare or Medicaid; some are repurposed ranch homes or one-story buildings; others locate as close to area hospitals as possible; some aim for a cozy or homelike atmosphere; and still others make do by aiming for sterile or institutional professionalism. Regardless, most offer beds, laundry, meals, and communal living spaces.[4]

People live in these establishments, but they also die there, whether they are called nursing homes, assisted living facilities, or luxury retirement communities. A time traveler from the nineteenth or early twentieth century might call them boardinghouses. Recalling Texie Gordon's early training as a nurse, as well as her willingness to let former residents return to her

Athens, Georgia, boardinghouse to recover from surgeries, today's assisted living communities trade on similar ideas of care, trust, and communal life. Much like Abbie Brooks witnessed, some facilities are kinder than others. Much in the news during the 2020 COVID pandemic, group living arrangements are necessary in the US health system.

Crucial differences have crept in, of course, as southern boardinghouses of the nineteenth and early twentieth centuries have become retirement communities, assisted living facilities, and nursing homes of the twenty-first century. Individual tasks, previously done by a single boardinghouse keeper and staff, are now more frequently subcontracted out to more formal businesses—from housekeeping and landscaping contracts to food supply to medical staff—each with its own structures of pay, profit, and accounting. Other changes were foreshadowed by some of the keepers profiled here: willingness to open kitchens on off hours or to allow residents to order à la carte rather than eat communal dishes, for instance. And, of course, the biggest difference of all: corporate structuring means that owners can access business loans and lines of credit offered by financial institutions in a way that the South's female boardinghouse keepers in earlier decades could never do. In fact, corporate banking has entered the retirement community in a big way; a growth industry, as it were, corporate retirement community companies are receiving investment capital, real estate development, and shareholder profit structures that rival those of any other resort or hospitality field. Eighteenth-, nineteenth-, and twentieth-century women who scraped and scrapped for resources to establish or expand their boardinghouses would recognize the forms but not the financial structures of today's caretaking boardinghouses in the assisted living world.

Another business model today, the side hustle, gets discussed as "innovative," "disruptive," and quintessentially millennial or Gen Z. Hallmarks of good side hustles in 2023 include the ability to make money off them around one's other work or life commitments. They generally arise from skills you already possess or can gain informally. Side hustles do not require major investments from formal banking or credit institutions. They can exist inside whatever living spaces or workplaces you inhabit—even or especially if those are virtual. Boardinghouse keepers throughout this study who began businesses on shoestrings, often while performing other home or paid work and with only resources and skills they had at hand, would find today's model familiar, continuous, and "millennial"—as long as the century's number started with an "18" or a "19."

Airbnb launched in 2008 as one of several businesses offering to connect people looking for vacation or short-term housing outside of big hotel chains to those with extra space in their own home spaces. Competitor Vrbo had begun a little more than a decade earlier, and others have opened subsequently. Food trucks and markets offer people the ability to sell dishes without needing brick-and-mortar stores for the variety, adventure, and economy of entrepreneurial cooks. Instagrammers, podcasters, and other social media lifestyle influencers turn their home kitchen spaces into places for recipe development, writing, and product recommendation, sometimes resulting in contracts for print cookbooks, television shows, or print magazine writing that all have the possibility of contributing to modern foodways and cuisines. Pop-up restaurateurs, pet sitters, personal assistants, and errand-runners for hire all propose to take care of the homelife needs of people willing to outsource domestic tasks.

The pop-up restaurant movement, closely tied to the resurgence of food trucks in US cultures, displays a similar ethos of finding resources without the help of formal sources of capital or permanent brick-and-mortar locations to maintain. In Asheville, the Blind Pig group connects pop-up meals with historical research and thoughtful ingredient sourcing. In Austin, Texas, live music and performance art combine with chefs in popular supper clubs serving underground meals around the city. One Long Table, Bread and Circus, and Foster ATX all offer good food meant to be shared and conversation, often with people who don't know each other. Like Della McCullers, though, the food, music, and conversation does not require a formal licensed restaurant space with a year's lease and all the concomitant inspections. Rather, caterers and pop-ups (while still needing to meet food safety and fire precautions) have more flexibility to create events and moments.

Boardinghouses are remembered fondly. Southern men who began their careers in sales, finance, or manufacturing stop to tell me about iconic tables when they hear I am researching boardinghouses. Bonding that occurred in remote camps and temporary town work assignments looms large in today's memories. Women recall tough-as-nails aunts and grandmothers who had the ability to cook for hundreds but still had a jar of cookies for the nieces and granddaughters to help themselves. Reminiscent self-published books recount scenes in company boardinghouses to hold onto the memories. It would be a mistake not to look underneath the nostalgia and romance.[5] When operating, boardinghouses were modern, new structures; women at their helm were innovating new business models for themselves and their communities.

Sometimes, a newer business spirit explicitly pulls in older boarding-house models, though at times the interpretation has a sheen of romantic nostalgia more than authentic historical experience. The "Wilkes Collection" affords visitors to Savannah, Georgia, the opportunity to stay in Sema Wilkes's former boardinghouse while still affording the ease of an online, mobile, short-term housing booking app. Wilkes, proprietor of the famed boardinghouse restaurant in Savannah, and author with southern food scholar John T. Edge of *Mrs. Wilkes' Boardinghouse Cookbook*, fits squarely in the center of nostalgic boardinghouse memories. The boardinghouse restaurant still serves daily, and reporters wax poetic over it. After being closed for a while, the old boardinghouse's rooms have now been reimagined as "an experience" you can rent through a boutique Airbnb program. "Stay in a Piece of History," the webpage orders (with inexplicable capitalization). Alternatively, you can stay in an affiliated pied-à-terre, which comes with "two gift cards for lunch" at Mrs. Wilkes's restaurant.[6] Rooms are located above the present-day restaurant, newly renovated and reorganized for the luxury audience. No longer aimed at working-class residents traveling through or looking for cheap options to sleep and be fed, rooms are now comfortable, with amenities including Wi-Fi and flat-screen televisions. So complete is the renovation that one reviewer commented, "I felt like a shipping magnate from the 1890s," a comment that surely would have surprised the tired, working-class railroad employees of the previous century. Sema Wilkes closed her railroad boardinghouse as soon as her restaurant was viable. She was eager to let go of the responsibility for laundry and lodgers. As far as we know, she never looked back. Today's Wilkes Collection website does. It is aimed at modern tourists, with the full ease of Airbnb scheduling and booking. But it also promises that you can smell breakfast from your rooms—and for a charge, they can arrange special seatings for you at the communal table down in the restaurant itself.[7] It's an oddly calibrated palimpsest of the boardinghouse spirit in the present day.

Similarly, in urban and rural locations across the South, communities are attempting to bring back the spirit of boardinghouses' role in launching careers of teachers and other underpaid middle-class workers whose presence are crucial for a community's success. North Carolina, for instance, is experimenting with how to keep young teachers in towns and cities by reestablishing teacherages strategically across counties. A partnership between the State Employees' Credit Union and Durham County garnered news headlines in 2017 for its attempt to bring back affordable teacher housing through a community-funded teacherage. Unlike the teacherage in which future actress Ava Gardner grew up, Durham's experiment would have had individual kitchens and no "second mother," the role Gardner's mother assumed in the 1920s for six young female teachers living in Smithfield, North Carolina's teacherage. Austin, Texas, floated a similar model to Durham's around the same time. There, rapid urban growth and escalating real estate prices were driving teachers away from a highly desirable southern city. City leaders wondered if the more rural teacherage model could be reworked for a southern city.[8] Nonetheless, the 2017 idea that communal living could make a job more viable—and that from the savings that boardinghouse living made possible teachers might be able to invest in their own homes quicker and thus commit to a longer career in the community—whether in urban or small-town sites looks a lot like the logic of boardinghouses across the nineteenth- and twentieth-century rural South.

In some places, new combinations of boardinghouse innovations are emerging. A competitor to the luxury assisted living facilities for retirement has emerged in college towns. Numerous magazine and newspaper articles tout the value of retiring to a college town—including access to teaching hospitals, free and daytime cultural events, and easily managed public transportation. Some take the idea further with the option of becoming a house mother (or, as some prefer, house director) of a sorority or fraternity.[9] It is an inversion of a caretaking model—not only are house directors taking care of college-age women and men living in communal spaces, but also directors are being taken care of by the town and community as they wind down their careers through shared housing and supported activities. Each future-looking scenario banks on nostalgia; contemporary spaces hold the spirit of boardinghouses past.

Malinda Russell translated her skills at laundry and pastry into a resort-town business and later cookbook to sell even while she was a refugee from war and violence. Alice Lee Larkins opened her family home to "quiet and steady" boarders despite her family telling her not to. Texie Gordon created a profitable catering business while embracing her boarders' needs for nursing and caretaking. Mary Ellen Pleasant put her boardinghouse profits toward the political change she wished to see. Lola Walker's aunts tried to reset their niece's reputation by putting the focus on the excesses of bachelor boarders. Jackie Mabley set the table for others when she came off the road to rest. Ida Beard found room to write after her marriage failed. Della McCullers figured out how to support grandchildren and community over

boardinghouse lunches and a jukebox. All might recognize today's side hus-
tlers and community spirit. As much as anything, these are descendants of
the South's many innovative and inventive boardinghouse keepers. Not only
were boardinghouse women hiding in plain sight in the historical record,
but they also left lessons and innovations for today's world in profound and
significant ways.

When you next sign up online for a themed supper club under the stars
on a warm spring night by a meandering river, when you find a cowork-
ing space that offers communal meals and Wi-Fi to remote workers in a
bustling southern city, when you find an Instagram or TikTok account that
teaches you how to cook or bake with items already at hand in your own
pantry or garden, when you join with your best friends and their partners
to figure out how to age in place but share the work in the Sunbelt, thank
a boardinghouse woman from the past. And when you think about living
well, taking care of community, preparing food for yourself and others that
nurtures and comforts in familiar ways, making political change, living
as your truest self, telling your story, and supporting yourself and others
with new ideas and flexible models, you pay those historical boardinghouse
women's energy forward to the next generation of keepers.

Notes

INTRODUCTION

1. Claiborne, *Feast Made for Laughter*, 13, 15, 21.

2. Claiborne, *Feast Made for Laughter*, 13.

3. Claiborne, *Feast Made for Laughter*, 21.

4. Craig Claiborne, "Sophistication Spices Southern Food," *New York Times*, June 26, 1985, C1.

5. The historical marker in Indianola reads in part, "Craig Claiborne (1920–2000) was born in Sunflower, Mississippi. In 1924 his family moved to Indianola, where his mother, Kathleen, ran a boarding house. After studying hotel and restaurant management in Switzerland, he became the first male food editor for the *New York Times* in 1957." "Craig Claiborne," City of Indianola, Mississippi (website), accessed April 5, 2023, https://www.indianolams.gov/media-gallery/detail/48/85. James Beard, another candidate for most influential food figure in twentieth-century America, grew up in his mother's boardinghouse too. Located in Oregon, the house run by Elizabeth Beard and Jue Let (a Canton-born chef who partnered with Elizabeth in more than one venture) indelibly shaped James's future palate as well. See Dan Q. Rao, "Who Was Jue-Let, the Unknown Chinese Chef Who Raised James Beard?," *Saveur*, May 18, 2017.

6. "Iva S. Whitmire," 1940 US Federal Census (database), 88–3, Brevard township, North Carolina, Ancestry.com.

7. Fitzsimons, *From the Banks of the Oklawaha*, 2:219.

8. Fitzsimons, *From the Banks of the Oklawaha*, 2:217–22. To Fitzsimons's credit, he interviewed Stephens and included his portrait in his volumes of town history written in the 1970s. The story of Jewish Hendersonville, however, is nowhere to be found in any of the three volumes.

9. Institute for Southern Jewish Life, "Hendersonville, North Carolina," *Encyclopedia of Southern Jewish Communities*, accessed April 5, 2023, https://www.isjl.org/north-carolina-hendersonville-encyclopedia.html.

10. Mabley's connections to Brevard and her subsequent housing are discussed in chapter 6.

11. On Galluchat, see Royall, *Southern Tour*, vol. 2, 19, 32. Royall uses various spellings, including Gallishot. To minimize confusion, I've silently amended each mention to "Galluchat." On Eliza Lee, see Myers, *Forging Freedom*, 94–100; and Shields, *Culinarians*, 84–88. On Sema Wilkes, see her *Mrs. Wilkes' Boardinghouse Cookbook*, 70; and "America's Classics Award Winners," James Beard Foundation (website), accessed March 1, 2020, https://www.jamesbeard.org/content/americas-classics-award -winners (page discontinued).

12. On New Orleans, see Long, *Great Southern Babylon*, 13–14, 40–53; James Rees, "The Gold Chain: A Passage in the Life of Lafitte," *New World: A Weekly Family Journal of Popular Literature, Science, Art, and News*, October 17, 1840, 305; and Reizenstein, *Mysteries of New Orleans*. Tennessee Williams's New Orleans queer boardinghouse play, *Vieux Carré*, is discussed in chapter 6. On West Virginia, see I. Beard, *My Own Life*, 212; Mary Nelson Stanard, "Two Women Writers of the South," *Bookman*, January 1921, 317; and Montague, *Deep Channel*.

13. Ferris's *Edible North Carolina* explores these economies, as does *The Food We Eat, the Stories We Tell*, which I edited.

14. Cooke and MacGowan, *Aunt Huldah*, preface, n.p.; "A Mismanaged Business," *Christian Union*, July 25, 1889, 104.

15. On the workarounds created by Black workers in otherwise white mill villages, see Dixon, "Building the White Right of Textile Work," on Danville, Virginia, or any of the six strike novels from the 1930s Gastonia mill strike, such as Dargan's *Call Home the Heart*.

16. On traces of boardinghouses in the architecture of a southern city, see Perkins, "Accommodating Strangers," a thesis examining the built environment of Wilmington, North Carolina.

17. Mary Hamilton's Delta boardinghouses are discussed in chapter 8. Historian Sharon Salinger described floating taverns with lodging in the James River in Virginia as early as 1619 in *Taverns and Drinking in Early America*, 90.

18. Strasser, *Never Done*, 145.

19. See all three volumes of Royall's *Southern Tour*. The bachelor running a cattery was Dr. Lanning, in Nashville; he had more than twenty cats when Royall visited (vol. 3, 192). Diarist Abbie Brooks encountered the same forty years later as she boarded in Ocala, Florida, though she dismissed the man's effort as an experiment "most novel and least money-making of all" (A. M. [Abbie M.] Brooks, Diary, 1872–1876, January 23, 1873, David M. Rubenstein Rare Book and Manuscript Library, Duke University, Durham, NC).

20. Robert O. King, "'Aunt' Della McCullers' Boarding House," Subseries 1.5 North Carolina, folder 583, Federal Writers' Project Papers, 1936–1940, #3709, Southern Historical Collection, Wilson Library, University of North Carolina at Chapel Hill. Scholars of northeastern boardinghouses include Gamber (*Boardinghouse in Nineteenth-Century America*) and Faflick (*Boarding Out*). Along with others, Strasser has noted, "With every census after 1910, fewer women described themselves as boardinghouse keepers, relative both to other women's occupations and to the population as a whole" (*Never Done*, 159), but her nationwide assessment is countered by Hirsch, analyzing the Federal Writers' Project of the 1930s. Hirsch found more continuity and

ongoing boarding in the region than was picked up in the census. He noted, "These interviews do not support the common tendency to make a sharp contrast between nineteenth- and twentieth-century family history. Much that is held to be typical of the nineteenth-century family fits equally well as a description of the twentieth-century southern families described in the FWP interviews" (*Portrait of America*, 159).

21. Examples of boardinghouse transformations are discussed in chapter 6. For examples of the same institution changing hands and the job of running it changing titles, see Perkins, "Accommodating Strangers," 48–50. Delia Bryson, for instance, took over the Farmer's Hotel previously managed by a man, and under her management it was advertised as a boardinghouse. Ida May Beard (*My Own Life*) gives several examples of Winston-Salem hotels and boardinghouses run by women and men, variously advertised.

22. These stories have been offered by friends Chuck Flynt, Drucie French, and Jay Oglesby; by an attendee of the Townsend lecture I was fortunate to deliver at the University of South Carolina in 2016; at various talks; and even in phone messages left at my University of North Carolina at Chapel Hill office. I thank every person who has shared a story from their life with me.

CHAPTER 1

1. For biographical details on Randolph, see Hess's "Historical Notes and Commentaries" in the facsimile edition of *The Virginia Housewife*.

2. Russell, *Domestic Cook Book*, 5. This could change. US archives have not systematically preserved ephemera like cookbooks well, and mainstream archives have not historically valued and collected materials from communities of color. As archival practices change, materials are being discovered. We cannot, however, know how many have been permanently lost. Only two copies of Russell's cookbook are known. None of Russell's papers or records have been found. Jan Longone detailed a thorough search for records of Russell's life in the introduction to the 2007 facsimile edition of Russell's *Domestic Cook Book*. Despite her lifetime as a curator and researcher, after failed research trips and genealogical work, Longone reluctantly concluded, "All we know about Malinda Russell is what she tells us" (vii). See also Monica Burton, Osayi Endolyn, and Toni Tipton-Martin, "The Legacy of Malinda Russell, the First African-American Cookbook Author," Eater.com, February 23, 2021, https://www.eater .com/22262716/malinda-russell-author-a-domestic-cookbook.

3. For biographical details, see "Leslie, Eliza, 1787-1858," Feeding America: The Historic American Cookbook Project website, Michigan State University Libraries, accessed April 5, 2023, https://d.lib.msu.edu/msul:41. See also Diamond, *Mrs. Goodfellow*; and Myers, *Forging Freedom*, 23, 94–99. Eliza Lee of Charleston, South Carolina, forged a similar career path in the 1820s. She learned pastry skills from her mother, and she passed them on to others. She ran at least four boardinghouses between 1840 and 1851 with her husband; after his death, she operated a restaurant and continued her baking and catering businesses. During this era, at least seven other Black women earned their living as pastry cooks in Charleston, as documented by Shields, *Southern Provisions*, 112–15, and *Culinarians*, 84–88. See

also Elias, *Food on the Page*, 11–15; John T. Edge's "Boardinghouse Ruminations" in Wilkes, *Mrs. Wilkes*, 11–14; Mitchamore, *Miss Mary Bobo's Boarding House Cookbook*, 9–12; and Claiborne, *Feast Made for Laughter*, 21–28. On Elizabeth Beard, see the "About James Beard" section on the James Beard Foundation website, accessed March 15, 2019, https://www.jamesbeard.org/about/james-beard; and James Beard, *Delights and Prejudices*. On Sarah Elliott, see Shields, *Culinarians*, 6.

4. Walden, *Tasteful Domesticity*, 82–112. Stokes and Atkins-Sayre make a parallel argument about the constitutive role of food in southern identities for individuals (*Consuming Identity*, 5, 21–49).

5. On the possibility of American cuisines, see Mintz, *Tasting Food*, 92–105. A recent version of the argument about southern cuisine comes from Kim Severson, "The North Carolina Way," *New York Times*, January 28, 2015, D1. Decades earlier, Egerton made similar claims about eating at home and slow restaurant development in *Southern Food*, 27–31.

6. Shields has led the counterargument on port cities and resorts in both *Southern Provisions* and *Culinarians*. Shields also has begun research on the role of early agricultural journals and nurseries. On celebrity chef cookbooks, see Tippen, *Inventing Authenticity*, 109–48.

7. On the movement of the idea of the South, see McPherson, *Reconstructing Dixie*, 1–37; and Taylor, *Circling Dixie*, 197–201. Boardinghouse examples include Holdredge, *Mammy Pleasant's Cookbook*; and James C. Young, "The Boarding-House Era Goes with 'Miss Mary's': Lodgings That Southerners Patronized on Their Way to Fortune Disappear before New Trends," *New York Times*, October 18, 1925, SM4. The Carolina House for American tourists in Havana, Cuba, was profiled in "A Trip to Cuba and the Southern States, No. 5" *Horticulturist and Journal of Rural Art and Rural Taste*, October 1, 1857, 442.

8. Hess, "Historical Notes and Commentaries," x–xii; Hess, "Mary Randolph"; Kierner, *Beyond the Household*, 203–7.

9. Hess, "Mary Randolph"; Leni Sorensen, "Queen Molly: The *Virginia Housewife* and the Unsung Heroines of Her Kitchen," unpublished talk, 2014, draft in author's possession, n.p.; Randolph, *Virginia Housewife*, 15, 129.

10. Mordecai, *Richmond*, 97; Sorensen, "Queen Molly," n.p.; Deetz, *Bound to the Fire*, 99–109; Randolph, *Virginia Housewife*, 17.

11. David was fired in 1801 or 1802. The biography "Randolph, Mary, 1762–1828," on the Feeding America: The Historic American Cookbook Project website, Michigan State University Libraries (https://d.lib.msu.edu/msul:52), gives the earlier date; Hess ("Historical Notes and Commentaries," xi), the later.

12. The dismissive sister-in-law is discussed in Sorensen, "Queen Molly," n.p. See also "Randolph, Mary, 1762–1828." Hess ("Historical Notes and Commentaries," xi) says 1808; the bio on the Feeding America website says 1807 for opening the house. Mordecai, *Richmond*, 97–98.

13. Ferris, *Edible South*, 88. The styling of the word "housewife" changes across the many editions, sometimes appearing as "house-wife" on the title pages; for consistency, I silently amend them all to "housewife."

14. Hess, "Mary Randolph"; Ferris, *Edible South*, 86–89; Egerton, *Southern Food*, 19; Shields, *Southern Provisions*, 145; Randolph, *Virginia Housewife* (facsimile ed.), 63 (barbecue shote), 37 and 72 (catfish), 135 (field peas). Rice recipes are throughout, as are other local fish and vegetable recipes. See Herman, *South You Never Ate* (119–36), on ducks in mid-Atlantic foodways.

15. Sorensen, "Queen Molly," n.p.; Mordecai, *Richmond*, 45.

16. Mordecai, *Richmond*, 45, 313–14. Shields traced more than 100 records of establishments across Virginia for the period 1785–1830 in the newspapers of the state. These show a robust marketplace of businesses, from suppliers to caterers to restaurants and boardinghouses (unpublished research, shared with the author).

17. Sorensen, "Queen Molly," n.p.; Randolph, *Virginia Housewife* (facsimile ed.), ix–xi, 142–43.

18. Walden is primarily interested in the "decidedly republican discussion of the role of women and domesticity in shaping American society" that Randolph emphasized. Walden, *Tasteful Domesticity*, 39; Vester, *Taste of Power*, 54–57.

19. Trollope, *Domestic Manners*, 283–84.

20. Trollope, *Domestic Manners*, 297.

21. Maria Georgina Milward, "Mrs. Sad's Private Boarding-House," *Southern and Western Literary Messenger and Review*, November 1846, 692. Milward signed her story "Oswichee, Ala." She wrote frequently for the publication, always identifying herself as a southerner. It is unclear in which city the story was set (the only clue: the main character travels by a two-day stage trip from his country home to it).

22. Gunn, *Physiology of New York Boarding-Houses*, xvi–xviii.

23. "An Unpleasant Reminiscence," *American Monthly Knickerbocker*, November 1864, 477–78.

24. On cartoons, songs, and jokes, see for instance O. Wilde Dusenbury and X. Tennyson Quackenbos, "Selections from Patience, or, The Impatient Starvelings," *Virginia University Magazine*, October 1882. Also, see Puck's Library, *Great American Boarding House*, 26. On Gilbert and Sullivan, see "If You Want a Receipt" from their operetta *Patience* (Gilbert & Sullivan Very Light Opera Company, accessed April 5, 2023, http://gsvloc.org/about-us/gilbert-sullivan-revised/patience/). See chapter 8 for Mary Hamilton's positive interpretation of hash.

25. As ubiquitous then as mother-in-law jokes were in the mid-twentieth century or viral memes are today. Quevedo, "Trotting Sausages: The Prime Country and the Boarding House Brand." *National Police Gazette*, December 28, 1889, 6. The author's pseudonym here roughly translates to "what I see." Puck's Library, *Great American Boarding House*, 4, 8, 25.

26. Pruneless dinners were a major selling point in "Found! The Ideal Boarding-house," *Chicago Daily Tribune*, July 21, 1912, F6. Puck's Library, *Great American Boarding House*, 4.

27. "A Domestic Euclid," compiled by the Students of Vassar College, *Good House-keeping*, August 1903, 181; "Brick Boarding-House Geometry," *Brick*, June 1, 1905, 303. The piece also appeared in *Life* magazine, the *Southern Pharmaceutical Journal*, and the *Unitarian Register*, among many other places. Moritz and Moritz, *Leacock*, 124–39; Gerald Lynch, "Stephen Leacock," Canadian Encyclopedia, June 17, 2010,

updated by Jules Lewis on March 1, 2019, https://www.thecanadianencyclopedia.ca /en/article/stephen-leacock.

28. See Longone's introduction to Russell, *Domestic Cook Book*, n.p.; and Tipton-Martin, *Jemima Code*, 18–20.

29. Russell, *Domestic Cook Book*, 3. The issue of Liberia in the nineteenth century is complex and much discussed. See, for instance, Clegg, *Price of Liberty*.

30. Russell, *Domestic Cook Book*, 3–4.

31. Aron, *Working at Play*, 16–19. Russell does not specify but for reasons outlined by Pryor in her *Colored Travelers*, I tentatively conclude that Russell's guests were most likely white or passing for white, not fellow free Black travelers on holiday. Pryor, *Colored Travelers*, 44–53.

32. Russell, *Domestic Cook Book*, 3–5. See also Sharpless, *Grain and Fire*, for a history of baking in the southern United States.

33. Russell, *Domestic Cook Book*, 3–5. On legacies of violence in Tennessee during and after the Civil War, see Tom Lee, "The Lost Cause That Wasn't," in Slap, *Reconstructing Appalachia*, 293–322.

34. Civitello, *Baking Powder Wars*, 15; Strasser, *Never Done*, 242–62; Goldstein, *Creating Consumers*, 23–34.

35. Russell, *Domestic Cook Book*, 7, 15, 24, 31–33.

36. Sharpless, *Cooking in Other Women's Kitchens*, 65–87.

37. Cobble, *Dishing It Out*, 34–58. Della McCullers, discussed in chapter 8, outlined struggles of isolated laundry workers in a changing midcentury south.

38. Randolph, *Virginia Housewife* (facsimile ed.), ix–xi. Cookbook scholars have also discussed the rising popularity among inexperienced housekeepers of printed cookbooks like Randolph's. While a white middle- or upper-class woman likely encountered cookbooks as "a reader, rather than a worker," in Elias's words (*Food on the Page*, 15), the texts could still serve to instruct. Reflecting increasing mobility of US consumers and concomitant shrinking of extended family connections, cookbooks filled in skills that previously may have been learned through conversation and mentorship. Whereas women living near older generations or family members could learn cooking or management skills and recipes because they could work at the elbow of more experienced cooks or senior women directing work in families, women who moved and who had nuclear family connections at most may have been more likely to learn those same lessons from a purchased cookbook. Other contributing factors to the rise of popularity for cookbooks in nineteenth-century US culture included armchair colonialism (see Hoganson, *Consumers' Imperium*, 105–51), community philanthropy (see, among others, Bower, *Recipes for Reading*, 1–14), and participation in food and protest movements (see Walden, *Tasteful Domesticity*, 113–42; and Shprintzen, *Vegetarian Crusade*, 134–39).

39. Sorensen, "Queen Molly," n.p.; Randolph, *Virginia Housewife* (1838), xi.

40. Randolph, *Virginia Housewife* (1838), xi–xii.

41. Walden, *Tasteful Domesticity*, 32, 49; Deetz, *Bound to the Fire*, 5; Ferris, *Edible South*, 87.

42. "Domestic Life in South Carolina," *Provincial Freeman* (Chatham, Canada West), February 16, 1856 (dateline Columbia, SC, January 8, 1856). Chapter 4 explores

Mary Ellen Pleasant and the political activism funded by her boardinghouses. She sent funds to Canada West, out of which Mary Ann Shadd Cary published the *Provincial Freeman*.

43. Smedes, *Memorials of a Southern Planter*, 33.

44. Shields, *Southern Provisions*, 114–15. Similar networks persisted in Virginia, as seen, for instance, in the work of fried chicken vendors for rail passengers documented in Williams-Forson's *Building Houses Out of Chicken Legs*. Tunis Campbell and Robert Roberts, hotel manager and butler, respectively, documented Black men's efforts to build networks as well. See Campbell, *Hotel Keepers*; and Roberts, *House Servant's Directory*. The memoir of Rhode Islander Elleanor Eldridge, who built a domestic service business in the 1830s, could also fit in this pantheon of documentarians of networks (Whipple with Eldridge, *Memoirs of Elleanor Eldridge*).

CHAPTER 2

1. This was, of course, none-too-subtle nineteenth-century code for being his mistress. See Houston diary, February 4 and 6, 1870, Alice Lee Larkins Houston Papers, 1859–1877, #05022, Southern Historical Collection, Wilson Library, University of North Carolina at Chapel Hill (hereafter Houston diary). Alice had several names over the course of her life: Larkins, Houston, and Quinn. Her family, who eventually donated her diary to the Southern Historical Collection, refers to her as Alice (or Allie) Larkins, so I have chosen to do so throughout as well. The identity of Fanny as "parlor maid" is added in pencil in a different hand on the first page of the diary; it is consistent with internal evidence in Larkins's diary entries. I have been unable definitively to determine Fanny's race. Thanks to KC Hysmith and the Blackwell family for research assistance.

2. Wolfe, *Look Homeward, Angel*, 16, 43.

3. Julia's papers are in archives at the Thomas Wolfe Memorial State Historic Site (and I am deeply grateful for the staff's help), and at the University of North Carolina at Chapel Hill. Papers related to Thomas are at Harvard and at UNC-Chapel Hill, and both Julia and daughter Mabel appear in the archives of Wilma Dykeman at the University of Tennessee. Thanks to Danielle Dulken for research assistance. Jim Clark and the Thomas Wolfe Society also deserve my thanks. "Thomas Wolfe's Parents: W. O. Wolfe and Julia E. Westall," *The Ledger* 8, no. 1 (January 2005): 1–7, Thomas Wolfe Memorial State Historic Site, Print Archives, Asheville, NC.

4. Houston diary, February 6, 1870. Her grave in Wilmington's Oakdale Cemetery records her birthdate as March 2, 1840. See New Hanover County Cemetery Records, Oakdale Cemetery, Wilmington, North Carolina, p. 47.

5. Houston diary, February 6, 1870, and March 4, 1870.

6. Houston diary, February 12 and 18, 1870. Silkenat has sorted out the family relations; I follow him and the Blackwell family research in naming Mr. and Mrs. B to be Larkins's cousins the Burnetts (Silkenat, *Moments of Despair*, 191). The Lillington referred to in the diary was most likely the family's Lillington Hall, about twenty miles from Wilmington, not the town further inland.

7. Houston diary, March 8, 1870, and May 6, 1870.

8. Houston diary, July 20 and 30, 1870, and August 18, 1870. I have not been able to confirm what the illness was, but given the era and the coastal location, typhoid, yellow fever, or a similar tropical summer disease is a good bet. It is possible Larkins's doctors feared she had consumption, given her descriptions of lung problems. See, for instance, Willoughby, *Yellow Fever*, for an exploration of diseases in southern port cities. While Willoughby studies New Orleans, cities like Wilmington suffered the same waves of illnesses and civic responses.

9. Houston diary, September 15 and 20, 1870, and November 10, 1870.

10. Archival traces of southern boardinghouse keepers almost always represent women well established in their careers, looking back on life, recounting old feelings and memories. Larkins's diary is important because we see her decision-making in real time. The Federal Writers' Project interviews of McCullers and Gordon discussed in chapters 3 and 8 and the cookbooks of Randolph and Russell are all examples of boardinghouse keepers looking back and remembering their state of mind when they opened their establishments. Larkins worried in her diary over a sister who had "fallen" or "strayed," so Larkins must have been keenly aware of the risks of being unprotected by southern patriarchal systems (see Houston diary, November 13, 1870, and May 12, 1871). That sister was the mother of Rose, the niece staying with Alice.

11. I have puzzled over the phrase "no sedentary life." Does Larkins mean her doctors told her to keep active? Is it a sentence revised midway through: "no [activity]" rethought as "sedentary life," meaning her doctors advised she should think of passing her days indoors? Regardless, the important details are, first, that a boardinghouse was her conclusion and, second, that her doctors seem to have been wrong at least in the sense that she would go on to live many more years. Houston diary, November 19, 1870.

12. Houston diary, November 19, 1870, and January 1, 1871.

13. Houston diary, January 10, 1871. On "Biddy" or Bridget stereotypes about domestic work, part of the general prejudice shared by many Americans against Irish immigrants, see Strasser, *Never Done*, 164–72. For Rose's relation to Alice, about which the diary is confusing, I am indebted to the Blackwell family's own research.

14. Mrs. Stayclose, "Household Economy: Trials of House-Keepers," *Southern Cultivator*, July 1872, 278–79. Written contemporaneously with Larkins's diary, Mrs. Stayclose (clearly a pseudonym) recommended ways to manage household tasks at a time when domestic help was in flux (as many Black men and women were seeking any job other than domestic work for white families in the post–Civil War South). Her comments countered "mistaken northern sisters" who were beginning to lobby for equal rights, instead suggesting that southern women should teach other southern women the art of managing hard work well. For more on *Mrs. Hill's Southern Practical Cookery and Receipt Book*, see Ferris, *Edible South*, 91.

15. Houston diary, July 25, 1870.

16. See Cecelski and Tyson, *Democracy Betrayed*; and Umfleet, *Day of Blood*.

17. Albert Rhodes, "Woman's Occupations," *Galaxy: A Magazine of Entertaining Reading*, January 1876, 45–55. Rhodes was a diplomat and man of letters; this piece discussed results of the 1870 Federal Census and his opinions about women wearing makeup, longing for nice houses, and choosing the wrong careers and his faith that

equal pay was not deserved yet but would "naturally" come about in the future. The *Galaxy* published literary lights like Mark Twain, Henry James, and Walt Whitman. That Rhodes and the *Galaxy* turned to boardinghouses showed their ubiquity in US culture. See "Rhodes, Albert, Obituary," *New York Sun*, April 6, 1894, 3. On the cultural impact of the *Galaxy*, see Scholnick, "'Culture' or Democracy."

18. Maria Georgina Milward, "Mrs. Sad's Private Boarding-House," *Southern and Western Literary Messenger and Review*, November 1846, 690–91.

19. Milward, "Mrs. Sad's Private Boarding-House," 692. Edgar, the young clerk, profoundly misunderstood codes of flirtation and love in the boardinghouse; rejection by a female boarder combined with the clerkship his mother forced him to take despite not being suited for it led to early death. In addition, Mrs. Sad's ministrations once he fell ill consisted of begrudging, poor-quality broth and willful neglect. No one mourned his death. Milward, "Mrs. Sad's Private Boarding-House," 697–98; Gunn, *Physiology of New York Boarding-Houses*, 54–57. These ideals were, of course, profoundly racially coded; they reflected few women's lived realities. But they were still powerful images and expectations. See Welter's classic "Cult of True Womanhood" for a recitation of nineteenth-century expectations that at least some women were prey to.

20. Rhodes, "Woman's Occupations," 45.

21. Sparks, *Capital Intentions*, 10.

22. For a history of domestic science and home economics, see Goldstein, *Creating Consumers*; and Shapiro, *Perfection Salad*. Marion Harland, "How to Be a Successful Boarding House Keeper," *Louisville Courier-Journal*, October 20, 1907, B4; Anna Green, "Making the Boarding-House a Business," *Boston Cooking School Magazine of Culinary Science and Domestic Economics* 18, no. 7 (1914): 542–45; Laurine Marion Krag, "How I Made a Boarding-House Successful: Based on Twenty Years' Experience," *Ladies' Home Journal*, April 1906, 34. Edward Bok, in the lead editorial for the October 1891 issue of *Ladies' Home Journal*, wrote,

> In brief, you must be a good financier; you must know how and what to buy; you must be versed on all the seasons and what those seasons bring to the market; you must have a correct knowledge of men and women, and know how to meet their tastes; you must be a manager in all that that term implies; you should be an expert housekeeper, as everything you have ever known about housekeeping will seem little enough to you; you must be economical and yet not parsimonious; your bump of executive ability must be unusually well developed; you must know how to perfect an excellent domestic system, and train others to adhere to it; you must be a thorough disciplinarian to your servants, and possess the utmost suavity for your boarders; you must have a mind to remember the past, think of the present, and look into the future; an artistic taste must be yours, and your knowledge how to please people must be keen and accurate.

One fears what he would say if not trying to be brief. Edward Bok, "At Home with the Editor," *Ladies' Home Journal*, October 1891, 12.

23. Mrs. S. T. (Sarah Tyson) Rorer, "The Boarding-House Table," *Ladies' Home Journal*, November 1899, 29.

24. Rorer, "Boarding-House Table," 29; Harland, "How to Be a Successful Boarding House Keeper." Rorer and Harland were two of the three leading lights in turn-of-the-century home and cooking advice columns. For biographies of each, see "Harland, Marion, 1830–1922," Feeding America: The Historic American Cookbook Project, Michigan State University Libraries, accessed April 5, 2023, https://d.lib.msu.edu/msul:47; and "Sarah Tyson Rorer," Pennsylvania Center for the Book, accessed April 5, 2023, https://pabook.libraries.psu.edu/literary-cultural-heritage-map-pa/bios/Rorer__Sarah_Tyson.

25. My favorite piece of advice from Krag is to make sure all your dresses have pockets (because you need to carry your purse with you at all times, she says, but really, just good advice in general). Krag, "How I Made a Boarding-House Successful," 34.

26. Green, "Making the Boarding-House a Business," 542–45.

27. Houston diary, January 25 and 28, 1871, and March 13, 1871. If "rattle-snake without the i" is a colloquialism or popular culture reference, it is lost to me today. I have left it in the text because it shows Larkins's wittiness and cutting assessment of her boarder's personality.

28. Scholars of northeastern boardinghouses agree, with Gamber and Faflik finding high proportions of single women keepers. Gamber, *Boardinghouse in Nineteenth-Century America*, 39, 50; Faflik, *Boarding Out*, 46; Gunn, *Physiology of New York Boarding-Houses*, 79, 86, 124.

29. In his study of debt in North Carolina, Silkenat estimated the Civil War created "20,000 widows in North Carolina and more than 100,000 across the Confederacy." Silkenat, *Moments of Despair*, 186–94; Houston diary, February 4, 1870, and July 10, 1871.

30. For biographical information, see Clapp, *Notorious Woman*.

31. Royall, *Southern Tour*, vol. 1, 122, 143; vol. 2, 6, 32.

32. Houston diary, February 21, 1870, and March 1 and 8, 1870. Marriage equality activists like Lucy Stone and even more radical free love theorists such as Victoria Woodhull were actively developing ideas of companionate marriage in which partners were intellectual and emotional equals, both contributing equally to their marriage (Goldsmith, *Other Powers*). See also Broussard, *Stepping Lively in Place*.

33. Houston diary, January 28, 1871, April 18, 24, and 26, 1871, and May 1 and 5, 1871.

34. Houston diary, April 22 and 29, 1871, and May 12, 1871. Perhaps she should have stuck with her first impression of S: "He is what I despise above all things—a regular fop, egotist and cynic with one of the most licentious faces I ever saw" (Houston diary, April 17, 1871).

35. Houston diary, May 7, 1871. The *Oxford English Dictionary* shows wider senses of the word "tasty" than today's uses: an example from 1905 deployed it as "fastidious"; earlier in the nineteenth century it was used to mean "displaying good taste, elegant"; and in 1899 it was being used as "attractive, pleasing." See, *OED* Online, s.v. "tasty (adj.)," accessed October 2016, http://www.oed.com/view/Entry/198070?redirectedFrom=tasty&.

36. Houston diary, June 16, 1871. Mr. S wasn't all bad. They had moments of delighted flirtation: Walking with Mr. S, "on the way some of my garments came unfastened and I executed what I considered a splendid coup de etat to cover the

accident but in vain—'Julian' (I like that name) gave me a quiet intimation that he *could* a 'tale unfold'" (May 23, 1871). The diary does not outline the precise events that precipitated Julian S's final exit from Larkins's life. On July 20, 1871, she wrote, "Another letter, like a sunbeam. . . . What am I to think? Surely fate must have a hand in this strange work? . . . What"—but the page is torn and four subsequent pages are missing from the journal. Larkins's next entry begins on September 20, 1871, and Larkins does not explicitly mention S again.

37. Houston diary, October 29, 1871, and November 6, 1871.

38. Della McCullers, subject of chapter 8, talked through her own economizing with food.

39. Silkenat's research showed Larkins disappears from city directories by 1872. She married John Quinn in June 1872 (North Carolina, U.S., Marriage Records, 1741–2011 [database], accessed April 5, 2023, Ancestry.com). It's likely she closed her boardinghouse after her remarriage.

40. "Thomas Wolfe's Parents," 5, 7; Joe Wakefield, "Recollections of Spruce Street," 1–2, Thomas Wolfe Memorial State Historic Site, Print Archives, Asheville, NC.

41. Wolfe, *Look Homeward, Angel*, 42; "Thomas Wolfe's Parents," 5, Thomas Wolfe Memorial State Historic Site, Print Archives, Asheville, NC.

42. Cobble, *Dishing It Out*, 49; Poley-Kempes, *Harvey Girls*, 57. As the life of Mary Ellen Pleasant will attest in chapter 4, Black women with cooking skills (or assumed ones) could find opportunities through travel as well.

43. "World's Fair Schemes," *Railway Age and Northwestern Railroader*, January 29, 1892, 81. I was fortunate to deliver the Townsend lecture at the University of South Carolina as I was working on this chapter. An audience member (I regret I did not get her name) told me the story of an aunt who wanted to visit Asheville but could not afford to go from her home in coastal South Carolina. The aunt rented a house in Asheville for the season and opened a boardinghouse; her plan was successful enough that she repeated it, summering in Asheville for many years. Julia would have been impressed.

44. Wolfe purchased real estate around Asheville as well as some in Miami, Florida. She also scouted locations in St. Petersburg, Florida, and Hot Springs, Arkansas, although she did not buy them. "Thomas Wolfe's Parents," 5, 7; Joe Wakefield, "Recollections of Spruce Street," 1–2, Thomas Wolfe Memorial State Historic Site, Print Archives, Asheville, NC.

45. For an overview of Old Kentucky Home, see "The House, 1880s–1950s," Thomas Wolfe Memorial State Historic Site webpage, accessed April 5, 2023, https://wolfememorial.com/history/the-house-1880s-1950s/.

46. Perkins, "Accommodating Strangers," 76.

47. Wolfe, *Look Homeward, Angel*, 103. "Gabular" here seems to simply mean a gabled roof.

48. North Carolina resorts often advertised "northern style" cooking and service. See also *Southern Pines, N.C.*

49. *Visitors Guide to Asheville, North Carolina*, 36, 45, 48, 51, 59, 65, 66.

50. "Thomas Wolfe's Parents," 5, 7.

51. Wolfe, *Look Homeward, Angel*, 56.

52. See Locklear, *Appalachia on the Table*; and Wolfe, *Look Homeward, Angel*, 106–12.

53. Wakefield, "Recollections of Spruce Street," 1–2.

54. Wakefield, "Recollections of Spruce Street," 1–2; "Thomas Wolfe's Parents," 7. In Wilma Dykeman's words, "With the usual perverseness of humanity, the people of Asheville did not seem shocked at much of the deceit and folly and wickedness and waste that Wolfe found—they were shocked only that he exposed it." She continued, "Whether or not the people of his home town appreciated or understood, they came alive, the family that lived in that rambling boardinghouse, the family that Tom Wolfe knew and distilled into another fictional family" (*French Broad*, 223–25).

55. Julia Wolfe, Ledgers, 1906–1920s, Thomas Wolfe Memorial State Historic Site, Print Archives, Asheville, NC.

56. Eliza Gant's racism and hard business approach made African Americans disinclined to work for her—here again, space between fictional character and woman is useful. Historian Jill Cooley wrote eloquently about the virulence of white southerners' Jim Crow era beliefs about how African Americans would contaminate foods in southern restaurants merely by being customers and the lengths to which white people's fantasies went—dangers of smoke or smells passing from a man's cigar or food into a woman's nose, for instance (*To Live and Dine in Dixie*, 62–63). Martha Hinton, who is discussed in chapter 5, had reactions that were more purely separatist: when her second husband wanted to hire a Black cook, she refused because "I wouldn't eat a biscuit they had their black hands in" (Travis Tuck Jordan, "Martha Hinton—A Good Woman," December 9, 1938, 9, Thaddeus Ferree Papers on the North Carolina Federal Writers' Project, 1935–1941, #4258, Southern Historical Collection, Wilson Library, University of North Carolina at Chapel Hill). Race in Wolfe's novel is fraught. On the surface, perhaps its greatest contribution was to document what census records and demographics hinted at: the landscape of class divisions and the physical layout of southern small cities, like Asheville, brought residents of different races and ethnicities in contact with each other, especially around support industries like boardinghouses, groceries, cafés and restaurants, general stores, laundries, and bars.

57. "Houston, Alice Larkins," marriage certificate, North Carolina, U.S., Marriage Records, 1741–2011 (database), Ancestry.com; Alice Lee (Mrs. George P.) Quinn, Oakdale Cemetery Burial Record, May 9, 1891, Wilmington, NC, accessed April 8, 2023, https://www.oakdalecemetery.org/burial-database; Houston diary, August 18, 1870, May 5, 1871, and June 10, 1871. I visited the cemetery where Larkins is buried; photos are in author's possession.

58. "Thomas Wolfe's Parents," 6; "Old Kentucky Home," North Carolina Historic Sites webpage, accessed March 15, 2018, http://www.nchistoricsites.org/wolfe/OldKyHome.htm.

CHAPTER 3

1. Cooke and MacGowan, *Aunt Huldah*; Cooke, *Power and the Glory*. For their time in New Jersey, see Buchan, *Utopia*; and for their time in California, see Dramov, *Carmel-by-the-Sea*.

2. The interview with Texie Gordon was conducted by Grace McCune for the Federal Writers' Project, "The Boarding House Operator," Subseries 1.3 Georgia, folder 223, Federal Writers' Project Papers, 1936–1940, #3709, Southern Historical Collection, Wilson Library, University of North Carolina at Chapel Hill.

3. On early college living arrangements, see Lindemann, "The School Day and the School Year," in *True and Candid Compositions*, https://docsouth.unc.edu/true /chapter/chp03-02/chp03-02.html.

4. Cooke and MacGowan, *Aunt Huldah*, 209.

5. Cooke and MacGowan, *Aunt Huldah*, 54–55. Labor arrangements in the boardinghouse reflected the casual racism of Texas and the wider South (including the authors'): "There was a Mexican hired for the kitchen work, or a Chinaman, or whatever the mistress of the house could secure, all the incumbents being temporary, and so regarded by her" (60).

6. Cooke and MacGowan, *Aunt Huldah*, 31–32, 206, 309–14.

7. Cooke and MacGowan, *Aunt Huldah*, 63, 213, 263–64.

8. Cooke and MacGowan, *Aunt Huldah*, 111, 255.

9. Leong, while focusing on early modern England, usefully defined the "household" as a site of people "living and working together as a collective," expansive enough for later centuries' boardinghouses too (*Recipes and Everyday Knowledge*, 10). Hill, *Mrs. Hill's Southern Practical Cookery*, 360–96, quote on 395, italics in original; Russell, *Domestic Cook Book*, 37–39.

10. Russell, *Domestic Cook Book*, 38–39.

11. Cooke and MacGowan, *Aunt Huldah*, 281.

12. Travis Tuck Jordan, "Martha Hinton—A Good Woman," December 9, 1938, Thaddeus Ferree Papers on the North Carolina Federal Writers' Project, 1935–1941, #4258, Southern Historical Collection, Wilson Library, University of North Carolina at Chapel Hill; Maria Georgina Milward, "Mrs. Sad's Private Boarding-House," *Southern and Western Literary Messenger and Review*, November 1846, 692.

13. Gaston, "MacGowan Girls," 119.

14. Buchan, *Utopia*, 10, 23–25; Gaston, "MacGowan Girls"; Cooke, *Power and the Glory*, x–xv. Earlier Alice had briefly worked in Texas as a governess, so some descriptions benefited from what she had seen there. *Aunt Huldah* went into its second edition three years later, in 1907. Note that Gilman did not necessarily agree with Sinclair's interpretation of her writings (Buchan, *Utopia*, 25).

15. See for instance the University of North Carolina at Chapel Hill's Southern Historical Collection's list of McCune interviews, https://finding-aids.lib.unc .edu/03709/#d1e1723.

16. McCune, "Boarding House Operator," 2–3. Census records show Gordon was married at age sixteen to Jim Gordon, six years her senior. "Gordon, Texie A.," Mill, Madison, Georgia, 1900 United States Federal Census (database); and "Gordon, Texie A.," Mill, Madison, Georgia, 1910 United States Federal Census (database), both accessed April 5, 2023, Ancestry.com. The 1910 census added that Gordon had four children, three of whom were living.

17. McCune, "Boarding House Operator," 3.

18. McCune, "Boarding House Operator," 11–12.

19. McCune, "Boarding House Operator," 11–12. Recall Jane Austen in *Persuasion* portrayed "Mrs. Smith," a school friend of Anne Elliott. Widowed and an invalid, Mrs. Smith spent her last money to get to Bath in hopes that the waters would cure her. She arrived already ill: "She had caught cold on the journey, and had hardly taken possession of her lodgings, before she was again confined to her bed, and suffering under severe and constant pain; and all this among strangers." Her landlady's kindness in taking her in and connecting her with a nurse, the landlady's sister, "proved to her that her landlady had a character to preserve, and would not use her ill" (Austen, *Persuasion*, 206). Nurse Rooke not only helped Mrs. Smith heal, but she also played a small role in revealing the negative character of Anne's cousin, who was bent on seducing Anne.

20. McCune, "Boarding House Operator," 12. Abbie M. Brooks, sick in a boardinghouse where the keeper was a drunk, wrote in her diary on July 15, 1870,

> Mr. Butler would give me no water or rather allow no one to do it. I had mine from yesterday dinner until today at about 12—nearly 24 hours. Mr. Butler came into the room about ten o'clock—my mouth so parched I could not speak. He got me some water. I told him to send for Miss Vick Wilson which he did. He met her and told her he believed I was crazy and to be careful of me. Miss Vick came in and gave me some water, sat by me. I kept trying to get better until evening just before sun set when she came for me and I went home with her.

Abbie M. Brooks, Diaries and Church Invitation, 1858–1870, ahc0039f-001, Kenan Research Center at the Atlanta History Center.

21. Salinger, *Taverns and Drinking in Early America*, 39.

22. James Rees, "The Gold Chain: A Passage in the Life of Lafitte," *New World: A Weekly Family Journal of Popular Literature, Science, Art, and News*, October 17, 1840, 305. The story as a whole is about an encounter between boarders and a notorious pirate, Lafitte, the "terror of the ocean."

23. In her interview titled *The Sunshine Lady*, Mrs. Neille Wesenger spoke to Ada Radford in Augusta, Georgia, in 1939 about keeping a boardinghouse and then finding herself kept in one. Wesenger had been in a wheelchair for thirty-seven years, but during that time she had "rented a house with twenty-nine rooms, and every bit of it that was not required for the family, I furnished for my boarders." Wesenger ran the house for fifteen years, but once her stepchildren were married and gone and her husband passed away, she ended up in the county home. Even though she was now a tenant, not the keeper or matron, Wesenger continued caring for others: "When one of them is seriously ill I stay awake at night and see that his medicine is given on time, measuring the dose myself to make sure it's right. When one dies, I have an electric switch on my bed, and I ring for the matron." She also provided spiritual counsel (Wesenger was Catholic; Radford's interview is shot through with the anti-Catholicism of her time, so this was presented as surprising). Almost completely immobile from debilitating degenerative arthritis and misguided treatments of it, she was still cheerful: "If I was a complaining, faultfinding person with a tale of woe to tell everyone, I would soon lose all of my friends and nobody would want to come

about me." Ada Radford, Leila H. Harris, and Neille Wesenger, *The Sunshine Lady*, Georgia, December 4 and 29, 1939, 9, 1–14, Federal Writers' Project Papers, Library of Congress, Washington, DC.

24. M. M., "The Old Landlady's Album," *Catholic World*, July 1891, 528–42.

25. Radford, Harris, and Wesenger, *Sunshine Lady*, 13–14. On Keckley's support, see "Merriweather Home for Children," Cultural Tourism DC (website), accessed April 5, 2023, https://www.culturaltourismdc.org/portal/merriweather --home-for-children/elizabeth-keckly-african-american-heritage-trail; Carleton Fletcher, "The Colored Home," Glover Park History (website), accessed April 5, 2023, https://gloverparkhistory.com/estates-and-farms/burleith/the-colored-home/; and Jordan Grant, "Elizabeth Keckly: Businesswoman and Philanthropist," *O Say Can You See? Stories from the Museum* (blog), National Museum of American History (website), March 22, 2016, https://americanhistory.si.edu/blog/elizabeth -keckly-businesswoman-and-philanthropist.

26. Southworth, *Self-Raised*, 80. For more on nineteenth-century concepts of the self-made man, see Rotundo, *American Manhood*. For an astute analysis of the interplay between women, men, and the law in *Ishmael* and *Self-Raised*, see Stockton, "E. D. E. N. Southworth's Reimagining." On Southworth's biography, see Homestead and Washington's introduction to *E. D. E. N. Southworth*.

27. Southworth, *Self-Raised*, 21, 37, 82. They communicated care with food: "The kind old maiden ladies also bestirred themselves earlier than usual this morning, that their young favorite should enjoy one more comfortable breakfast before he left." Rather than "weak, muddy coffee and questionable bread and butter of the railway restaurant," Ishmael "received a summons to the dining room, where he found his two hostesses presiding over a breakfast of Mocha coffee, hot rolls, buckwheat cakes, poached eggs, broiled salmon, stewed oysters, and roast partridges." Never one to land a subtle point, Southworth made it obvious: "Our young man had a fine healthy appetite of his own, and could enjoy this repast as well as any epicure alive; but better than all to his affectionate heart was the motherly kindness that had brought these two delicate old ladies out of their bed at this early hour to give him a breakfast. They had their reward in seeing how heartily he ate." They sent him off with a packed hamper of food. Jenny Downing handed it to him saying, "There's ham sandwiches and chicken pie, and roast partridges and fried oysters, and French rolls and celery, and plenty of pickles and pepper and salt and things. And I have put in some plates and knives and napkins, all comfortable" (Southworth, *Self-Raised*, 78–79).

28. McCune, "Boarding House Operator," 6, 10.

29. McCune, "Boarding House Operator," 7, 11–12.

30. McCune, "Boarding House Operator," 13.

31. McCune, "Boarding House Operator," 13–14.

32. In fact, the rival keeper "kept going from bad to worse, and a few years ago she was so up against it that she drank poison and died before they could get her to the hospital," a sobering moment in the interview. McCune, "Boarding House Operator," 4.

33. Royall, *Southern Tour*, vol. 1, 84–87, 140–42. Smaller schools also created close ties with nearby boardinghouses. Louisburg, North Carolina, had both male and female academies from the early 1800s onward (the female academy's formation in

1815 put it among the first wave of women's higher education efforts in the nation). President Matthew Smart Davis, who had worked with the male institution beginning in the 1870s, took the reins of the female academy in 1896. He worked hard to outline "Boarding House Regulations" for his rowdy boys boarding. Get twenty-five "faults" and one was kicked out of school; take longer than ten minutes to dress, receive two faults; miss church on Sunday, three faults; "go out with any serenading party or go down street after night," a full ten faults (Matthew Smart Davis, "Boarding House Regulations," Matthew Smart Davis Papers, 1851–1914, #4125, Southern Historical Collection, Wilson Library, University of North Carolina at Chapel Hill).

34. Silkenat, *Moments of Despair*, 178–79; Eyre, *Profiles of Chapel Hill*, 295–97.

35. Eyre, *Profiles of Chapel Hill*, 296.

36. Chapel Hill, for instance, admitted women in 1897 but did not build its first female dorm until Spencer Hall in 1925; in this the school was not unusual. Eyre, *Profiles of Chapel Hill*, 250–51, 265, 316. Fraternities and sororities are in many ways still boardinghouses. They offer food, lodging, and the emotional support this chapter discusses.

37. Dudley W. Crawford, Ethel Deal, and Joe Matheson, "Joe Matheson. North Carolina, 1939," 1–6, Federal Writers' Project Papers, Library of Congress, Washington, DC.

38. Even when most students moved into dormitory housing, some held to the boardinghouse model. Fraternity and sorority houses (which pointedly kept the name "house") retained a house mother, as well as full kitchens, headed up by cooks. Those persist into the present day.

39. McCune, "Boarding House Operator," 19.

40. Texie Gordon first appeared in Athens, Georgia, city directories as a nurse in 1923–24 (*Piedmont Directory Company's Athens . . . 1923–1924*, 243); she was listed as a boardinghouse keeper by 1926–27 (*Piedmont Directory Company's Athens . . . 1926–1927*, 167); she remained listed as such until 1958, after which she disappeared from the directories On her death and burial location, see "Texie Gordon," Georgia, U.S. Death Index, 1919–1998 (database), Certificate 27195; and Find a Grave Index, 1600s–Current (database), both accessed April 8, 2023, Ancestry.com. My thanks to Kimber Symone Thomas for research help.

41. Cooke, *Power and the Glory*; for biographical details, see my introduction to Cooke, vii–xxxii.

CHAPTER 4

1. Hudson, *Making of "Mammy Pleasant,"* 34, 58. I rely heavily on Hudson's excellent work for the biographical research that follows, as she is such a thoughtful interpreter of the myriad myths and stories that circle Mary Ellen Pleasant. By contrast, a day's wage in New York City at the time was around two dollars. Steve Boggan, "Gold Rush California Was Much More Expensive than Today's Tech-Boom California," *Smithsonian Magazine*, September 30, 2015, https://www.smithsonianmag.com/history/gold-rush-california-was-much-more-expensive-todays-dot-com-boom-california-180956788/). On the million-dollar figure, see Hudson, *Making of "Mammy Pleasant,"* 97.

2. For biographical details on Surratt, see Larson, *Assassin's Accomplice*. The story of Booth and the conspiracy has received popular and scholarly treatment in almost every decade since the assassination; some of the works have aged better than others.

3. Hudson, *Making of "Mammy Pleasant,"* 18–22. Mary Ellen first married a man named Smith with whom she shared abolitionist work. She was soon widowed, but he left her with money. Her second husband was John James Pleasants (at some point in their journey to California, both Mary Ellen and John dropped the final *s* from their now-shared last name). John Pleasant is also difficult to trace in the historical record, but we can document that he worked as a cook in the sailing industry. They had a long marriage, but Mary Ellen spent her final years on her own after he passed away.

4. Sparks, *Capital Intentions*, 51; Hudson, *Making of "Mammy Pleasant,"* 32.

5. Hudson, *Making of "Mammy Pleasant,"* 32–35.

6. Hudson, *Making of "Mammy Pleasant,"* 56–61.

7. Hudson, *Making of "Mammy Pleasant,"* 24–43.

8. Tubman's and Jacobs's stories are (rightly) well celebrated. Brown and the Crafts both published narratives (as *Narrative of the Life of Henry Box Brown* and *Running a Thousand Miles for Freedom*, respectively). Still's work is *Underground Railroad*. Colson Whitehead's 2016 novel and now television adaptation, *Underground Railroad*, has brought the story much more into public discourse.

9. Still, *Underground Railroad*, 235–40, 112–17, 182–87. This was a twist on the exploration of boardinghouse transformations that will be discussed in chapter 6.

10. Hudson, *Making of "Mammy Pleasant,"* 37–39. See also McGinty, *Archy Lee's Struggle for Freedom*, 117–18; and Lapp, *Archy Lee*, 27–28, 63–64. The historic marker was erected by the African American Historical and Cultural Society; see "Mary Ellen Pleasant Memorial Park, 1814–1904," Historical Marker Database, February 7, 2023, https://www.hmdb.org/m.asp?m=85557.

11. Hudson, *Making of "Mammy Pleasant,"* 38–41. Another side of the politics in boardinghouses involved labor rights. As Strasser wrote, "People who both lived and worked together enjoyed an intimacy that united them, making them more likely to resist their employers; homes full of boarders furnished safe places for workers to plan strikes or sabotage or simply to offer each other support" (*Never Done*, 156). The politics discussed in this chapter share boardinghouse space if not eras with such strike planning.

12. Hudson, *Making of "Mammy Pleasant,"* 51–55. Pryor tracked cases in the Northeast in the prewar era that established "Jim Crow cars" on railroads and ships; Pleasant's later case centered on San Francisco streetcars but shared a core resistance to "legalized foreclosure on free black access to public space" (*Colored Travelers*, 95). Hudson, *Making of "Mammy Pleasant,"* 45–47, 63–78.

13. Hudson, *Making of "Mammy Pleasant,"* 4.

14. Versions of Pleasant's story that traded in stereotypes included Holdredge's *Mammy Pleasant's Cookbook* and Asbury's *Barbary Coast*. Hudson devoted her final chapter to popular culture representations of Pleasant after her death (*Making of "Mammy Pleasant,"* 98–116).

15. Hudson, *Making of "Mammy Pleasant,"* 60–61.

16. Asbury, *Barbary Coast*, 14; "Mammy Pleasant: Angel or Arch Fiend in the House of Mystery," *San Francisco Call*, May 7, 1899. Asbury specialized in crime writing.

Perhaps best-known today as the author of *Gangs of New York*, he turned his attention to the San Francisco underworld. Hudson, *Making of "Mammy Pleasant,"* 33.

17. Hudson, *Making of "Mammy Pleasant,"* 33–34.

18. Wallace-Sanders, *Mammy*, 4, 59. Note that Wallace-Sanders did not discuss Pleasant specifically. Manring had earlier argued that the "literary and historical" mammy always contained "a nest of internal contradictions," which created space under its rubric for many women even when they exhibited characteristics outside central stereotypes. While Wallace-Sanders distinguished between the early nurse-maid mammy and the later cook Aunt Jemima, sometimes called a mammy, Manring suggested the cooking remained consistent from earliest appearances of a mammy figure. It does not especially matter here, as Pleasant was technically neither and yet was assumed to be both. Manring dated the creation of the Aunt Jemima character to slightly earlier minstrel stage performers upon which Quaker Oats based its advertising campaign. Manring, *Slave in a Box*, 8, 20, 61.

19. The cultural fascination with voodoo, Marie LaVeau, and sensational stories of African American hidden knowledge has persisted through 1970s Blaxploitation films, post-*Roots* Pan-Africanism, and scholarly and community explorations of circum-Atlantic networks. See, for instance, Missouri, *Black Magic Woman*; and Cartwright, *Sacral Grooves*.

20. Holdredge, *Mammy Pleasant's Cookbook*, 5, 26–39. The finding aid for the Holdredge Collection (at the San Francisco History Center, San Francisco Public Library) lists recipe books purported to be by Pleasant. Hudson, *Making of "Mammy Pleasant,"* 5. Walden made a similar point in her chapter "Taste and Race." Black women were constrained by a "history of domestic service and cultural associations with physicality, instinct, and sexuality" that excluded them from conversations about taste as an intellectual marker of class and accomplishment. Walden, *Tasteful Domesticity*, 144.

21. Note that Tipton-Martin took *Mammy Pleasant's Cookbook* mostly at face value as a document of Pleasant's travels and recipes learned through them (*Jemima Code*, 2, 102). At the same time that Nancy Green debuted at the 1893 World's Fair in Chicago acting the part of a quintessential natural cook Aunt Jemima, New York gadfly Ward McAllister staged a cooking competition between an unnamed "southern cook" (probably a Black man in Savannah whose food McAllister had eaten earlier that year) and a French-trained New York chef. McAllister declared the chef the clear winner, calling him an "artist" while giving the losing cook a backhanded compliment. The cook was "as nature made him," merely possessing "wonderful natural taste." McAllister figured himself as the arbiter of taste in New York, at one point deeming there to be only 400 people who mattered. He, of course, was one of them. Levenstein, *Revolution at the Table*, 14–15; McAllister, *Society as I Have Found It*, 99–101.

22. For details on Hercules and Hemings, see A. Miller, *President's Kitchen Cabinet* (60–76), but note the more recent analysis that has disproved the portrait used on the cover. Craig Laban, "George Washington's Enslaved Chef," *Philadelphia Inquirer*, March 1, 2019, https://www.inquirer.com/food/craig-laban/george-washington-slave -chef-cook-hercules-gilbert-stuart-painting-wrong-20190301.html. See also Shields's *Culinarians* and Tipton-Martin's profiles of early publications (*Jemima Code*, 10–21).

23. Hudson, *Making of "Mammy Pleasant,"* 57–58; Shields, *Culinarians*. Additional manuscript resources shared with author; my deepest thanks to David for this generosity.

24. On Pleasant's access to San Francisco's dirty laundry, see Hudson, *Making of "Mammy Pleasant,"* 55–57; and Asbury, *Barbary Coast*, 14–15. On "dirty laundry" and the association of Black women with it in American culture, see Engelhardt, "Listening to Black Appalachian Laundrywomen."

25. Hudson, *Making of "Mammy Pleasant,"* 34–35.

26. Sharpless, *Cooking in Other Women's Kitchens*, 16.

27. Cooper, *Voice from the South*, 254. As Sparks said, "Women who sold boarding and cooking services provided a kind of 'commercial domesticity' that substituted for the more-personal kind of domestic nurturing that most men received from their sisters, mothers or wives" (*Capital Intentions*, 119–20). Of course, significant numbers of women—poor, unmarried, not mothers, women of color, and women from certain religions or regions—were seen to not take care of their own families correctly. For more on the rhetorical attempt, see Collins, *America's Women*, 208–11.

28. Hudson, *Making of "Mammy Pleasant,"* 9.

29. Hudson, *Making of "Mammy Pleasant,"* 57–62.

30. Hudson, *Making of "Mammy Pleasant,"* 57–58.

31. James C. Young, "The Boarding-house Era Goes with 'Miss Mary's': Lodgings That Southerners Patronized on Their Way to Fortune Disappear before New Trends," *New York Times*, October 18, 1925, SM4. On the concept of southern hospitality, see Szczesiul, *Southern Hospitality Myth*, especially 130–67.

32. Gunn, *Physiology of New York Boarding-Houses*, 124–25. Jefferson Williamson profiled two southern hotels well known in New York City: the Planters and the New York Hotel (*American Hotel*, 264). Later in life, Mary Todd Lincoln tried to convince her former dressmaker Elizabeth Keckley to accompany her to New York, avoiding the nicest hotels while selling her clothing to support herself. Keckley, *Behind the Scenes*, 93. On the undercurrent of untidiness, Olmsted found the same. He came south expecting to find southern hospitality, and much of his tour involved his horror at not finding luxury but instead only meager food and rough lodgings of working-class folks just getting by (and occasional land- and person-rich enslavers whose greed or cash-poor existence led to the same outcome). His fantasy of New England hospitality was a "family room . . . curtained and carpeted and glowing softly with the light of sperm candles or a shaded lamp. When I entered it, I could expect that a couch or an armchair, and a fragrant cup of tea, with refined sugar, and wholesome bread of wheaten flour, leavened, would be offered me." He dreamed of music, a good book, "a clean, sweet bed, where I could sleep alone and undisturbed, until possibly in the morning a jug of hot water should be placed at my door, to aid the removal of a traveller's rigid beard." His dream was capped off with "a royal breakfast," sending him back onto the road. But in the South, he found

not only none of those things, received none of those attentions, but I saw and met nothing of the kind. Nine times out of ten, at least, after such a promise, I slept in a room with others, in a bed which stank, supplied with but one sheet, if with any; I washed with utensils common to the whole household; I found no garden, no flowers, no fruit, no tea, no cream, no sugar, no bread (for corn pone—let me assert in parenthesis, though possibly as tastes differ, a very good thing of its kind for ostriches—is not bread: neither does even flour, salt, fat, and water, stirred together and warmed, constitute bread); no curtains, no lifting windows (three times out of four absolutely no windows), no couch—if one reclined in the family room, it was on the bare floor—for there were no carpets or mats. For all that, the house swarmed with vermin. There was no hay, no straw, no oats (but mouldy corn and leaves of maize), no discretion, no care, no honesty.

It was a hard lesson to swallow for the intrepid traveler. Olmsted, *Cotton Kingdom*, 519–20.

33. "Boarding-house Keepers from the South," *Atlanta Constitution*, May 7, 1871, 2, signed "Cor. N. Y. Times." Such emphasis extended to establishments in other locations that touted "southern hospitality." Miss Rosie, for example, was too delicate to settle disagreements among her staff at her New York boardinghouse, so she either shipped all back to Kentucky (summarily replacing them with people unwillingly relocated from there) or relied on "hoping" that boarders "got sumpin' to eat at lunch" when cooks refused to make dinner. "Mis' Rosie," *Milwaukee Journal*, June 30, 1899, 7. See also Halttunen, *Confidence Men and Painted Women*.

34. The growing popularity of advertising's Aunt Jemima and the "cozy racial nostalgia" she embodied "extends an invitation for all Americans to remember a time when Aunt Jemima cooked for the national family." The Jemima figure "is attributed with awakening a national remembrance of southern domesticity." Wallace-Sanders, *Mammy*, 62.

35. Steers, *Blood on the Moon*, details in photo essay following 176.

36. Steers, *Blood on the Moon*, 228–30.

37. Larson, *Assassin's Accomplice*, 18, 21. The twists and turns of the conspiracy are complex and a subject of much debate by historians and writers. I'm far from an expert, nor is my goal here to make a definitive claim about the unfolding events of the plot. However, the high-level pass I do give is to foreground the boardinghouse and Surratt's use of it for political purposes.

38. The Maryland structure is now a historical site and museum ("About the Museum," Surratt House Museum [website], accessed April 5, 2023, https://www .surrattmuseum.org/surratt-house-museum).

39. Larson, *Assassin's Accomplice*, 39–42, 56.

40. Larson, *Assassin's Accomplice*, 3.

41. Royall, *Southern Tour*, vol. 1, 42, 51–52. All italics in the original unless otherwise noted.

42. *Directory of the Names*.

43. Carson, *Ambitious Appetites*, 138–42.

44. Gelderman, *Free Man of Color and His Hotel*, 46–51, 106–9.

45. DeForest, *Honest John Vane*, 67.

46. See, for instance, Marszalek, *Petticoat Affair*.

47. Steers, *Blood on the Moon*, 138–39, 177, 228–29. As I worked on this project, a different Washington, DC, place of lodging from which political activities were planned entered the national news cycle. That hotel, the Trump Hotel, is located less than three-quarters of a mile away from Surratt's house.

48. Hudson, *Making of "Mammy Pleasant,"* 93–98.

49. Hudson, *Making of "Mammy Pleasant,"* 10. The converse assumption was also true: Americans, especially in the nineteenth century, had a hard time seeing the Black population of Nantucket. Mainstream media, from novels to music to theater, put African Americans in the South and did not center Black lives elsewhere in the United States. Sojourner Truth's Afro-Dutch, New York childhood disappeared into her abolitionist activism, much as Pleasant's New England–Canadian one vanished into the San Francisco millionaire's stories. See Painter, *Sojourner Truth*, 6–8.

50. Karen Cox, "Remembering the Civil War with Confederate Hair," UNC Press Blog, April 13, 2011, https://uncpressblog.com/2011/04/13/remembering-the-civil-war-with-confederate-hair/. See also her full-length book *Dixie's Daughters*.

51. A Sufferer, "A Plea for Poor Boarding-house Keepers," *Louisville Courier-Journal*, October 18, 1874, 2.

52. Hudson, *Making of "Mammy Pleasant,"* 99–116. See also Yerby, *Devilseed*; Cliff, *Free Enterprise*; and Asbury, *Barbary Coast*.

CHAPTER 5

1. Travis Tuck Jordan, "Martha Hinton—A Good Woman," 1, December 9, 1938, in the Thaddeus Ferree Papers on the North Carolina Federal Writers' Project #4258, Southern Historical Collection, Wilson Library, University of North Carolina at Chapel Hill.

2. Jordan, "Martha Hinton," 15. While most white southerners of Hinton's era were racist by today's standards, she was even by standards of her time. She wouldn't touch or eat anything touched by a Black person. Her family enslaved people whom she claimed did not want to be freed, and she had a bad experience with a Black midwife who drank through a long night of Hinton's labor; her venom from those experiences was profound.

3. Jordan, "Martha Hinton," 1, 15. Many of the Federal Writers' Project interviews assigned pseudonyms. Sometimes (as with Texie Gordon in chapter 3), both name and pseudonym were listed in archival cover material for the interview. That was not the case with Hinton.

4. I am working on a longer project about Walker and the trial ("Hopping Down the Line: The Life and Times of Lola Walker," work in progress); here I focus on how her aunt's boardinghouse was the gravitational center of a life-changing moment in a teen girl's life.

5. "A Sensation Was Started," *Robesonian* (Lumberton, NC), June 30, 1905, 1; "High Jinks Told of by Witness in Walker-Edwards Case," *Nashville American*, July 22, 1906, 7; "Kissing and Hugging," *Nashville American*, July 24, 1906, 6.

6. "Kissing and Hugging," 6; "Orators at Bar at Union City," *Nashville American*, July 28, 1906, 5; "Stories about Lola Edwards," *Nashville American*, July 29, 1906, 10.

The *Nashville American* assigned a reporter to the trial, and his columns were printed daily through its duration, although he did not get a byline for them. Coverage can also be found in the *Asheville (NC) Citizen-Times*, *Charlotte Observer*, *New York Times*, *Chicago Tribune*, and *Louisville Courier-Journal*, among others.

7. Travis Tuck Jordan Papers, 1929–1941, #3503, Southern Historical Collection, Wilson Library, University of North Carolina at Chapel Hill. Jordan's papers cross the era of her Federal Writers' Project work, but the poems are undated.

8. Even in this white-to-white interview, Jordan "interrupted her here to ask if she remembered anything about the Civil War"—a forced moment in the story as Hinton was three when the war began. For a full discussion of the racial politics at play, see Stewart, *Long Past Slavery*, 11–61. At least one assistant in the national office voiced criticisms of Jordan's style of writing up particularly her African American interviews (the assistant mistook Jordan for a man), saying Jordan "misjudges the subject of the enterprise, and gives himself to the compilation of blood-and-thunder yarns" (Hirsch, *Portrait of America*, 158).

9. Jordan, "Martha Hinton," 1.

10. Jordan, "Martha Hinton," 1.

11. Jordan, "Martha Hinton," 1–2.

12. Jordan, "Martha Hinton," 3.

13. Jordan was from Person County as well, but sharing this did not seem to connect the two women. Jordan Papers, 1929–1941, newspaper clipping, folder 1; Jordan, "Martha Hinton," n.p., insert between 3 and 4.

14. Jordan, "Martha Hinton," 5–6, 10, 16.

15. See, for instance, Bone and Link, *Creating and Consuming the American South*; Huber, *Linthead Stomp*; Hale, *Making Whiteness*; and Ownby, *American Dreams in Mississippi*. For portraits of the emotional draw of such items, see Anderson, *Kit Brandon*; and Cooke, *Power and the Glory*. Jordan, "Martha Hinton," 9–10.

16. Jordan, "Martha Hinton," 11–15.

17. Jordan, "Martha Hinton," 16.

18. Jordan clearly asked Hinton about "diet"; Hinton interpreted that as "dieting." That would not have been an uncommon shift for the time. See, for instance, de la Peña, *Empty Pleasures*; Levenstein, *Revolution at the Table*; and Biltikoff, *Eating Right in America*. DuPuis wrote about changes to and fortification of milk in the United States in *Nature's Perfect Food*. Cabbage, fried onions, and collards were an "everybody knows how to cook" option, with boiling for long hours the most common choice. They fell into the category of smelly country foods, the very ones Flannery O'Connor's characters with social class aspirations try to get away from in "A Good Man Is Hard to Find," *Complete Stories*, 117–33. Related to Hinton's reluctance to embrace new food preparation technologies (gas or electricity), she probably would judge shortcuts and pre-processed foods promoted in those early twentieth-century "diets" sinful as well. This deeply conservative woman saw no need for change, for time saving, or for vanity. Diets for slimming, strengthening, and health were reaching mainstream audiences through magazines, radio, university outreach programs, and advertising, the very sources she studiously avoided. While 1939 was near the

beginning of what would become a tidal wave of such attention, Hinton signaled her resolve to resist even the early stages of food and body consciousness.

19. Jordan, "Martha Hinton," 15.

20. Jordan, "Martha Hinton," 15.

21. Engelhardt, *Mess of Greens*, 32–39. See also Odem, *Delinquent Daughters*, 95–127; Stoneley, *Consumerism and American Girls' Literature*, 2–4; Nash, *America's Sweethearts*; and Hunter, *How Young Ladies Became Girls*.

22. Zipf, *Bad Girls at Samarcand*, 4; Jordan, "Martha Hinton," 15.

23. Zipf, *Bad Girls at Samarcand*, 45, 54.

24. Jordan Papers, 1929–1941. Jordan lived much of this time in one of Raleigh's hotels that offered long-term accommodations. Her correspondence was on stationery from the Bland Hotel. When she wrote of the interior lives of boardinghouses, she knew some of which she spoke.

25. Jordan "Martha Hinton," 10–16; Jordan Papers, 1929–1941, folder 13.

26. Jordan, "Martha Hinton," 11–13; Jordan Papers, 1929–1941, folders 7, 12. Cooke also used the image of shoes meant not for work but for pleasure to stand in for a young girl's dreams of a different life. Mavity Bence saved her daughter's dancing slippers, shoes worn when she committed suicide in despair about being trapped for life in cotton mills, to remember her (*Power and the Glory*, 136).

27. Asheville society was nervous about what the trial would reveal. See "Little Lola's Suit for Big Damages Is Now on Trial," *Asheville Citizen-Times*, January 7, 1906, 5; and "New Features in Lola Walker Case," *Asheville Citizen-Times*, October 3, 1905, 14.

28. "Lively Time in the Court Room," *Nashville American*, July 25, 1906, 2. Dr. G. S. Tennent testified that he knew Lola by sight; he saw her out late at night a couple of times and feared she was on her way to the Battery Park Hotel but never subsequently saw her there. Finally, he weighed in on her horseback riding activities (the defense was trying to use that to argue her wildness).

29. Alexander, *Around Biltmore Village*, 14; "Mrs. Gilbert Tennent Dead," *Asheville (NC) Daily Citizen*, July 17, 1899, 1. Mrs. S. S. Tennent is hard to find in the historical record, but she appears to be the Marianne R. Martin who married Samuel Tennent in Buncombe County on September 6, 1877 ("Martin, M. R.," North Carolina, U.S., Marriage Records, 1741–2011 [database], accessed April 8, 2023, Ancestry.com). He later married Ada Henry on July 4, 1893 ("Samuel S. Tennent," Tennessee, U.S., Marriage Records, 1780–2002 [database], accessed April 8, 2023, Ancestry.com). By the time Walker came to live with her aunt on Montford, the author Mrs. S. S. Tennent had passed away and her widower, Samuel, had moved to Georgia with his new wife. "Sam'l. S. Tennent Died Yesterday," *Asheville Citizen-Times*, April 7, 1908, 5. But in the 1880s, *Godey's* celebrated Marianne Tennent as one of its star authors, advertising that "original tales, novels, short stories and serials will be given during the year by the following writers of national reputation" and listing Mrs. S. S. Tennent prominently ("To Subscribers for 1887," *Godey's Lady's Book*, November 1886, n.p.); however, she does not seem to have published beyond their pages. Historian Nan Enstad argued that working girls like Lola were more likely to grab dime novels and sensational

newspapers than middle-class aspirational "high" culture magazines like *Godey's*, the *Atlantic*, or *Harper's* (Enstad, *Ladies of Labor*).

30. Mrs. S. S. Tennent, "Among the Mountains," *Godey's Lady's Book*, September 1882, 219.

31. Tennent, "Among the Mountains," 220.

32. Tennent, "Among the Mountains," 223.

33. Virginia Gunn Fick and Richard D. Starnes, "Resorts, Part 2: The Resorts of Western North Carolina," NCPedia, 2006, https://www.ncpedia.org/resorts-part -2-resorts-western. Tennent detailed her knowledge of the region, both the city life of Asheville and the wilderness opportunities for fashionable day trips in the surrounding mountains. Characters discussed streetcars, neighborhood amenities, and railroad connections. Caesar's Head, Buck Forest (now called DuPont State Forest), Beaucatcher Mountain, Pisgah, and the Blue Ridge ("stretched forth in all the beauty of its soft changing hues from the dark blue . . . to the hazy purple, and overtimes pink, thrown over mountains and valleys by the freaks of sun and sky and clouds") made appearances in the piece. The group traveled to Caesar's Head through the town of Brevard, by "Conistee" (now Connestee Falls), up Cedar Mountain, and then down to the hotel at Caesar's Head. Tennent listed the waterfalls in Buck Forest—"Bridal Veil Falls, the Triple Falls, and last the High Falls," all places still called by the same names and still places both locals and tourists visit for hikes, picnics, and romance. Tennent, "Among the Mountains," 244–48.

34. Tennent, "Among the Mountains," 252.

35. Rob Neufeld, "Visiting Our Past: First Battery Park Hotel Opens in 1866," *Asheville Citizen-Times*, July 6, 2014.

36. The menu collection of the New York Public Library offers ample evidence of the decadence Asheville offered. See "What's on the Menu?," New York Public Library Labs, accessed April 5, 2023, http://menus.nypl.org/.

37. Both Cullen and Walker are included in *Hill Directory Company's Directory of Asheville, N.C., 1904–1905*, 82, 258. Cullen was living at 103 Montford but perhaps working for her mother, Mrs. Abbie Overton, listed as primary for the street address in 1902, according to *Hill Directory Company's Directory of Asheville, N.C., 1902–1903*, 63, 163. By 1906, Cullen identified herself as "proprietor" (*Hill Directory Company's Directory of Asheville, N.C., 1906–1907*, 76. Overton was discussed in "Evidence Is Being Piled Up at Union City," *Asheville Citizen-Times*, July 31, 1906, 6.

38. "Fair Plaintiff Ends Her Story of Wrongs," *Nashville American*, July 15, 1906, 20; "Walker-Edwards Case Drags On," *Nashville American*, July 27, 1906, 5; "High Jinks Told Of by Witness in Walker-Edwards Case," 7; "Edwards on the Stand," *Nashville American*, July 26, 1906, 8; "Mas. [*sic*] Cullen's Reputation Is Now Assailed," *Asheville Citizen-Times*, July 20, 1906, 2.

39. Walker claimed Edwards requested the photos "for his den at home." She posed in fencing clothing and in reenactments of famous works of art such as *The Model's Rest*. In rebuttal, lawyers wrangled over whether she was "in the all-together" for other photographs. "Fair Plaintiff Ends Her Story of Wrongs," 20. See also "Defendant's Inning," *Nashville American*, July 21, 1906, 3, in which the photographer, C. F. Ray, testified. On horseback rides, see "High Jinks Told Of by Witness in Walker-Edwards

Case," 7; and "Lively Time in the Court Room," 2, in which Dr. G. S. Tennent added that the red skirt was "divided." The trial was a veritable list of turn-of-the-century transportation options, buggies, carriages, coupes, tallyhos, bikes, and horses. New York City plans were discussed on the stand by all sides, with Edwards and Walker joined by testimony from Cullen, Weaver, a railroad porter, Edwards's New York friends, and more.

40. For Cullen's testimony of the dramatic night elopement, see "Walker-Edwards Case," *Nashville American*, July 18, 1906, 8. The "Pullman conductor," Paul Jones, confirmed Cullen's actions and said Lola told him she was "on her way to New York to meet and marry a man named Edwards." See "For the Plaintiff," *Nashville American*, July 19, 1906, 2. Examples of the articles Cullen placed during Walker's flight include "Seeking a Trace of Her Eloping Niece," *Raleigh News and Observer*, August 27, 1903, 5; and "Girl Elopes from Asheville," *Raleigh Morning Post*, August 25, 1903, 2. Boardinghouses were often a first stop for eloping couples. Two decades later, Montague wrote a poignant scene in her 1923 novel *Deep Channel* where the main character fled her small West Virginia town for the anonymity of larger Richmond, Virginia. Julie and Bixby, the married man with whom she eloped, posed as a married couple and experienced happiness, living in a modest boardinghouse, with three rooms of their own: "a sitting room, a kitchen, and at the back a bedroom." But it was not sustainable. Soon, their life in Richmond faced "complete shattering." Bixby was arrested as a draft dodger; Julie went home (167–68).

41. "Asheville Girl Jilted," *Charlotte News*, August 2, 1905, 3. The Asheville papers covered the elopement as it happened, in "Eloped from Asheville," *Asheville Citizen-Times*, August 25, 1903, 5; "Wants to Be a Leading Lady," *Asheville Citizen-Times*, September 8, 1903, 8; and "Stage-Struck Girl," *Charlotte News* via *Asheville Daily Citizen*, September 9, 1903, 3. Others picked up the story once she was found in New York, such as "Miss Lola Walker," *Wilmington (NC) Messenger*, September 10, 1903, 2; and "Little Lola's Suit for Big Damages Is Now on Trial," *Asheville Citizen-Times*, January 7, 1906, 5.

42. Mary Barrel's testimony was reported in "Orators at Bar at Union City," 5. Agnes Dasmann and Josephine Sawyer followed her; see "Stories about Lola Edwards," 10. The suit brought in 1905 was reported in papers across the South, such as "Breach of Promise Suit," *North Carolinian* (Raleigh), June 29, 1905, 3; and "Special to the Washington Post," *Wilmingtonian* (Wilmington, NC), February 18, 1905, 2, which had the dateline of Union City, Tennessee. Dick Avesta Edwards married Lulie Gibbs on October 5, 1904 (Tennessee, U.S., Marriage Records, 1780–2002 [database], accessed April 8, 2023, Ancestry.com).

43. The threat was reported in "Dragging Along," *Nashville American*, July 13, 1906, 9. "Lively Time in the Court Room," 2, detailed a fistfight that broke out between sheriffs and spectators during the trial, during which Walker fainted and the *Nashville American* reporter rescued two stenographers from the fray.

44. Will Beard, "Why Boarding-House Keepers Sigh for the Coming of Spring," *Nashville American*, December 13, 1897, 3. Names in the piece were crafted for humor—Mrs. Butterine (evoking controversial margarines sweeping the country), Mr. Cornfield (who ate too much chicken until he fell in love), and perhaps even Will Beard

(if he followed the tradition of humor columnists taking pseudonyms—Doesticks or Mark Twain, for instance).

45. "High Jinks Told Of by Witness in Walker-Edwards Case," 7.

46. In the early decades of the 1900s, Asheville city directories listed two Black women named Hattie Morgan who identified their profession as "cook." One, Hattie A. Morgan, was married to Charles E. Morgan (who is listed over time as a laborer, waiter, and butler). The other Hattie Morgan appeared unmarried and was listed separately. See, for instance, *Piedmont Directory Company's Asheville . . . 1914*, 344; "Kissing and Hugging," 6.

47. "Kissing and Hugging," 6. The man Morgan referenced may have been W. N. Cooper, who also gave a deposition and was also discussed as a suitor of Cullen's. See "Defendant's Inning," 3; and "For the Plaintiff," 2.

48. Given that she was referred to with the honorific "Miss," Willis was most likely a white woman in the house. "Servant Did Not Know of Her Husband," *Asheville Citizen-Times*, July 19, 1906, 1; "For the Plaintiff," 2. Both reporters agreed that Willis also testified that women frequently rode astride rather than sidesaddle in Asheville. Lawyers for Edwards were attempting to use Lola's horsemanship as evidence of her wild and loose temperament. Merish, *Archives of Labor*, 27–28.

49. "Depositions in Plenty," *Nashville American*, July 20, 1906, 3; "Walker-Cullen Given Good Names," *Nashville American*, August 1, 1906, 3; "Defendant's Inning," 3; "High Jinks Told Of by Witness in Walker-Edwards Case," 7.

50. Reynolds's deposition, including his lemonade drinking, was covered in "Lively Time in the Court Room," 2. On lemonade, see the 1914 cookbook by Members of the Bradford District Union of the National British Women's Temperance Union's, *Recipes for Temperance Drinks, for Winter and Summer*. In another Asheville neighborhood, Helen Morris Lewis might have had quite an opinion about the drinking choices made by Lola and Mrs. Cullen. Lewis and her sister ran a boardinghouse across town from Cullen's Lynnoaks on what was then Bailey Avenue (today's Asheland Avenue) until 1906. In 1894, Lewis founded the first suffrage organization in North Carolina. Temperance and suffrage work were deeply connected; speakers from the Woman's Christian Temperance Union soon were canvassing North Carolina. See Joyner, "Helen Morris Lewis."

51. "Edwards on the Stand," 8; "Lively Time in the Court Room," 2.

52. Moss's overall argument was that whiskey brands "played an instrumental role in shaping American trademark law." Moss, *Southern Spirits*, 160–62; "Edwards on the Stand," 8; Battery Park Hotel, Asheville, NC, Menu, March 19, 1900, "What's on the Menu?," New York Public Library Labs, accessed April 5, 2023, https://menus.nypl .org/menus/13167. Newspaper accounts of the trial discussed other cocktails being consumed, but they did not specify type. A New York bartender in the second half of the nineteenth century claimed, "North Carolina, Alabama, Louisiana, Tennessee, and other southern states send us great fancy drinkers." He listed "sherry cobblers, mint juleps, brandy smashes, brandy juleps, and bourbon sours" as particular favorites of customers who identified as southerners (Moss, *Southern Spirits*, 177).

53. "Orators at Bar at Union City," 5; later in the trial Walker testified that she did not know what "hopping down the line" was—and she certainly never did it. See "Lola

Walker Takes the Stand," *Nashville American*, August 4, 1906, 2. Comedian George Sidney developed the character "Bizzy Izzy," and, according to a career retrospective article published in the *Louisville Courier-Journal*, he took "his own companies over the burlesque wheels"—in other words, graduated to promoting troupes such as the one Walker joined. "Do You Remember 'Bizzy Izzy' in which George Sidney Was Star?," *Louisville Courier-Journal*, March 21, 1915, C4. He was honored in Louisville at a dinner club and with the article in 1915. In 1917 Tom Bullock, an expert bartender, published his landmark book, *The Ideal Bartender*, the first cocktail book by an African American. In its pages is the Bizzy Izzy High Ball. See Bullock, *Ideal Bartender*, 14.

54. Chudacoff, *Age of the Bachelor*, 7 and 75–76. "The boarder problem" is Addams's term; the description of the threat posed is Chudacoff's summary of Addams's writing on the topic.

55. Chudacoff, *Age of the Bachelor*, 150–52, 166–70; "Special to the *Washington Post*," *Wilmingtonian*, February 18, 1905, 2; Rotundo, *American Manhood*, 124–26; "Kissing and Hugging," 6.

56. On "disorderly houses," see *Oxford English Dictionary*, definition 2.b., accessed April 5, 2023, https://www.oed.com/. In America, the term was in use in the colonial era, with women occasionally being charged with running a disorderly house when they operated taverns where the drinking surpassed community standards. Association with prostitution or simply unmarried sex could be related to such a charge. See Salinger, *Taverns and Drinking in Early America*, 126–29. Silkenat discussed how "Southerners had long associated boardinghouses with prostitution" (*Moments of Despair*, 187).

57. They cannot so easily exclude people who frequented them from town histories, of course, as they are often "town fathers," lawyers, doctors, mayors, senators, and wealthy landowners.

58. Coggeshall, *Liberia, South Carolina*, 77.

59. Wolfe, *Look Homeward, Angel*, 118; "High Jinks Told of by Witness in Walker-Edwards Case," 7. I have yet to find the records of Weaver's arrest in Asheville. Ida Beard (discussed in chapter 7) had a sister who seems to have fallen (or escaped) into prostitution. Beard wrote of Nellie, "I will not go into details in regard to Nellie's flight, as I deem it sufficient to say that she had quite a hazardous one; was found in a penniless condition, and on account of being hatless was held a prisoner at the Cortenia Hotel in Covington, Ky., and was more than glad to be released from her situation." Later, Nellie hesitantly visited her sister late at night to learn details of their father's death. Beard gave her "a piece of good advice" before she left; seven months later Beard received a letter from Nellie saying "she would like to send the children and I something." But Ida "told her that, owing to circumstances, I could not accept the things she had offered me, and hoped that she would not become offended." The evidence of Nellie's "circumstances" is thin, admittedly, but suggestive. Going hatless signaled shame, scandal, and loss of status for women. Being unaccompanied in a hotel in a booming financial and industrial town such as Covington (on the outskirts of the even larger Cincinnati) also was risky for women in the late 1800s. Ida's efforts to maintain her reputation as a respectable mother regardless of financial struggles would have been made more difficult if her sister was known to engage in sex work.

Nellie's perspective was missing—could she have been happy and prosperous once free of her family? Or was her life brutal and dangerous? We do not know. Beard, *My Own Life*, 59, 184–85. On the perils of going without a hat, see Steinberg, *Hatless Jack*.

60. Wall, *Madam Belle*. See Landau, *Spectacular Wickedness*, 138–43, on photography; and Long, *Great Southern Babylon*, 102–47, on efforts to establish Storyville specifically for the purpose of containment. For a sensationalist but contemporary perspective, see Reizenstein, *Mysteries of New Orleans*. See also Guralnick, *Sam Phillips*, 28.

61. Broussard, *Stepping Lively in Place*, 61–67; Myers, *Forging Freedom*, 21. And, of course, not all sex workers identified as women; see, for instance, characters in T. Williams's *Vieux Carré*, discussed in chapter 6.

62. Potter, *Hairdresser's Experience in High Life*, 144.

63. Wall, *Madam Belle*, 61–62.

64. "Large Verdict for Breach of Promise," *Louisville Courier-Journal*, August 8, 1906, 3; "Miss Walker Wins," *Nashville American*, August 8, 1906, 3.

65. On the value of the judgment in today's dollars, see Consumer Price Index Inflation Calculator, Official Data Foundation, Alioth Finance, www.in2013dollars .com, accessed April 6, 2023, https://www.officialdata.org/1906-dollars-in-2018? amount=21000. "A Tennessee Jury," *North Carolinian*, August 16, 1906, 5.

66. Circuit Court Minutes, August 9, 1906, Obion County, roll A-1927, book H, 432–33, 436–37, Tennessee State Library and Archives, Nashville. The judge's phrasing is awkward to nonlegal ears, but the meaning is clear. Interestingly, two pages immediately after the jury verdict and before the judge's overturning of it are missing in the court records. Nonetheless, that records survive at all is remarkable. On their deaths, see "Dick Avesta Edwards," Tennessee, U.S., Deaths and Burials Index, 1874–1955 (database); and "Lulie Gibbs Edwards," Tennessee, U.S., Death Records, 1908–1965 (database), both accessed April 8, 2023, Ancestry.com.

67. "Lola Walker Married," *Charlotte Observer*, January 4, 1907, 1; "Jilted Actress Won by a Printer," *Chicago Daily Tribune*, August 31, 1906, 4; "Chorus Girl Marries Star Witness," *Louisville Courier-Journal*, August 31, 1906, 1. George and Lola had at least one son, William, born in 1909. See Cook County birth records on Ancestry.com. "George Lieferman," *Nashville American*, August 2, 1906, 7.

68. Jordan, "Martha Hinton," 15–16.

69. For details on Cullen's life after the trial, see "Cullen, Lynn," *Piedmont Directory Company's Asheville . . . 1912*, 132, where she was running the Richelieu Hotel. She may have been dividing her time between North Carolina and Florida, because she was also listed in *R. L. Polk and Company's Jacksonville*, 340. She was listed as the proprietor of the Grand Hotel in Miami by 1920, according to the *R. L. Polk and Company's Miami*, 309. In the 1930 federal census, she was living with her mother, brother, and two lodgers in Miami. 1930 United States Federal Census (database), accessed April 5, 2023, Ancestry.com. By the 1935 state census, she listed her occupation as hotel owner: "Cullen, Lynn M.," Florida, U.S., State Census, 1867–1945 (database), accessed April 5, 2023, Ancestry.com. Miami is the city on her death record as well: "Cullen, Lynn M.," Florida, U.S., Death Index, 1877–1998 (database), accessed April 5, 2023,

Ancestry.com. Each entry identified her as the widow of C. J. Cullen, born in Illinois, or as living with people whose family names match those listed in the trial.

70. Jordan, "Martha Hinton," 16.

CHAPTER 6

1. The anecdote about disappearing food came from Slappy White, another of the film's actors, as related in E. Williams's excellent *Humor of Jackie Moms Mabley*, 47.

2. The last name "Gibert" appears only once in the *Washington Post* article. Could it be a typo for Gilbert? Perhaps. The nature of boardinghouses, which was the very reason Frank and Cora were there, has made my efforts to trace them beyond the story unsuccessful. Regardless, for this discussion, I have chosen to stick with the spelling given in the article, "Woman in Guise of a Man: Razor and Revolver Found in Her Trunk by the Police," *Washington Post*, June 28, 1902, 5.

3. On Ward, see "In the Wrong House: A Colored Man's Imposition on a Boarding-house Keeper," *Louisville Courier-Journal*, March 28, 1885, 8. For the heiress story, see "Flare Up at a Fashionable Boarding House," *Baltimore Sun*, March 8, 1849, 1, signed "N.Y. Star." Also, see T. Williams, *Vieux Carré*.

4. Mabley later changed her date of birth to 1894; she used both dates as needs required. Census data supports the later 1897 as accurate; see "Loretter Aiken," 1900 United States Federal Census (database), accessed April 5, 2023, Ancestry.com, which lists "Loretter Aiken" as three years old. Mrs. S. S. Tennent, "Among the Mountains," *Godey's Lady's Book*, September 1882, 244. What would become Brevard Institute in 1903 began in 1895 as the Epworth School. Today's Brevard College, on the same site, was formed in the 1930s by consolidating several regional small colleges. "The History of Brevard College," Brevard College website, accessed April 6, 2023, https://brevard.edu/our-history/. On education for Black Brevard residents, see Reed, *Brevard Rosenwald School*, 43–44. Today the Rosenwald school serves as a community center; a column of news and history called "Rosenwald News" runs regularly in the *Transylvania Times*.

5. M. L. Shipman, "James P. Aiken," *French Broad Hustler* (Hendersonville, NC), September 2, 1909, 4; Hall, "Negroes of Transylvania County," in McCrary, *Transylvania Beginnings*, 173; Reed, *Brevard Rosenwald School*, 139–42.

6. "Chemical Engine Explodes: J. P. Aiken Instantly Killed and Several Others Injured," *Brevard (NC) News*, August 27, 1909, 4. The newspaper was uncertain about what exactly caused the disaster. For my understanding of the equipment, thanks go to Robert Delwiche, chemical engineer and technical research assistant, who is also my father.

7. "Chemical Engine Explodes," 4; Shipman, "James P. Aiken," 4. Such remembrances track with the work of scholars of African American western North Carolina such as Darin Waters or Latoya Eaves. Eaves drew upon Waters's work to point out that race was often figured as invisible and thus unproblematic in the twentieth-century mountains. That invisibility could effectively marginalize Black individuals' contributions. See, for instance, Eaves, "Outside Forces," 147. Eaves extended her

analysis to rural queer Black women in present-day Asheville, thirty miles from Mabley's Brevard.

8. "J. P. Aiken," North Carolina, U.S., Wills and Probate Records, 1665–1998 (database), accessed April 5, 2023, Ancestry.com. See also "Card of Thanks," *Brevard News*, September 10, 1909, 5; "Mary Aiken (successor to J. P. Aiken)," advertisement, *Brevard News*, October 22, 1909, 8; and "Mary M. Aiken," 1910 United States Federal Census (database), accessed April 5, 2023, Ancestry.com.

9. "New Hygienic Restaurant," *Brevard News*, March 18, 1910, 7. Bowen had "leased the rooms at the rear of Mary Aiken's store" for "an up-to-date restaurant" offering "quick lunches and meals on short order" ("Local Paragraphs," *Brevard News*, December 17, 1909, 2). Three months later, Bowen placed a longer ad, saying, "You can get anything the market affords, served in a nice, clean and warm dining room or sent to your place of business in nice style. Call phone 48 or call and be served." He added that fresh breads and cakes were in stock, and he was willing to serve "early or late." The ad was attached to one by Aiken and again noted his location at the rear of her store. See "New Hygienic Restaurant" and "I Have on Hand," *Brevard News*, March 18, 1910, 7. By 1911, Aiken's advertisements offered not only dry goods but also "Fish and Oysters each Wednesday and Saturday" ("What Are You Looking For?," *Brevard News*, January 20, 1911, 7).

10. Hall, "Negroes of Transylvania County," in McCrary, *Transylvania Beginnings*, 173; E. Williams, *Humor of Jackie Moms Mabley*, 42; Leslie Bennetts, "The Pain behind the Laughter of Moms Mabley," *New York Times*, August 9, 1987, H5; Reed, *Brevard Rosenwald School*, 142; Hine, "Rape and the Inner Lives of Black Women," 914–15.

11. Mabley maintained her ties to Brevard for the rest of her life; she may well have had good reason to obscure details of the tumultuous years between her father's death and her exit from town. Two frustratingly brief newspaper entries suggested some of what Loretta faced. In a "Recorder's Court" column in August 1913, the following appeared: "State v. Bunyan Mills, seduction under promise of marriage. Only a superficial examination was made by the recorder in this case. Loretta Aiken, the prosecuting witness, being the only witness examined. The defendant was bound to Superior court under a $400 bond" ("Recorder's Court," *Brevard News*, August 29, 1913, 1). The case appeared a second time, in the newspaper report of superior court: "State v. Bunyan Mills, seduction under promise of marriage. Only the prosecuting witness, Loretta Aiken, was examined in this case[;] after her testimony it was shown that a marriage contract had never existed, and that therefore the defendant was not guilty. The case was dismissed" ("Superior Court," *Brevard News*, September 5, 1913, 1). It was four years, almost to the day, of her father's death.

12. E. Williams, *Humor of Jackie Moms Mabley*, 11, 22.

13. E. Williams, *Humor of Jackie Moms Mabley*, 43–48.

14. Pryor, *Colored Travelers*, 2–3. Recall Mary Ellen Pleasant had sued for access to San Francisco's streetcars in 1867 (Hudson, *Making of "Mammy Pleasant,"* 50–55), the major form of transportation across that booming city. Across the nation, railroad lines and roads made possible the movement of people, ideas, and industry. Women and people of color fought to be included.

15. *Negro Motorist Green Book* (1948), 1, Green Book Collection, Schomburg Center for Research in Black Culture, Manuscripts, and Rare Books Division, New York Public Library, accessed April 8, 2023, https://digitalcollections.nypl.org/collections /the-green-book#. Spanish-language radio in my state of North Carolina today performs similar service, breaking in to note immigration checkpoint locations as well as spreading the word about local yard sales and flea markets where necessities and furnishings might be found for families setting up homes, whether across town or across borders (personal communication, Bill Smith, Chapel Hill, NC, 2017).

16. *Negro Motorist Green Book* (1948), 1; S. M. Fleischman, "Impressions of Asheville," *Jewish Exponent*, December 23, 1892, 2. Geographical descriptions began his article, followed by reviews of Battery Park Hotel, Kenilworth Inn, and the growing Biltmore estate. Reflecting complications of the times, it does include an unfortunate foray into stereotypical and racist descriptions of Black and poor white Asheville "natives," positioning Asheville's substantial and well-established Jewish population as fundamentally still outsiders. Nonetheless, his piece guided fellow travelers.

17. Institute for Southern Jewish Life, "Hendersonville, North Carolina," *Encyclopedia of Southern Jewish Communities*, accessed April 5, 2023, https://www .isjl.org/north-carolina-hendersonville-encyclopedia.html; and advertisement for a Jewish boardinghouse, Jacksonville, 1878, Florida Memory Project, State Library and Archives of Florida, Tallahassee. Long discussed ties between New Orleans and Jacksonville for mixed-race couples in the late 1800s, with comparatively welcoming boardinghouses and neighborhoods (*Great Southern Babylon*, 29–40).

18. Lauterbach, in his study of musicians in the South, pointed out the "term *chitlin' circuit* was strictly a word-of-mouth phenomenon." He found a first use of it in print in 1972 but lots of oral history and lyrical evidence of it circulating earlier in the century. Lauterbach carefully distinguished the story of musicians from that of vaudeville performers such as those with the Theater Owners Booking Association. Business models were related, but performers and managers did not overlap all that much (*Chitlin' Circuit*, 303–4n8, 305n10).

19. Steans, "Black Film Classics"; E. Williams, *Humor of Jackie Moms Mabley*, 47–48. For a full cast list, see *Boarding House Blues*, IMDb, accessed April 6, 2023, https://www.imdb.com/title/tt0040176/.

20. Herbert Ward Wind, "The House of Baedeker," *New Yorker*, September 14, 1975, 42–62; Hatchett, *Duncan Hines*, 53.

21. On the cost of gas in 1935, see "The Cost of Living 1935," The People History website, accessed April 5, 2023, http://www.thepeoplehistory.com/1935.html. Volumes of Green Books cited here can be found in the Green Book Collection, Schomburg Center for Research in Black Culture, Manuscripts, Archives, and Rare Books Division, New York Public Library, accessed April 8, 2023, https://digitalcollections .nypl.org/collections/the-green-book#/?tab=about.

22. Hatchett, *Duncan Hines*, 90–96, 108–9. Gender coding of spinning wheels and quilts needs hardly be unpacked. Hines, *Adventures in Good Eating* and *Lodging for a Night*.

23. Like Green, Hines regularly evoked "danger" as a reason to purchase his *Adventures in Good Eating*. However, the danger that Hines promised to help readers navigate—and that he suggested was life-threatening—was food poisoning. A self-confessed stickler for cleanliness and sanitation, Hines assessed food establishments first and foremost on hygiene practices. But those practices could be found anywhere in the United States, according to Hines, and he urged readers who associated cleanliness with modernity and upscale urban life to venture farther afield. Hatchett, *Duncan Hines*, 43, 53. On racial codes for hygiene and cleanliness, see Cooley, *To Live and Dine in Dixie*, 19–42.

24. Olive Ruth Neal, Autograph Book, 1926–1930, n.p., David M. Rubenstein Rare Book and Manuscript Library, Duke University, Durham, NC. On the fierce competition between baking powder companies, see Civitello, *Baking Powder Wars*.

25. *Negro Motorist Green Book* (1939), 2, and *Negro Motorist Green Book* (1949), 10–11, "The Green Book Collection," Schomburg Center for Research in Black Culture, Manuscripts, Archives, and Rare Books Division, New York Public Library, accessed April 8, 2023, https://digitalcollections.nypl.org/collections/the-green-book#.

26. "Woman in Guise of a Man," 5.

27. Jackson, Keller, and Flood, "Tenderloin," in *Encyclopedia of New York City*, 1289.

28. "Woman in Guise of a Man," 5.

29. Williamson, *American Hotel*, 170–73; "American Boarding-House Sketches," *Catholic World*, July 1885, 455–63. A footnote in part 1 identified "Lady Blanche Murphy" as the posthumous author of the articles. See also "American Boarding-House Sketches. (Concluded.)," *Catholic World*, August 1885, 657–73. When Keckley traveled to New York with Mary Todd Lincoln, she encountered a particularly racist hotel clerk who also "was exquisitely arrayed, highly perfumed, and too self-important to be obliging or even courteous" (*Behind the Scenes*, 93).

30. "She Drew Line on Charge of Taking Men's Apparel," *Atlanta Constitution*, August 2, 1907, 4.

31. "Woman in Guise of a Man," 5.

32. "Miss Medcalf Was after Her Trunk," *Atlanta Constitution*, September 30, 1899, 12. Trunks were big business in the United States around the turn of the century; companies patented new designs, advertisements for the latest were in newspapers and magazines weekly, and their size and weight were fiercely regulated and debated by transport companies. See, for instance, "To Protest Trunk Ruling: Salesmen Call Meeting to Fight New Railroad Excess Charge," *New York Times*, September 12, 1912, 12. In Louisa May Alcott's sensational story "Behind a Mask: or, A Woman's Power," Jean, the main character, knelt "before the one small truck which held her worldly possessions" in the novella's opening pages. The truth hidden in her trunk included fake hair, makeup, false teeth, and drugs to make her pass as significantly younger than she was in order to secure a wealthy marriage and her revenge (*Louisa May Alcott Unmasked*, 367).

33. "In the Wrong House: A Colored Man's Imposition on a Boardinghouse Keeper," *Louisville Courier-Journal*, March 28, 1885, 8. Ward's comment that he was "as white as anybody" may have been a simple statement; it is tempting to read it as a comment

on the inherent mess of definitions of race in the United States, especially given that he paired it with saying he had "not a drop of negro blood in his veins."

34. "In the Wrong House," 8. Scholars working to bring attention to this nuanced practice include Allyson Hobbs with *Chosen Exile*.

35. In 1875, hoteliers in Chattanooga received news coverage for "converting" their establishments into boardinghouses to avoid having to abide by new "civil rights" legislation. See "Civil Rights: Converting Hotels into Boardinghouses in Chattanooga," *Republican Banner* (Nashville), March 7, 1875, 1. Also see Cooley, *To Live and Dine in Dixie*, for a study of how restaurants fought integration over the century; and see Wiltse, *Contested Waters*, on segregated swimming pools and bathing in America.

36. "Mr. Clarence Gower, or, a Peep into a 'Genteel' Boarding House," *United States' Telegraph*, December 10, 1834, 9, 34.

37. "Flare Up at a Fashionable Boarding House," 1, signed "N.Y. Star." Halttunen explored the anxieties and possibilities inherent in anonymity and reinvention in American culture in the second half of the nineteenth century in *Confidence Men and Painted Women*.

38. "Duplicity Punished: 'It Was Love as Did It,' a True Incident of Lowly Life," *Huntsville (AL) Gazette*, June 6, 1885, 4.

39. E. Williams, *Humor of Jackie Moms Mabley*, 11, 43–48.

40. On *Stage Door* and the Rehearsal Club, see Bordman and Hischak, *Oxford Companion to American Theatre*. See also Catherine Van Dyke, "Boarding Houses I Have Met," *Ladies' Home Journal*, January 1917, 12–13.

41. "Famous Bell House Ends Its Career: Mrs. Bell Dismissed Sixty-Four Boarders Tuesday, and Has Retired," *Atlanta Constitution*, June 17, 1897, 5. There are long histories of people in American life enjoying, seeking, and creating homosocial spaces for themselves.

42. Robert Bray, introduction to *Vieux Carré*, by T. Williams, viii.

43. Landau, *Spectacular Wickedness*, 199–206; Long, *Great Southern Babylon*, 103–47. On the long history of the play's creation, see Bray, introduction to *Vieux Carré*, ix.

44. T. Williams, *Vieux Carré*, 4, 36–39, 44, 116.

45. Bray, introduction to *Vieux Carré*, x; T. Williams, *Vieux Carré*, 18–19, 69.

46. Harker, *Lesbian South*; E. Johnson, *Sweet Tea*; Bibler, *Cotton's Queer Relations*.

47. We could fill in a litany of other Black headliners, from bandleader Louis Armstrong to religious and political leader Martin Luther King Jr. to Oscar-winning actress Hattie McDaniel, who faced discrimination at hotels or on the road throughout the mid-twentieth century. For a college town, see Ferris on Martin Luther King Jr.'s visit to Chapel Hill (*Edible South*, 262).

48. Those reputed lovers included the writer Zora Neale Hurston, who had logged many miles in the US South conducting interviews and gathering material for her academic work and novels. Hurston and Mabley performed a skit together in cheerleading outfits, both stepping out of roles of serious writer and old lady to which they have been consigned by history. E. Williams, *Humor of Jackie Moms Mabley*, 46.

49. Mabley's mother continued to offer financial support, especially in the early years as Mabley incurred off-season expenses. Her mother's funds helped with food

and rent not only for Mabley but also for the people living with her. Later, she returned her mother's love and support by moving her to Washington, DC, after the death of George Parton, Mabley's stepfather. E. Williams, *Humor of Jackie Moms Mabley*, 43, 48.

CHAPTER 7

1. Clapp, *Notorious Woman*, 11, 126–45, 148–65, 191. For coverage of the trial, also see Biggers, *Trials of a Scold*, 111–67.

2. Beard, *My Own Life*.

3. The folk medicine was application of a madstone on wounds such as those caused by rabies-infected bites, which Ida used both before and after John deserted her. Beard, *My Own Life*, 108, 170.

4. Died or disappeared, Clapp and Biggers disagree (Clapp, *Notorious Woman*, 15–16, 23; Biggers, *Trials of a Scold*, 11).

5. Clapp, *Notorious Woman*, 24–25.

6. Clapp, *Notorious Woman*, 27–31; Biggers, *Trials of a Scold*, 17–23.

7. Clapp, *Notorious Woman*, 36–37, 46–49. There is even speculation that she may have spent a year or two in debtors' prison during this time (Biggers, *Trials of a Scold*, 26). Royall discussed becoming a writer in *Letters from Alabama*, which is quoted in Biggers, *Trials of a Scold*, 31.

8. Overall, Royall published nine travel volumes and one novel, plus her later newspapers.

9. Clapp, *Notorious Woman*, 76–79, 105; see also Royall, *Southern Tour*, vol. 2, 207. Target of Royall's particular ire were those she found to be religious zealots, especially "Blue-skins," the derogatory epithet Royall and others used to dismiss Presbyterians (Bartlett, *Dictionary of Americanisms*, 39).

10. Harriet Martineau traveled through counties in which Royall lived, and she stayed in Sweet Springs, saying, "Never shall I forget those tufty purple hills!" (*Society in America*, 190). Frances Trollope traveled half of the route Royall did, going from New Orleans up to Cincinnati, across Pennsylvania, and down to Baltimore and Washington; see her *Domestic Manners*. Alexis de Tocqueville and later Frederick Law Olmsted also used their travels across the United States to frame pointed commentary. For a discussion of the possibilities the travel narrative held for politically minded women, including Frances Wright and Royall during this era, see Steadman, *Traveling Economies*. Biggers pointed to Washington Irving and James Paulding as writers who influenced Royall. Paulding in particular traveled south and west; he made much of exaggeration, outlandish tales, and biting satire. He and Irving indulged in what Biggers aptly called "embellished language" and a "smirking sense of aggrandizement" that made its way into Royall's voice as well. Biggers, *Trials of a Scold*, 32–35.

11. Pryor outlined the "transportation revolution" in the nation between the 1790s and 1860s, especially pointing out the difference that race made in how Americans experienced changes (*Colored Travelers*, 44–48). Royall's quotes, from *Southern Tour*, are as follows: steamboat prostitutes, vol. 2, 76; "infamous house," vol. 3, 88. See, for instance, *Venus in Boston*, George Thompson's 1849 novel, or Baron Ludwig von

Reizenstein's 1854 German-language *Mysteries of New Orleans*. Royall herself would likely have been appalled by the comparison, but city mysteries were similarly animated by providing glimpses into back rooms and backstreets of cities and towns.

12. On respectability and Sparta, Georgia, see Royall, *Southern Tour*, vol. 2, 114.

13. Royall, *Southern Tour*, vol. 1, 58, 68.

14. Royall, *Southern Tour*, vol. 1, 99, 130, 156.

15. Royall, *Southern Tour*, vol. 1, 110, 122; vol. 3, 5; vol. 2, 37–38.

16. Royall, *Southern Tour*, vol. 2, 141–42, 132–33. Royall was an avid supporter of Andrew Jackson, so her sojourn to Creek and Cherokee territories included her suggestion that not only should Native Americans be relocated but perhaps they should be moved to parts of eastern Virginia where the land was already worn out and unproductive. While she supported Frank here, it should be seen as the kind of white privilege that could tolerate individual high-achieving African Americans while dismissing—in racially targeted ways—most others. At the Bayou Sarah "infamous house," Royall was particularly nasty about a mixed-race woman nicknamed Betsy Brig (vol. 3, 88).

17. Royall, *Southern Tour*, vol. 2, 209. Her complaints about franking went throughout the *Southern Tour* volumes.

18. I do not mean that Brooks read Royall or knew of her track through the South; what she did was travel in similar ways through states Royall had passed through earlier. Abbie M. Brooks, Diaries and Church Invitation, 1858–1870, frontispiece and November 2, 1870, MSS 39F, Kenan Research Center, Atlanta History Center. Details about Brooks's early days and her child come from the finding aid for the Atlanta History Center. Boardinghouse food quality and quantity was hit-or-miss when Brooks traveled. In a diary entry from Centre, Cherokee County, Alabama, on August 17, 1870, she wrote, "Mrs. C. seems so stingy with everything and food is cooked over so many times that my stomach does not relish anything, for instance light bread that looked sad as a November sky in its lightest day—was soaked for toast, not eaten and then made into pudding with no sugar scarcely—not eaten—and made into batter cakes with all-spice. I did not eat any. The different cooking had not improved them any." Food in Florida boardinghouses made her much happier—in Live Oak, Florida, she was greeted at the dock with "sentinels waiting for orders to furnish coffee from black looking pots. A table with potato puddings bread and fish was set upon this plank-covered piece of earth" (A. M. [Abbie M.] Brooks, Diary, 1872–1876, December 10, 1872, David M. Rubenstein Rare Book and Manuscript Library, Duke University, Durham, NC). Backyard citrus on boardinghouse tables gave her joy throughout the later volumes of her diaries. Like Royall, Brooks was ready to call out overcharging and poor quality. Fifteen miles outside of Ocala, Florida, she fumed, "What messes have I not tried to eat in Florida. Fritters dripping with grease, batter cakes tough enough to make pocket handkerchiefs, coffee thick as swamp mud, amber colored biscuits, meal beyond the mastication of human teeth" (Diary, January 29, 1873).

19. Clapp, *Notorious Woman*, 100–101; Royall, *Southern Tour*, vol. 2, 200; Brooks, Diary, November 2–3, 1872.

20. Brooks, Diaries and Church Invitation, October 28, 1870; Royall in Biggers, *Trials of a Scold*, 24, 70.

21. Royall, *Southern Tour*, vol. 1, 9. Julia bought her first real estate from money she had saved as a teacher and a book agent. More than that, she met W. O. when he purchased "a book entitled *Thorns in the Flesh*, and when she went to deliver the book to him, he asked her to marry him" ("Thomas Wolfe's Parents: W. O. Wolfe and Julia E. Westall," *Ledger* 8, no. 1 [January 2005]: 1–7, Print Archives, Thomas Wolfe Memorial State Historic Site, Asheville, NC). Beard, *My Own Life*, 196–209.

22. Hart, *Travelling Book-agent's Guide and Instructor*, 11. Note: this guide did not imagine either female agents or southern routes. The latter made sense given its publication year was 1865. Brooks, Diaries and Church Invitation, April 20, 1870; Beard, *Mississippi Lawyer*, 3. Fictional portraits of southern sales professionals included Clyde Edgerton's novel *Bible Salesman* and the Coen brothers' movie *O Brother, Where Art Thou?* Cooke's *Power and the Glory*, discussed in this project's conclusion, and Sherwood Anderson's novel *Kit Brandon* both featured characters who were traveling salespeople, a chiropractor and liquor salesman, respectively.

23. Beard, *My Own Life*, preface, 3–4.

24. John Beard is difficult to find in the historical record. As befits a man who needed to disappear from creditors, lawyers, and other women, he covered his tracks. Beard's racial or ethnic background was equally hard to pin down. Ida's mother called him "that little black John Beard" and said he reminded her "more of an Indian than anything else." For the most part, Ida did not make much of John's skin color, focusing more on his character, though she did use her mother's terms once herself. Beard, *My Own Life*, 8–9, 17–20.

25. Beard, *My Own Life*, 104.

26. Brooks also witnessed the spread of opium, especially in the form of morphine taken by women ("a slave chained by habit," she called one woman) (Diary, April 12, 1874). Lola Walker's "hopping down the line" carried accusations of drug use, as did courtroom testimony about her Chicago aunt's boardinghouse and the "hop fiends" who stayed there ("Walker-Edwards Case Nearing End," *Nashville American*, July 31, 1906, 3). Rothman's *Flush Times and Fever Dreams* explored the hanging of five professional gamblers in Mississippi in the 1830s, a story of capitalism but also of drinking and licentiousness. Beard, *My Own Life*, 74–75, 82. For a discussion of masculine cultures of drink and sin on the main streets and at public entertainments in southern towns, see Ownby, *Subduing Satan*, 38–66. The antagonist in Beard's second book, William Maybin, is addicted to "powerful opiates" (*Mississippi Lawyer*, 14–15).

27. "A Story of Strength; Writing about Her Hard Life Let Ida May Beard Support Her Children," *Winston-Salem Journal*, January 7, 2001, B2; Beard, *Mississippi Lawyer*, 4.

28. Catherine Owen's cookbook-as-novel, *Ten Dollars Enough*, devoted itself to countering prevailing narratives that life in boardinghouses for young couples was "easier" and more "restful," the same argument John Beard mounted to Ida here (*Ten Dollars Enough*, 7–11). Beard, *My Own Life*, 60.

29. Beard, *My Own Life*, 62, 65–68, 82, 87–91, 97, 113–14.

30. Beard, *My Own Life*, 122–23.

31. Beard, *My Own Life*, 162, 168–73.

32. Beard, *My Own Life*, 174. Brooks's experiences agreed. For one two-month period she found herself in boardinghouses with thin walls, ones where she had the

run of a whole floor, and ones where she had to share with baggage or other women or suffer from poorly vented smoke from parlors below; see Diary, entries from April and May 1872.

33. Silkenat, *Moments of Despair*, 198; Beard, *My Own Life*, 169–70.

34. Beard, *My Own Life*, 169–70. It is interesting to contrast Texie Gordon, a highly successful keeper, who had easily cleaned fake flowers on the dining room table (Grace McCune, "The Boarding House Operator," 2, Subseries 1.3 Georgia, folder 223, Federal Writers' Project Papers, 1936–1940, #3709, Southern Historical Collection, Wilson Library, University of North Carolina at Chapel Hill), or Laurine Marion Krag's descriptions of inexpensive ferns in the center of the table ("How I Made a Boarding-House Successful: Based on Twenty Years' Experience," *Ladies' Home Journal*, April 1906, 34). Both successful keepers understood that money was better spent on food or labor, not on decorations.

35. Uriah Slipskin, "Keeping Boarding-House: The Sad Experience of One Who Tried It," *Louisville Courier-Journal*, September 11, 1870, 2.

36. Slipskin, "Keeping Boarding-House," 2.

37. In the 1910 US Federal Census, Beard is listed as an "authorist"; her son Basil and three other lodgers (a "fancy horseshoer," a Swiss electrician, and a shoemaker) lived with her. "Ida M. Beard," 1910 United States Federal Census (database), accessed April 8, 2023, Ancestry.com. In volumes of the *Piedmont Directory Company's Winston-Salem, N.C. City Directory*, from 1911 until 1915, Beard was listed as a widow who had furnished rooms. See, for instance, *Piedmont Directory Company's Winston-Salem . . . 1911*, 75; *Piedmont Directory Company's Winston-Salem . . . 1915*, 117. Beard, *Mississippi Lawyer*, 3–63.

38. Ralp [*sic*] Burns, "Virginia's 'Super-Reno' Holds Early Clean-up Day," *Nashville Tennessean*, February 20, 1922, 5.

39. Burns, "Virginia's 'Super-Reno' Holds Early Clean-up Day," 5. A hotel in the Great Dismal Swamp straddled the North Carolina–Virginia line in the 1830s and served a similar purpose for young couples wishing to elope in North Carolina, where the marriage age was younger (Pugh and Williams, *Hotel in the Great Dismal Swamp*, 18–19).

40. Burns, "Virginia's 'Super-Reno' Holds Early Clean-up Day," 5; the judge was named the day before, in "Tells of Divorce Warning to Judge," *Washington Post*, February 19, 1922, 2. One wonders whether the dates of this news story pointed to discomfort over the Nineteenth Amendment and suffrage for women as they positioned the scheme stretching from 1919 to 1922.

41. "Tells of Divorce Warning to Judge," 2.

42. "Free Mrs. Baggett in Alexandria Case," *Washington Post*, March 7, 1922, 5; "Charges Divorce Papers Are Gone." *Washington Post*, February 22, 1922, 15; "Question Moncure on Divorce Clients," *Washington Post*, March 11, 1922, 19.

43. Biggers, *Trials of a Scold*, 29.

44. Carr, *Lonely Hunter*, 75–78. On the historic marker and Charlotte's relationship to McCullers, see "Honoring Charlotte's Writers: Mary Norton Kratt's Bulldog Tenacity Got the Job Done," *Charlotte Observer*, December 20, 1988, ED. Cooke and MacGowan, *Aunt Huldah*; Cooke, *Power and the Glory*, 358–59; finding aid,

Travis Tuck Jordan Papers, 1929–1941, #3503, Southern Historical Collection, Wilson Library, University of North Carolina at Chapel Hill.

45. Woolf, *Room of One's Own*, 3, 49, 112.

46. Clapp, *Notorious Woman*, 176–77.

CHAPTER 8

1. Mary Hamilton worked with Helen Dick Davis to write her memoir in the early 1930s. Lost for many years, it was finally published in 1992 as *Trials of the Earth: The Autobiography of Mary Hamilton*.

2. Robert O. King, "'Aunt' Della McCullers' Boarding House," 1, Subseries 1.5 North Carolina, folder 583, Federal Writers' Project Papers, 1936–1940, #3709, Southern Historical Collection, Wilson Library, University of North Carolina at Chapel Hill.

3. Hamilton, *Trials of the Earth*. A new edition of the work has recently been released, attesting to its endurance.

4. Hamilton, *Trials of the Earth*, 3–4. On the timber industry in the Delta, see Walker and Cobb, *Agriculture and Industry*, 325–27.

5. Hamilton, *Trials of the Earth*, 52, 64–65. Threats of sexual violence were absent in Hamilton's autobiography. Memories from my grandmother Iva Whitmire, who spent time in the logging camps of Washington State as a child after the logging industry of western North Carolina shrank, included a large pot of water her mother kept boiling on the stove—a weapon hidden in plain sight to ward off unwanted advances from men when her husband was out on work crews. Well before she was a boarding-house keeper herself, young Iva saw the downside of male-dominated work cultures. Such background violence would seem more common than Hamilton's idyll. Skilled workers followed jobs in the timber industry—Appalachians to the Pacific Northwest, eastern Europeans to the Delta, and, in a short news item in an industry magazine called *Timberman*, Finns to Texas. J. E. D., "Southern Observations," *Timberman*, December 15, 1888, 6. That story noted that foreign workers were accepted at camps but that labor tensions arose when they came to work in the town of Orange, Texas, at the sawmill itself. Suronda Gonzalez, "Cornbread and Fabada: Savoring a West Virginia Story," in Engelhardt, *Food We Eat*, 156–64.

6. Hamilton, *Trials of the Earth*, 10–11. Frank unfortunately drank, which led to economic challenges for them as a family (but did not, according to her memoir, result in violence or infidelity or other all-too-frequent consequences of alcohol for men of his generation). His mysterious past, which was never revealed to Mary, also became a family challenge that all just worked around. However, theirs was a successful marriage as Mary told it. Meals that Mary Hamilton described sounded a lot like a meal Wilma Dykeman described from an Appalachian drovers' tavern run by a woman a hundred years earlier. There, in the early 1800s, "Steaming bowls of sweet-smelling cabbage boiled in an iron kettle half the day, platters of spareribs and sausage sharp with sage and seasoning, pots of dried beans rich with grease, sweet potatoes baked to a yellow crumble, plates of hot biscuits, golden nutty-smelling corn bread and pungent cracklin' bread" were served. Meals were "washed down with pitchers of fresh-churned buttermilk, sweet milk, pot after pot of strong black coffee." Altogether

it was, according to Dykeman, "heavy, hearty fare that would stick to a man's ribs through heavy, hearty work." Despite decades separating them, Hamilton's cooking and kitchen management and Dykeman's tavern keeper shared much. Dykeman, *French Broad*, 145–46.

7. Hamilton, *Trials of the Earth*, 16.

8. Mrs. Stayclose, "Household Economy: Trials of House-Keepers," *Southern Cultivator*, July 1872, 278; Mrs. S. T. (Sarah Tyson) Rorer, "The Boarding-House Table," *Ladies' Home Journal*, November 1899, 29; Laurine Marion Krag, "How I Made a Boarding-House Successful: Based on Twenty Years' Experience," *Ladies' Home Journal*, April 1906, 34. On her mother's experiences, see Krag, "Boarding House Defended by Woman on the Inside," *Chicago Daily Tribune*, October 1, 1905, E8. Marion Harland, "How to Be a Successful Boarding House Keeper," *Louisville Courier-Journal*, October 20, 1907, B4. Sarah Tyson Rorer and Marion Harland pioneered home economics and domestic science; both wrote multiple cookbooks and advice columns over the course of their careers; that they weighed into boardinghouse debates made sense, though neither had firsthand experience. By far, the best line in Harland's piece was, "Have all the daintiness you can achieve. I approve of that; but be sure your ambition as a caterer is satisfied before you transfer your ideals to furbelows."

9. Bradley, *Cooking for Profit*, 196–97. Other boardinghouse cooks dealt with similar rough conditions. One of fictional Huldah Sarvice's Wagon-Tire Houses was called by her "a picket house." Huldah explained, "A picket house is sorter like a Mexican *jacal*; it's jest poles driv' in the ground, clost together, an' chinked, fer a wall; the dirt fer a floor; an' a roof put over of some sort." The front door was a "frame with a cowskin stretched over it" (Cooke and MacGowan, *Aunt Huldah*, 210).

10. Hamilton, *Trials of the Earth*, 30–31.

11. Hamilton, *Trials of the Earth*, 121. Stine is hard to find in archives, but his work likely resembled that of chefs behind a Memphis hotel dining room whose menu Frederick Law Olmsted included in his travel narrative from 1857. D. Cockrell's name was on the Commercial Hotel's printed bill of fare that Olmsted described as the only literature available in the establishment. Unfortunately for Olmsted, it was largely a work of fiction. He was late to dinner, so, "beginning with the soup, and going on by the fish to the roasts, the first five dishes I inquired for—when at last I succeeded in arresting one of the negro boys—were 'all gone'; and as the waiter had to go to the head of the dining-room, or to the kitchen, to ascertain this fact upon each demand, the majority of the company had left the table before I was served at all." Frustrated, Olmsted said he would "take anything that was still to be had, and thereupon was provided immediately with some grimy bacon, and greasy cabbage." He continued, "This I commenced eating, but I no sooner paused for a moment, than it was suddenly and surreptitiously removed, and its place supplied, without the expression of any desire on my part, with some other Memphitic chef d'œuvre, a close investigation of which left me in doubt whether it was that denominated 'sliced potato pie,' or 'Irish pudding.'" A simple meal of cabbage, bacon, and potatoes could have been fine, but it was insulting next to the promise of such choice and delicacy. Driving home the point, Olmstead printed the full menu of the hotel; it included those dishes and seventy-nine other offerings. "Pastry" is one of the largest categories; "Memphitic" chefs claimed mastery of baking savory

and sweet. Olmsted, *Cotton Kingdom*, 336–38. Olmsted was ten years too early in his assessment of Memphis cuisine. Under John Gaston, "one of the finest French chefs in nineteenth-century America," according to Shields, Memphis after 1866 became an "exalted standard of cuisine in the region for half a century" (*Culinarians*, 241). Frank Hamilton may have been influenced by this reputation when he went to Memphis seeking a chef. Frank's success in hiring someone like Stine points out a truth still operational: while top chefs may have disdained "ordinary boardinghouses" (as Shields terms them), their many employees did not have such a luxury. The travels of a trained chef like Stine, moving back and forth between haute cuisine and backwoods kitchens, might have been extreme, but they likely were not unique. Just as owners moved between hotels and boardinghouses over their careers, employees too must have followed jobs rather than enforced lines of distinction between cooking work.

12. Hamilton, *Trials of the Earth*, 122.

13. Hamilton, *Trials of the Earth*, 124.

14. Hamilton, *Trials of the Earth*, 122–24.

15. US Bureau of Labor Statistics, *Descriptions of Occupations*, 11–12.

16. US Bureau of Labor Statistics, *Descriptions of Occupations*, 17.

17. Hamilton, *Trials of the Earth*, 66. In the extreme environment in which she was baking and cooking, even water was an issue. Cooking required more than ingredients, fire, and skill. In camp conditions, Hamilton struggled to supply a frequently invisible but crucial part of cooking: acquiring good water. Hamilton remembered, "When we first came to this country, to get water we had to drive iron pipes in the ground, thirty to sixty feet. If the water threw white sand, it was soft; but if it threw black sand and mud, it was alkali and iron." If it was the latter, "it had to be broken for washing clothes or dishes. To break it we pumped it into a barrel and put in it about three tablespoonfuls of concentrated lye or about two pounds of sifted ashes. We filtered it to drink, to cook rice, potatoes, or make coffee." Safe to consume, the resulting water nonetheless "turned potatoes black, rice almost red; coffee made of it without first being boiled or filtered was black as ink and tasted flat." She vividly recalled, "When lye was used to soften it, it would, after standing overnight, be clear and ready to use, but there would be about three inches of feathery yellow settlings in the bottom of the vessel." I checked with a chemical engineer—this seems a remarkably accurate recounting of the process.

18. Hamilton, *Trials of the Earth*, 84.

19. Bendele, "Food, Space, and Mobility"; Weiner, *Coalfield Jews*; Gabi Mendick, "For More Than a Decade, the Durham Green Flea Market Has Been a Taste of Home for the Triangle's Hispanic Community," *Indy Week* (Durham, NC), December 8, 2021.

20. Hamilton, *Trials of the Earth*, 30–31, 94.

21. Hamilton, *Trials of the Earth*, 93–94.

22. Carroll, *Three Squares*, 114–15.

23. Carroll, *Three Squares*, 103–5.

24. King, "'Aunt' Della McCullers' Boarding House," 2–3. It was a familiar story for many families in North Carolina. A Southern Oral History Program interview almost forty years later in 1977 with Josephine Turner described a similar combination of skills making up a family industry. Turner's mother took in boarders who were in their

area building Camp Butner. But the family also did laundry for residents in the area; quite reasonably, later in life, Turner said, "The day would begin at three o'clock in the morning and end at night. So I don't iron at all now. I won't even pick up an iron." Her interviewer laughed in agreement, repeating, "Three in the morning, she'd begin?" Turner sang the praises of bologna sandwiches—a critical time saver for busy families. Josephine Turner, interview with Karen Sindelar, June 7, 1976, 5, Southern Oral History Program Collection, Southern Historical Collection, Wilson Library, University of North Carolina at Chapel Hill.

25. King, "'Aunt' Della McCullers' Boarding House," 3–5.

26. King, "'Aunt' Della McCullers' Boarding House," 5. Death certificates for "Dela Harris (December 20, 1909)," "Wilbert McCullers (July 23, 1929)," and "Ruffin McCullers (January 16, 1924)" can be found in North Carolina, U.S., Death Certificates, 1909–1976 (database), accessed April 8, 2023, Ancestry.com. An enduring family mystery surrounds John's death. In the interview with Robert O. King, McCullers said he died "about 1916." His death certificate (with her name on it) lists his death in 1924. While pneumonia is the main cause of death, the "drayman" employed by "several" also had a contributory illness listed: "insanity." Whether that was from a short-term high fever that can accompany pneumonia or whether Della was hinting at something more with her revised timeline, I do not know.

27. King, "'Aunt' Della McCullers' Boarding House," 5–6; *Hill Directory Company's Raleigh . . . 1926*, 381; *Hill Directory Company's Raleigh . . . 1931*, 563.

28. King, "'Aunt' Della McCullers' Boarding House," 6; *Hill Directory Company's Raleigh . . . 1933*, 246.

29. King, "'Aunt' Della McCullers' Boarding House," 1, 6, 8.

30. *Hill Directory Company's Raleigh . . . 1935*, 564. Southern food studies readers will remember Shaw as the location of Ella Baker's "Bigger than a hamburger" speech in 1960, which further energized the lunch counter sit-ins and resulted in the founding of the Student Nonviolent Coordinating Committee, the student arm of the organized civil rights movement (Moye, *Ella Baker*, 109–34). See *Hill Directory Company's Raleigh . . . 1939*, 186 (for Gooch); and *Hill Directory Company's Raleigh . . . 1940*, 512 (for Waddell).

31. On the Pure Food and Drug Act, see Veit, *Modern Food, Moral Food*, 37–38, 142; "Meals Must Be Pure," *Washington Post*, November 2, 1908, 18; Williams-Forson, *Building Houses Out of Chicken Legs*, 34–37. Some white proprietors trying to keep Black patrons out of their hotels also reorganized as boardinghouses to avoid complying with laws that they integrate. An article in Nashville, Tennessee's *Republican Banner* from 1875 called out two "principal hotels" in the city of Chattanooga for resisting change for themselves and guests, united by beliefs in white superiority and segregation. The one-sentence news item under the headline "Civil Rights" read, "Owing to the passage of the civil rights bill, the proprietors of the two principal hotels here have surrendered their licenses, and will conduct their establishments as private boardinghouses." "Civil Rights," *Republican Banner*, March 7, 1875, 1. The change from publicly licensed to privately conducted had everything to do with exempting themselves from laws requiring equal treatment of African Americans in the brief era of post–Civil War expansion of civil rights. This strategy came back in the 1950s and

1960s as restaurants tried to redefine themselves as "social clubs" and hotels as private establishments to preserve the segregation that the 1875 article foreshadowed. See also Cooley, *To Live and Dine in Dixie*, 128–47.

32. Y. Johnson, *Song and the Silence*, 156–59. For footage of Wright, see "Booker Wright Interview—Mississippi: A Self Portrait," posted by user JSF1 on YouTube, accessed April 5, 2023, https://www.youtube.com/watch?v=93iz98-BDvw.

33. King, "'Aunt' Della McCullers' Boarding House," 6.

34. King, "'Aunt' Della McCullers' Boarding House," 8.

35. King, "'Aunt' Della McCullers' Boarding House," 1–2.

36. Bradley, *Cooking for Profit*, 199, 232. Today, hot dog stands are a crucial food legacy in North Carolina. Along with Raleigh, Charlotte and Winston-Salem all have long-standing and beloved hot dog restaurants with Greek roots. And Greek residents did not stay in the realm of street-side or quick food service. In places like Greensboro, Chapel Hill, and Asheville, the food scene was forever changed.

37. King, "'Aunt' Della McCullers' Boarding House," 2, 7.

38. For a contemporary take on North Carolina foodways, see McKimmon, *When We're Green We Grow*. On coffee in the South, see Engelhardt, "Cookbook Story." Today's North Carolina food cultures are expertly explored in Ferris's *Edible North Carolina*.

39. Grace McCune, "Susie Ray," 2, 6–7, Subseries 1.3 Georgia, folder 237, Federal Writers' Project Papers, 1936–1940, #3709, Southern Historical Collection, Wilson Library, University of North Carolina at Chapel Hill. McCune and her editor renamed Favors "Susie Ray" for the title of her story; however, as with Gordon, her full name was given in the heading.

40. Grace McCune, "The Boarding House Operator," 17, Subseries 1.3 Georgia, folder 223, Federal Writers' Project Papers, 1936–1940, #3709, Southern Historical Collection, Wilson Library, University of North Carolina at Chapel Hill.

41. McCune, "Boarding House Operator," 9, 18.

42. Williamson, *American Hotel*, 207–9; Strasser, *Never Done*, 155.

43. Anne Winn Stevens, Douglas Carter, and Junius Allison, "Public School Teachers," 6, North Carolina, 1939, Federal Writers' Project Papers, Library of Congress, Washington, DC.

44. Bradley, *Cooking for Profit*, 8, 177–78, 192.

45. Hamilton, *Trials of the Earth*, xv–xxii.

46. King, "'Aunt' Della McCullers' Boarding House," 8; "Deaths: McCullers, Della," *Evening Star* (Washington, DC), May 5, 1954, A-32.

CONCLUSION

1. David Sedaris, "This Old House," *New Yorker*, July 9, 2007.

2. Cooke, *Power and the Glory*, 359.

3. Largest is the Villages. See also "Shanghai's Elderly Elite Flock to Luxury Nursing Homes," Sixthtone (website), accessed March 15, 2020, http://www.sixthtone.com/news/1001284/shanghais-elderly-elite-flock-to-luxury-nursing-homes; and Bill Kress, "'Grand Reveal' at the Vi at Aventura Celebrates Newly Transformed Spaces,"

Miami Community News, May 30, 2018, http://communitynewspapers.com/aventura /grand-reveal-at-the-vi-at-aventura-celebrates-newly-transformed-spaces/.

4. See, for example, Brevard, North Carolina's Tore's Homes ("Locations," Tore's Homes website, accessed April 5, 2023, https://toreshome.com/locations/). Not unrelated are the recovery homes for people struggling with addictions and so-called halfway houses for people transitioning out of incarceration.

5. See, for instance, Sink and Doyal, *Boarding House Reach*; Gift, *Feeding Generations*; or even Ahern, *Our Boarding House*. The latter was a popular newspaper cartoon series that appeared in the 1920s and was reprinted for fans in 2005.

6. Wilkes, *Mrs. Wilkes' Boardinghouse Cookbook*. Also "Wilkes Pied-a-Terre" and "Wilkes House," Wilkes House (website), accessed April 5, 2023, https://mrswilkes .com/lodging/pied-a-terre/ and https://mrswilkes.com/lodging/wilkes-house/.

7. Comment left by Andy W. of Marion, OH, on March 6, 2019; that and other details of the Wilkes Collection are all on the Lucky Savannah vacation rentals website, "The Wilkes Collection," Lucky Savannah website, accessed April 6, 2023, https:// www.luckysavannah.com/wilkes-collection.

8. "The Teacherage Gets an Update in North Carolina," *Times News* (Burlington, NC), February 16, 2017, https://www.thetimesnews.com/opinion/20170216/editorial -the-teacherage-gets-update-in-north-carolina. On Gardner and the Smithfield teacherage, see Doris Rollins Cannon, "Ava Gardner," NCpedia, January 1, 2012, https://www .ncpedia.org/gardner-ava. On Austin, Texas, see Melissa Taboada, "Austin School Leaders Pitch Housing Plan for Teachers, Civil Servants," *Austin American-Statesman*, September 25, 2018, https://www.statesman.com/story/news/2016/10/13/austin-leaders -pitch-housing-plan-for-teachers-civil-servants-today/10076433007/.

9. There are many examples of such articles. See Emily Brandon and Rachel Hartman, "10 Best College Towns for Retirement," *US News and World Report*, updated March 31, 2023, https://money.usnews.com/money/retirement/baby-boomers /slideshows/the-best-college-towns-for-retirement; Anne Fields, "10 Great Places to Live and Learn," *AARP Magazine*, accessed April 5, 2023, https://www.aarp.org /retirement/planning-for-retirement/info-2016/ten-ideal-college-towns-for -retirement-photo.html#slide1; "Why You May Want to Retire to a College Town," *MarketWatch*, July 29, 2019, https://www.marketwatch.com/story/why-you-may -want-to-retire-to-a-college-town-2019-07-29. Some colleges are investing in their own retirement properties, aimed at former faculty, staff, or alumni (the MarketWatch story touched on this phenomenon). On the house director model, including helpful tips for how to apply for such jobs, see "Second Career: Becoming a Sorority or Fraternity House Director," *Forbes*, August 6, 2019, https://www.forbes.com/sites/nextavenue /2019/08/06/second-career-becoming-a-sorority-or-fraternity-house-director /#a5632ab69fc4. See also the Sorority Mom website (https://sororitymom.com), a site dedicated to encouraging and supporting "the Ideal Career for Single, Mature Women," according to its tagline.

Bibliography

PRIMARY SOURCES

Archives

David M. Rubenstein Rare Book and Manuscript Library, Duke University,
    Durham, NC
Kenan Research Center, Atlanta History Center, Atlanta, GA
Library of Congress, Washington, DC
    Federal Writers' Project
        Folklore Project: Life Histories, 1936–39
New York Public Library, New York City, NY
    NYPL Labs
        "What's on the Menu?," https://menus.nypl.org/
    Schomburg Center for Research in Black Culture, Manuscripts, Archives,
        and Rare Books Division
        Green Book Collection, 1936–1967
State Library and Archives of Florida, Tallahassee, FL
    Florida Memory Project
Tennessee State Library and Archives, Nashville, TN
    Circuit Court Minutes, Obion County
Thomas Wolfe Memorial State Historic Site, Asheville, NC
    Print Archives
Wilson Library, University of North Carolina at Chapel Hill, Chapel Hill, NC
    Southern Historical Collection
        Alice Lee Larkins Houston Papers, 1859–1877
        Federal Writers' Project Papers, 1936–1940
        Matthew Smart Davis Papers, 1851–1914
        Southern Oral History Program Collection
        Thaddeus Ferree Papers on the North Carolina Federal Writers' Project,
            1935–1941
        Travis Tuck Jordan Papers, 1929–1941

Magazines and Newspapers

American Monthly Knickerbocker
Asheville (NC) Citizen-Times
Asheville (NC) Daily Citizen
Atlanta Constitution
Baltimore Sun
Bookman
Boston Cooking School Magazine of
    Culinary Science and Domestic
    Economics
Brevard (NC) News
Brick
Catholic World
Charlotte News
Charlotte Observer
Chicago Daily Tribune
Christian Union
Evening Star (Washington, DC)
French Broad Hustler (Hendersonville,
    NC)
Galaxy: A Magazine of Entertaining
    Reading
Godey's Lady's Book
Good Housekeeping
Horticulturist and Journal of Rural Art
    and Rural Taste
Huntsville (AL) Gazette
Indy Week (Durham, NC)
Jewish Exponent
Ladies' Home Journal
Louisville Courier-Journal

Milwaukee Journal
Nashville American
Nashville Tennessean
National Police Gazette
New World: A Weekly Family Journal of
    Popular Literature, Science, Art, and
    News
New Yorker
New York Sun
New York Times
North Carolinian (Raleigh)
Provincial Freeman
Railway Age and Northwestern
    Railroader
Raleigh Morning Post
Raleigh News and Observer
Republican Banner (Nashville)
Robesonian (Lumberton, NC)
San Francisco Call
Saveur
Southern and Western Literary
    Messenger and Review
Southern Cultivator
Timberman
United States' Telegraph
Virginia University Magazine
Washington Post
Wilmington (NC) Messenger
Wilmingtonian (Wilmington, NC)
Winston-Salem Journal

Books

Ahern, Gene. *Our Boarding House, with Major Hoople, 1927.* Classic Reprint Series.
    Almonte, ONT: Leonard G. Lee, 2005.
Alcott, Louisa May. *Louisa May Alcott Unmasked: Collected Thrillers.* Edited by
    Madeleine Stern. Boston: Northeastern University Press, 1995.
Alexander, Bill. *Around Biltmore Village.* Images of America Series. Charleston:
    Arcadia, 2008.
Anderson, Sherwood. *Kit Brandon: A Portrait.* New York: Arbor House, 1985. Origi-
    nal work published 1936.
Asbury, Herbert. *The Barbary Coast: An Informal History of the San Francisco
    Underworld.* Garden City, NY: Knopf, 1933.

Austen, Jane. *Persuasion: An Annotated Edition*. Edited by Robert Morrison. Cambridge, MA: Belknap Press, 2011. Original work published 1817.

Bartlett, John Russell. *Dictionary of Americanisms: A Glossary of Words and Phrases Usually Regarded as Peculiar to the United States*. 2nd ed. Boston: Little, Brown, 1859.

Beard, Ida M. *The Mississippi Lawyer, or, Was It All a Dream?* Winston-Salem: Winston Print Company. 1911.

——. *My Own Life; or, A Deserted Wife*. 5th ed. North Carolina: n.d. [1898?].

Beard, James. *Delights and Prejudices*. New York: Atheneum, 1964.

Bradley, Alice. *Cooking for Profit: Catering and Food Service Management*. Chicago: American School of Home Economics, 1922.

Brooks, Abbie M. [Silvia Sunshine]. *Petals Plucked from Sunny Climes*. Introduction by Richard A. Martin. Gainesville: University Presses of Florida, 1976. Original work published c. 1879.

Brown, Henry. *Narrative of the Life of Henry Box Brown*. Edited and with an introduction by John Ernest. Chapel Hill: University of North Carolina Press, 2008. Original work published 1851.

Bullock, Thomas. *The Ideal Bartender*. St. Louis: Buxton and Skinner, 1917.

Campbell, Tunis G. *Hotel Keepers, Head Waiters, and Housekeepers' Guide*. Boston: Coolidge and Wiley, 1848.

Claiborne, Craig. *Craig Claiborne's A Feast Made for Laughter*. New York: Doubleday, 1982.

Cliff, Michelle. *Free Enterprise*. New York: Dutton, 1993.

Cooke, Grace MacGowan. *The Power and the Glory*. With an introduction by Elizabeth S. D. Engelhardt. Boston: Northeastern University Press, 2003. Original work published 1909.

Cooke, Grace MacGowan, and Alice MacGowan. *Aunt Huldah: Proprietor of the Wagon-Tire House and Genial Philosopher of the Cattle Country*. London: Hodder and Stoughton, 1904.

Cooper, Anna Julia. *A Voice from the South*. Schomburg Library of Nineteenth Century Black Women Writers. Introduction by Mary Helen Washington. New York: Oxford University Press, 1988. Original work published 1892.

Craft, William, and Ellen Craft. *Running a Thousand Miles for Freedom; or, The Escape of William and Ellen Craft from Slavery*. London: William Tweedie, 1860. Electronic edition online at Documenting the American South, University Library, University of North Carolina at Chapel Hill, 2001. https://docsouth.unc .edu/neh/craft/craft.html.

Dargan, Olive Tilford (Fielding Burke, pseud.). *Call Home the Heart: A Novel of the Thirties*. New York: Feminist Press, 1983. Original work published 1932.

DeForest, John William. *Honest John Vane*. Introduced by Joseph Jay Rubin. State College, PA: Bald Eagle Press, 1960. Original work published 1875.

A Directory of the Names of the Members of the Senate and House of Commons of the Present Legislature, Their Respective Boarding Houses, Politics, &c. &c. [Raleigh, NC]: n.p., 1838.

Dunlap, William. *Thirty Years Ago; or, the Memoirs of a Water Drinker*. 2 vols. Vol. 1. New York: Bancroft and Holley, 1836.

Edgerton, Clyde. *The Bible Salesman*. New York: Little, Brown, 2008.

Gift, Helen C. *Feeding Generations: Boarding House Fare and Family Oral Tradition*. Brevard, NC: Brevard Printing Company, 2001.

Gunn, Thomas Butler. *The Physiology of New York Boarding-Houses*. Edited and with an introduction by David Faflik. New Brunswick, NJ: Rutgers University Press, 2009. Original work published 1857.

Hamilton, Mary. *Trials of the Earth: The Autobiography of Mary Hamilton*. Edited by Helen Dick Davis. With a foreword by Ellen Douglas. Jackson: University of Mississippi Press, 1992.

Hart, William. *The Travelling Book-agent's Guide and Instructor: Containing the Simple Rules and Method Pursued with Such Well-known Success*. Boston: D. C. Colesworthy, 1865.

Hill, Annabella P. *Mrs. Hill's Southern Practical Cookery and Receipt Book*. Historical commentary by Damon Fowler. Columbia: University of South Carolina Press, 2011. Original work published 1872.

Hill Directory Company's Directory of Asheville, N.C., 1902–1903. Richmond: Hill Directory Company, 1902.

Hill Directory Company's Directory of Asheville, N.C., 1904–1905. Richmond: Hill Directory Company, 1904.

Hill Directory Company's Directory of Asheville, N.C., 1906–1907. Richmond: Hill Directory Company, 1906.

Hill Directory Company's Raleigh City Directory, Wake County, N.C. 1926. Richmond: Hill Directory Company, 1926.

Hill Directory Company's Raleigh City Directory, Wake County, N.C. 1931. Richmond: Hill Directory Company, 1931.

Hill Directory Company's Raleigh City Directory, Wake County, N.C. 1933. Richmond: Hill Directory Company, 1933.

Hill Directory Company's Raleigh City Directory, Wake County, N.C., 1935, Richmond: Hill Directory Company, 1935.

Hill Directory Company's Raleigh City Directory, Wake County, N.C., 1939, Richmond: Hill Directory Company, 1939.

Hill Directory Company's Raleigh City Directory, Wake County, N.C., 1940, Richmond: Hill Directory Company, 1940.

Hines, Duncan. *Adventures in Good Eating*. Ithaca: Duncan Hines Institute, 1936.
——. *Lodging for a Night*. Bowling Green, KY: Adventures in Good Eating Inc., 1938.

Holdredge, Helen, ed. and comp. *Mammy Pleasant's Cookbook*. San Francisco: 101 Productions, 1970.

Keckley, Elizabeth. *Behind the Scenes; or, Thirty Years a Slave, and Four Years in the White House*. New York: G. W. Carleton, 1868.

Lumpkin, Grace. *To Make My Bread*. Urbana: University of Illinois Press, 1995. Original work published 1932.

Martineau, Harriet. *Society in America.* Vol. 1. New York: Saunders and Otley, 1837.

McAllister, Ward. *Society as I Have Found It.* New York: Cassell, 1890.

McKimmon, Jane Simpson. *When We're Green We Grow.* Chapel Hill: University of North Carolina Press, 1945.

Members of the Bradford District Union of the National British Women's Temperance Union. *Recipes for Temperance Drinks, for Winter and Summer.* Bradford [Great Britain]: Wilkinson and Woodhouse, 1914.

Mitchamore, Pat. *Miss Mary Bobo's Boarding House Cookbook: A Celebration of Traditional Southern Dishes That Made Miss Mary Bobo's an American Legend.* Recipes edited by Lynne Tolley. Nashville: Thomas Nelson, 1994.

Montague, Margaret Prescott. *Deep Channel.* Boston: Atlantic Monthly Press, 1923.

Mordecai, Samuel. *Richmond in By-Gone Days: Being Reminiscences of an Old Citizen.* Richmond: George M. West, 1856.

O'Connor, Flannery. *The Complete Stories.* New York: Farrar, Straus and Giroux, 1986. Original work published 1946.

Olmsted, Frederick Law. *The Cotton Kingdom: A Traveller's Observations on Cotton and Slavery in the American Slave States, 1853–1861.* Edited with an introduction by Arthur M. Schlesinger. New York: Da Capo Press, 1966.

Owen, Catherine D. *Ten Dollars Enough: Keeping House Well on Ten Dollars a Week; How It Has Been Done, How It May Be Done Again.* Boston: Houghton Mifflin, 1889.

Piedmont Directory Company's Asheville, N.C. City Directory, 1912. Asheville: Piedmont Directory Company, 1912.

Piedmont Directory Company's Asheville, N.C. City Directory, 1914. Asheville: Piedmont Directory Company, 1914.

Piedmont Directory Company's Athens, GA, City Directory, 1923–1924. Asheville: Piedmont Directory Company, 1924.

Piedmont Directory Company's Athens, GA, City Directory, 1926–1927. Asheville: Piedmont Directory Company, 1926.

Piedmont Directory Company's Winston-Salem, N.C. City Directory, 1911. Asheville: Piedmont Directory Company, 1911.

Piedmont Directory Company's Winston-Salem, N.C. City Directory, 1915. Asheville: Piedmont Directory Company, 1915.

Potter, Eliza. *A Hairdresser's Experience in High Life.* Edited by Xiomara Santamarina. Chapel Hill: University of North Carolina Press, 2009.

Puck's Library. *The Great American Boarding House, Being Puck's Best Things about That Abode of Happiness.* Vol. 8. New York: Keppler and Schwarzmann, 1888.

R. L. Polk and Company's Jacksonville City Directory, 1911. Jacksonville, FL: R. L. Polk and Company, 1911.

R. L. Polk and Company's Miami City Directory, 1920. Jacksonville, FL: R. L. Polk and Company, 1920.

Randolph, Mary. *The Virginia House-wife.* Washington: Davis and Force, 1824. A facsimile of the first edition, 1824, along with additional material from the editions of 1825 and 1828. Columbia: University of South Carolina Press, 1984.

——. *The Virginia Housewife: Or, Methodical Cook.* Stereotype ed. Baltimore: Plaskitt and Cugle, 1838. Available through Feeding America: The Historic American Cookbook Project, Michigan State University Libraries, https://d.lib.msu.edu/fa/71#page/1/mode/2up.

Reizenstein, Baron Ludwig von. *The Mysteries of New Orleans.* Translated and edited by Steven Rowan. Baltimore: Johns Hopkins University Press, 2002. Original work published 1854–55.

Roberts, Robert. *The House Servant's Directory, or A Monitor for Private Families: Comprising Hints on the Arrangement and Performance of Servants' Work.* Boston: Munroe and Francis, 1827.

Royall, Mrs. Anne. *Mrs. Royall's Southern Tour, or Second Series of the Black Book in Three or More Volumes.* Vol. 1. Washington, 1830. Ulan Press, facsimile edition.

——. *Mrs. Royall's Southern Tour, or Second Series of the Black Book in Three or More Volumes.* Vol. 2. Washington, 1831. Nabu Public Domain Reprints, facsimile edition.

——. *Mrs. Royall's Southern Tour, or Second Series of the Black Book in Three or More Volumes.* Vol. 3. Washington, 1831. Ulan Press, facsimile edition.

Russell, Malinda. *A Domestic Cook Book: Containing a Careful Selection of Useful Receipts for the Kitchen.* Introduction by Jan Longone. Paw Paw, MI: Printed by the author by T. O. Ward at the "True Northerner" Office, 1866. Facsimile edition.

Sink, Alice E., and Nickie Doyal. *Boarding House Reach: North Carolina's Entrepreneurial Women.* Wilmington, NC: Dram Tree Books, 2007.

Smedes, Susan Dabney. *Memorials of a Southern Planter.* Baltimore: Cushings and Bailey, 1887.

Southern Pines, N.C.: Cottages, Hotels and Boarding Houses. Southern Pines, NC: n.p., 1900.

Southworth, E. D. E. N. *Ishmael or, In the Depths.* Chicago: M. A. Donohue, [1876].

——. *Self-Raised or, From the Depths.* New York: Grosset and Dunlap, [1876].

Still, William. *The Underground Railroad: A Record of Facts, Authentic Narrative, Letters, &C., Narrating the Hardships, Hair-Breadth Escapes and Death Struggles of the Slaves in Their Efforts of Freedom, as Related by Themselves and Others, or Witnessed by the Author; Together with Sketches of Some of the Largest Stockholders, and Most Liberal Aiders and Advisers, of the Road.* Philadelphia: Porter and Coates, 1872. Revised ed. published in 1878.

Thompson, George. *Venus in Boston and Other Tales of Nineteenth-Century City Life.* Edited by David S. Reynolds and Kimberly R. Gladman. Amherst: University of Massachusetts Press, 2002.

Trollope, Frances. *Domestic Manners of the Americans.* Edited by Donald Smalley. New York: Knopf, 1949. Original work published 1832.

US Bureau of Labor Statistics. *Descriptions of Occupations: Logging Camps and Sawmills.* Prepared for the US Employment Service and US Department of Labor. Washington: Government Printing Office, 1918.

Visitors Guide to Asheville, North Carolina: Including Hotels, Boarding Houses, Schools and General Information. Asheville: Asheville Print. Co., n.d. (between 1893 and 1918).

Whipple, Frances Harriet, with Elleanor Eldridge. *Memoirs of Elleanor Eldridge*. Edited by Joycelyn K. Moody. Morgantown: West Virginia University Press, 2014. Original work published 1838.

Wilkes, Sema. *Mrs. Wilkes' Boardinghouse Cookbook: Recipes and Recollections from her Savannah Table*. With a history by John T. Edge. Berkeley: Ten Speed Press, 2001.

Williams, Tennessee. *Vieux Carré*. With a new introduction by Robert Bray. New York: New Directions Books, 2000. Original work published 1977.

Williamson, Jefferson. *The American Hotel: An Anecdotal History*. The Leisure Class of America. New York: Arno, 1975. Original work published 1930.

Wolfe, Thomas. *Look Homeward, Angel: A Story of the Buried Life*. With introductions by Robert Morgan and Maxwell E. Perkins. New York: Scribner, 2006. Original work published 1929.

Yerby, Frank. *Devilseed*. Garden City, NY: Doubleday, 1984.

SECONDARY SOURCES

Books

Aron, Cindy S. *Working at Play: A History of Vacations in the United States*. Oxford: Oxford University Press, 1999.

Bibler, Michael P. *Cotton's Queer Relations: Same Sex Intimacy and the Literature of the Southern Plantation, 1936–1968*. Charlottesville: University of Virginia Press, 2009.

Biggers, Jeff. *The Trials of a Scold: The Incredible True Story of Writer Anne Royall*. New York: St. Martin's Press, 2017.

Biltikoff, Charlotte. *Eating Right in America: The Cultural Politics of Food and Health*. Durham: Duke University Press, 2013.

Bone, Martyn, and William Link, eds. *Creating and Consuming the American South*. Gainesville: University Press of Florida, 2015.

Bordman, Gerald, and Thomas S. Hischak. *The Oxford Companion to American Theatre*. 3rd ed. Oxford: Oxford University Press, 2012.

Bower, Anne L., ed. *Recipes for Reading: Community Cookbooks, Stories, Histories*. Amherst: University of Massachusetts Press, 1997.

Broussard, Joyce Linda. *Stepping Lively in Place: The Not-Married, Free Women of Civil-War-Era Natchez, Mississippi*. Athens: University of Georgia Press, 2016.

Buchan, Perdita. *Utopia, New Jersey: Travels in the Nearest Eden*. New Brunswick, NJ: Rivergate Books, 2007.

Carr, Virginia Spencer. *The Lonely Hunter: A Biography of Carson McCullers*. Foreword by Tennessee Williams. Athens: University of Georgia Press, 2003.

Carroll, Abigail. *Three Squares: The Invention of the American Meal*. New York: Basic Books, 2013.

Carson, Barbara. *Ambitious Appetites: Dining, Behavior, and Patterns of Consumption in Federal Washington*. Washington, DC: American Institute of Architects Press, 1990.

Cartwright, Keith. *Sacral Grooves, Limbo Gateways: Travels in Deep Southern Time, Circum-Caribbean Space, Afro-Creole Authority.* Athens: University of Georgia Press, 2013.

Cecelski, David C., and Timothy B. Tyson, eds. *Democracy Betrayed: The Wilmington Race Riot of 1898 and Its Legacy.* Chapel Hill: University of North Carolina Press, 1998.

Chudacoff, Howard P. *The Age of the Bachelor: Creating an American Subculture.* Princeton: Princeton University Press, 1999.

Civitello, Linda. *Baking Powder Wars: The Cutthroat Food Fight That Revolutionized Cooking.* Urbana: University of Illinois Press, 2017.

Clapp, Elizabeth. J. *A Notorious Woman: Anne Royall in Jacksonian America.* Charlottesville: University of Virginia Press, 2016.

Clegg, Claude A., III. *The Price of Liberty: African Americans and the Making of Liberia.* Chapel Hill: University of North Carolina Press, 2004.

Cobble, Dorothy Sue. *Dishing It Out: Waitresses and Their Unions in the Twentieth Century.* Urbana: University of Illinois Press, 1992.

Coggeshall, John M. *Liberia, South Carolina: An African American Appalachian Community.* Chapel Hill: University of North Carolina Press, 2018.

Collins, Gail. *America's Women: 400 Years of Dolls, Drudges, Helpmeets, and Heroines.* New York: William Morrow, 2003.

Cooley, Angela Jill. *To Live and Dine in Dixie: The Evolution of Urban Food Culture in the Jim Crow South.* Athens: University of Georgia Press, 2015.

Cox, Karen L. *Dixie's Daughters: The United Daughters of the Confederacy and the Preservation of Confederate Culture.* Gainesville: University Press of Florida, 2003.

Deetz, Kelley Fanto. *Bound to the Fire: How Virginia's Enslaved Cooks Helped Invent American Cuisine.* Lexington: University Press of Kentucky, 2017.

de la Peña, Carolyn. *Empty Pleasures: The Story of Artificial Sweeteners from Saccharin to Splenda.* Chapel Hill: University of North Carolina Press, 2010.

Diamond, Becky. *Mrs. Goodfellow: The Story of America's First Cooking School.* Chicago: Westholme Publishing, 2012.

Dramov, Alissandra. *Carmel-by-the-Sea, the Early Years (1903–1913): An Overview of the History of the Carmel Mission, the Monterey Peninsula, and the First Decade of the Bohemian Artists' and Writers' Colony.* Bloomington, IN: Author-House Books, 2012.

DuPuis, Melanie. *Nature's Perfect Food: How Milk Became America's Drink.* New York: New York University Press, 2002.

Dykeman, Wilma. *The French Broad.* 1955. Newport, TN: Wakestone Books, 1999.

Eaves, Latoya E. "Outside Forces: Black Southern Sexuality." In *Queering the Countryside: New Frontiers in Rural Queer Studies,* edited by Mary L. Gray, Colin R. Johnson, and Brian J. Gilley, 146–57. New York: NYU Press, 2016.

Egerton, John. *Southern Food: At Home, on the Road, in History.* 1987. Chapel Hill: University of North Carolina Press, 1993.

Elias, Megan J. *Food on the Page: Cookbooks and American Culture.* Philadelphia: University of Pennsylvania Press, 2017.

Engelhardt, Elizabeth S. D. "The Cookbook Story: Transitional Narratives in Southern Foodways." In *Writing in the Kitchen: Essays on Southern Literature and Foodways*, edited by David A. Davis and Tara Powell, 69–85. Jackson: University Press of Mississippi, 2014.

———. "Listening to Black Appalachian Laundrywomen: Teaching with Photographs, Letters, Diaries, and Lost Voices." In *Appalachia in the Classroom: Teaching the Region*, edited by Teresa L. Burriss and Patricia M. Gantt, 33–49. Athens: Ohio University Press, 2013.

———. *A Mess of Greens: Southern Gender and Southern Food*. Athens: University of Georgia Press, 2011.

———. ed. *The Food We Eat, the Stories We Tell: Contemporary Appalachian Tables*. Athens: Ohio University Press, 2019.

Enstad, Nan. *Ladies of Labor, Girls of Adventure: Working Women, Popular Culture, and Labor Politics at the Turn of the Twentieth Century*. New York: Columbia University Press, 1999.

Eyre, John Douglas. *Profiles of Chapel Hill since 1900*. Chapel Hill: Chapel Hill Historical Society, 2009.

Faflik, David. *Boarding Out: Inhabiting the American Urban Literary Imagination, 1840–1860*. Evanston, IL: Northwestern University Press, 2012.

Ferris, Marcie Cohen. *The Edible South: The Power of Food and the Making of an American Region*. Chapel Hill: University of North Carolina Press, 2014.

———. ed. *Edible North Carolina: A Journey across a State of Flavor*. Chapel Hill: University of North Carolina Press, 2022.

Fitzsimons, Frank L. *From the Banks of the Oklawaha*. Vols. 1–3. Hendersonville, NC: Golden Glow Publishing, 1976–79.

Gamber, Wendy. *The Boardinghouse in Nineteenth-Century America*. Baltimore: Johns Hopkins University Press, 2007.

Gelderman, Carol. *A Free Man of Color and His Hotel: Race, Reconstruction, and the Role of the Federal Government*. Washington, DC: Potomac Books, 2012.

Goldsmith, Barbara. *Other Powers: The Age of Suffrage, Spiritualism, and the Scandalous Victoria Woodhull*. New York: Knopf, 1988.

Goldstein, Carolyn M. *Creating Consumers: Home Economists in Twentieth-Century America*. Chapel Hill: University of North Carolina Press, 2012.

Guralnick, Peter. *Sam Phillips: The Man Who Invented Rock 'n' Roll*. New York: Little Brown, 2015.

Hale, Grace Elizabeth. *Making Whiteness: The Culture of Segregation in the South, 1890–1940*. New York: Vintage Books, 1999.

Hall, Jacquelyn Dowd, et al. *Like a Family: The Making of a Southern Cotton Mill World*. New York: W. W. Norton, 1989. First published 1987 by University of North Carolina Press.

Halttunen, Karen. *Confidence Men and Painted Women: A Study of Middle-Class Culture in America, 1830–1870*. New Haven: Yale University Press, 1982.

Harker, Jamie. *The Lesbian South: Southern Feminists, the Women in Print Movement, and the Southern Literary Canon*. Chapel Hill: University of North Carolina Press, 2018.

Hatchett, Louis. *Duncan Hines: The Man behind the Cake Mix*. Macon, GA: Mercer University Press, 2001.

Herman, Bernard. *The South You Never Ate*. Chapel Hill: University of North Carolina Press, 2020.

Hess, Karen. "Historical Notes and Commentaries on *The Virginia House-wife*." In *The Virginia House-wife*, by Mary Randolph, ix–xlv. A facsimile edition. Columbia: University of South Carolina Press, 1984.

———. "Mary Randolph." *Oxford Companion to American Food and Drink*, edited by Andrew F. Smith, 491. Oxford: Oxford University Press, 2007.

Hirsch, Jerrold. *Portrait of America: A Cultural History of the Federal Writers' Project*. Chapel Hill: University of North Carolina Press, 2003.

Hobbs, Allyson. *A Chosen Exile: A History of Racial Passing in American Life*. Cambridge, MA: Harvard University Press, 2014.

Hoganson, Kristin L. *Consumers' Imperium: The Global Production of American Domesticity, 1865–1920*. Chapel Hill: University of North Carolina Press, 2007.

Homestead, Melissa J., and Pamela T. Washington, eds. *E. D. E. N. Southworth: Recovering a Nineteenth-Century Popular Novelist*. Knoxville: University of Tennessee Press, 2012.

Huber, Patrick. *Linthead Stomp: The Creation of Country Music in the Piedmont South*. Chapel Hill: University of North Carolina Press, 2008.

Hudson, Lynn M. *The Making of "Mammy Pleasant": A Black Entrepreneur in Nineteenth-Century San Francisco*. 2003. Urbana: University of Illinois Press, 2008.

Hunter, Jane H. *How Young Ladies Became Girls: The Victorian Origins of American Girlhood*. New Haven: Yale University Press, 2002.

Jackson, Kenneth T., Lisa Keller, and Nancy Flood, eds. *The Encyclopedia of New York City: Second Edition*. New Haven: Yale University Press, 2010.

Johnson, E. Patrick. *Sweet Tea: Black Gay Men of the South*. Chapel Hill: University of North Carolina Press, 2008.

Johnson, Yvette. *The Song and the Silence: A Story about Family, Race, and What Was Revealed in a Small Town in the Mississippi Delta while Searching for Booker Wright*. New York: Atria, 2017.

Kierner, Cynthia A. *Beyond the Household: Women's Place in the Early South, 1700–1835*. Ithaca: Cornell University Press, 1998.

Landau, Emily Epstein. *Spectacular Wickedness: Sex, Race, and Memory in Storyville, New Orleans*. Baton Rouge: Louisiana State University Press, 2013.

Lapp, Rudolph M. *Archy Lee: A California Fugitive Slave Case*. Foreword by Shirley Ann Wilson Moore. Berkeley: Heydey Books, 2008.

Larson, Kate Clifford. *The Assassin's Accomplice: Mary Surratt and the Plot to Kill Abraham Lincoln*. New York: Basic, 2009.

Lauterbach, Preston. *The Chitlin' Circuit and the Road to Rock 'n' Roll*. New York: W. W. Norton, 2011.

Leong, Elaine. *Recipes and Everyday Knowledge: Medicine, Science, and the Household in Early Modern England*. Chicago: University of Chicago Press, 2018.

Levenstein, Harvey. *Revolution at the Table: The Transformation of the American Diet*. Berkeley: University of California Press, 2003.

Lindemann, Erika. *True and Candid Compositions: The Lives and Writings of Antebellum Studenta at the University of North Carolina*. Documenting the American South, University Library, University of North Carolina at Chapel Hill. 2005. https://docsouth.unc.edu/true/index.html.

Locklear, Erica Abrams. *Appalachia on the Table: Representing Mountain Food and People*. Athens: University of Georgia Press, 2023.

Long, Alecia P. *The Great Southern Babylon: Sex, Race, and Respectability in New Orleans, 1865–1920*. Baton Rouge: Louisiana State University Press, 2004.

Manring, M. M. *Slave in a Box: The Strange Career of Aunt Jemima*. Charlottesville: University Press of Virginia, 1998.

Marszalek, John F. *The Petticoat Affair: Manners, Mutiny, and Sex in Andrew Jackson's White House*. New York: Free Press, 1997.

McCrary, Mary Jane, ed. *Transylvania Beginnings: A History*. [Brevard, NC]: Transylvania County Historic Properties Commission, 1984.

McGinty, Brian. *Archy Lee's Struggle for Freedom: The True Story of California Gold, the Nation's Tragic March toward Civil War, and a Young Black Man's Fight for Liberty*. Guilford, CT: Lyons Press, 2020.

McPherson, Tara. *Reconstructing Dixie: Race, Gender and Nostalgia in the Imagined South*. Durham: Duke University Press, 2003.

Merish, Lori. *Archives of Labor: Working-Class Women and Literary Culture in the Antebellum United States*. Durham: Duke University Press, 2017.

Miller, Adrian. *The President's Kitchen Cabinet: The Story of the African Americans Who Have Fed Our First Families, from the Washingtons to the Obamas*. Chapel Hill: University of North Carolina Press, 2017.

Mintz, Sidney. *Tasting Food, Tasting Freedom: Excursions into Eating, Culture, and the Past*. Boston: Beacon, 1996.

Missouri, Montré Aza. *Black Magic Woman and Narrative Film: Race, Sex and Afro-Religiosity*. New York: Palgrave Macmillan, 2015.

Moritz, Albert, and Theresa Moritz. *Leacock: A Biography*. Toronto: Stoddart Publishing, 1985.

Moss, Robert F. *Southern Spirits: Four Hundred Years of Drinking in the American South, with Recipes*. Berkeley: Ten Speed Press, 2016.

Moye, J. Todd. *Ella Baker: Community Organizer of the Civil Rights Movement*. Lanham, MD: Rowman and Littlefield, 2013.

Myers, Amrita Chakrabarti. *Forging Freedom: Black Women and the Pursuit of Liberty in Antebellum Charleston*. Chapel Hill: University of North Carolina Press, 2011.

Nash, Ilana. *America's Sweethearts: Teenage Girls in Twentieth-Century Popular Culture*. Bloomington: Indiana University Press, 2006.

Odem, Mary E. *Delinquent Daughters: Protecting and Policing Adolescent Female Sexuality in the United States, 1885–1920*. Chapel Hill: University of North Carolina Press, 1995.

Ownby, Ted. *American Dreams in Mississippi: Consumers, Poverty, and Culture, 1830–1998*. Chapel Hill: University of North Carolina Press, 1999.

———. *Subduing Satan: Religion, Recreation, and Manhood in the Rural South, 1865–1920*. Chapel Hill: University of North Carolina Press, 1990.

Painter, Nell Irwin. *Sojourner Truth: A Life, a Symbol*. New York: Norton, 1997.

Poley-Kempes, Lesley. *The Harvey Girls: Women Who Opened the West*. New York: Marlowe, 1991.

Pryor, Elizabeth Stordeur. *Colored Travelers: Mobility and the Fight for Citizenship before the Civil War*. Chapel Hill: University of North Carolina Press, 2016.

Pugh, Jesse F., and Frank T. Williams. *The Hotel in the Great Dismal Swamp and Contemporary Events Thereabouts*. Richmond: Garrett and Massie, 1964.

Reed, Betty Jamerson. *The Brevard Rosenwald School: Black Education and Community Building in a Southern Appalachian Town, 1920–1966*. Contributions to Southern Appalachian Studies 11. Jefferson, NC: McFarland, 2004.

Rothman, Joshua D. *Flush Times and Fever Dreams; A Story of Capitalism and Slavery in the Age of Jackson*. Athens: University of Georgia Press, 2012.

Rotundo, E. Anthony. *American Manhood: Transformations in Masculinity from the Revolution to the Modern Era*. New York: Basic, 1994.

Salinger, Sharon V. *Taverns and Drinking in Early America*. Baltimore: Johns Hopkins University Press, 2002.

Shapiro, Laura. *Perfection Salad: Women and Cooking at the Turn of the Century*. New York: Farrar, Straus and Giroux, 1986.

Sharpless, Rebecca. *Cooking in Other Women's Kitchens: Domestic Workers in the South, 1865–1960*. Chapel Hill: University of North Carolina Press, 2010.

———. *Grain and Fire: A History of Baking in the American South*. Chapel Hill: University of North Carolina Press, 2022.

Shields, David S. *The Culinarians: Lives and Careers from the First Age of American Fine Dining*. Chicago: University of Chicago Press, 2017.

———. *Southern Provisions: The Creation and Revival of a Cuisine*. Chicago: University of Chicago Press, 2015.

Shprintzen, Adam D. *The Vegetarian Crusade: The Rise of an American Reform Movement, 1817–1921*. Chapel Hill: University of North Carolina Press, 2013.

Silkenat, David. *Moments of Despair: Suicide, Divorce, and Debt in Civil War Era North Carolina*. Chapel Hill: University of North Carolina Press, 2011.

Slap, Andrew, ed. *Reconstructing Appalachia: The Civil War's Aftermath*. Lexington: University Press of Kentucky, 2010.

Sparks, Edith. *Capital Intentions: Female Proprietors in San Francisco, 1850–1920*. Chapel Hill: University of North Carolina Press, 2006.

Steadman, Jennifer Bernhardt. *Traveling Economies: American Women's Travel Writing*. Columbus: Ohio State University Press, 2007.

Steers, Edward, Jr. *Blood on the Moon: The Assassination of Abraham Lincoln*. Lexington: University Press of Kentucky, 2001.

Steinberg, Neil. *Hatless Jack: The President, the Fedora, and the History of an American Style*. New York: Plume Books, 2004.

Stewart, Catherine A. *Long Past Slavery: Representing Race in the Federal Writers' Project*. Chapel Hill: University of North Carolina Press, 2016.

Stockton, Elizabeth. "E. D. E. N. Southworth's Reimagining of the Married Women's Property Reforms." In *E. D. E. N. Southworth: Recovering a Nineteenth-Century Popular Novelist*, edited by Melissa J. Homestead and Pamela T. Washington, 243–64. Knoxville: University of Tennessee Press, 2012.

Stokes, Ashli Quesinberry, and Wendy Atkins-Sayre. *Consuming Identity: The Role of Food in Redefining the South*. Jackson: University Press of Mississippi, 2016.

Stoneley, Peter. *Consumerism and American Girls' Literature, 1860–1940*. New York: Cambridge University Press, 2003.

Strasser, Susan. *Never Done: A History of American Housework*. 1982. New York: Henry Holt, 2000.

Szczesiul, Anthony. *The Southern Hospitality Myth: Ethics, Politics, Race, and American Memory*. Athens: University of Georgia Press, 2017.

Taylor, Helen. *Circling Dixie: Contemporary Southern Culture through a Transatlantic Lens*. New Brunswick, NJ: Rutgers University Press, 2001.

Thorp, Daniel B. "Taverns and Communities: The Case of Rowan County North Carolina." In *The Southern Colonial Backcountry: Interdisciplinary Perspectives on Frontier Communities*, edited by David Colin Crass et al., 76–86. Knoxville: University of Tennessee Press, 1998.

Tippen, Carrie Helms. *Inventing Authenticity: How Cookbook Writers Redefine Southern Identity*. Fayetteville: University of Arkansas Press, 2018.

Tipton-Martin, Toni. *The Jemima Code: Two Centuries of African American Cookbooks*. Forewords by John Egerton and Barbara Haber. Austin: University of Texas Press, 2015.

Umfleet, LeRae Sikes. *A Day of Blood: The 1898 Wilmington Race Riots*. North Carolina Office of Archives and History. Rev. ed. Chapel Hill: University of North Carolina Press, 2020.

Veit, Helen Zoe. *Modern Food, Moral Food: Self-Control, Science, and the Rise of Modern American Eating in the Early Twentieth Century*. Chapel Hill: University of North Carolina Press, 2013.

Vester, Katharina. *A Taste of Power: Food and American Identities*. Berkeley: University of California Press, 2015.

Walden, Sarah. *Tasteful Domesticity: Women's Rhetoric and the American Cookbook, 1790–1940*. Pittsburgh: University of Pittsburgh, 2018.

Walker, Melissa, and James C. Cobb, eds. *Agriculture and Industry*. Vol. 11 of *The New Encyclopedia of Southern Culture*, edited by Charles Reagan Wilson. Chapel Hill: University of North Carolina Press, 2008.

Wall, Maryjean. *Madam Belle: Sex, Money, and Influence in a Southern Brothel*. Lexington: University Press of Kentucky, 2014.

Wallace-Sanders, Kimberly. *Mammy: A Century of Race, Gender, and Southern Memory*. Ann Arbor: University of Michigan Press, 2008.

Weiner, Deborah R. *Coalfield Jews: An Appalachian History*. Urbana: University of Illinois Press, 2006.

Welter, Barbara. "Cult of True Womanhood." In *Dimity Convictions: The American Woman in the Nineteenth Century*, 21–41. Athens: Ohio University Press, 1976.

Williams, Elsie A. *The Humor of Jackie Moms Mabley: An African American Comedic Tradition*. Studies in African American History and Culture. New York: Garland, 1995.

Williams-Forson, Psyche. *Building Houses Out of Chicken Legs: Black Women, Food, and Power*. Chapel Hill: University of North Carolina Press, 2006.

Willoughby, Urmi Engineer. *Yellow Fever, Race, and Ecology in Nineteenth-Century New Orleans*. Baton Rouge: Louisiana University Press, 2017.

Wiltse, Jeff. *Contested Waters: A Social History of Swimming Pools in America*. Chapel Hill: University of North Carolina Press, 2010.

Woolf, Virginia. *A Room of One's Own*. Annotated and introduced by Susan Gubar. 1929. Orlando: Harcourt, 2005.

Zipf, Karin L. *Bad Girls at Samarcand: Sexuality and Sterilization in a Southern Juvenile Reformatory*. Baton Rouge: Louisiana State University Press, 2016.

Journal Articles, Theses, and Dissertations

Bendele, Marvin. "Food, Space, and Mobility: The Railroad, Chili Stands, and Chophouses in San Antonio and El Paso, 1870–1905." PhD diss., University of Texas at Austin, 2015.

Chapman, Georgeanna Milam. "Craig Claiborne: A Southern-Made Man." MA thesis, University of Mississippi, 2008.

Dixon, Elsabe C. "Building the White Right of Textile Work: Dan River Mills and the Development of Schoolfield Village, 1882–1931." PhD diss., University of North Carolina at Chapel Hill, 2021.

Gaston, Kay Baker. "The MacGowan Girls." *California History* 59, no. 2 (Summer 1980): 116–25.

Hine, Darlene Clark. "Rape and the Inner Lives of Black Women in the Middle West." *Signs* 14, no. 4 (1989): 912–20. http://www.jstor.org/stable/3174692.

Joyner, Ann. "Helen Morris Lewis: Biography of a Suffragist." MLA thesis, University of North Carolina at Asheville, 1996.

Perkins, Glenn Stuart. "Accommodating Strangers: Mid-Nineteenth-Century Wilmington, N.C., Boardinghouses." MA thesis. University of North Carolina at Greensboro, 2004.

Petlewski, Mary Katherine. "Taverns in Eighteenth Century North Carolina." MA thesis, University of North Carolina at Chapel Hill, 1972.

Scholnick, Robert J. "'Culture' or Democracy: Whitman, Eugene Benson, and *The Galaxy*." *Walt Whitman Quarterly Review* 13 (Spring 1996): 189–98.

Steans, Natia L. "Black Film Classics: *Boarding House Blues* (1948): A Film Review." *Black Camera* 16, no. 2 (2001): 8.

Index